THE COLUMN OF MARCUS AURELIUS

STUDIES IN THE HISTORY OF GREECE AND ROME

Robin Osborne, P. J. Rhodes, and Richard J. A. Talbert, editors

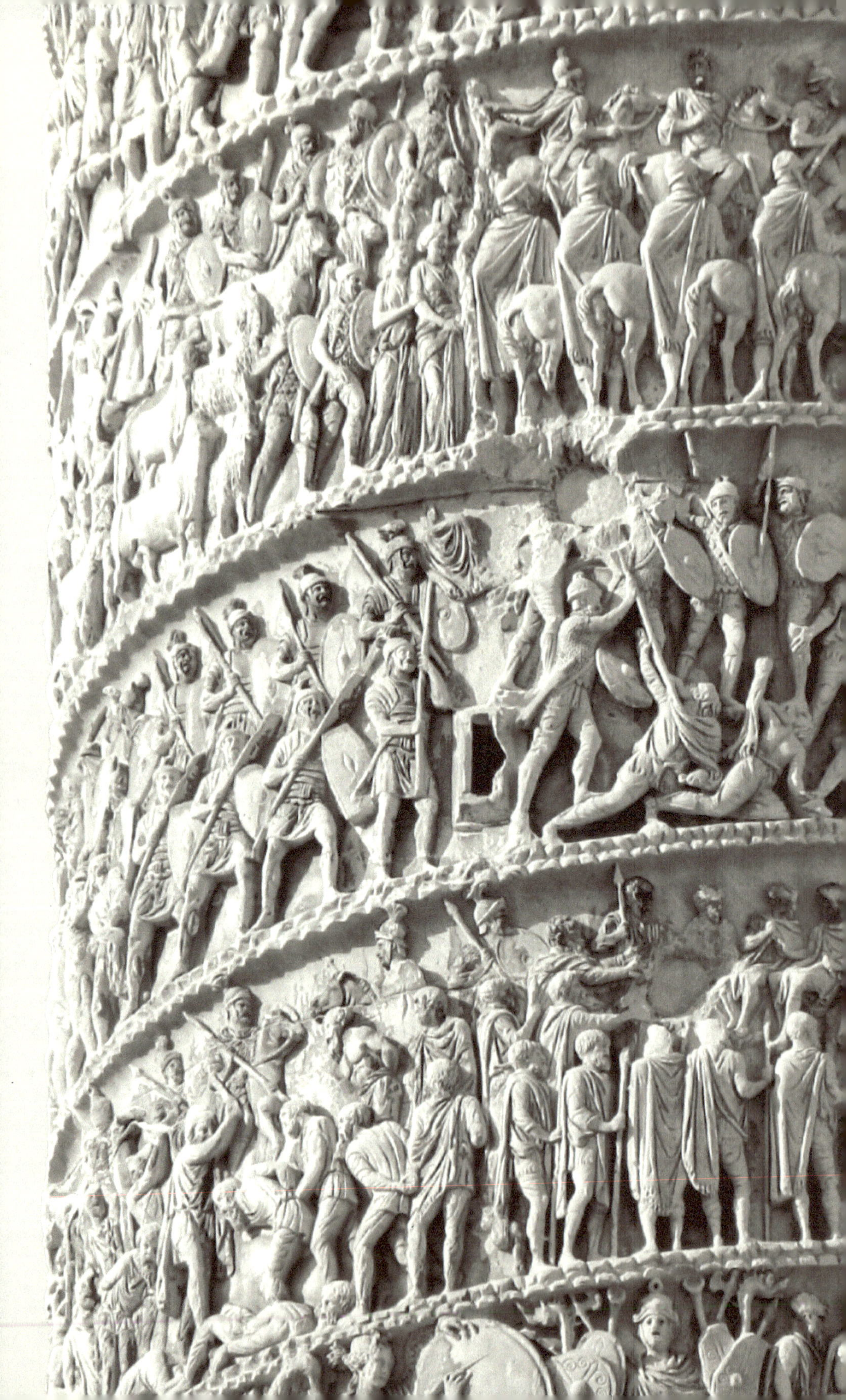

THE COLUMN OF MARCUS AURELIUS

The Genesis & Meaning of a Roman Imperial Monument

Martin Beckmann

The University of North Carolina Press · Chapel Hill

 Designed by Kimberly Bryant and set in Warnock Pro with Trajan Pro and Castellar display by Tseng Information Systems, Inc.

The paper in this book meets the guidelines for permanence and durability of the Committee on Production Guidelines for Book Longevity of the Council on Library Resources. The University of North Carolina Press has been a member of the Green Press Initiative since 2003.

Library of Congress Cataloging-in-Publication Data
Beckmann, Martin.
The Column of Marcus Aurelius : the genesis and meaning of a Roman imperial monument / Martin Beckmann.
p. cm. — (Studies in the history of Greece and Rome)
Includes bibliographical references and index.
ISBN 978-0-8078-3461-9 (cloth: alk. paper)
ISBN 978-1-4696-6863-5 (pbk: alk. paper)
ISBN 978-0-8078-7777-7 (ebook)
1. Column of Marcus Aurelius (Rome, Italy) 2. Column of Marcus Aurelius (Rome, Italy)—History. 3. Rome (Italy)—Buildings, structures, etc. 4. Relief (Sculpture), Ancient—Italy—Rome. 5. Friezes—Italy—Rome. 6. Monuments—Social aspects—Rome—History. 7. Monuments—Political aspects—Rome—History. 8. Imperialism—Social aspects—Rome—History. 9. Rome—History—Marcus Aurelius, 161–180. 10. Rome—History—Empire, 30 B.C.–284 A.D. I. Title.
NA9340.R4B43 2011
725'.940945632—dc22 2010047523

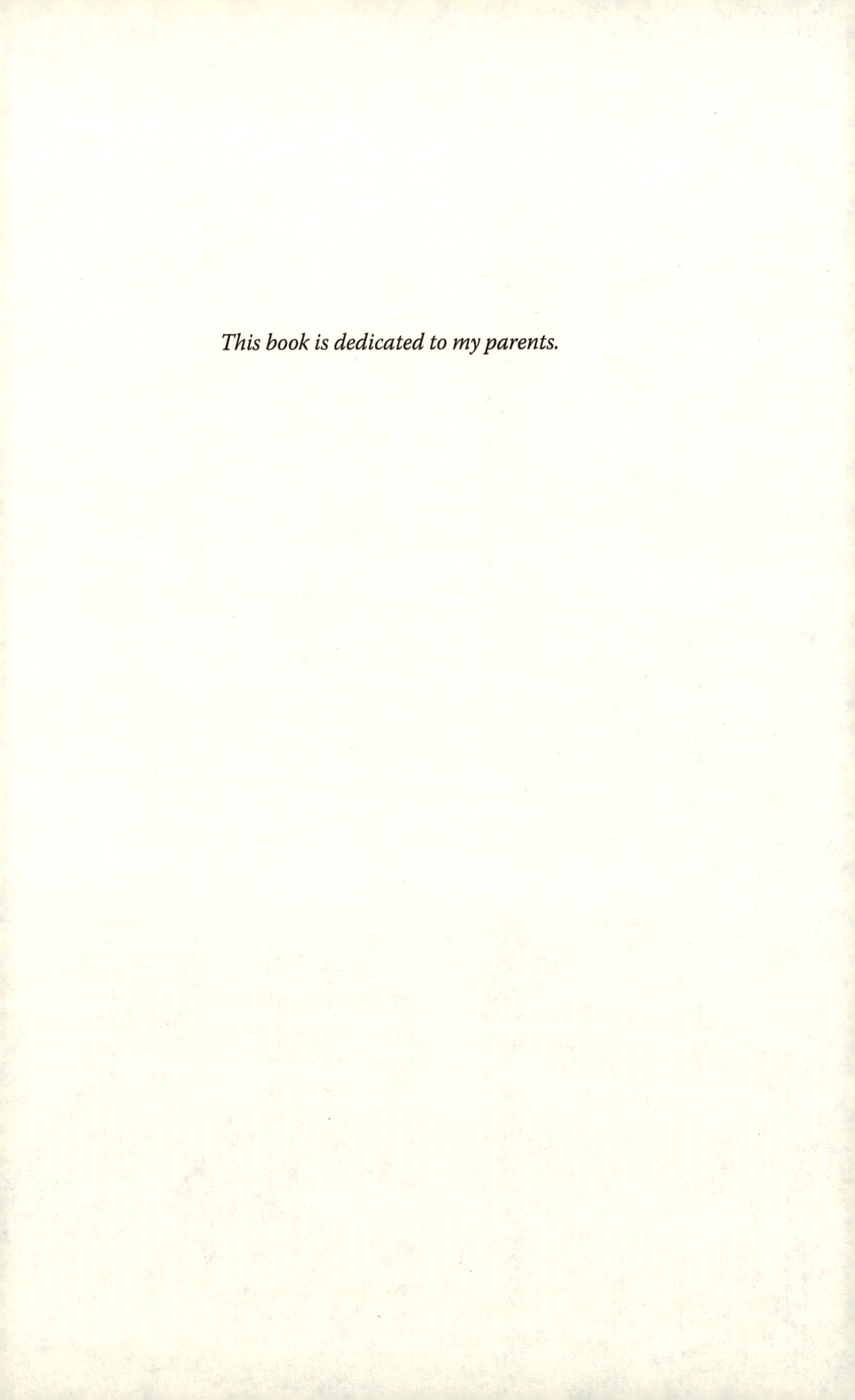

This book is dedicated to my parents.

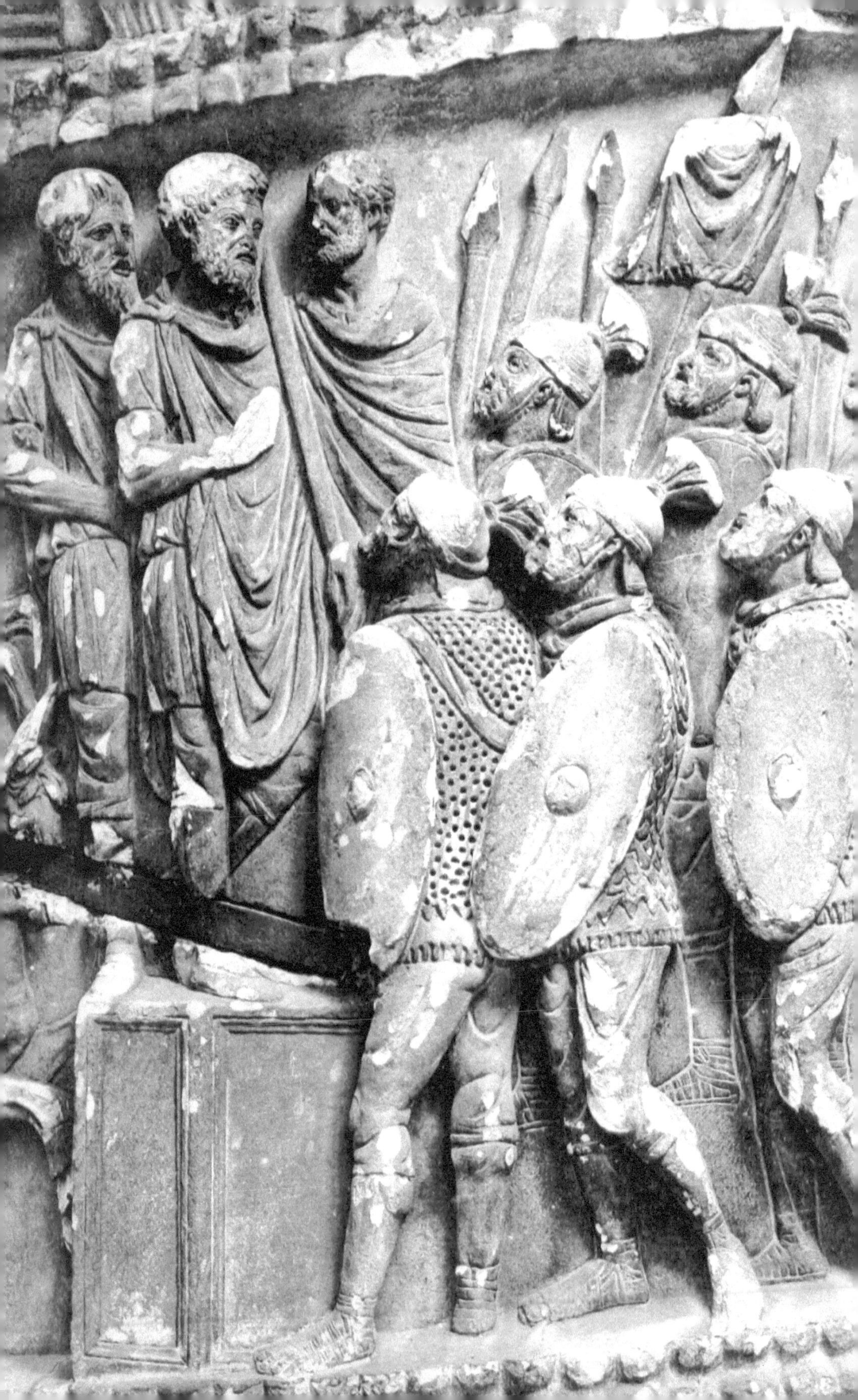

Contents

Acknowledgments ix

Introduction 1

1 · The Date & Purpose of the Column 19

2 · The Dust of Northern Warfare: Choice of Location 37

3 · Form & Function 55

4 · Planning & Construction 68

5 · The Frieze: Concept & Draft 84

6 · Carving the Frieze 110

7 · The Frieze as History 128

8 · The Frieze as Art 156

9 · Viewing the Column 187

EPILOGUE · The Columns of Trajan, Marcus Aurelius, & Arcadius 207

Notes 215 Bibliography 233 Index 243

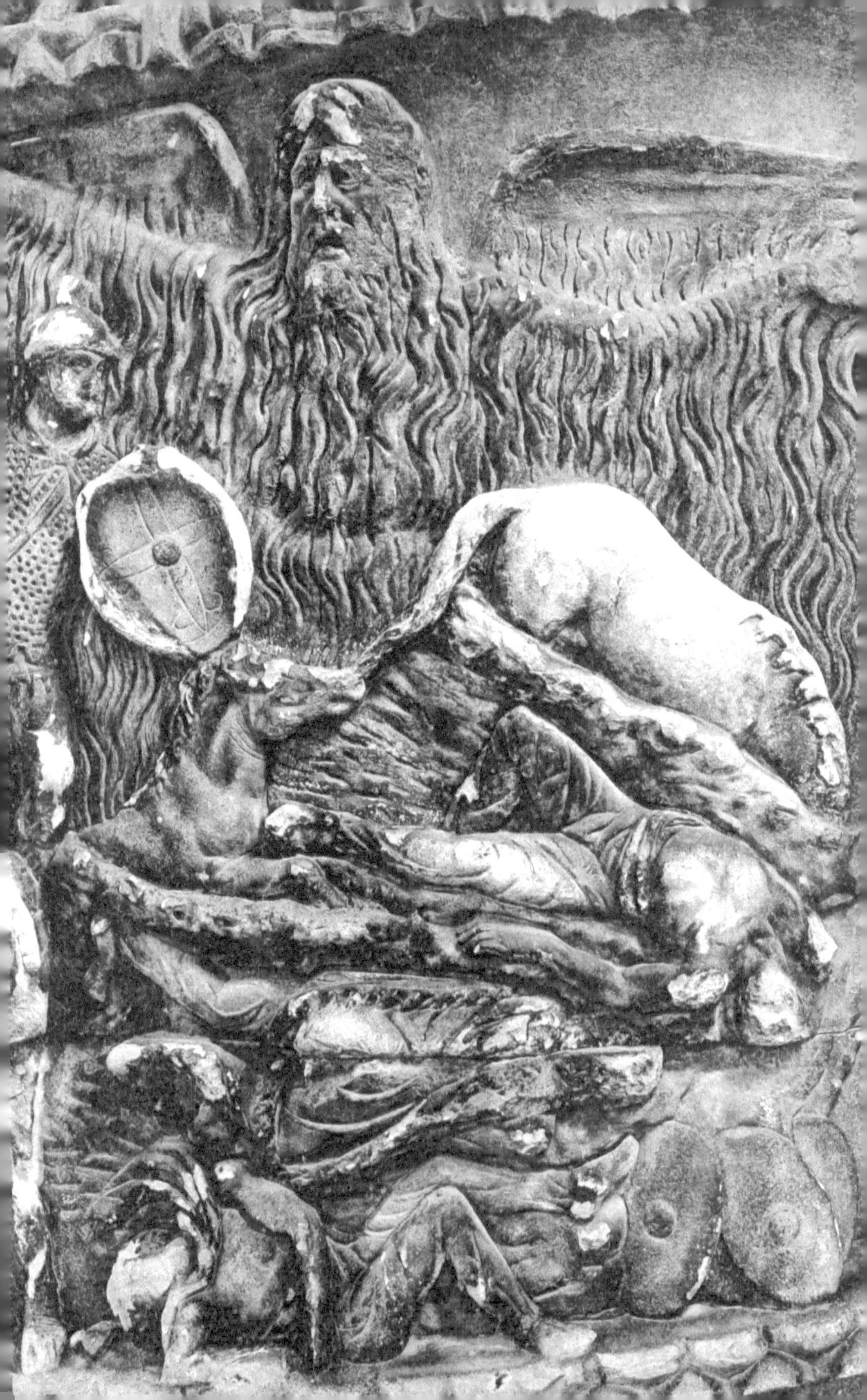

Acknowledgments

The idea for this book grew slowly, as over the course of a number of years spent investigating particular details of the monument it gradually became clear to me how little was known about how the Column of Marcus Aurelius was created. I have the great pleasure of thanking Katherine Dunbabin for encouraging my early research on this subject. Many of the questions that are addressed in this book first arose in discussions with Peter Rockwell, who also explained the practicalities of carving marble and opened my eyes to the fundamental importance of the relationship between the processes of carving and design. In a similar way I am grateful to Lynne Lancaster for conversations and correspondence on issues involved in architectural design and the process of construction. Most of the research and writing of this book took place in the library of the Institute for Classical Archaeology at the University of Heidelberg; I thank my friends and colleagues there, especially Tonio Hölscher and Jens-Arne Dickmann, for much stimulating discussion. I am especially grateful to the editors and staff at the University of North Carolina Press, and particularly to Richard Talbert, who both encouraged this project and supported it consistently through the editorial process. I also happily acknowledge the support of the Social Sciences and Humanities Research Council of Canada, which funded my stay in Germany. Many others also helped make this a much better book, and I thank you all here.

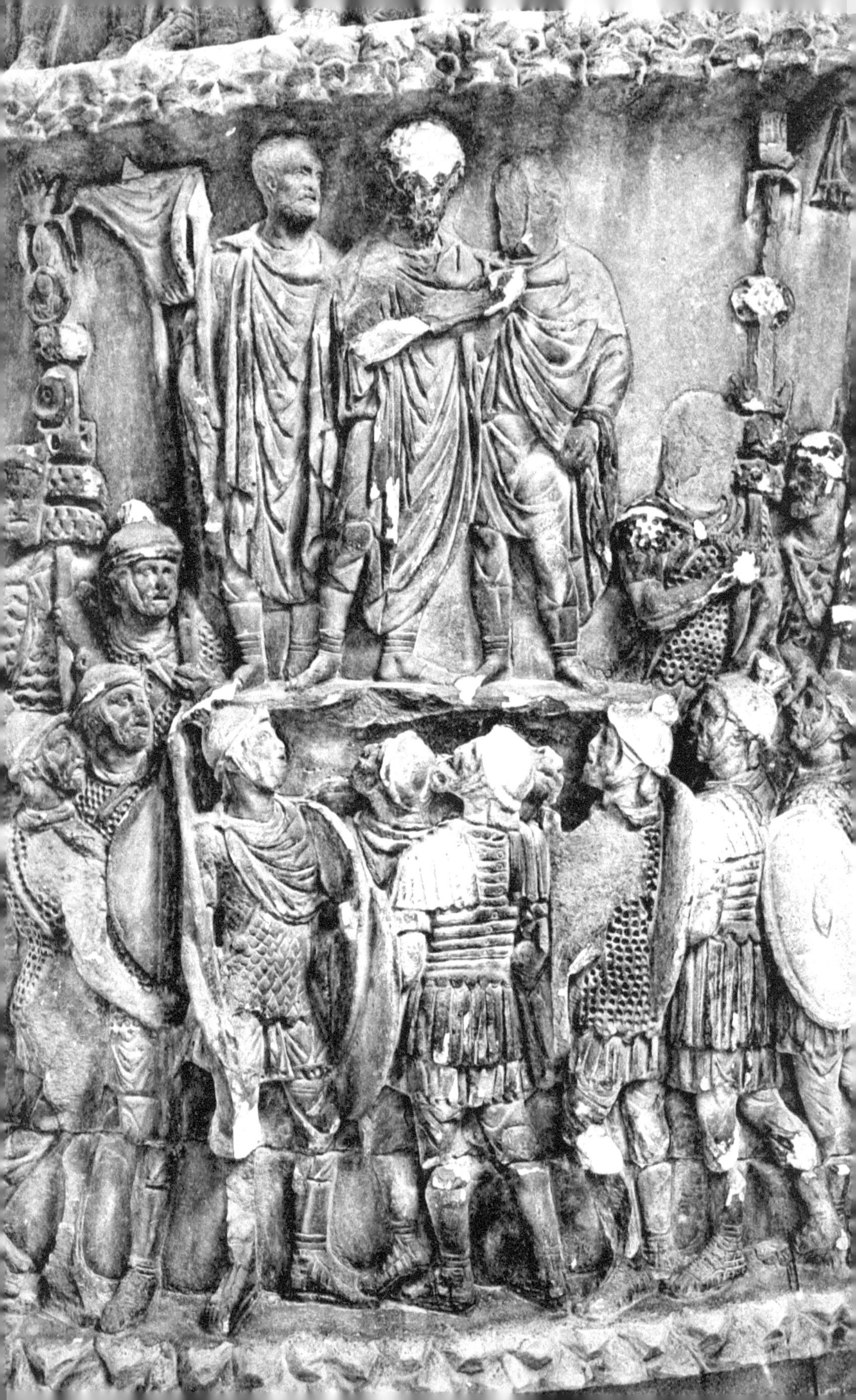

THE COLUMN OF
MARCUS AURELIUS

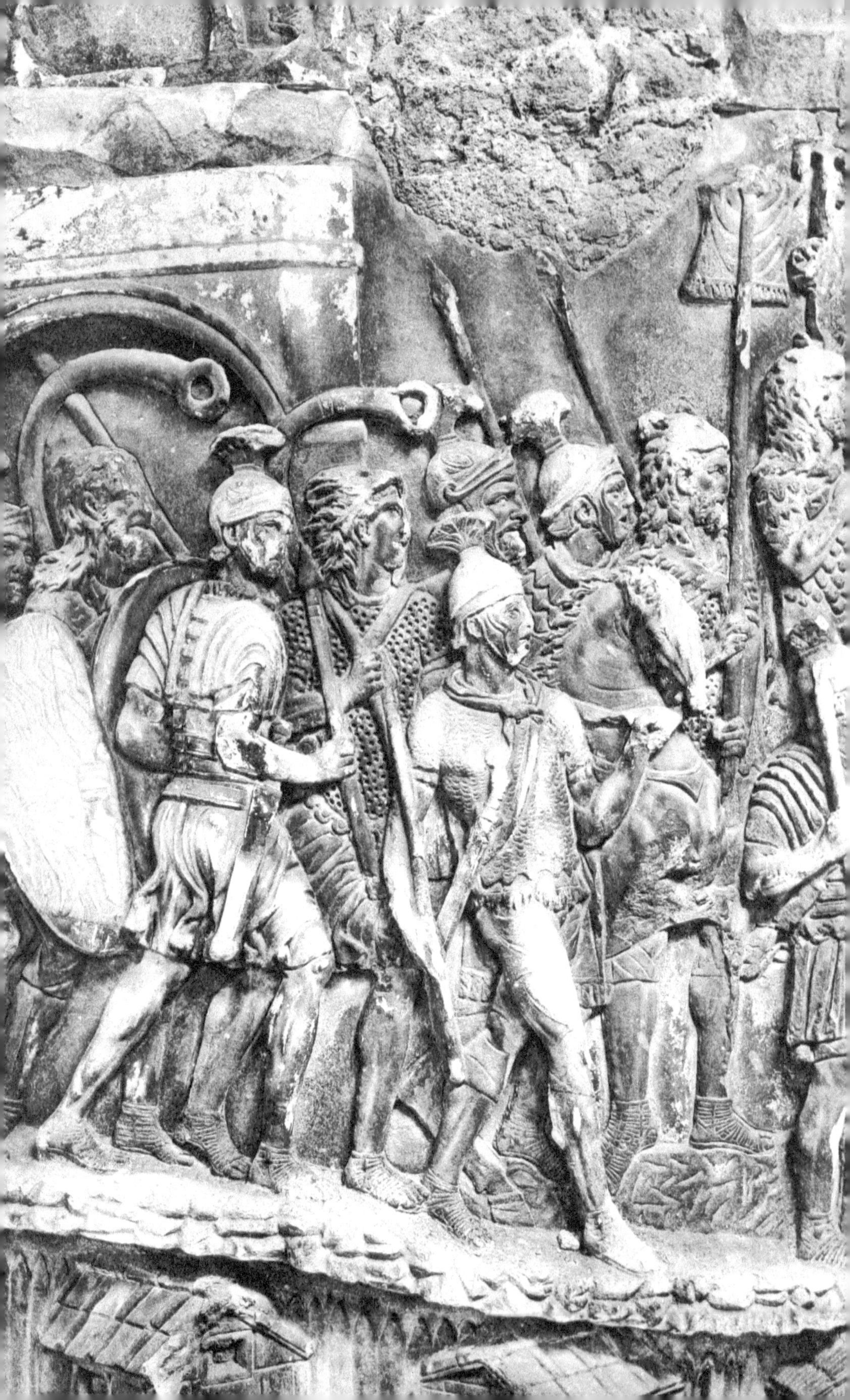

INTRODUCTION

"If a man were called to fix the period in the history of the world during which the condition of the human race was most happy and prosperous, he would, without hesitation, name that which elapsed from the death of Domitian to the accession of Commodus."[1] This is the well-known verdict of Edward Gibbon on the condition of life in the Roman Empire between A.D. 96 and 180, a happy period of stable government, benevolent rulers, and more or less peaceful frontiers. It ended, in Gibbon's opinion, with the death of the last of the good emperors, Marcus Aurelius. But a strong argument can be made that things had ceased being "happy and prosperous" well before the philosopher-emperor passed the throne to his delinquent son. By far the most vivid illustration of this dramatic and depressing change in the circumstances of the empire is the remarkable decoration of a monument in the heart or Rome: the Column of Marcus Aurelius.

Life and Times of Marcus Aurelius Antoninus

Marcus Aurelius (fig. i.1) was born in a villa on the Caelian Hill in Rome in April of A.D. 121.[2] He was raised by his grandfather, a holder of three consulships (a rare honor) and a relative of Hadrian. Hadrian took Marcus under his wing and eventually ordered his own chosen successor, Antoninus Pius, to adopt him. On Pius's death in 161, Marcus became emperor; he promptly raised his adoptive brother Lucius Verus to the position of coemperor and took his adoptive father's name. Thereafter he was known as Marcus Aurelius Antoninus. But all was not smooth: various peoples beyond the Roman frontiers seized the opportunity offered by the imperial transition to stir up trouble. Marcus and Verus were ill prepared to deal with these developing crises: neither had gained any practical military experience in their youth, and one of them—Marcus—had never even been outside of Italy.[3] The most pressing problem was an invasion of the eastern provinces by the Parthians, successors to the Persian Empire and the only single power of the time capable of rivaling Rome. This attack was so threatening that the junior emperor, Verus, personally took charge of the military response—

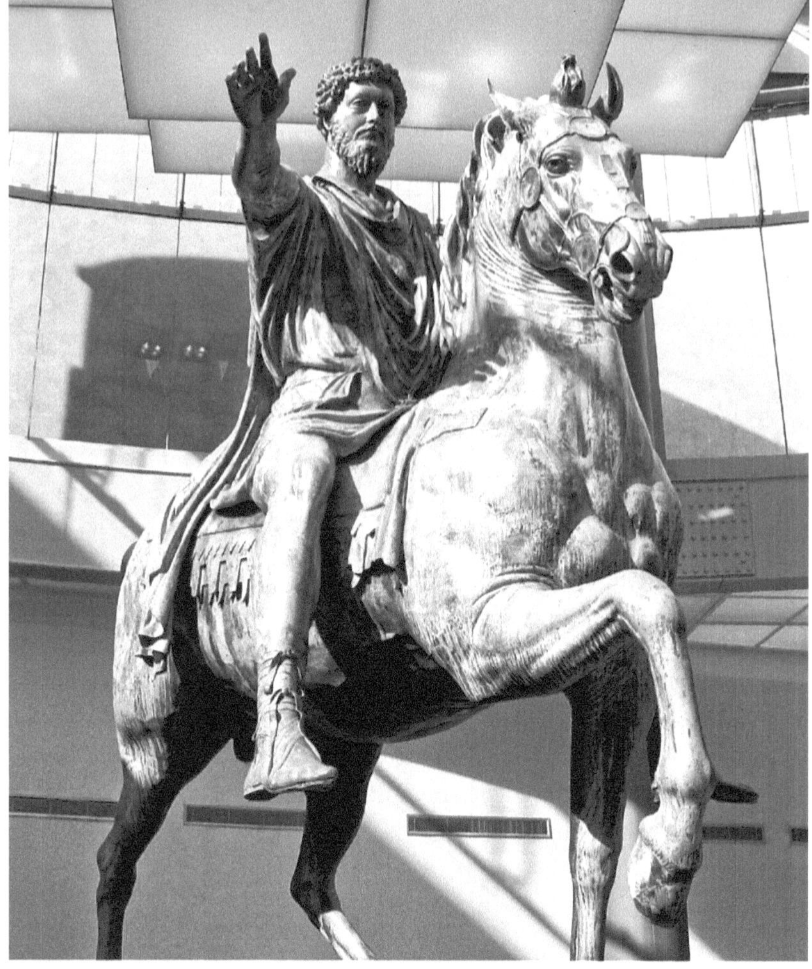

FIGURE i.1. Marcus Aurelius on horseback (ancient bronze statue, Rome, Capitoline Museum). Photo by author.

either because he was healthier and stronger, or because Marcus wanted his uncouth brother out of the Roman public eye. After initial setbacks, the Parthian capital of Ctesiphon was captured and its royal palace put to the torch in 165; Verus returned to Rome in 166 and the emperors celebrated a common triumph. Marcus also used the opportunity to raise his son, Commodus, to the rank of Caesar.

But the war with Parthia had drawn crucial military resources away from the Danube frontier. The Germanic tribes saw this as their chance to attack, and they seized it. This touched off a long, exhausting war against various Germanic barbarians north of the Danube that occupied the last decade of Marcus's life almost without stop. This war, which the Romans called the *bellum Germanicum* or, sometimes, the *bellum Marcomannicum* (after the largest, fiercest, and most feared of the Germanic tribes), is recorded in all its violence and desperation on the Column of Marcus Aurelius. The chronology of Marcus's Germanic wars is notoriously complex: it can only be partly reconstructed from fragmentary and scattered sources, and no more than the bare outlines are clear.[4] Open conflict along the Danube frontier began just as the Parthian War ended. But a deadly plague, brought back to Italy by Roman soldiers returning from the east, devastated the army and terrified the urban population of Rome. "Many thousands" of citizens, including nobles, died, according to the fourth-century A.D. *Historia Augusta*, so many that their bodies had to be carried off in carts and wagons.[5] This disaster delayed the imperial response to the new German threat. And when the Romans finally countered, in 168, the plague followed the emperors and the army into the field and forced them to withdraw to Italy after no more than a partial victory had been achieved. Then Verus himself died, succumbing to a stroke while riding in the imperial coach. One ancient story goes so far as to say that he was cleverly poisoned by his brother. When Marcus got back to Rome, so little money was left in the imperial treasury that he was compelled to auction off imperial possessions to fund the defense of the empire. With the finances in a disastrous state and plague having ravaged the populace, the emperor was forced to enroll slaves and gladiators in the army—some accounts say that even common criminals were enlisted.[6]

Again, the emperor, this time alone, marched north and prepared for a great offensive across the Danube. It was the year 170. But this time, too, disaster: Marcus's army was repulsed with as many as 20,000 casualties. A contemporary tale alleges that the emperor had followed the bad advice of a charlatan prophet, one Alexander, who published an oracle saying that if Marcus threw a great mass of offerings, including a pair of lions, into the Danube, victory would be won. The offering was made, but the lions swam to the other side, where the barbarians clubbed them to death. Disaster followed for the Romans, but the false prophet escaped censure by claiming that he had not predicted which side would be victorious.[7] The story may be fiction, but the defeat it referred to was real enough. This calamity both weakened the Romans and encouraged their enemies, the Marcomanni and their allies, the Quadi, who surged across the frontiers and stormed over the Alps. They ravaged the countryside of northeast Italy, besieged Aquileia, and destroyed at least one major city, Opitergium.[8] But despite these disasters, the Romans still held the Danube, and when the barbarians tried to return home with their plunder in 171, the Roman forces trapped and destroyed them. Marcus Aurelius, true to his moral upbringing, returned the plunder to the provincials from whom it had been seized.[9] This put an end to the threat posed by the Marcomanni, and the emperor celebrated a formal victory over the Germans, taking "Germanicus" as part of his name in 172. He pressed on, advancing to Carnuntum in Panonnia (modern Austria), where he made his headquarters as he persecuted the war against the Quadi and another tribe, the Sarmatians (also known as the Iazyges). The unknown author of the *Historia Augusta*, a collection of imperial biographies written in the fourth century, claimed that Marcus intended to create two new provinces, Marcomannia and Sarmatia, on the far side of the Danube.[10]

But it was not to be. In July 175 the emperor, still engaged on the northern front, received disastrous news: the Roman governor of Syria and up to now a trusted friend, Avidius Cassius, had launched a rebellion. Marcus was compelled to make peace with the Germans and set out for the east to suppress the insurrection.[11] Although he was hailed victor for the second time, taking the name "Sarmaticus" in 175, the acclamation must have rung hollow. The rebel Cassius was slain before Marcus could reach Syria, but the emperor continued his march through the eastern provinces all the way to Alexandria. During the return journey to Rome, further tragedy struck in the form of the death of Faustina, Marcus's beloved wife, causing the emperor great grief.[12] On his arrival in the capital Marcus had the double duty of celebrating his triumph over the Germans and Sarmatians and of mourning at the funeral of his wife. Faustina's body was cremated on a great pyre on the Campus Martius, and her ashes laid to rest in the Mausoleum of Hadrian; on the site of her cremation a commemorative funerary altar was built.[13] Trouble on the frontier began again almost immediately, and Marcus was compelled to return to the Danube in 178. With him on this second campaign he took his son and coemperor, Commodus, and there the both of them remained until the death of Marcus Aurelius in the year 180.[14]

One can only imagine how these events—war from the beginning of his reign, plague, treachery, and multiple deaths in his family—affected the emperor. *Fuit a prima infantia gravis*, says the writer of the *Historia Augusta*: "he was from earliest infancy a serious person."[15] The intensity of Marcus's seriousness is revealed in a remarkable document from his own hand: a journal, known today as his *Meditations* but titled originally, in Greek, *To Himself*. This philosophical diary offers rare insight into Marcus's mind, especially in the first book, which consists of a list of various members of his family, friends, and teachers and what he learned from each.[16] From this we learn that Marcus was (or at least tried to be) mild, thoughtful, and reserved. He strove to be just and kind and to do all that he was required to do diligently and without complaint. He did not involve himself with base or superstitious concerns (the circus races, for example, or magic), and he turned a deaf ear to rumor. In fact, the entire work gives the impression of a man detached: at least part of it was written in the north during the Germanic war (the first book of the *Meditations* concludes with the terse remark: "among the Quadi, on the River Gran"), but, throughout, Marcus makes almost no reference at all to the events of the brutal conflict in which he was engaged.

What's in a Name? Terminology and the Column

The Column of Marcus Aurelius (fig. i.2) is, if anything, even more puzzling than the character of Marcus himself. To make matters worse, we are also very poorly informed about the monument. The column was first mentioned (at least, it first appears among our surviving literary sources) near the end of the third century A.D., when an unknown Roman topographer compiled a list of the monuments of the imperial capital.[17] The topographer's method was to proceed through the fourteen regions of the city, listing the most notable sights and providing some limited details about their appearance—how tall a structure was, for example, or how many seats a theater had. He began with the First Region, in the south; by the time he reached the Eighth Region, the Imperial Fora, he had described an arc around the eastern half of the city. The next region on his list encompassed the land east of the Tiber, north of the city center: the Campus Martius. "The Ninth Region contains the temple of Antoninus," he wrote, "and a snail-column, which is one hundred seventy-five and a half feet tall." The column in question is of course the Column of Marcus Aurelius, and today it is one of the best-preserved monuments of imperial Rome and the single most important to have survived from the reign of the philosopher-emperor. Exactly one hundred Roman feet tall and perched atop a forty-foot pedestal, it was once topped by a bronze statue of the emperor. Column, statue, and pedestal together presumably added up to produce the total height given by the topographer of 175½ feet. But what inspired his description of the monument as a *columna cochlis*: a "snail column"? How is the Column of Marcus Aurelius anything like a snail, and why was such a monument built in the emperor's honor?

This puzzle—how we today are to understand this strange-sounding Ro-

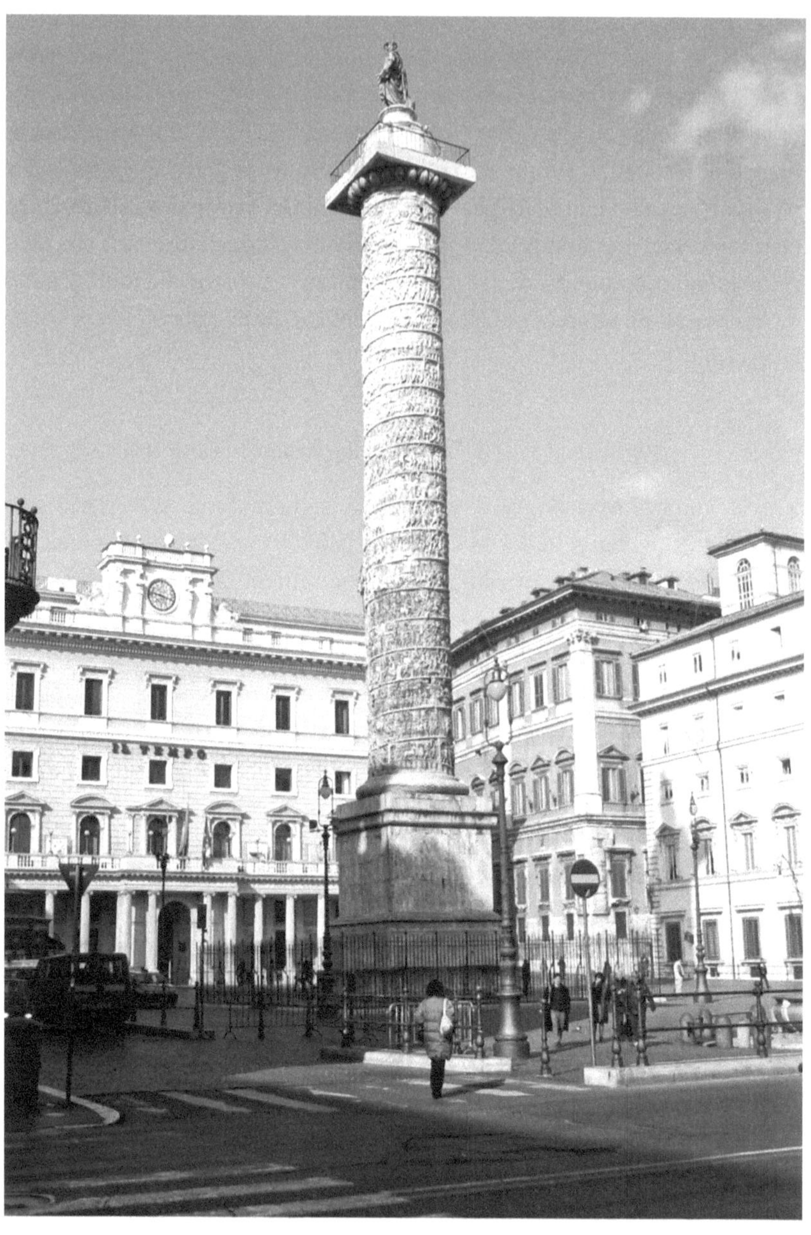

FIGURE i.2. The Column of Marcus Aurelius in Piazza Colonna, Rome, looking northwest across the Via del Corso (the ancient Via Flaminia). Photo by author.

man term—is representative of the many problems of interpretation that surround the Column of Marcus Aurelius. The form of the monument is relatively simple, at least when looked at from the exterior: it consists of a single Doric column (a fluted shaft with a plain, pillowlike capital—the fluting is visible only at the very top, where a raised border divides it from the carved figural frieze below—see fig. i.4) standing atop a tall pedestal and surmounted by a statue. The pedestal is built from large rectangular blocks of marble, the column from twenty marble drums. However, a number of remarkable features set this monument apart from the ordinary. First of these is its size. Including its partly buried pedestal the column is 135½ feet tall, and with its statue was once much taller. Even today it towers above the multistory *palazzi* that surround it. Its individual components are also impressively scaled: the marble drums from which the column is built measure five feet tall and weigh over forty tons; the monolithic capital is even more massive, weighing in at over seventy tons of solid stone. The second noteworthy feature is the complex interior architecture. Within the pedestal and column a spiral stairway winds its way up inside the structure (fig. i.3) to emerge on a platform atop the capital (fig. i.4). Encircled by a guardrail, this belvedere was by far the highest point on the Campus Martius. The third remarkable feature is the exterior decoration: the column was adorned with detailed relief sculpture. The decoration of the pedestal was fairly ordinary, including depictions of Victories, garlands, and a scene of the emperor receiving the submission of barbarians. The decoration of the column shaft proper, however, was decidedly out of the ordinary. It consists of a continuous helical band of narrative relief sculpture that winds around the shaft twenty times from bottom to top. At over 700 feet in length, it is the second-longest narrative frieze known from the ancient world (the Parthenon frieze measures just over 500 feet; the longest is the frieze of Trajan's Column). Given these novelties, it is not surprising that even modern scholars cannot settle on a name for the Column of Marcus Aurelius. The monument combines aspects of a freestanding architectural element (the column) with those of a full-blown building (doors, interior space, a stairway, and a balcony). It also serves as a support for a single piece of unified narrative relief carving of almost-unprecedented length. It is sometimes called a "historical" column, highlighting the overwhelming modern interest in the historical content of the helical frieze carved on its shaft. But this is not really helpful, for it tells us nothing about how the Romans viewed and understood the monument. "Snail column," on

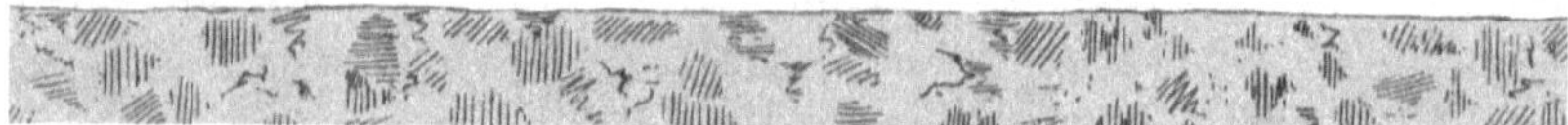

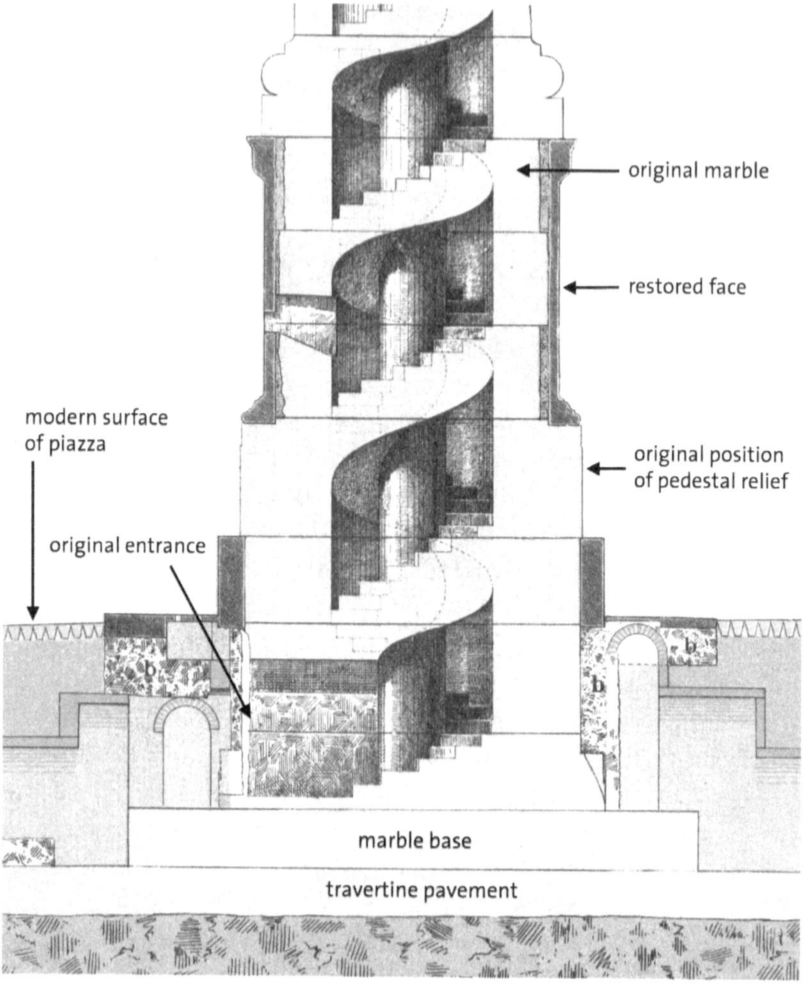

FIGURE i.3. Cutaway view (west to east, seen from the north) of the pedestal of the column, showing the modern ground level and, below it, the ancient entrance. From Petersen et al. 1896, pl. 3.

the other hand, might indeed be very helpful—if we can understand its meaning.

Documenting and Interpreting the Column

Until the late nineteenth century, the only resources available to the scholar interested in the reliefs of the column (besides the original itself) were two drawings: one made in the 1670s by Pietro Santi Bartoli, and another exe-

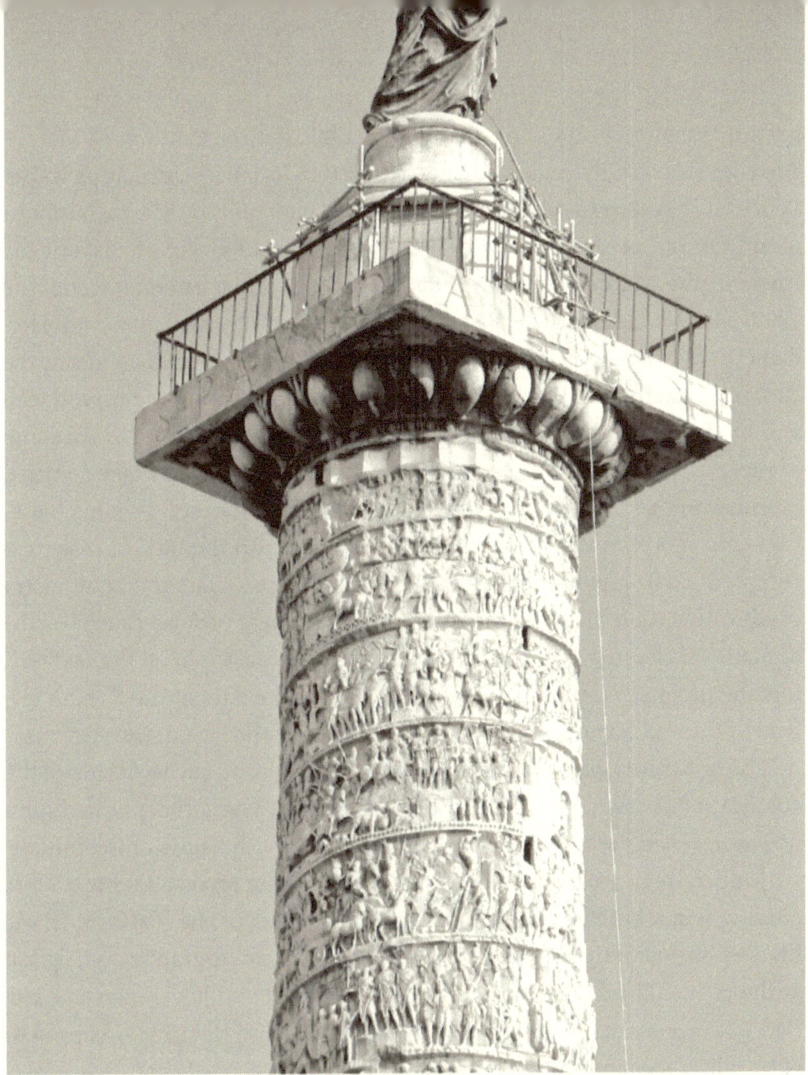

FIGURE i.4. View of the upper portion of the column, showing the upper doorway opening onto the surface of the capital. Photo by author.

cuted in 1758 by Piranesi. Bartoli drew the entire frieze, and his drawings were translated into prints in which the frieze is divided into rectangular segments in an artificially horizontal alignment; Piranesi's drawing, which was also published as a print, presented a complete view of the column, but only from the east. Both drawings are flawed, incomplete, and sometimes misleading, especially Bartoli's. And since Piranesi based his drawing of the upper parts of the frieze on Bartoli's prints, he incorporated some of Bartoli's errors into his own work.[18] In the nineteenth century, while research on the Column of Trajan forged ahead with a project beginning in 1861 to make casts of the entire frieze—and from these casts to make and publish a complete photographic record of the sculpture—the Column of Marcus Aurelius stood sadly neglected. It took a visit to Rome by Germany's Kaiser Wilhelm II in 1893 to rekindle professional excitement for Marcus's monument. On the occasion of the Kaiser's visit, a small group of casts of the frieze of the Marcus column, centered around one particular scene, the "Rain Miracle," was made. The next year, a group of "learned men from Heidelberg" decided that "these oldest images of German life" (they meant the barbarian enemies of Rome shown on the column) should be reproduced and made available to the scholarly public. In 1894 a committee made up of representatives from various German states was ready to make a formal presentation to the Kaiser. On 30 May 1894, His Majesty gave his blessing—and more important, his financial support—to the task of making a complete photographic record of the column's frieze. The Italian ministry of education then gave its permission, and after a year of delay caused by the difficulty of clearing enough space in Piazza Colonna to set up the scaffolding, the project was ready to begin on 21 April, the date of the Roman festival of the Pallilia and the traditional birthday of the city, in the year 1895.

The apparatus used (see fig. i.5) was remarkable: on the west side of the column, a tall, narrow scaffold tower was erected. The actual photography, however, was done from a single giant platform with a hole in the middle, suspended by ropes from the column's capital. The ropes attached to tall, curving metal brackets at each of the four corners of the platform (these brackets are sometimes visible at the edges of the photographs, e.g., fig. 5.9 at the right). This entire platform could be raised and lowered as needed. Bad weather hindered the start of photography, and the time was used to clear out cracks in the column and to fix loose pieces of marble in place. Finally, in the middle of June, photography got underway. The original plan was to take four images per winding of the frieze, and to do this by turning the entire platform around the column; this plan was soon abandoned in favor of tripling the number of photographs, these taken from twelve carefully marked places on the surface of the platform. The camera was covered with a tent roof and the pictures taken on glass plates using reflected light: the resulting quality of the images speaks for both the extreme care and the outstanding technique with which they were made. No photographic images of either the Column of Marcus Aurelius or of Trajan come anywhere near to rivaling those made by Petersen's photographer, D. Anderson, in June and July 1896. And, in one important way, no better images can ever be produced, because this series of photographs records the column before it faced the ravages of twentieth-century pollution. Comparison of

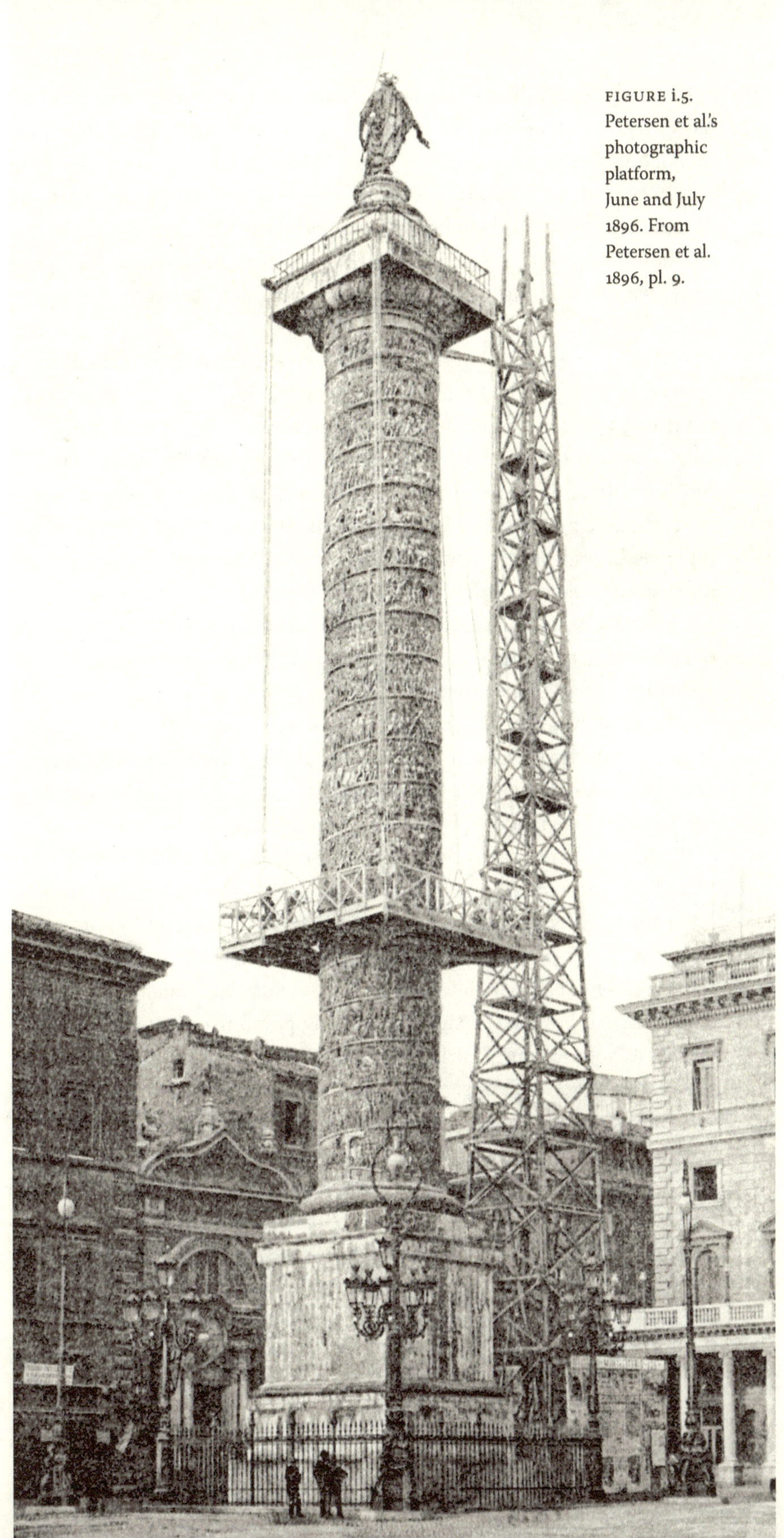

FIGURE i.5. Petersen et al.'s photographic platform, June and July 1896. From Petersen et al. 1896, pl. 9.

Petersen's photos to more recent ones shows only too clearly how the original surface of the marble has been eaten away over the span of little more than a hundred years.

The primary scholarly interest in all of this was—from the German point of view at least—the documentation of early German peoples, societies, and conditions of life. Some German scholars of the late nineteenth and early twentieth century felt a very close connection between themselves and the barbarians on the column. The Nobel Prize–winning historian Theodor Mommsen was very moved by the circumstances of the Kaiser's project, in which he had the role of writing the historical commentary on the frieze. In his introduction he noted with some sentimentality that this great new photographic work was being produced by the descendants of the same Romans and Germans who were depicted on Marcus's monument.[19] These men were very optimistic about what they could learn about their ancestors from the frieze: in the course of his detailed description of the scenes, Petersen felt that his main task was to distinguish different races of Germans, based on dress and facial characteristics: "the most important thing for us is to observe the enemies of the Romans and to classify them according to their appearance."[20]

The most important effect of Petersen's publication was that it made it possible to study the column's frieze in great detail in more or less its original appearance, rather than via the dubious medium of Bertoli's or Piranesi's prints. This made it possible to examine not only the general content of the scenes, but to study the form of the carving itself. Still, it took more than thirty years for the column to be comprehensively addressed from an art historical perspective, in the form of Max Wegner's lengthy study of its style.[21] Wegner's purpose was not to study the art of the Marcus column per se, but rather to compare it with that of the Column of Trajan in an attempt to define what he saw as a shift or a turning point in artistic style (what he termed a "style-change," or in German a *Stilwandel*) in Roman art in the second century A.D. Petersen's evaluation of the style of Marcus's Column was simplistic: he pronounced it vastly inferior to the artistic style of the frieze on Trajan's Column.[22] Wegner avoided making subjective judgments and instead focused on defining clearly the style of the column: painterly rather than sculptural, with emphasis on the play of shadows in the deep drill cuts and figural modeling and a striving to express motion and power in the twisting and turning of figures.[23] He noted that architecture and landscape elements were subordinated to these emotive figures, and much more of the background was simply left blank. But it was left to Gerhard

Rodenwaldt to take the next step, from definition to explanation. Rodenwaldt firmly linked the art of the Marcus column with a wider and deeper artistic trend of the late second century.[24] He focused on seeking out the main characteristics of this new trend in the funerary reliefs of the lower classes, and almost as an aside he identified many of the same features in the art of the Marcus column. Thus the Column of Marcus Aurelius soon came to be identified as the key monument of a sweeping artistic change in Roman art known widely as the Antonine *Stilwandel*.[25] Rodenwaldt's own words provide the best summary of his view of the column and its art:

> On the Column of Marcus some essentially new and peculiar elements, unknown to Flavian or Trajanic art, are apparent. In place of broad presentation there is a concentration of action, Roman pride of conquest, helpless barbarian submission, the solemn representation of the Emperor himself are strongly stressed, and a transcendental element comes into the scene depicting the [Rain] Miracle. The Italic centralizing method of composing single scenes and the un-classical repetition of identical figures, like those of marching legionaries, are employed to intensify effect. Lines and alternations of light and shadow heighten the expressive character of the whole work, the merit and artistic significance of which have for long been underrated. It is no transition, but rather a prelude to the last phase of ancient art. Its roots are struck deeper in the spiritual heritage of Rome than those of Trajan's Column, and yet it points towards the art of the future.[26]

Rodenwaldt suggested that this new style was more than a natural development in art, removed from other concerns. To him, it was a manifestation of a change in mentality, in how the Romans viewed the world, precipitated by a crisis of confidence and identity in the late second century. In his view, formed in the uncertain environment of the years between the First and Second World Wars, the column's art was an antidote to uncertain times.

The uncertain times of the 1930s soon culminated in global war. For the Column of Marcus Aurelius, this meant being photographed again prior to being encased in a protective covering of sandbags to avoid damage from bomb blasts and flying debris. These photographs were eventually published in 1955, along with a series of essays designed to cover in general, if not in detail, the main features of the column: its architecture, historiography, art, military representations, and historical associations.[27] The authors of this Italian study duly addressed these and other themes, but none of the contributions succeeded in breaking substantially new ground. In his 1956 review of this compilation, C. Vermeule wrote that a "comprehensive study of the Marcus Column . . . must surely result from so many recent skirmishes."[28] This, however, was not to be, and instead the column's study again lapsed into inactivity. Recently this has begun to change—one can point to the work of Pirson on the message of the frieze, Hölscher on the organization of its scenes, the various contributors to a multiple-author volume loosely focused on the subject of the use of gesture in the column's frieze, and Coarelli's republication of Petersen's photographs.[29] But one can still write, as Vermeule did in the 1950s, that the Column of Marcus Aurelius remains sorely in need of new, comprehensive treatment.

Method and Material

Considering the great range of specialized approaches to ancient monuments and art that are in use today, the task of producing a comprehensive treatment of the column may be beyond any single author. What is attempted here is deliberately limited: an examination of the creative process behind the monument with the goal of trying to piece together a picture of how and what the Romans themselves—architects, artists, and the Roman public—thought of the Column of Marcus Aurelius. This goal extends far beyond discovering the meaning of the term *columna cochlis*: it encompasses an investigation not only of how the column was viewed, but also of how it was created. The main underlying premise of the book is that an understanding of this creative process, how a monument was conceived, planned, and executed, is a fundamental step toward truly understanding the intent behind it and its eventual public reception. Unfortunately, there are problems with this approach. There are no records of construction, no archive of plans, no copies of decrees ordering the building of the column. Nor are there any substantial descriptions of the finished monument by contemporaries. Nevertheless, the situation is far from hopeless: parallel evidence is available, and many aspects of the creative process have left traces on the column itself. Careful study of the final form of the column can yield many clues to the process of its creation.

In spite of a tradition of scholarly research over a century old, many aspects of the various stages in the column's planning process—the concept of the frieze, the creation of its individual scenes, even the place of the monument in topography and time—remain uncertain or unknown. The list of questions is long. What occurred at the time the initial decision was made to build the column? When was this decision made? (Surprisingly, not even this most basic fact about the column can be stated unequivocally.) Why was this particular form of monument chosen to honor Marcus Aurelius? Why was the column placed where it was in the urban landscape? What were the steps in its planning? Who designed the frieze, and how did he go about it? Where did the individual images come from? To what extent were these images historical? How exactly was the sculpture on the column executed, and by whom? And, finally, what did contemporary viewers see and think when they looked at the column? How did they approach and experience it?

The opportunity to solve these problems would make taking a deeper look at the Column of Marcus Aurelius rewarding enough, but in fact the monument has even more to offer. The column is also a work of emulation and, to some extent, interpretation. Most Roman monuments were in general heavily indebted to their predecessors, and a comparison between a monument and its forerunners can often reveal the sources of inspiration and the nature and extent of changes and refinements in the new monument. This in turn might reveal developments and changes in the thinking of the designers and in the ideals and standards of the times. A major problem with this method is often that of knowing whether or not we have evidence of all the forerunners for any particular monument. In the case of the Column of Marcus Aurelius this problem does not exist, for it had only one forerunner, the Column of Trajan. Elements derived from Trajan's Column are easy to identify, as are those that were novel. The value of this opportunity—of being able to directly compare the column and its unique, well-known, and well-preserved model—is difficult to overstate. It provides on one hand a critique of Trajan's Column through Roman eyes, and on the other a chance to study the working methods of a design team responsible for creating an imperial public monument of the highest importance. It may perhaps even be possible to view the Column of Marcus Aurelius as, in effect, a work of Roman artistic and architectural criticism, the result of deliberate improvements made by its designers on the model of its predecessor. For example, the frieze is taller and carved to a greater depth than that on Trajan's Column. Was this the result of a deliberate attempt by the designers of Marcus's Column to increase the visibility of the frieze? Or is there another explanation for this change?

On the other hand, the Column of Marcus Aurelius labors under a number of disadvantages, especially when compared to the Column of Trajan. At first glance its state of preservation appears nearly perfect. It has stood exactly in its original location in Rome down to this very day, and it still bears most of its original elaborate sculptural decoration. We can still follow its remarkable helical frieze in its original course from the bottom of the column to its top. There is no need to reconstruct the original location of its display, as, for example, in the case of the Great Trajanic Frieze, or to debate the order of its scenes, as we must for the Tropaeum Traiani. However, all is not perfect. We have almost no evidence above modern ground level about what surrounded the column in Roman times. In addition, the Column of Marcus Aurelius has not survived the years entirely intact. It lost its surmounting statue (and the uppermost stone block of its construction) sometime in the Middle Ages, likely in one of the earthquakes that shook the shaft and left many of its drums shifted awkwardly out of place. Even the metal clamps that held the drums together were robbed, chiseled out of the stone, leaving gaping wounds that have in the past been confused with cannonball damage from the time of Napoleon.

Ironically, this damage may have helped ensure the survival of the column. Free to move independently, the drums have been shifted by earthquakes, but the entire column remains standing. Still, the quakes and fires took their toll and drums suffered damage, some losing substantial pieces. The pedestal, worn and already stripped of its original veneer in the Renaissance period, was entirely refinished in the sixteenth century by Pope Sixtus V (who also added a statue of St. Paul to the top, the one we see today). This obliterated the remaining traces of the pedestal's sculptural decoration, which are now preserved only in a few drawings and prints. At the same time, gaps in the shaft of the column were carefully patched with marble and many worn and damaged areas were chiseled away and replaced with fresh-carved stone. Even the ground-level doorway to the column's internal staircase is no longer in its original location: it is now a diminutive portal, moved from the primary eastern to the secondary southern face of the pedestal and substantially elevated to compensate for rising ground levels. The final and perhaps most frustrating impediment to our modern understanding of the column is the paucity of contemporary Roman references to it. Only once did an ancient Roman stop to record a description of the Column of Marcus Aurelius, or at least only one such record is preserved today. That was by the snail-column topographer, the author of the Regionary Catalogues at the starting point for this study.

Our lack of knowledge about the Column of Marcus Aurelius really cannot be overemphasized. But at the same time it is important to remember that our state of knowledge might not be so different from that of the people who created Marcus's monument. Many of the questions that we ask of the Column of Marcus Aurelius were probably some of the same questions that the designers of this very monument asked about Trajan's Column. These were not generic Romans living in a vaguely defined "imperial" period, steeped in a thorough knowledge of art and architecture as practiced from Augustus to Constantine. Rather, they lived at the end of the second century A.D., at a time when no one who had taken part in the construction of Trajan's Column was still alive. Architectural plans may have existed, but plans for the frieze almost certainly did not (see chapter 5). Oral history may have conveyed some of the thinking behind the design of Trajan's Column but could not have preserved it all. The designers of the Marcus column would have had to puzzle out many of its details themselves and must have asked themselves questions like: What exactly were Trajan's architects trying to accomplish? What were his artists aiming at? Here we may, paradoxically, have an advantage over Marcus's own experts: we have detailed studies of the architecture of Trajan's Column and comprehensive photographic surveys of its frieze at our disposal. Modern scholars have made careful studies of the individual scenes in the frieze, and of their composition and arrangement. It is likely that we know more today about many aspects of the content and organization of the frieze of Trajan's Column than the Romans of the late second century themselves did, only eighty years after Trajan's monument was built.

This book begins with an examination of the background of the Column of Marcus Aurelius, before proceeding into a discussion of its most famous component, the frieze. One of the main premises of this book is not to project modern knowledge onto late-second-century artists and craftsmen. Instead, an attempt is made to determine what resources they likely had, and how they might have used them. The Romans of Marcus's time were better informed than us on certain points: the meaning, for example, of *columna cochlis* would have been clear to them, as would the occasion and purpose of the erection of Marcus's monument. This basic, fundamental question—when was the column decreed, and why?—is the starting point of this study. From there, chapters 2 and 3 consider the significance both of the column's location within the topography of late-second-century Rome and of its architectural form. The next two chapters look at the planning process in greater detail and examine the creative process behind the monument and its sculptural decoration. Chapter 6 then turns from planning to doing and attempts to determine exactly how the column's carvers went about their work. The last three chapters look in turn at three related aspects of the frieze: its historical accuracy, its status as art, and its meaning. Finally, the epilogue attempts to put the creation of the Column of Marcus Aurelius into historical perspective by considering what happened when a team of artists and architects arrived in Rome from Constantinople in the late fourth century A.D., looking for inspiration for a major project, the Column of Arcadius, to be built in the new capital. Their choices and decisions provide a remarkable ancient commentary on the two Roman columns, and throw new light on the relative success of each.

chapter one

THE DATE & PURPOSE OF THE COLUMN

At the end of the second century A.D., in the early years of the reign of the emperor Septimius Severus, a Roman official named Adrastus—a former slave but now a freedman of the emperor—moved into a new house. Adrastus was not just any official, and his was not just any house. He was the *procurator* or caretaker of the Column of Marcus Aurelius, and his new residence was built just behind the column. The remains of his house were found in the year 1777 during excavations beneath the Piazza di Montecitorio, about one hundred meters to the west of the Piazza Colona and the column itself.[1] We know a lot about Adrastus's house because he recorded its construction in a pair of remarkable inscriptions, dating to the year 193, that reproduce letters that Adrastus exchanged with the emperor and his servants.[2] The letters were inscribed on a tall marble block that formed the doorpost to the new house (fig. 1.1). In the first letter, Adrastus asked for official permission to replace the little hut, *cannaba*, in which he had heretofore been living, with a more substantial dwelling, described as a *hospitium*. Since he knew the area well, Adrastus also suggested a specific location for his new house, a certain distance "behind the hundred-foot column of the divine Marcus and Faustina, on public ground" (*post colu*[*mnam centenariam divorum*] *Marci et Faustina*[*e . . . loco publico*] *pedibus plus min*[*us*] . . .). In reply, Adrastus was not only given permission to build his new *hospitium*, but also to pass it on to his heirs.

But Adrastus got even more: in one of the letters, three imperial treasury officials instruct another administrator to assign to Adrastus "all the bricks and building materials" (*tegulas omnes et inpensam*) "from the little houses, huts and suitable buildings" (*de casulis item cannabis et aedificiis idoneis*).[3] The location of these little houses, huts, and buildings is not specified, but because no other specific details are given, it must be assumed that they would have been known to Adrastus. They presumably were located near the *cannaba*, or hut, that Adrastus wanted to replace with his new *hospitium*. Adrastus was explicitly permitted to build his *hospitium* in the place

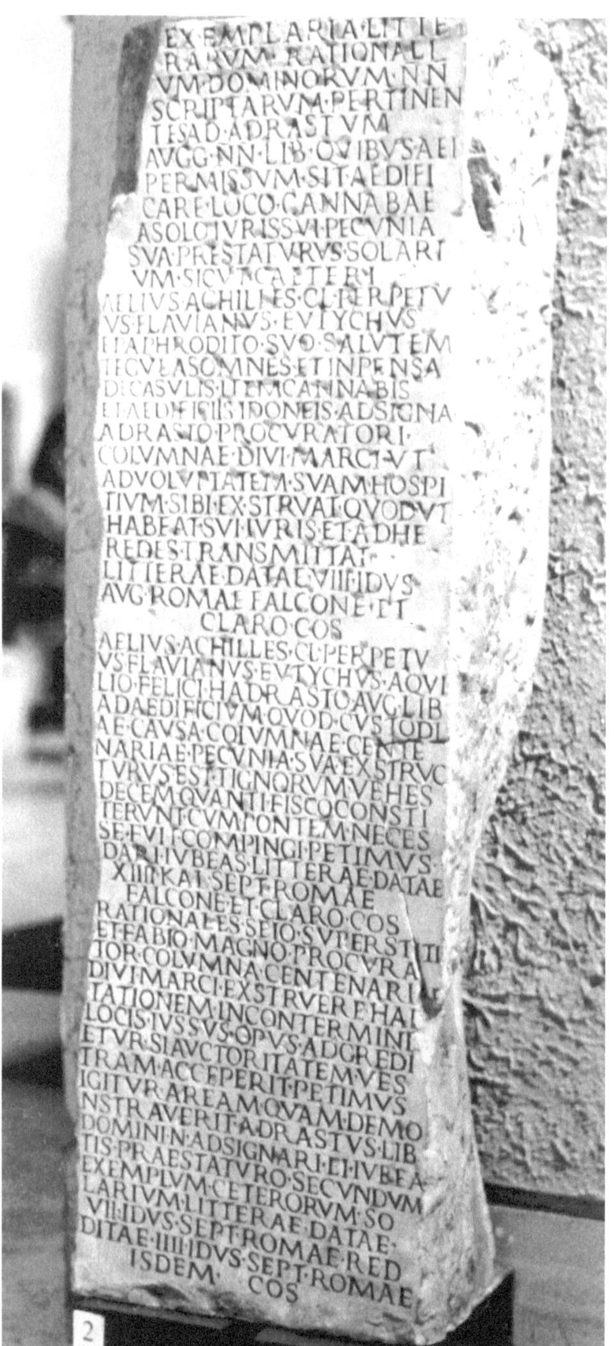

FIGURE 1.1.
Inscription of Adrastus (copy in Museo della Civiltà Romana, Rome). Photo by author.

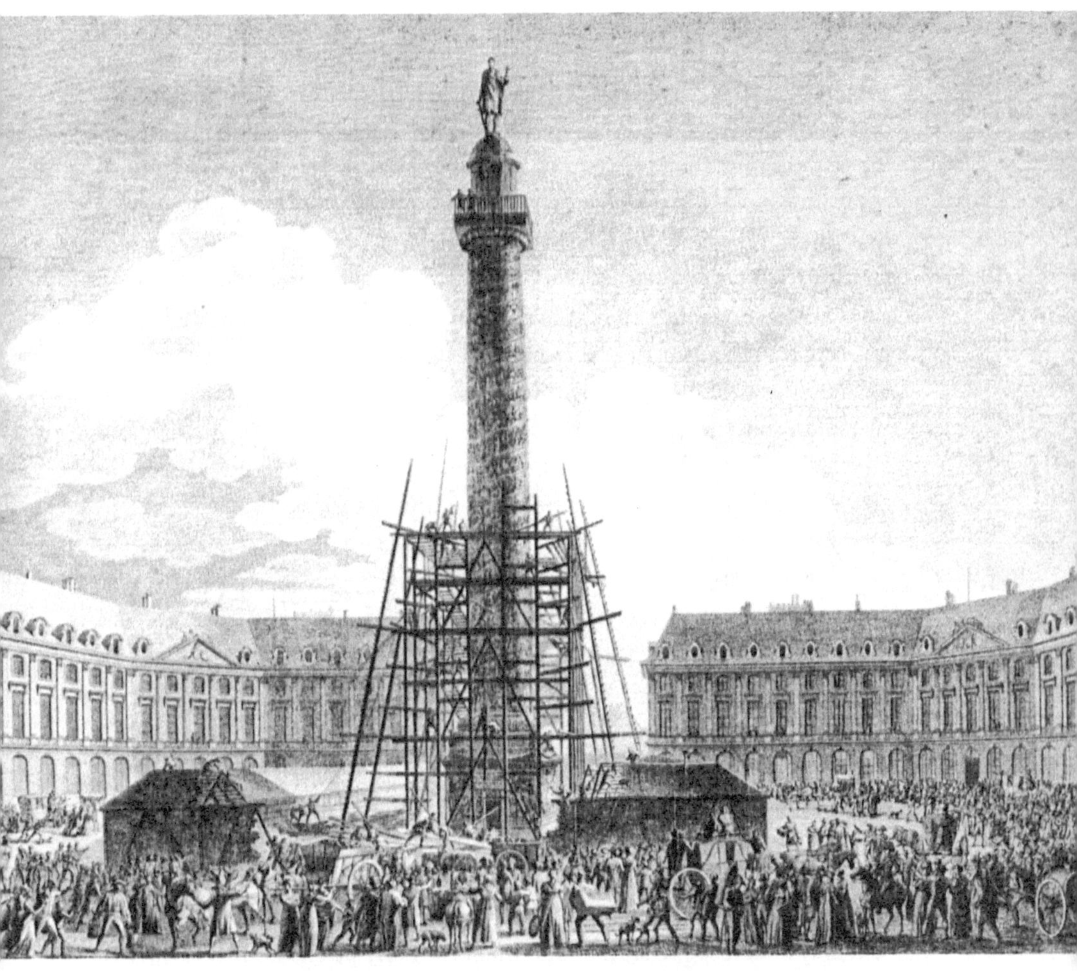

FIGURE 1.2. The Colonne de la Grande Armée, Paris, during demolition of surrounding workshops just after its completion in 1810. Bibliothèque nationale de France.

where his hut already stood (*loco cannabae*), a certain distance behind the Column of Marcus Aurelius. The "little houses, huts and suitable buildings" mentioned in the letter therefore likely stood near the column too. A sensible conclusion is that they were temporary structures of various sizes that had been built to act as storerooms, workshops, and perhaps even barracks during the construction of the column itself. An impression of what these structures may have looked like is given by an etching of the Colonne de la Grande Armée on Place Vendôme in Paris (fig. 1.2). The column, still partly surrounded by scaffolding, stands in the middle of a small courtyard formed by brick buildings, which are in the process of being torn down.

The timbers are being collected and the bricks taken away in carts. A similar situation can be imagined at the conclusion of work on the Column of Marcus Aurelius. If Adrastus was being given permission to cannibalize the materials of service buildings to construct his own house, then their useful life was over and their purpose—to support the construction of the Column of Marcus Aurelius—was complete. Therefore it seems more or less certain that the column was completed in the year 193.

Unfortunately the date of completion is much less helpful for our understanding of the column than the date of its decree. This is the single most important unresolved question about the Column of Marcus Aurelius, and a difficult one to solve, because the evidence is by no means clear. There are two main contenders: 180, the date of the death of Marcus Aurelius and the ascension of his son Commodus; and 176, when Marcus returned to Rome after a multiyear absence and celebrated a triumph for his German and Sarmatian victories.

In the late nineteenth century, both dates were considered equally possible, but since then the trend has been toward accepting a date of 180, thus attributing the decision to Commodus.[4] This is no more than a four-year difference, but the identification of the proper date could hardly be of greater importance. At stake is our understanding of the fundamental function of the monument: is it primarily funerary (A.D. 180), or is it primarily honorary (A.D. 176)? In the inscription of Adrastus, the column is called *columna divi Marci*, "the column of the deified Marcus," suggesting on the face of things that its primary purpose was to honor the emperor after he had died and been deified. But unfortunately this is not as helpful as it may at first seem. At the time when the inscription was made, the year 193, Marcus Aurelius was thirteen years dead and long-since deified. Thus any reference at that time to a monument to Marcus could have called him a *divus*, regardless of whether the monument was set up during his lifetime or posthumously. By way of comparison, the Column of Trajan was certainly commissioned and completed during that emperor's lifetime, but was also known as "the Column of the deified Trajan" after his death.

There are no other preserved inscriptions (the pedestal of the column surely carried one, but it was removed after antiquity and before the earliest modern drawing was made), and textual sources of any sort are few and far between. The most-often quoted is a problematic reference in the text of a fourth-century writer of abbreviated imperial biographies, Sextus Aurelius Victor. Concerning the events after Marcus's death, Victor wrote: *denique, qui, seiuncti in aliis, patres ac vulgus soli omnia decrevere, templa columnas sacerdotes* (*Liber de Caesaribus*, 16.15): "then, the Senate and the People, who in the cases of other emperors acted independently, decreed everything together, temples and columns and priests." At first glance, this reference seems to give evidence that the Column of Marcus Aurelius was erected in his honor and after his demise by decree of the Senate and people of Rome. But there are problems. The main question is, what are we to understand by the plural noun *columnas*? What is Victor referring to? Does he mean that Marcus Aurelius was honored by the column we know today, in addition to an unspecified number of others?

This numerical ambiguity is only one of the problems with Victor. Also dubious are his qualifications as an expert on Roman topography and his overall accuracy. Sextus Aurelius Victor was born in North Africa, around A.D. 320.[5] He moved from North Africa to Rome, where he served, perhaps, as a bookkeeper in the imperial service. He then moved to Sirmium, where he was (again, perhaps) fiscal secretary to the praetorian prefect; later he was made governor of Pannonia by the emperor Julian. At Sirmium, between about 358 and 360, he wrote his *Liber de Caesaribus*. Victor's position as urban prefect of Rome is sometimes appealed to as an argument in support of the accuracy of his statements about the city—but he did not take on this office until 388, a quarter of a century after his wrote his history.[6] Thus Victor had some experience in Rome but wrote his imperial history in a city far away from the capital. He would have relied, presumably, on memory for any details of Roman topography, and had no opportunity to check the facts for himself. He could not have visited the column in person, and thus he could not have read its inscription and confirmed its date of dedication even if he had wanted to. Also problematic is Victor's record of inaccuracy. His work is full of errors and misunderstandings. For our period he records, for example, that Marcus Aurelius gave citizenship to all the inhabitants of the Roman empire, when in fact this happened much later, under Caracalla.[7] Victor also reports that Commodus was made Caesar on the death of Verus, but in fact Verus died in 169, and Commodus had already been made Caesar in 166.[8] The latter error might be forgiven, the result presumably of an assumption that when Verus had died, Marcus would have immediately wanted a colleague to fill his shoes. The former is more serious—but it too has a likely explanation, which I will return to later in this chapter. For now it is enough to say that Victor's reference to *columnas* in the *Liber de Caesaribus*, a poor source in general, cannot be taken with any degree of confidence as evidence for the date of the Column of Marcus Aurelius.

This exhausts our literary sources. The next-best evidence for the date of the column comes from the monument itself, or more precisely from the content of its relief decoration.

Visual Evidence: Dating the Frieze

In the absence of solid written evidence for the date of the decision to build the Column of Marcus Aurelius, most scholars have turned to its sculpture. Two elements of the relief decoration of the column are potentially useful as dating tools: clearly historical scenes in the frieze, and the presence or absence of Commodus in the overall decoration. The rationale behind each is simple: if it were possible to determine what time period is represented by the images on the column, whether the main helical frieze or the pedestal relief, it would be possible to use this to help date the monument. The basic argument for using the frieze to date the column is this: if the events shown on it only cover the period up to 175, then a date of 176 would be highly likely. If however the relief shows events from the campaigns down to 180, that would support a postmortem dating for the monument. Crucial here is the presence or absence of Commodus: if Commodus is certainly absent from the column's decoration, this would be a strong argument for a date of 176 (before Commodus became directly involved in his father's wars), but if his image can be shown to have existed anywhere in the relief decoration, this would be a near-certain guarantee of a date of 180.

In the main helical frieze, three scenes above all others are generally thought to be historical—that is, to represent specific historical events: the Danube Crossing at the base of the column; the Victoria in the middle; and the Rain Miracle, located between the two. Figure 1.3 shows the lowest of these scenes, the Danube Crossing and the Rain Miracle, as they appear from the perspective of a viewer standing at the base of the column today (the ancient view would have been more distant, as the ground level has since risen by approximately three meters—see chapters 2 and 9). Marcus Aurelius and his troops certainly crossed the Danube at the beginning of the war, and must have done so at other, later times during the course of various campaigns during the 170s. But there is no specific characteristic of this scene that allows us to decide when the crossing depicted took place, except for its appearance at the start of the frieze, which would seem to suggest a date sometime at the beginning of the campaigns. The Victoria, on the other hand, does not represent in a realistic fashion a particular event in the wars, but rather alludes to victory through a personification. Marcus

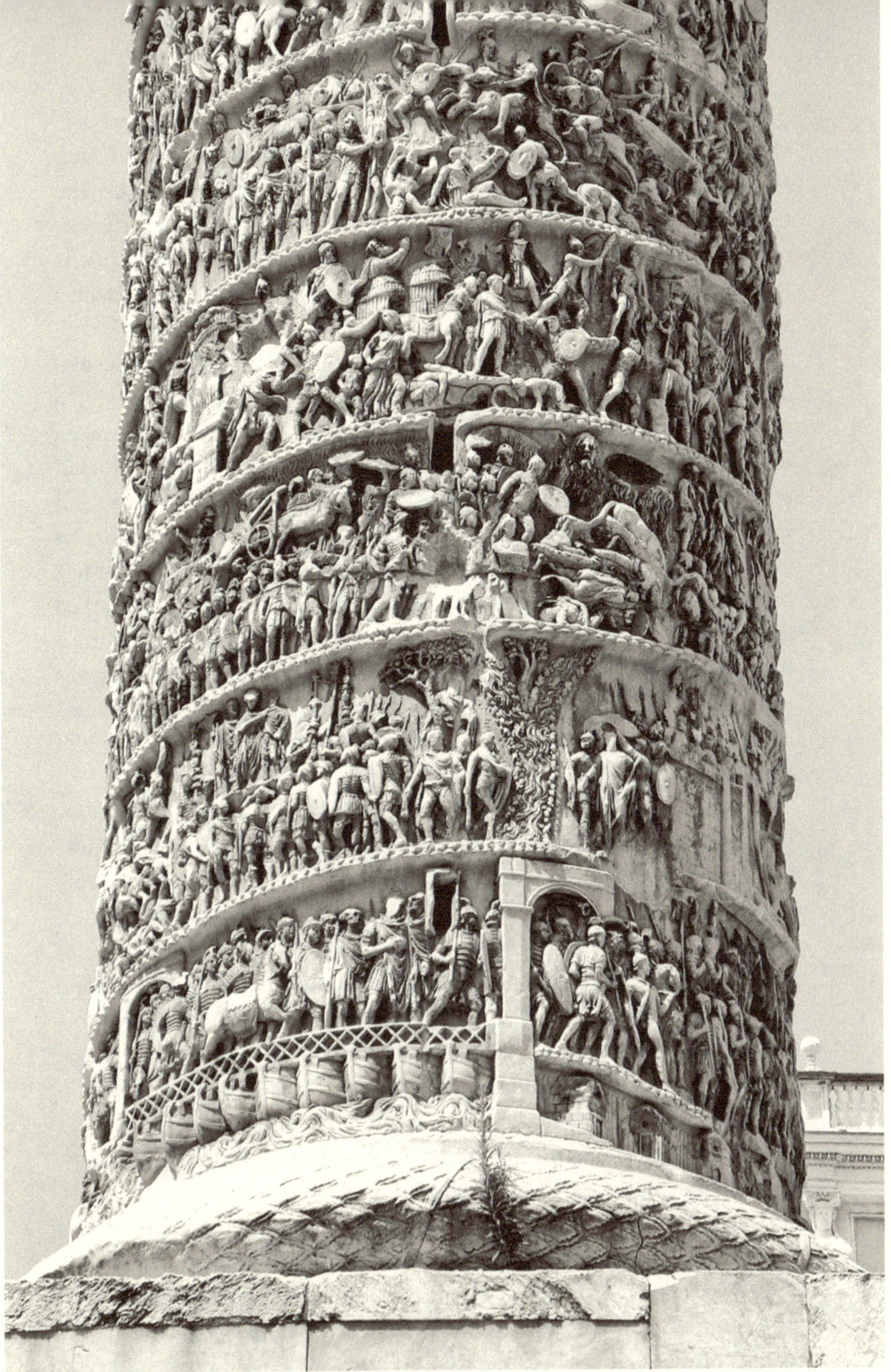

FIGURE 1.3. Lower portion of the column, seen from the east. In the first winding, Marcus crosses the Danube on a boat bridge; in the third is the Rain Miracle. Photo by author.

Aurelius celebrated two victories during the 170s: one over the Germans in 172, the other over the Sarmatians in 175. Both are commemorated on coins and led to Marcus being titled *Germanicus* and *Sarmaticus*. The general trend has been to interpret the Victoria as representing Marcus's first victory and thus serving as a divider between his two main campaigns, just as the Victoria on Trajan's Column stands between that emperor's two Dacian wars.

The Rain Miracle, unlike the Danube Crossing and the Victoria scenes, definitely represents a specific historical event. Records are preserved in a number of sources, including the work of the historian Dio (see the detailed discussion of the scene in chapter 7), that tell the story of how a Roman army was saved from thirst and barbarian attack by a lightning storm and a torrential downpour. We even have an apparently reliable date for the event: Dio says that as a result of this victory Marcus was saluted *imperator* by the troops for the seventh time; this title first appears on coins marked as struck during his eighteenth tenure of the tribunician power and thus dating to the year 174.[9] This creates a problem: if the Danube Crossing was intended to represent an event that occurred in 170 or 171, and the Victoria an event that occurred in 172, then the Rain Miracle is very much out of place in a supposedly chronologically organized frieze.

A number of solutions to this problem have been put forward, most involving detailed arguments for the redating of one or more of the Danube Crossing, Victoria, or Rain Miracle scenes.[10] The most convincing solution, however, is this: that the content of the frieze is *not* a strictly chronological account of the wars of Marcus Aurelius. The strongest evidence in favor of such an interpretation is to be found in the Danube Crossing and Victoria scenes themselves. At first glance, they seem to be there because they commemorate specific events in Marcus's campaigns. But this is in fact not the case. These two scenes, so often taken as chronologically fixed points, are in fact copied from the Column of Trajan (the Danube Crossing in particular is an exact copy of the corresponding scene on Trajan's column—see chapter 5). This connection is usually ignored, and even in the rare cases where it is acknowledged (for example by Wolff with regard to the Victoria), it is most often simply assumed that these scenes still must have a specific historical meaning on Marcus's Column.[11] There is no sound reason for such an assumption to be made, and the evidence of the strong parallels in the details of these scenes between the two columns speaks strongly against it. The Danube and Victoria scenes may well have brought to mind for the viewer events in Marcus's campaigns (the emperor and his army did cross the Danube, and Marcus did win victories), but the fact that they are copied from Trajan's Column, and copied in exactly the same positions and precisely in a number of details, indicates that the act of copying, not any historical relevance, is the reason for their presence and, most important, for their exact positioning on the column. Thus they have no value as specific historical evidence for events in Marcus's wars.

Further evidence of the nonhistoric nature of the Victoria in the frieze of the Column of Marcus Aurelius can be found in its setting within the column's narrative, by which I mean the nature of the various scenes immediately before and after it. On Trajan's Column, the Victoria stands in a genuine and clearly visible break between two wars. Before it, the events in Dacia surrounding the victory of A.D. 102 are clearly and dramatically shown: an entire Dacian army offers itself in submission to Trajan in a scene that occupies one-half of a complete winding of the frieze; Dacian fortifications are demolished and populations evicted; and, finally, Trajan is hailed by his troops. After the Victoria the second campaign (A.D. 105–106) begins with a sequence of twelve travel and greeting scenes that continues for two complete windings of the frieze before the first scene of field operations appears. The frieze of Trajan's Column could be divided at the figure of Victoria and each of the resulting two segments could be easily understood as a distinct campaign with a clear and well-developed beginning and end. On the Column of Marcus Aurelius, on the other hand, before the Victoria there is simply a battle (scene LIV) followed by a scene of Marcus on a podium reading a document to his troops (LV). After the Victoria, the war appears to pick up again immediately, as if it had never left off, with a scene (LVI) of the emperor receiving barbarian envoys; this in turn is followed by a skirmish in a forest (LVII). There is no indication that Marcus has left the field and then returned to it later, as would have been the case if the Victoria represented the victories for which Marcus earned a triumph in Rome in the year 176. There are also no opening scenes of the *expeditio Germanica secunda* of 178. It seems strange for the designer of Marcus's Column, who clearly studied the Column of Trajan closely enough to copy the Victoria scene, to have dispensed with such a preamble, especially since he did include one at the beginning of the frieze. An argument could be made on this basis that the Victoria scene might have been conceived of by the designers of the column as representing the German victory of 172, won when Marcus was in the field and followed immediately by campaigns against the Sarmatians. However, there are none of the sort of images that we might expect to find associated with such an event: defeated Germans being led off into captivity, their houses destroyed, etc. Again, the best interpretation of this scene, along with the Danube Crossing, is that it is positioned here mainly because it was also present in the same spot on Trajan's Column.

This renders the place of the Rain Miracle in the frieze more or less irrelevant, for the purpose of precise dating at least. If the Danube Crossing and the Victoria are there in their specific form and locations because they were copied from scenes of the same content and location on Trajan's Column, then the position of the Rain Miracle relative to them does not say anything about its date. It may however say something about the concerns of the column's designers. The Rain Miracle was clearly a very famous event, as is made clear by the number of different sources that have preserved an account of it (see chapter 7). The low placement of this scene on the column, apparently out of chronological order, may be the result of a desire to increase its visibility. This interpretation is reinforced by the alignment of the Rain Miracle scene (along with the figure of Marcus Aurelius crossing the Danube and the personification of Victoria above) along the main east axis of the column. A visitor approaching the column would have seen this axis, and the important scenes on it, first. The low position of the Rain Miracle would have greatly aided a visitor in making out what it represented. The fact that a famous event is involved, and a god is represented, makes such a motivation all the more plausible. An added reason for putting this scene of divine intervention low on the column may have been to make clear to the viewer that the gods were on the emperor's side from the beginning of the campaign.[12] This scene might be compared with the representation of Zeus in scene XXIV of Trajan's Column, another low-placed scene, where the god is shown joining the Romans and helping them in their battle.

In summary, two of the three most important "historical" scenes on the Column of Marcus Aurelius are not actually historical at all. Instead, both their form and their location in the frieze were copied from identical scenes in identical locations on the Column of Trajan. This copying, and not any historical connection, determined their appearance and position. The single truly historical scene—the Rain Miracle—loses its chronological relevance when this copying is recognized, a conclusion that also suggests that a great deal of caution should be used when seeking specific historical meaning in either the content or location of other scenes in the frieze.

The Presence or Absence of Commodus

What of Commodus? Marcus's son remained in Rome for the first half of the 170s and did not join his father on the front until 175, when he was summoned after the revolt of Avidius Cassius.[13] He triumphed along with Marcus in Rome in 176, then accompanied his father to the front during his second series of campaigns (177–180) and was there with him when he died.[14] Therefore, if the column was commissioned after Marcus's death, then its sculpture would logically have chronicled events up to that point, and we would expect to see Commodus on it. If, on the other hand, the column was commissioned in 176 and records only events up to 175, Commodus should be absent. This argument is reinforced by the series of monumental reliefs (the "Panel Reliefs") thought to have once decorated a triumphal arch erected to Marcus Aurelius in honor of his triumph in 176. The reliefs include scenes from the wars up to 175 and scenes from Marcus's triumph in Rome after his return in 176. Commodus was present on panels showing scenes of triumph and largesse in Rome, but not on any of the panels showing scenes from the war abroad (more on this below).[15]

So is Commodus present on the column, or is he not? There are two possible places where he might be found: first, in the main helical frieze; and second, in the relief that once decorated the pedestal. Birley believes that Commodus may be seen in the frieze and tentatively identifies him in a number of scenes; XLIX, illustrated here as figure 1.4, is one of the best-preserved examples, where the man standing to the left of (behind) Marcus Aurelius is identified as Commodus.[16] However, each of Birley's "Commoduses" is a fully bearded man, a man not noticeably younger than Marcus himself. Commodus was born in 161, which would have made him a teenager throughout the 170s. On coins from this period he is always shown as youthful and beardless.[17] The contemporary contrast between Marcus's mature image and the child Commodus is abundantly clear on a double-headed coin of the year 175, were the boyish bust of the *augusti filius* stands in bold contrast to that of his bearded father on the obverse (fig. 1.5).[18] Sestertii of 177 show Marcus and his son seated on a platform, in a *liberalitas* scene, where Commodus is identifiable by his round, beardless head and his shorter stature.[19] Even as late as 180 Commodus is shown wearing only sideburns (fig. 1.6); a full beard first appears in 185.[20] Birley suggests that Commodus "would appear looking as he was at the time the Column was being made"—that is to say, during the 180s.[21] But contem-

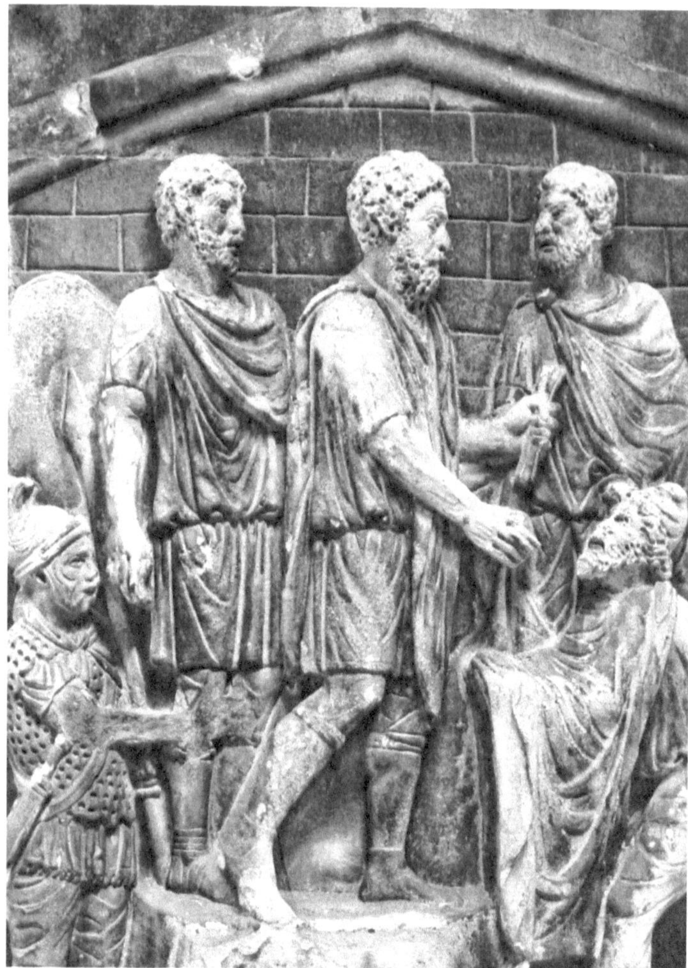

FIGURE 1.4. Marcus and companions on a podium (scene XLIX); the figure behind Marcus has been identified as Commodus. From Petersen et al. 1896, detail of pl. 56A.

porary Romans—including the artists who worked on the column—would have been aware of how old Commodus was during his father's campaigns, not least from seeing depictions of him together with his father from this period. An image showing him bearded and fully-grown in a scene from a time when he certainly was not would have come across as curious and jarring. There is no known instance of such retrospective aging in the entire repertoire of Roman historical art. It cannot be that the Romans of the 180s had lost the ability to render a young Commodus; they were certainly capable of producing youthful busts of older emperors. In fact, it appears that youthful busts of Commodus himself were produced long after he had grown into adulthood—and perhaps even after his death. The evidence for

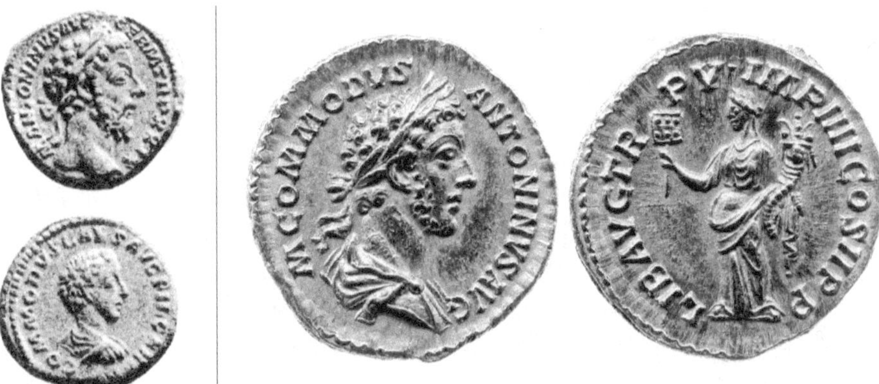

(left) FIGURE 1.5. Denarius of A.D. 175, showing Marcus Aurelius on the obverse and a very youthful, beardless Commodus on the reverse. Mattingly 1923–62, Marcus 625. Copyright Trustees of the British Museum.

(right) FIGURE 1.6. Aureus of Commodus from his first year as sole emperor, A.D. 180. Mattingly 1923–62, Commodus 1. Copyright Trustees of the British Museum.

this comes from a series of marble busts belonging to his first portrait type and showing a young, beardless Commodus, but identifiable on stylistic grounds as Severan rather than Antonine in date.[22] These portraits may be part of a series of newly created busts connected with the rehabilitation of Commodus's memory under Septimius Severus, intended to replace earlier portraits destroyed during the brief period after his death when he suffered *damnatio memoriae*.[23] The Romans possessed the capacity to execute portraits in whatever style the situation required, and had they wanted to depict Commodus on the Column of Marcus Aurelius, they would surely have done so in an appropriate manner.[24]

The helical frieze is not the only place where Commodus has been "sighted." The column also bore figural decoration in the form of carvings that adorned its pedestal. An entire band of this decoration on the pedestal has been preserved in Renaissance drawings; there may in fact have been more such decoration, in the form of panels attached to other parts of the pedestal, but this has long since been lost without record. Although the majority of the pedestal's substance is antique, its exterior was entirely refaced by Domenico Fontana, under orders of Pope Sixtus V, between the years 1588 and 1589. Even before this the base was already in a serious state of decay, with only a portion of its original surface surviving; this much at least we know from a small selection of drawings made before 1588.[25] Relief carving decorated a single preserved block of stone projecting beyond the main body of the pedestal. On three sides it was adorned with images of Victories holding up garlands, and on the fourth, eastern side it bore a figural frieze. An etching by Antonio Lafreri, circa 1550, preserves the only known depiction of this relief (fig. 1.7). It shows the emperor (just left of center, in armor and cloak) receiving the submission of two kneeling barbarians (for a complete description of the relief, see the conclusion of chapter 9). This much is clear. But one prominent figure, a male in armor standing between the emperor and the barbarians, defies easy identification. He balances the figure of the emperor in the composition and his full frontal pose marks him out as being similar to Marcus in importance. The most common theory (dating back to Petersen in the late nineteenth century) is that this figure represents Commodus, shown in the act of presenting prisoners to his father.[26] If this were the case, it would be a strong argument for a date of 180 for the decision to build the column.

But there is one major problem with the theory: the fact that after Commodus's murder on New Year's Eve 192 the Senate abolished his memory and declared him an enemy to the country and the gods. Anger that could not be vented on his person was expressed on his images. Both the Senate and the people, reported Dio, "wanted to drag off his body and tear it limb from limb, as they did do, in fact, with his statues."[27] His statues were overthrown; his name was erased from inscriptions both public and private. The busts of Commodus that survive today were either movable images placed in storage, ones safely exhibited in private houses, or images created after his rehabilitation by Septimius Severus. Inscriptions and fixed images in public places (including relief sculpture) faced the full wrath of *damnatio memoriae* and were duly obliterated. This is most clearly visible on the so-called Panel Reliefs of Marcus Aurelius, created to honor Marcus on the occasion of his triumph in 176.[28] Commodus's image was once present in two of these scenes, one where he was shown riding in his father's triumphal chariot (the Triumph panel) and another where he was shown seated with his father on a podium, distributing money to the people (the Liberalitas panel). The *damnatio memoriae* of Commodus in these works of relief sculpture did not involve merely the reworking of his portrait or the replacement of his head, but the entire removal of every part of his body. On the Triumph panel, all that remains is a roughly chiseled patch of stone at the top of the chariot in front of Marcus, visible only from above. On the Liberalitas panel there is the low outline of one of his feet (which would not have been visible from the ground), and the space where he once sat has been awkwardly filled by enlarging the bodies of two figures who once were

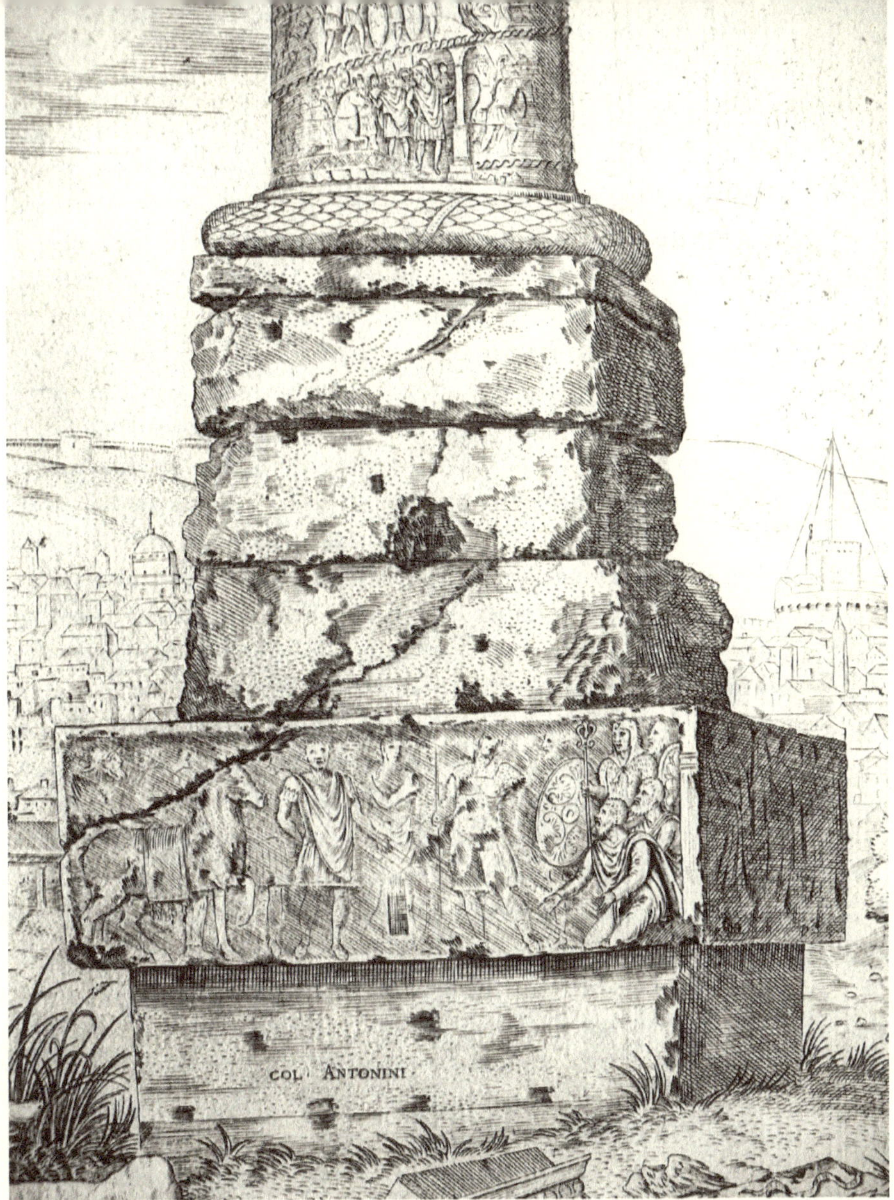

FIGURE 1.7. The pedestal of the column in the sixteenth century. From A. Lafreri, *Speculum Romanae Magnificentiae*, ca. 1550 (no date), p. 34 (no pagination).

in the background. There are no known instances of Commodus's image being merely reworked; in each case it was entirely removed. The implication of all this is that had the figure on the pedestal of the column been Commodus it could not have survived his *damnatio memoriae*, but rather would have been chiseled from the face of the monument. In light of this it seems highly unlikely that the figure in question could be Marcus's son.

If Commodus cannot be convincingly identified among the figures on the pedestal relief, nor among the extant figures on the column, what then of the possibility that his image once existed in the main frieze but was later removed, as on the Panel Reliefs? Morris believed he could identify two such instances on the column, in scenes CXII and in CXIV.[29] These are cases where whole sections of the frieze have been chiseled out and replaced with inserted blocks of stone. This is entirely unlike any known example of *damnatio memoriae* in relief sculpture, and the excellent state of preservation of these inserts suggests that these figures have spent much less time exposed to the open air than the heavily eroded and damaged ancient surfaces surrounding them. The style of the figures in these insertions is unlike anything known from the Roman period, and they are, in fact, the work of Renaissance restorers operating under Domenico Fontana. Comparison with other examples of Fontana's restoration clearly marks them as belonging to this project.[30] If this is not enough, Fontana's chief sculptor kept careful records of this restoration work including detailed accounts of the nature and number of figures that were executed as new work. His records for scenes CXII and in CXIV can be convincingly connected to Morris's presumed excisions of Commodus.[31] With these scenes eliminated, there is no further possible evidence for the *damnatio memoriae* of Commodus on the Column of Marcus Aurelius. This lends significant weight to the argument that the frieze covers events prior to Commodus's arrival on the front, meaning essentially that it concludes with events dating no later than 175, the year in which Marcus concluded his first set of northern campaigns.

The final chronological factor to consider is the overall decorative theme of the monument. Everywhere are representations of military activity and victory, either realistic (on the column frieze) or allegoric (on the pedestal relief). Nowhere is there even a hint of funerary or apotheosis imagery. Compare this to the pedestal of the Column of Antoninus Pius, which is decorated exclusively with representations of the funeral and subsequent deification of the emperor and his wife. Moreover, Marcus Aurelius is represented on his column as very much mortal. He engages in normal terrestrial activities, attended exclusively by humans, and dressed like the officers that surround him. This is unlike any known representation of a deified Roman emperor, and is not the imagery that one would expect to have been used on a posthumous monument. Rather, it is the imagery we would expect on an honorific monument erected—or at least commissioned and planned—while an emperor was alive.

Although the content of the relief (and what it does not contain, namely Commodus) argues strongly for a date of 176, Victor's *columnas* still require some sort of explanation. As noted above, Victor's work includes many errors. These errors often appear in generic-sounding lists, for example regarding Augustus: *hinque, uti deo, Romae provinciisque omnibus per urbes celeberrimas vivo mortuoque templa, sacerdotes et collegia sacravere*: "moreover, like for a god, in Rome and in all the provinces, in the most populous cities, during his life and after his death, temples and priests and priestly colleges were consecrated to him."[32] The latter part of this statement is wrong, at least as pertains to Rome: Suetonius, a much more reliable source, tells us that Augustus allowed temples in the provinces as long as they bore the name of Roma along with his, but *in urbe quidem pertinacissime abstinuit hoc honore*: "in the city itself he refused this honour most resolutely."[33] Victor was very fond of constructing impressive lists of honors for emperors he favored. However, he was not scrupulous in choosing what he included, and in the case of Augustus he introduced an error: temples dedicated to the emperor in Rome during his lifetime.

A similar piece of carelessness may have been responsible for the lumping of *columnas* into a generic list of honors voted on the death of Marcus Aurelius. But why add this plural noun at all? There is a very plausible explanation, and it has to do with the confusingly similar nomenclature of the emperors of the late second and early third centuries. The emperors known commonly today as Antoninus Pius, Marcus Aurelius, Commodus, Caracalla, and Elagabalus were known to the Romans as Aelius Aurelius Antoninus, M. Aurelius Antoninus, L. Aurelius Commodus Antoninus, M. Aurelius Antoninus, and M. Aurelius Antoninus. Each shares the name Antoninus, and three (Marcus, Caracalla, and Elagabalus) share praenomen, nomen, and cognomen. The potential for confusion was great. In another of his erroneous lists, Victor states that under Marcus Aurelius *data cunctis promiscue civitas Romana, multaquae urbes conditae, deductae, repositae ornataeque . . .* : "citizenship was given to everyone, and many cities were founded, settled, restored or adorned . . ."[34] Close, but not exactly right: the true donor of universal citizenship was Caracalla, or as the Romans knew him, Marcus Aurelius Antoninus. Victor's mistake appears to have stemmed not solely from carelessness but also from a confusion of names. He appears to have been unsure exactly which Antoninus issued the

Constitutio Antoniniana. He chose Marcus, perhaps based on his generous reputation, and so introduced an error into his history.

A similar potential for name confusion existed among the monuments of the northern Campus Martius. Two columns, both erected in honor of an Antoninus, stood within clear sight of one another near the Via Flaminia just north of the Temple of Divine Hadrian and the Pantheon: the Column of Aelius Aurelius Antoninus and the Column of Marcus Aurelius Antoninus. We have no literary mention of Aelius's (Antoninus Pius's) Column, but Marcus's Column was known in the early-fourth-century *Notitia Urbis Romae* as the "Column of Antoninus." Victor, writing his history in the 360s A.D., far from Rome, may have recalled the existence in Rome of two "Antonine" columns in the Campus Martius, both in close proximity to a number of imperial funerary monuments (see chapter 2). It would then be a short step to assume that both columns honored a single emperor, and to choose the wrong Antoninus: Marcus instead of Aelius, much as he chose Marcus instead of Caracalla as the author of the grant of universal citizenship. Thus both Pius's and Marcus's columns may have come in Victor's mind to belong to Marcus Aurelius, and he was in no position to check the evidence for himself and correct the error.

Conclusion: The Verdict of Cassius Dio

One author who *was* in a position to check for himself was the Roman senator and historian Cassius Dio. Dio, who sat in the Senate during the reign of Commodus and wrote his imperial history in the early third century, was the best placed of all our surviving authors to know the events surrounding the death of Marcus Aurelius. The surviving text of his history unfortunately is fragmentary, but the portion dealing with the honors voted to Marcus after his demise is preserved. But Dio mentions no column (or columns). Instead he records: "After his death he received many marks of honour; among other things a gold statue of him was set up on the senate-house itself."[35] His silence on the column in this context speaks volumes and reinforces the conclusion reached here: that the decision to build the Column of Marcus Aurelius does not belong among Marcus's posthumous honors, but rather to the time of his German and Sarmatian triumph in the year 176.

chapter two

THE DUST OF NORTHERN WARFARE

CHOICE OF LOCATION

The Column of Marcus Aurelius stood in the northern part of the Campus Martius, the flat expanse of land bounded by the Capitol to the south, the wide bend of the Tiber to the west, and the Via Flaminia to the east. To be more precise, its ancient location was on the west side of the Via Flaminia just north of a road sometimes called the Via Tecta or Via Recta, though in ancient times it almost certainly was called something else altogether, that led west past the Pantheon and the Stadium of Domitian to the Tiber and to Nero's bridge to the Ager Vaticanus. This area was traditionally associated with funerary monuments: the Mausoleum of Augustus lay to the north, the Column of Antoninus Pius not far to the west. But to call this area of the Campus Martius a funerary landscape is far too simple a characterization. The northern Campus Martius was a highly varied and sometimes puzzling monumental area. I have already touched on one of the puzzles: the house of Adrastus, procurator of the Column of Marcus Aurelius. Adrastus had apparently been living on-site during construction of the column; at least, the inscription on his doorposts records that his new house was intended to replace a smaller dwelling that had previously stood on the spot, presumably while the column was being built. Perhaps Adrastus had been an overseer, maybe the main controller, of the construction project. But Adrastus did not leave the site after construction was complete. Instead, he appealed for—and received—permission to build a new, permanent dwelling, one that he could pass on to his heirs, just behind the newly finished column. So, a short distance behind the Column of Marcus Aurelius, in the middle of an otherwise monumental landscape, a private residence was occupied by a contemporary Roman and his family. The topography of the Campus Martius defies simple classification.

Understanding the rationale behind the location of Adrastus's house is but one of the problems one faces when trying to reconstruct the ancient surroundings of the Column of Marcus Aurelius. Our understanding of the function of the column in its broad historical and political context depends in large part on an understanding of the meaning and use of the spaces and structures that surrounded it. Did the column stand in the open, or was it surrounded by other buildings? What sort of buildings? And what relationship, if any, did the column have with these structures? Rapid changes in this area of the Campus Martius during the second century A.D. make answering these questions a challenge. These changes did not involve new buildings alone (although many new buildings were indeed erected): they also relate to the very substance of the Campus itself, for the ground level rose continuously throughout the early imperial period. This means that it is impossible to reconstruct the area by simply adding new buildings to a plan of an older period. Monuments sank, disappeared, and were overlapped by later structures. The best way to understand the function of the Column of Marcus Aurelius in its ancient landscape is to see it within the broader picture of the evolution and development of the area since the time of Augustus.

From Augustus to Hadrian on the Campus Martius

The geographer Strabo, writing in the time of Augustus, provided a lucid description of the Campus Martius:

> Indeed, the size of the plain is remarkable, since it affords space at the same time and without interference, not only for the chariot-races and every other equestrian exercise, but also for all that multitude of people who exercise themselves by ball-playing, hoop-trundling, and wrestling; and the nearby works of art, and the ground, which is covered with grass throughout the year, and the crowns of those hills that are above the river and extend as far as its bed, which present to the eye the appearance of a stage-painting—all this, I say, affords a spectacle that one can hardly draw away from. And near this field [that is, to the south] is still another field, with colonnades round about it in very great numbers, and sacred precincts, and three theatres, and an amphitheatre, and very costly temples, in close succession to one another, giving you the impression that they are trying, as it were, to declare the rest of the city a mere accessory. For this reason in the belief that this place was holiest of all, the Romans have erected in it the tombs of their most illustrious men and women. The most

noteworthy is what is called the Mausoleum, a great mound near the river on a lofty foundation of white marble, thickly covered with ever-green trees to the very summit. Now on top is a bronze image of Augustus Caesar; beneath the mound are the tombs of himself and his kinsmen and intimates; behind the mound is a large sacred precinct with wonderful promenades; and in the centre of the Campus is the wall, this too of white marble, around his crematorium; the wall is surrounded by a circular iron fence and the space within the wall is planted with black poplars. And again, if, on passing to the old Forum, you saw one forum after another ranged along the old one, and basilicas, and temples, and saw also the Capitolium and the works of art there and those of the Palatium and Livia's Promenade, you would easily become oblivious to everything else outside. Such is Rome.[1]

Strabo gives not only a powerful impression of the appearance of the Campus, but also a clear idea of what it was used for: exercise and sport in the west, public life and entertainment in the center, and garden promenades among the funerary monuments to the north. The description is concerned exclusively with the area to the west of the Via Flaminia; east of this road was an open plain usually referred to as the Campus Agrippae, which Dio says was owned by Agrippa and willed after his death to the Roman public. During the first century A.D. it seems to have contained no substantial buildings; Aulus Gellius reports that it was popular for strolling.[2]

Strabo omits some buildings from his description, particularly from the area between the Mausoleum and the Via Recta. Most important of these were the Horologium and the Ara Pacis, the latter located directly near the Via Flaminia, the former further to the west of it. The Horologium, dedicated in 10 B.C., consisted of an Egyptian obelisk forming the gnomon of a massive sundial, mounted at the south-center of a trapezoidal expanse of travertine paving measuring 160 meters east to west and 75 meters north to south.[3] Suetonius records that the space between the Horologium and the Mausoleum (and north to Piazza del Populo) was laid out by Augustus with elaborate public gardens.[4] The space to the south of the Horologium and Ara Pacis, all the way south to the Via Recta at the north edge of the built-up monumental area of the Campus, appears to have been largely empty, perhaps with a similarly parklike character. This whole area would have provided outdoor recreation for the many thousands of visitors to the baths, theaters, and porticos immediately to the south.

The Campus Martius developed dramatically during the first century A.D. Claudius inserted a triumphal arch into the Aqua Virgo at the point where it crossed over the Via Flaminia, transforming this waterway into a monumental entrance to the center of the city.[5] Nero constructed a massive bath complex in the area to the northwest of the Pantheon, and most likely built a new road (the Via Recta) along the front (north face) of his baths, from the Via Flaminia west to the Pons Neronianus and over the river to his circus in the Ager Vaticanus.[6] The great fire of A.D. 80 destroyed many buildings in the area, including the Pantheon of Agrippa and the theater of Balbus.[7] Domitian used the opportunity to rebuild and enlarge the complex, most importantly by building a temple (the Divorum) to his deceased father and brother between the baths of Agrippa and the Via Flaminia, a great new stadium immediately to the west of the baths of Nero with spaces for 30,000 spectators, and an odeon (perhaps south of the stadium) that could accommodate 11,000. Naturally, this amount of construction would have required extensive work areas. One of these, attested by rough stones with quarrymen's inscriptions of Domitianic date, was located near the Tiber immediately north of Domitian's stadium.[8]

The earth itself was also on the move. By the time of the great fire in the year 80, the ground level over the entire area from the Via Recta to the Mausoleum had risen by about 1.6 meters from Augustan levels. In the aftermath of the fire, Domitian reconstructed the entire sundial of Augustus at a new, higher level, using new paving stones but reusing the old bronze lettering from the Augustan monument.[9] This almost doubled the height of this area of the Campus above the Tiber, giving it much better protection from flooding.

After the massive efforts of Domitian, building activity in the Campus Martius slowed. Nerva's reign was short, and Trajan focused his energy elsewhere, in his new Forum complex just southeast of the Campus. It was left to Hadrian to make the next major additions to the area. Like Domitian, he both renovated and restored old and damaged buildings (many, including the Pantheon, must have lain in ruin through Domitian's reign) and constructed new ones. The *Historia Augusta* credits him with restorations to the Pantheon, the Saepta, the Baths of Agrippa, and the Basilica of Neptune (apparently between the Baths and the Pantheon), and emphasizes that that he did not write his own name on any of these structures; the surviving evidence bears this out.[10] Hadrian commemorated Matidia, his mother-in-law, with a large temple just east of the piazza before the Pantheon.[11] He also made plans for his own eternal rest, building a great new mausoleum in the style of that of Augustus, across the Tiber, upstream from the Pons Neronianus. This he joined to the Campus Martius by a new bridge, the Pons Aelius, set on the main south axis of approach to the mausoleum.[12] Much of the preparatory work for these substantial building projects must have taken place in the area north of the Via Recta. The northwestern Campus Martius was certainly the location of major stonemasons' workshops, most vividly attested by the one-to-one scale plans carved into the paving in front of the Mausoleum of Augustus showing elements of the capitals and pediment of the Hadrianic Pantheon.[13] It appears that these massive architectural elements were prepared in front of the Mausoleum and then transported overland directly south to the Pantheon building site just to the south.

The ground level of the northern portion of the Campus Martius, including the Via Flaminia, had risen dramatically by the time of Hadrian. The increase in ground level was even greater than that which had occurred between Augustus and Domitian: the ground surface in the area of the Horologium and Ara Pacis rose by almost three meters, and the level of the Via Flaminia was increased by about two meters.[14] This change had striking effects on the topography of the Campus Martius. The Ara Pacis was now located in a well, the surrounding earth held back by a brick retaining wall (the stamps on the bricks in the wall can be dated to Hadrian's reign).[15] The Horologium of Augustus simply disappeared—except, of course, for the obelisk. In an attempt to preserve some small aspect of the monument, a basin was constructed along the length of the old meridian line; the remainder of the monument, however, was forever lost from view. While it seems that some parts of the new Hadrianic ground level were paved (in front of the Mausoleum, for example), most of it was likely left as a natural, grassy field, perhaps planted in part with trees and gardens.

But the most dramatic change was the appearance of the first houses, in the form of massive, multistory brick apartment blocks (insulae) reminiscent of Hadrianic construction at Ostia. A row of insulae was built lining the east side of the Via Flaminia opposite Piazza Colonna, the future site of the Column of Marcus Aurelius.[16] These were constructed of brick-faced concrete and some travertine blocks; brick stamps found in the walls date to around A.D. 123.[17] Another large insula was built west of the Via Flaminia just north of the Ara Pacis, where its remains have been found beneath the church of San Lorenzo in Lucina.[18] This structure, which is on the same level as the new retaining wall around the Ara Pacis, partly overlapped the former location of the Horologium. Together, these new, massive, multistory brick structures rising from a previously flat and open landscape would have drastically changed the appearance of the northern Campus Martius.

The Age of the Antonines: An Apotheosis Landscape?

Immediately after Hadrian's death, his adoptive son and successor, Antoninus Pius, constructed in his father's honor a temple, located in a large colonnaded courtyard east of the Pantheon, along the Via Flaminia.[19] As a monument to a deceased imperial relative, it followed the example set by Hadrian's temple of Matidia (likely located just to the west) and Domitian's temple for his father, Vespasian, and brother, Titus, located along the Via Flaminia to the south.

The next additions to the area were different (fig. 2.1). These were a series of travertine and marble enclosures, square in plan and measuring 100 feet to a side, each with two concentric walls enclosing a square central structure. Three such monuments have been found, one in the eighteenth century at the southwest corner of the Palazzo Montecitorio (also known by its later name, Palazzo del Parlamento, a very short distance northwest of the Piazza Colonna), and two altars, side by side, in the twentieth century beneath the palazzo itself. The single altar in the southwest had an outer wall (about thirty meters or one hundred feet a side) of travertine pillars with iron fencing, an inner wall of marble with a door in its north face, and a solid central structure measuring thirteen meters a side.[20] Of the twin altars beneath the palazzo, the easternmost had two enclosure walls of travertine pillars and iron fencing with an entrance on the south side, inside of which was marble wall measuring 10.5 meters a side.[21] The western altar, more poorly preserved, abuts its eastern counterpart and appears to have been similar in plan, although one of its walls is curved.[22] Substantial portions of the eastern altar have been found. The most notable feature is the set of acroteria, deeply carved with an elaborate vegetal pattern in a style that points to an Antonine date.[23]

These structures have been interpreted as commemorative altars (*arae consecrationis*) marking the sites of the imperial funerary pyres (*ustrina*), which were originally wooden and would have been consumed during cremation.[24] These pyres were, by the second century at least, massive structures of at least three stories, built of timber, covered with cloth woven with gold thread, and adorned with ivory statues and paintings. In the early third century A.D., the historian Herodian compared them to lighthouses, which

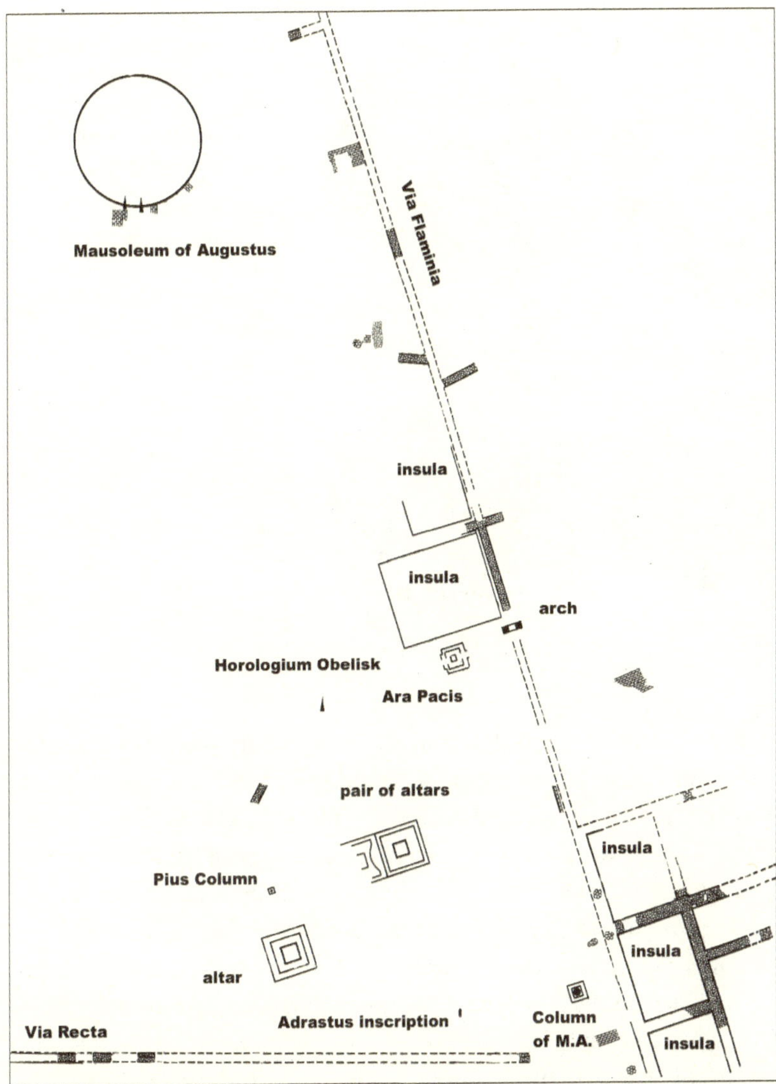

FIGURE 2.1. Plan of the northern Campus Martius in the time of Septimius Severus. Shaded areas represent archaeologically attested road surfaces. Drawing by author.

in the ancient world were built in a form resembling a steep, square-sided wedding cake.[25] Cassius Dio, contemporary of Septimius Severus, gives a vivid description of the cremation of Pertinax on a three-story pyre in the Campus Martius:

> All the rest of us, now, marched ahead of the bier, some beating our breasts and others playing a dirge on the flute, but the emperor fol-

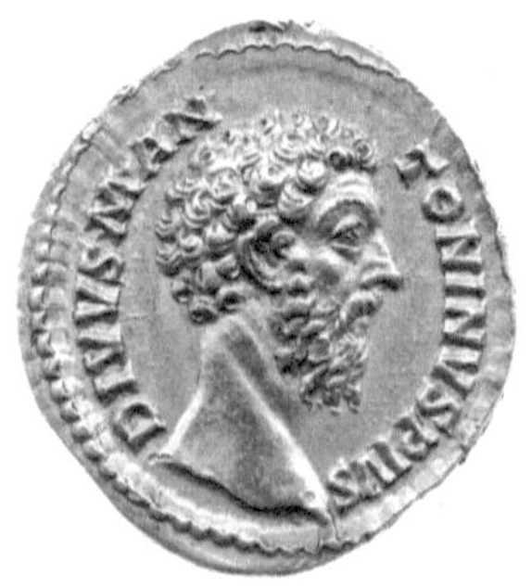

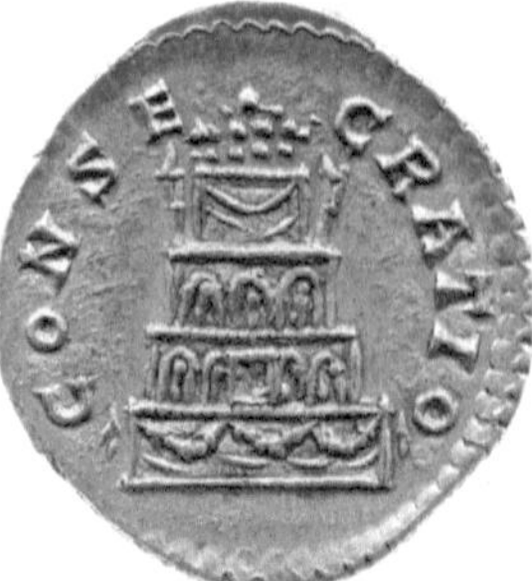

(above) FIGURE 2.2.
Aureus struck under Commodus showing funeral pyre of Marcus Aurelius. Mattingly 1923–62, Commodus 25. Copyright Trustees of the British Museum.

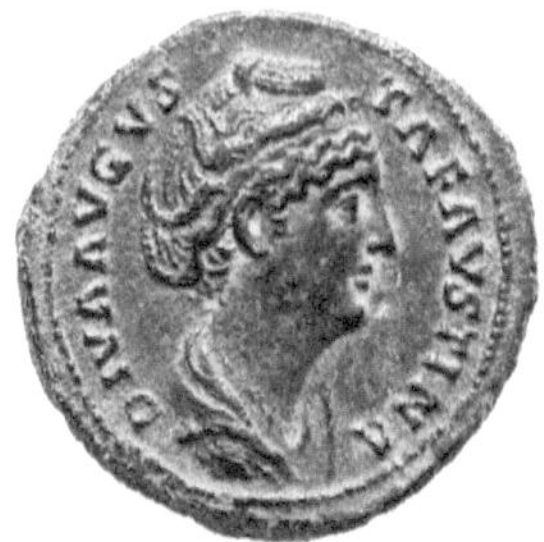

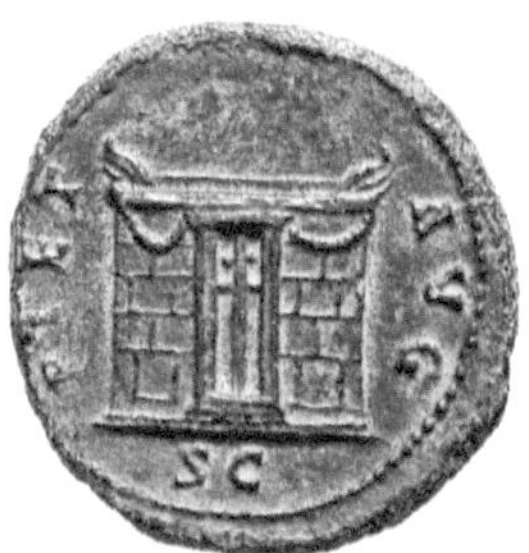

(below) FIGURE 2.3.
Dupondius showing the funerary altar of Faustina the Elder, ca. A.D. 141. Vienna, Kunsthistorisches Museum, photo by author.

> lowed behind all the rest; and in this order we arrived at the Campus Martius. There a pyre had been built in the form of a tower having three stories and adorned with ivory and gold as well as a number of statues, while on its very summit was placed a gilded chariot that Pertinax had been wont to drive. Inside this pyre the funeral offerings were cast and the bier was placed in it, and then Severus and the relatives of Pertinax kissed the effigy. The emperor then ascended a tribunal, while we, the senate, except the magistrates, took our places on wooden stands in order to view the ceremonies both safely and conveniently. The magistrates and the equestrian order, arrayed in a manner befitting their station, and likewise the cavalry and the infantry, passed in and out around the pyre performing intricate evolutions, both those of peace and those of war. Then at last the consuls applied fire to the structure, and then this had been done, an eagle flew aloft from it. Thus was Pertinax made immortal.[26]

These pyres are shown on the posthumous coinage of a number of second- and third-century emperors and imperial family members (fig. 2.2). The altars found on the Campus Martius are different from these pyres, but they are strikingly similar to another and less common structure

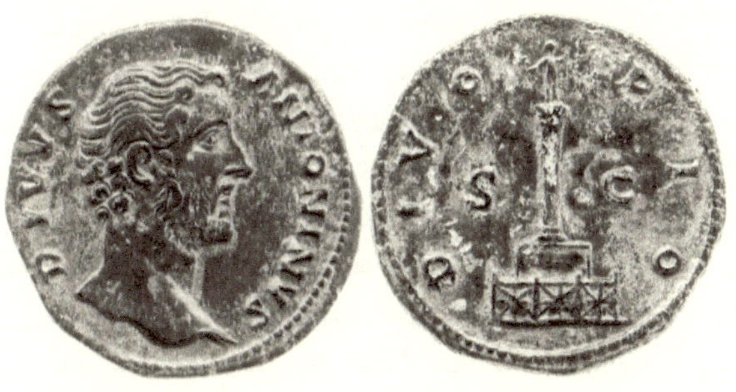

FIGURE 2.4. Sestertius of Marcus Aurelius struck in the name of Divus Antoninus Pius, showing the latter's column on the Campus Martius. Mattingly 1923–62, Marcus 881. Copyright Trustees of the British Museum.

seen on posthumous coinage (fig. 2.3), an altar and an enclosure in stone masonry.

The key question is, of course, to whom did these altars belong? Whose consecrations did they mark? Their decoration and their elevation atop the Hadrianic ground level suggests that they belong to the Antonine period, but which of the Antonines exactly did they honor?[27] Central to answering this question is the Column of Antoninus Pius (fig. 2.4). The granite column, fifty feet tall and topped by a statue of the deceased Pius, was mounted atop a massive base formed from a solid block of marble. The base is decorated on three sides with carving in very high relief; on the fourth the dedicatory inscription *Divo Antonino Aug Pio / Antoninus Augustus et / Verus Augustus filii*: "To the Deified Antoninus Pius, from his sons Marcus Aurelius and Lucius Verus."[28] Two of the sculpted sides depict images of one of the central rituals of the imperial public funeral: the *decursio*, a procession by riders around the pyre (although in this case a group of soldiers is shown at the center of the procession). The remaining face is carved with a remarkable allegoric scene representing the culminating event of the funeral, the apotheosis of the emperor (and his wife, although they died on different dates) in the Campus Martius. The landscape setting, the Campus itself, is represented as a reclining figure supporting himself on the obelisk of Augustus's sundial.

The remains of the Column of Antoninus Pius were excavated and removed from their original location in the early eighteenth century, but the original site is still known.[29] The pedestal of the column was aligned precisely with the facing wall of the altar to its south and placed exactly one hundred Roman feet from the center of its north side. The inscribed side faced away from the altar; the side showing the apotheosis toward it. The altar facing Pius's column has been identified as belonging to his wife Faustina I, who predeceased him, or to Antoninus Pius himself.[30] The other two altars, the ones beneath the Palazzo del Parlamento, present a greater problem of identification. The eastern and more completely preserved of the two has generally been identified with Marcus Aurelius,[31] due mainly to its relative proximity to the Column of Marcus Aurelius and the precedent supposedly set by Pius's altar-column complex. However, two important factors give cause for doubt. First, the distance (ca. 420 feet) between the Column of Marcus Aurelius and the twin altars is out of all proportion to the exact one-hundred-foot separation between Pius's column and its nearby altar. Second, while the column base, the nearby altar, and the twin altars are all aligned to exactly the same grid, the Column of Marcus Aurelius is aligned instead to the Via Flaminia. These factors have caused more than one scholar to express serious reservation about the connection between the Marcus column and the altars under the Palazzo del Parlamento.[32] This in turn throws doubt on the identification of the better-preserved altar as that of Marcus, and of the neighboring altar as that of Lucius Verus or Faustina.[33]

The evidence of coinage can be used to help solve this riddle. Posthumous coin issues were at their most popular in the second century and show not only symbolic references to an emperor's or empress' death and deification (eagles or peacocks, for example), but also representations of physical objects used in the ceremonies (carts or pyres) or dedicated to the Divus or Diva afterwards (temples or altars, for example). On all the divus and diva coinage of the second century, only four altars are recorded. The first appears on coins of Diva Sabina, wife of Hadrian, as part of a relatively small posthumous issue.[34] The second appears on coins of Faustina I, wife of Antoninus Pius, who was honored with a very large and long-lasting series of posthumous coinage that also included representations of her funerary pyre and numerous images of her temple in the Roman Forum.[35] The third funerary altar appears on the coinage of Divus Pius, where not only his altar but also his funeral pyre and his column are depicted. Lucius Verus's posthumous coinage, on the other hand, shows only a pyre.[36] This imbalance is consistent with the common public image of the two emperors: Pius, serious and respected, and Verus, the buffoon who entertained himself by, among other things, getting into fights with common brawlers and throwing heavy coins through wine-shop windows to see if he could break the cups inside.[37] Pius was honored with an altar and a column after his death, while Verus received neither. The fourth and final altar to appear on posthumous coinage of the Antonines (and the last to be depicted for over a century) was that of Faustina II; her pyre is also represented.[38] For Marcus Aurelius, her husband, the only architectural depiction on his *divus* coinage was his pyre.[39]

Thus there is a firm record of four funerary altars being dedicated to members of the imperial family—Sabina, Faustina I and II, and Antoninus Pius—and we have three altars datable by their carving to the Antonine period, all in close proximity to a column that is clearly identified by an inscription as having been set up in honor of the deified Pius. Since both column and altar appear on the posthumous coinage of Antoninus Pius, we can conclude that the altar directly aligned with the Column of Antoninus Pius was his. The pair of altars beneath the Palazzo del Parlamento might then sensibly be assigned to Faustina I and II, mother and daughter. The altar of Sabina is thus still to be found, but we need not look for it within our cluster of Antonine monuments. The coinage suggests that these altars were a particular fashion of the Antonine period, and it is possible that with Marcus the tradition of erecting such altars died out.[40] There is no compelling reason to expect that there is any more than one more altar—Sabina's—waiting to be found in the Campus.

Paul Zanker has proposed that the three known altars, together with the two columns and the nearby temples of Hadrian, Matidia, and Marcus Aurelius are but the tip of an archaeological iceberg, hinting at further altars, columns, and temples dedicated to later deified emperors and empresses lying unseen beneath the surface of the Campus.[41] The resulting "apotheosis landscape" would have constituted a religious center to rival the Capitol. But evidence for this is lacking. Certainly the three altars, together with Pius's column, formed an apotheosis landscape of sorts. It was, however, a relatively small, focused, and short-lived one. The northern Campus Martius never became the exclusive site of monuments to deceased and deified imperial family members. Antoninus Pius chose the Roman forum as the site of the temple in honor of his wife, Faustina the Elder, who died in 141. When Pius died, Marcus Aurelius rededicated this temple to honor the imperial pair together, erasing part of the extant decoration to add a new inscription. Marcus Aurelius, after setting up a column and altar to Pius and an altar to his own wife Faustina in the Campus Martius, then erected a temple to the latter in another location altogether, perhaps on the Palatine.[42] After the temple of the Divine Marcus (whose location is by no means certain—see below), we have no record of any other imperial temple erected in this area of the Campus.

The Placement of the Column of Marcus Aurelius

To understand why this particular location was chosen in the year 176 for a new monument to honor the victories of Marcus Aurelius, it is not enough merely to create a general picture of the function of the area. Rather, the precise situation and orientation of the column must be taken into consideration. Two aspects are especially important: first, the column's orientation to the Via Flaminia; second, its relationship to other monuments, especially the funerary altars, to the west of this road.

The relationship between the column and the Via Flaminia was of primary importance to its designers, a point made abundantly clear both by the column's architecture and by its decoration: the column's designers considered the eastern side to be the primary axis of approach and interaction with the monument. First, the pedestal of the column is oriented so that its east side parallels the adjacent road. Moreover, the doorway giving access to the column's internal staircase faces the street, inviting passersby to enter. Artistically, the most important scenes of the column's helical frieze are oriented in the same direction: Marcus's crossing of the Danube, the Rain Miracle, and the central scene of Victoria inscribing her shield. All these scenes would have been immediately discernable to a person entering the area of the column, and some scenes—particularly the Victoria with its extremely large central figure—may have been visible from the road. The Column of Marcus Aurelius was meant primarily to be both seen and approached from the Via Flaminia.

The column is set back from the Via Flaminia, which suggests that it was the centerpiece of a large, open area, perhaps a colonnaded court with more or less the same dimensions as the modern Piazza Colonna.[43] One main difference between the ancient and the modern situation would have been the elevation of the column compared to the elevation of the road. The column sat on a marble platform, about thirty feet square and three feet tall, which rested in turn on a layer of travertine blocks.[44] The top of the marble platform was about two and a half to three meters higher than the surface of the Via Flaminia.[45] From the road, a passerby would not have been able to see the bottom of the column pedestal, and there must have been steps to provide access from the road. The area around the column was apparently open to casual visiting and varied use: on the top of the marble platform in front of the door giving access to the column, excavators found a *tabula lusoria*, an ancient Roman gaming board in the shape of a circle divided with pielike slices, incised into the marble.[46]

The area surrounding the Column of Marcus Aurelius would have been substantially larger than the one in which the Column of Trajan stood. This would have both increased the relative prominence of the monument and given visitors a much better opportunity to observe it. Unfortunately there is no evidence to show how exactly the Via Flaminia and the column complex were articulated, and we can only consider the possibilities. One is that the entire side of the complex lay open to the street. Another is that there was a barrier, either in the form of a colonnade or a solid wall. If there was a colonnade or a wall, an entryway would be needed. This could have been relatively simple in form, or it could have been grand—perhaps even in the form of a triumphal archway, such as possibly stood at the entrance to the courtyard in front of the Hadrianeum just to the south.[47] Whatever structure existed here, it would have appeared all the grander for its elevation above the Via Flaminia.

Despite this direct, primary orientation of the column with the Via Flaminia, the column also had a connection, clever and narrowly focused, to the funerary altars to the west. By climbing the internal staircase a visitor could ascend to the platform atop the capital of the column, from which he would have an unparalleled view of the city. From the top of the column a visitor would have been able to see all of the major monuments of the northern Campus Martius: the temples of Divine Hadrian and Matidia to the south, the Column of Antoninus Pius and the funerary altars to the west, and the Horologium and Ara Pacis to the north. Elevation alone would not have been enough to draw a visitor's attention directly to the altars of Marcus and Faustina. The temple of Hadrian would have loomed much larger and closer, and the visitor would also have had all the rest of the Campus Martius to distract him. However, a clever refinement in the column's design compelled a visitor to direct his attention toward the altars: the upper doorway of the staircase faced directly onto them.[48] Stepping from the upper doorway onto the capital platform, the visitor would find himself exactly facing the two marble altars. Examination of the first block of the superstructure atop the capital shows that this alignment is anything but coincidental. The column's designer could have placed a door immediately at the end of the stairway, as on Trajan's Column, in which case it would have opened to the north. Instead, they chose to carve a passage horizontally through the solid marble of the statue base in a westward direction until the point had been reached where the door could be opened in the proper alignment with the altars.

The effect of this forced direction of the visitor's sight must have been profound. If the Column of Marcus Aurelius was surrounded by a colonnaded courtyard that could be entered only from the Via Flaminia, a visitor at the base of the column would have been entirely cut off from the rest of the Campus Martius. After taking in all the impressive sights in the courtyard, he could ascend the inner stairway of the column. The climb was lit only by small and infrequent windows placed low in the wall of the stairwell. This arrangement was more practical than that in Trajan's Column, where the windows are high up and thus do not illuminate the steps effectively, but it would have been no more useful for keeping the visitor oriented with the outside landscape. The climb would have been dark and disorienting, which was perhaps part of the intended effect. The very first sight that would have greeted the visitor when he emerged into daylight at the top of the column would have been the two altars, a complex of white marble walls covering 20,000 square feet.

If the designer wanted to create a connection between the Column of Marcus Aurelius and the two funerary altars to its northwest one must ask why a more direct relationship was not established, like for instance the precise alignment between the Column of Antoninus Pius and that emperor's funerary altar. The reason seems to have been that the relationship between the Column of Marcus Aurelius and the Via Flaminia was considered more important. All the most important iconographic features of the column faced this road, as did the entrance to its internal stairway, and the entire structure was aligned with it. Only one aspect of the column, its upper doorway, faced the altars.

It is possible that this remarkable feature of the column (the alignment of the upper doorway with the funerary altars to the west) was connected with the funeral celebrations of the Younger Faustina, wife of Marcus Aurelius. These were held in 176 when the emperor returned to Rome from his eastern journey, on the return leg of which his beloved wife had died. This was also most likely the occasion on which the column itself was voted by the Senate, to honor the emperor for his great victories north of the Danube. Everything about the column suggests an honorary monument to a military victor; only the orientation of the upper doorway imparts a funerary association. In a way this is similar to Trajan's Column, which also incorporated a combination of honorific and funerary function with Trajan's burial in its pedestal. But in the case of the Column of Marcus Aurelius it was not a two-stage process, requiring the death of the emperor to occur before the funerary function was fulfilled. Instead the two functions would have been immediately relevant at the time the monument was commissioned, the honorific focused on Marcus and the funerary on Faustina and her altar. It is even possible that the alignment of the upper door was a detail added at the suggestion of the emperor himself, as a mark of commemoration for his wife in what was otherwise a purely honorary monument focused on the victories of the emperor.

The Problem of the Temple of the Divine Marcus

Both of the late third-/early fourth-century Regionary Catalogues, the *Curiosum urbis Romae* and the *Notitia urbis Romae*, list in the same breath a *templum Antonini* (*divi Antonini* in the *Notitia*) *et columnam coclidem*: "a temple of (the divine) Antoninus and a cochlid column."[49] It has often been suggested (and sometimes simply assumed) that this temple stood immediately west of the column.[50] The Adrastus inscription poses a problem for this argument. Adrastus's inscribed doorposts were found, along with the remains of his house, on the east side of the Piazza di Montecitorio, about twice the distance from the column as that by which the column is set back from the Via Flaminia.[51] The potential problems are two. First, the location of the house of Adrastus relative to the column does not leave a great deal of space for a temple—certainly not for one as large as the Hadrianeum just to the south or of the temple of Divine Antoninus and Faustina in the Roman Forum. The second problem involves the terminology used to define the location of Adrastus's residence: *post columnam*. If a temple to Marcus did in fact stand between Adrastus's house and the column, why did Adrastus not ask to build his house *post templum*?[52]

One possible alternative explanation is that the temple may have stood to the north of the column. But this orientation would have been odd, and there are no archaeological finds to support its existence in that location. The best explanation is that a quirk of the catalogue's compiler is to blame, and that the temple of Divus Marcus was in fact located elsewhere and was simply grouped with Marcus's Column by the compilers of the *Curiosum* and the *Notitia* as a matter of convenience. This sort of grouping is not uncommon in the regionary catalogues: for example, three triumphal arches, those of Verus, Trajan, and Drusus, are grouped together as the fourteenth entry in Regio I, and the theatres of Balbus, Marcellus, and Pompey are listed in a single line in Regio IX, even though they did not stand side by side. Likewise, in Regio IX the baths of Nero and those of Agrippa are listed together as the sixteenth entry, while in reality they stood a great distance apart, with the Pantheon and the Basilica Neptuni lying between them. The temple of the divine Marcus Aurelius may simply have been grouped together with his column by the compiler of the catalogue because they belonged to the same emperor and stood in the same general area—not side by side in the same complex.

The Dust of Northern Warfare

For the contemporary Roman the main orientation of the Column of Marcus Aurelius was to the Via Flaminia, though it had a secondary, almost invisible connection to the pair of funerary altars just over 400 feet to the northwest. But if the column was primarily honorific in function, why then did its designers place it here in this location, in the company of various Antonine funerary monuments? These neighboring monuments suggest a predominantly funerary association for the area in the Antonine period, but their presence often draws attention away from other monuments, very different in function, in the same area. This part of the Campus Martius was also a popular choice for victory monuments, and in particular monuments commemorating victories achieved in the north. The key element here was the Via Flaminia, which was the main road taken by armies setting out in that direction—and by successful generals returning to the capital. When Augustus noted that Rome's roads were sorely in need of repair, he entrusted all but one of them to various senators, reserving for himself the restoration of the Via Flaminia—according to Dio, "since he was going to lead an army out by that route."[53] When the work was done he built arches at each end, at the Pons Mulvius just north of the city and at the far terminus of the Via Flaminia, Ariminum (modern Rimini), just south of Ravenna.[54] When Augustus returned to Rome from Gaul in 13 B.C. the Senate voted to build an altar to Peace—the Ara Pacis—in the Campus Martius alongside the Via Flaminia, at the point one mile from the *pomerium* where military authority (*imperium*) ceased.[55] The direction from which Augustus entered the city was clearly seen as important, just as when, in 19 B.C., the Senate ordered the erection of the altar of Fortuna Redux to celebrate Augustus's return from the east.[56] On that occasion, Augustus returned by ship and then entered Rome from the south by the Via Appia, and thus the altar was built near or in the precinct of the Temple of Honos and Virtus at the Porta Capena, near the south end of the Circus Maximus where this road entered the old walls of Rome.

The point of return to the city was crucial to determining where an honorific monument was built. The Arch of Claudius, built across the Via Flaminia and into the Aqua Virgo, was situated with exactly the same concept in mind. Voted by the Senate in 51/52, it commemorated Claudius's victories in Britain and therefore spanned the very road by which the emperor would have made his triumphal return to the city.[57] Domitian was similarly honored with a triumphal arch in this area, in return for his northern victories. His return from these wars is vividly described by the first-century poet Martial:

> Here, where shines far and wide the gleaming temple of Fortune the Home-bringer, was but lately a lucky space. Here stood Caesar, beauteous with the dust of northern warfare, pouring brilliant radiance from his countenance. Here Rome, her hair wreathed with laurel and clothed in white, saluted her Leader with voice and hand. Another gift attests the signal merit of the spot: a sacred arch stands exultant over subjugated nations. Here twin chariots number many an elephant, and himself in gold suffices for the colossal cars. This gate, Germanicus, is worthy of your triumphs; Mars's city deserves such an entrance.[58]

Martial's description of the temple of Fortuna Redux as having been built in an open space in which the emperor stood, dusty but victorious upon his arrival at the end of his journey back to Rome from Germany, is powerfully evocative. Domitian was likely standing in the Campus Agrippae, on the east side of the Via Flaminia, where he and his troops rested before their triumph.

Martial's poem has a direct connection to Marcus Aurelius. The Profectio or "setting-out" scene of the Panel Reliefs of Marcus Aurelius shows, in the background, an arch topped with four elephants, almost certainly the same arch described by Martial.[59] In the bottom-right corner, a half-draped female reclines on a wheel—the Via Flaminia, the road to the north and, eventually, the Danube frontier. The Adventus or "arrival" relief in the Panel Relief series also shows a scene in the Campus Martius. In the background are a temple and an arch. The arch bears no elephants, but the sculpture in the pediment of the temple is clear. A goddess stands between two figures reclining on wheels—almost certainly the temple of Fortuna Redux. In the lower part of the scene Marcus, with Mars at his side, is welcomed and led into the city by Roma. Marcus may not have returned directly from the north by the same route by which he departed (unless he circled the city to make his official reentry by the Via Flaminia, mustering on the Campus Martius before his triumph), but his return was depicted in art as if that were the case.

Therefore the Campus Martius was exactly the proper place for the Senate to erect a new monument in honor of Marcus Aurelius's victories over the Germans and the Sarmatians. This monument, the column, was placed alongside the Via Flaminia where it would be seen by any passersby traveling in or out of the city to or from the north. It was in good company: the arches of Claudius and Domitian, the Ara Pacis, and the Temple of Fortuna Redux also graced the same important section of road. It was near, and had some connection to, the Antonine funerary monuments to the west, but its main orientation was to the Via Flaminia, route of departure for and triumphal return from the northern provinces.

chapter three

FORM & FUNCTION

One of the most common expressions used by the Romans to describe the Column of Marcus Aurelius was *columna cochlis*: "snail column." This appears not just in one obscure author, but in many sources over centuries. Its meaning was obviously clear to the Romans but is, at first glance at least, extremely obscure to us. What kind of a monument was the Column of Marcus Aurelius, exactly? None of the words the Romans used to describe it—including "snail column"—seem to reflect the overwhelming modern interest in the historical frieze that adorns its exterior. But these expressions hold our only genuine clues as to how the column was viewed by its contemporaries. The focus of this chapter is deliberately restricted to one goal: to understand how the ancient Romans themselves understood the monument. What kind of a structure, in their minds, was the Column of Marcus Aurelius?

The Romans had a tradition, if an inconsistent one, of erecting monumental columns topped by statues dating back at least to the fourth century B.C.[1] Just how great a debt the Romans owed to the Greeks for this tradition is debatable, but it seems that even the Greeks themselves did not begin placing portrait statues atop columns before the fourth century.[2] The earliest such monument in Rome appears to have been a column and statue erected to Gaius Maenius, consul in 338 B.C., for his victory over the Latins.[3] In the third century B.C. there was an important development: the first rostral columns, *columnae rostratae*, a type of columnar monument particularly intended to honor the victor in a naval battle. The name comes from the bronze rams—*rostra*—of captured enemy ships that were fixed to the column; the first seems to have been erected in honor of Gaius Diulius in 260 B.C.[4] More followed: a rostral column set up on the Capitol to honor Marcus Aemilius Paulus, also in the third century, a similar monument to honor Octavian after his victory over Sextus Pompey in 36 B.C.[5] Another rostral column appears on coins of Vespasian and Titus (fig. 3.1), although

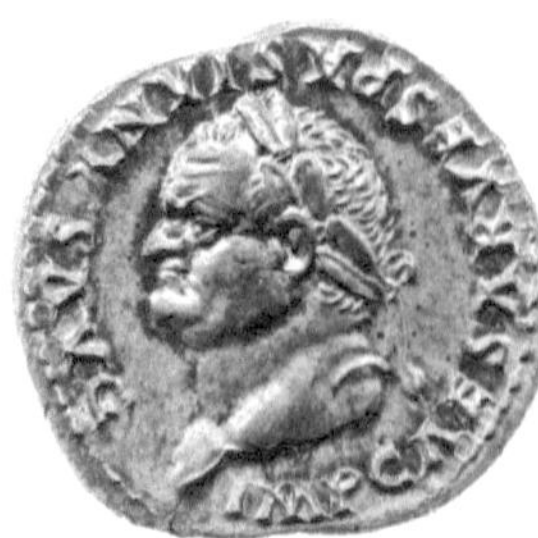
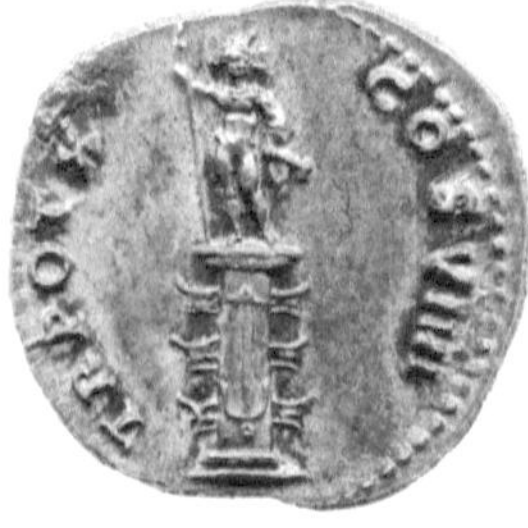

FIGURE 3.1. Rostral column on a denarius of Vespasian. Mattingly 1923–62, Vespasian 253. Copyright Trustees of the British Museum.

it is unclear whether this represents a new monument or is merely a repetition of a numismatic type from the time of Augustus.[6] So the honorary column, and especially the rostral column surmounted by a statue, was by the end of the first century A.D. an established if rare honor for a Roman military victor. Such a column served as more than an exalted statue base: it was also often used as a support on which to display symbols of victory: spoils taken from the enemy, the very prows of his warships.

A Novel Forerunner: The Column of Trajan

Against the background of the rostral column, the form of the next major columnar monument—the Column of Trajan (fig. 3.2)—is not entirely startling. This was erected by the Senate and the people to honor the emperor for his two victories over the Dacians achieved in A.D. 102 and 105; its construction was completed and the column dedicated by the year 113.[7] Trajan's Column is not a rostral column, but there are strong conceptual similarities. The pedestal of Trajan's Column was covered with carvings depicting armor and weapons taken from the Dacians, bringing to mind the enemy spoils that would be heaped at the bottom of a battlefield trophy. The idea behind this collection of arms is very similar to that behind the display of captured bronze rams on a *columna rostrata*; only on Trajan's Column sculpted versions of captured arms take the place of the originals. As ships' rams were eminently appropriate on a monument meant to honor a naval victor, so armor, weapons, and military standards were perfectly suited to honor a general who won his campaigns on land. The designer of the column chose the pedestal rather than the column shaft for this display because he had a greater purpose in mind for the latter. This was to display images of Trajan's victorious campaigns, making clear to the viewer that the

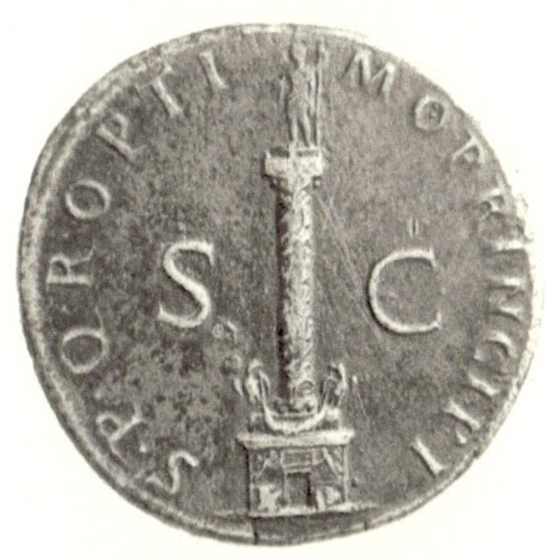

FIGURE 3.2.
Trajan's Column on a sestertius of Trajan, A.D. 113. Note the eagles at corners of the pedestal (now missing), the statue (also missing), and the detail of the relief on both the pedestal and the column shaft. Paris, Bibliothèque Nationale, photo by author.

spoils on the pedestal were not won in a single battle but rather as the result of a series of arduous campaigns.

Thus the exterior of the Column of Trajan reflected the essential function, if not the precise form, of earlier honorific columns and especially the *columnae rostratae*. However, Trajan's Column also had important novel aspects. The most important of these was the addition of interior space, including a rectangular chamber at the bottom of the column and a stairway through its entire height. Visitors entered the column by means of a door in the south face of the pedestal. This must have been a striking act, stepping *into* a monument that, in the visitor's mind, had always been thought of as solid. In Trajan's Column an object that had earlier been used as an architectural component or as a support for statuary had become a complete building in and of itself. Once inside, the visitor could turn right to climb the stairs or turn left around a corner to enter the chamber that occupies the north half of the pedestal. The chamber is lit by a small slit window in the west wall and originally contained a platform along its northern wall. According to both Dio and Eutropius, this room served as the final resting place for Trajan's ashes. In the words of Eutropius, "he was deified and alone among the Romans was buried within the city. His bones were collected in a golden urn and placed under the column, which is 147 feet tall, in the forum which he built."[8] Whether this was decided before or after the death of the emperor is debatable (the room may originally have contained more ordinary objects such as spoils from the Dacian campaigns), but the chamber itself was clearly no afterthought. The stairway was carefully routed around it, ascending through the pedestal in right-angled flights instead of proceeding straight up in a helix from the entrance.

Literary and epigraphic sources reveal another major and novel function of Trajan's Column—though not precisely how it was achieved. Dio says that Trajan's Column was designed on the one hand as his tomb and on the other "to show the work done on the forum."[9] How exactly was it meant to do this? The column's inscription provides a clue: it makes a similar and slightly more specific claim, namely that the column was dedicated by the Senate and the people *ad declarandum quantae altitudinis / mons et locus tant . . . ribus sit egestus*. The break in the inscription (*tant . . . ribus*) is caused by a medieval cutting made in the marble of the pedestal to anchor a roof above the door of the column. This makes translating what is already a difficult inscription even harder. The most common reconstruction is *tantis operibus*, giving a rough translation for the phrase as "to show the height of the mountain and place that were removed for the sake of these great works."[10] What does this mean? Did a mountain the height of the column once stand on the site? This is highly unlikely, especially since archaeological finds suggest that much of the area was no higher before the column's construction. The answer may lie in another novelty of Trajan's Column: the provision of the internal stairway, by means of which a visitor could climb to the top of the capital. From this privileged vantage point he could survey at once all of the glories of Trajan's new forum and basilica complex, of which the column formed only a part. The general view over the Basilica Ulpia, markets, and colonnades would have fulfilled Dio's purpose of showing "the work that had been done on the forum." It is also probable that the designers had a specific view in mind: the view that a visitor saw when he first emerged from the upper doorway atop the capital. The doorway opened facing east (fig. 3.3), and the visitor would first see the Quirinal Hill and the vast tiered expanse of Trajan's markets, cut into and built up on its slope. If this was the *mons et locus* referred to in the column's inscription then one of the functions of the column was to confront visitors with a clear and uninterrupted view of this accomplishment and to give a clear impression of the massive amount of earth and rock removed in the construction process.

In size, decoration, and architectural form Trajan's Column was an entirely novel monument. The designers of the Column of Marcus Aurelius imitated or copied each of these features when they came to construct a monument for their own emperor. No longer was Trajan's Column unique; rather, it would have stood together with Marcus's in the mind of any Roman looking at either. This, then, is the perspective I want to follow below, with the goal of identifying, as closely as possible, the thinking of the Romans with regard to these monuments. What did they see when

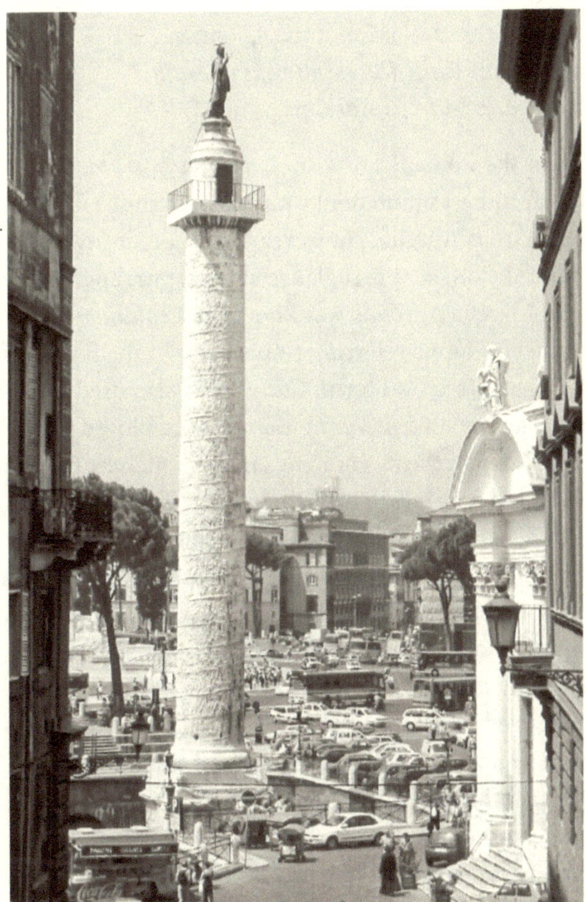

FIGURE 3.3.
Trajan's Column seen from the Quirinal Hill. Photo by author.

they looked at the columns of Trajan and Marcus Aurelius? More to the point, what did they think when they saw them, and how did they describe this thinking to others? We have very few sources and no full descriptions at all, but useful clues can be gained even from the brief mentions that do exist, particularly if we examine closely the descriptive words that were employed. It should be made clear that the impression created by these two monuments, similar though they were, would not have been exactly the same. The Column of Marcus Aurelius did not contain a tomb, nor did it serve to clarify the extent and scale of a greater surrounding complex. It is nonetheless clear that both monuments did make common impressions on their viewers, and this is reflected in the words used to describe them.

Columna Centenaria, Columna Cochlis: *What the Romans Called the Columns of Trajan and Marcus Aurelius*

Before the time of Trajan the Romans knew the *columna rostrata*, a term whose meaning is as clear today as it no doubt was then. In the case of the columns of Trajan and Marcus Aurelius, however, we encounter two new terms, one fairly clear but the other, at first glance at least, puzzling. To the Romans, the Column of Marcus Aurelius was known as a *columna centenaria* or as a *columna cochlis*, terms referring respectively to the height of the monument and to its architectural form. *Cochlis* was also used to describe Trajan's Column, and though *centenaria* was not so employed (in our sources, at least), it is reflected in the monument's measurements (Trajan's Column is also one hundred feet tall). The Romans were fascinated with the height of both of these columns, and most of our sources make some reference to this feature, often relating the total height of the monument in feet as if it was understood as being of natural interest. Cassiodorus writes of Trajan, "whose column reached a height of one hundred and forty feet." Eutropius, when mentioning the burial of Trajan's ashes in a golden urn beneath his column, felt obliged to tell the reader how high the whole monument is. Numbers were important to the Romans, and the more apparently the better. The term *centenaria* (which appears only in the inscription of Adrastus) is a specific and technical manifestation of this fascination. Translating as "hundred-footer," it refers to the height of the column itself, including its base and capital but not including the pedestal or the statue. This at least is its technical sense but, as Martines points out, it also had a more general significance: it uses an ideal mathematical figure to denote a monument of unparalleled, even divine, proportions.[11] One hundred feet may as well have been one thousand, since there was no other column in Rome that came near this height. The use of the term *centenaria*, occurring as it does at about the time when the column was completed, gives us a clear impression of what contemporary Romans appreciated about it: its remarkable—and remarkably precise—height.

The term *centenaria*, however, is only used in one source, with reference only to the Column of Marcus Aurelius, and does not appear to have gained general use. To find a term that was commonly used in reference to both monuments one must turn to slightly later sources and to the expression *columna cochlis*. This term is found first in the Regionary Catalogues, the *Curiosum urbis Romae* and the *Notitia urbis Romae*.[12] Rome was divided into geographic regions, and the *Curiosum* and *Notitia* list the contents (sometimes oddly selected) of each region in order. (The Column of Trajan was located in the Eighth Region of Rome, the Column of Marcus Aurelius in the Ninth.) The catalogs are an unparalleled, if sometimes mysterious, source for the ancient topography of the city. For example, from the *Curiosum*:

> *REGIO VIII FORVM ROMANVM MAGNVM continet . . . forum Caesaris / Augusti / Nervae / Traiani / templum / Traiani / et columnam coclidem / altam pedes CXXVII s. / grados intus habet / CLXXX / fenestras XLV*: "The Eighth Region, Forum Romanum, contains the forum of Caesar, of Augustus, of Nerva, and of Trajan, the temple of Trajan, and a cochlid column one hundred and twenty seven and a half feet tall; it has one hundred and eighty steps inside it and forty-five windows."
>
> *REGIO IX CIRCVS FLAMINEVS continet . . . templum Antonini / et columnam coclidem / altam pedes CLXXV s. / gradus intus habet CCIII / fenestras LVI*: "The Ninth Region, Circus Flamineus, contains the temple of Antoninus and a cochlid column one hundred seventy-five and a half feet tall; it has two hundred and three steps inside and fifty-six windows."

The term *columna cochlis* is not nearly as easy to understand as *columna centenaria*, but it is crucial to our knowledge of how the Romans themselves viewed both these monuments. *Cochlis* (spelled *coclis* in some sources) is a very rare word, an adjective derived from a Greek word for snail shell. The implication is that the columns are snail-shell-like. Two features of the columns could conceivably have warranted such a description: the external sculpted frieze, which runs up the column in a spiraling manner from bottom to top, or the internal spiral staircase, which runs the height of the column and provides access to a viewing platform on top of the wide capital. The question is, did the Romans, in using this term, mean to allude to the internal aspect of a snail shell, the external appearance, or both?

Most recent opinion has settled on a double meaning: the Romans saw the columns as reflecting both the external and internal appearance of a snail shell. However, close study of the ancient usage of the word *cochlis* and its relatives in both Latin and Greek points to another conclusion. *Cocleae*, wrote Isidore of Seville in the seventh century A.D., *sunt altae et rotundae turres et dictae cocleae quasi cycleae, quod in eis tamquam per cir-*

culum orbemque conscendatur: "*cocleae* are high, round towers and they are called *cocleae* like *cycleae*, because in them one ascends just as through a circle and a coil."[13] Thus, to Isidore, what made a *cochlea* a *cochlea* was what was inside: a winding passage going up. Other sources reinforce this interpretation. In the Vulgate Bible (circa A.D. 400) access to various levels in Solomon's new temple is described using the words *per cocleam ascendebant in medium cenaculum et a medio in tertium*: "they ascended through a *cochlea* into the middle room and from the middle into the third."[14] Here the *cochlea* is an internal architectural feature facilitating ascent. Placidus, a glossographer who lived in the fifth or sixth century A.D., defined the word thus: *coclea ascensus qui circiit*: "a *coclea* is an ascent which circles."[15] This is exactly what the stairway in the Column of Marcus Aurelius is: a circling ascent. A *columna cochlis* was therefore a column with a circling stairway inside it, like the interior of a snail shell. Significantly, the ancient understanding of *columnam cochlidem* appears also in the work of medieval and Renaissance topographers. Particularly revealing is a comment by Pierre Gilles, a sixteenth-century traveler to Constantinople, in a retort directed at a contemporary topographer on the subject of the porphyry Pillar of Constantine: *haec columna porphyretica non gradibus pervia est, sed solida. itaque falso tradit Fulvius antiquarius coclide esse*: "This porphyry column not does have stairs in it, but is solid. Thus Fulvius the antiquarian wrongly called it *coclide*."[16]

These two terms, *columna centenaria* and *columna cochlis*, emphasize the aspects of the Column of Marcus Aurelius that ancient Romans thought most important: height and the internal staircase. These interests appear repeatedly in later writings that refer to this monument, to Trajan's Column, to their twins in Constantinople, or even to imaginary columns. When Ammianus Marcellinus describes the structures that caught Constantius's attention during his visit to Rome in A.D. 357, he remarks on the *elatosque vertices scansili suggestu concharum, priorum principum imitamenta portantes*: "the exalted heights with rising platforms of conch-like quality bearing likenesses of previous emperors." Such "heights" of "conch-like quality" (mollusk imagery again) bearing statues of emperors and graced with viewing platforms can only be the columns of Trajan and Marcus Aurelius. The *Notitia urbis Constantinopolitanae* (late fourth/early fifth century, a later companion to the Roman equivalents just quoted) describes the columns of Theodosius and of Arcadius each as *columnam . . . intrinsecus usque ad summitatem gradibus perviam*, "a column accessible by stairs inside up to the summit," and *columnam . . . intra se gradibus perviam*, "a column accessible by means of stairs inside it." Again, it is the stairway that draws attention; the frieze is not mentioned. *Cochlis* (and its Greek equivalent) is used to describe the same columns in sources of the sixth and seventh centuries.[17]

Thus while height was clearly a noteworthy feature of these columns for the ancient Romans, only one descriptive term (*centenaria*) was ever used to make reference to this aspect of its appearance, and that only in one source. In comparison, the number and variety of the uses of *cochlis* and its equivalents, continuing over centuries, suggest that the internal stairway was an object of constant admiration for Roman viewers. Why was this?

The Importance of the Internal Stairway

None of our sources tell us why exactly the stairs in the columns were considered worthy of special attention, but at least three explanations can be suggested with some confidence. The first is that the stairway, cut inside the otherwise solid shaft of a column, represented a remarkable technical achievement. Before the construction of Trajan's Column, such a project had never before been attempted. The stairway required very careful planning, especially because a remarkably inconvenient ratio of fourteen steps per turn was chosen over one of twelve or sixteen steps, which would have been much simpler to execute. The importance of the stairway to the overall design of the *columna cochlis* is underlined by the way in which the designers of the Column of Marcus Aurelius copied the dimensions of the stairway in Trajan's Column with great fidelity, while at the same time taking liberties with other aspects of the design (see chapter 4).

A second factor was the overall rarity of spiral staircases of any sort in the city of Rome—and, for that matter, in the ancient world in general. Such structures are relatively uncommon in most places in the world today, but in ancient Rome they were extremely rare. Besides the columns, two spiral stairways are found in the Baths of Caracalla (A.D. 212–16), four in the Baths of Diocletian (298–305), and one in the Mausoleum of Constantia (circa 350). In other ancient buildings outside of Rome spiral staircases are similarly uncommon: there is, for example, one spiral staircase in the third-century Round Temple at Ostia, two in the Mausoleum of Galerius at Thessalonike (early fourth century), and eight in the Imperial Baths at Trier (also of the early fourth century). These examples show a clear pattern: the Romans used spiral staircases mainly in massive brick buildings, only from the third century onwards, and never in towers. The two column staircases in Rome were, in the city at the time of their construction, apparently unique. Even outside the capital, earlier parallels are exceedingly rare. One is in a fifth-century B.C. temple in Selinus, Sicily. While staircases in the *cellae* of Greek temples are not uncommon, the spiral example at Selinus is unique among them. Moreover, the unusual form of the Selinus staircase, with curving edges on each step, is not reflected in any later staircases. Another example is found in the first-century A.D. temple of Bel at Palmyra in Syria. It is appealing to imagine that the designer of Trajan's Column, Apollodorus of Damascus, was inspired by this potential Syrian prototype. Whether or not this was the case, the primary reason for choosing a spiral staircase was that this is the only type of stairway that one could possibly fit inside a column. The novelty of the staircase in Trajan's Column for most Romans would have been absolute.[18]

Interestingly, it seems that it was only after the construction of the two cochlear columns that spiral staircases appear in other buildings in Rome. Did the column staircases influence later architects? The influence could not have been instant: the Baths of Trajan and the Pantheon of Hadrian both employ staircases with straight flights and landings, even in restricted, oddly shaped areas such as angles and corners where in later monuments spiral stairs would eventually appear. But Trajan's Column must have been highly admired by Roman architects, and the building of the Column of Marcus Aurelius could only have made this form of stair better known. In its later incarnations it remained a practical solution rather than a means of proud display of architectural skill, employed in areas more likely to be frequented by maintenance workers than by the general public.

The final important feature of the staircases was their function. They were intended to provide a way for visitors to reach the viewing platform atop the columns. From the top of the Column of Trajan a person would have been able to inspect from an unparalleled vantage point the entire layout of Trajan's vast new forum and thus appreciate fully his incredible accomplishment (fig. 3.4). In the case of the Column of Marcus Aurelius the effect would have been similar, but this time the view would have encompassed the Via Flaminia, the Antonine funerary monuments, and other structures of the Campus Martius. How often the stairways were actually used, and who was allowed to ascend them, is not known. Considering the role of the pedestal of Trajan's Column as a resting place for the emperor's

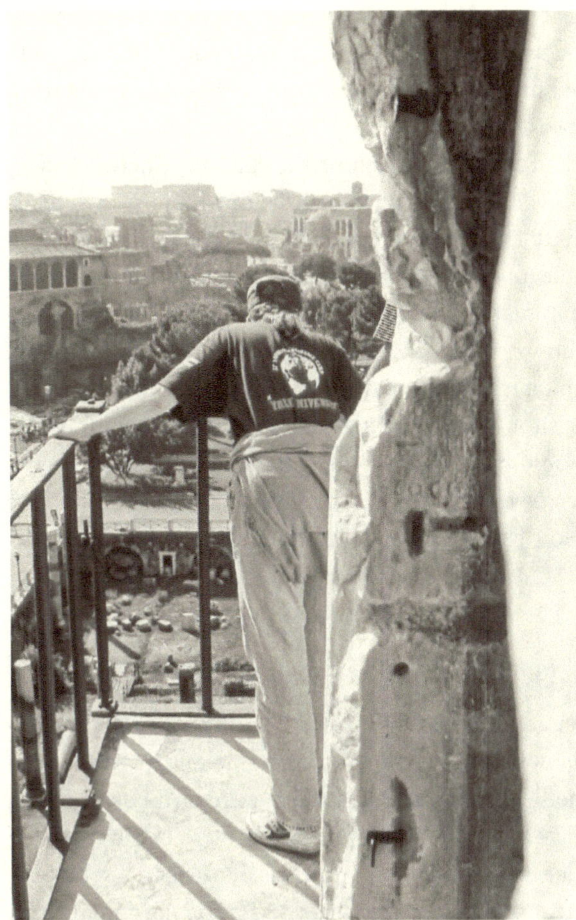

FIGURE 3.4. View from atop the capital of the Column of Trajan, with the Forum of Trajan below and the Colosseum in the distance. Photo by author.

ashes, access in Roman times may have been carefully regulated. Marcus's Column had no funerary chamber: one entered the pedestal and was faced immediately with the beginning of the stairway. In the Middle Ages, at least for the Column of Marcus Aurelius, the function of the stairs seems to have been fundraising. An inscription of the year A.D. 1119 in the church of S. Silvestro gives evidence that the column was leased and that revenue was derived from it for the leaseholders.[19] What could the possessor of the Column of Marcus Aurelius have derived revenue from, if not entrance fees to climb the staircase? An intriguing parallel can be drawn with Adrastus: the *procurator* appealed to the emperor for permission to build his new house using the argument that this would allow him to do his job better ([*ut rectius fungar of*]*icio meo*).[20] We do not know what exactly the job of

Adrastus was, but possibly, in addition to general maintenance and upkeep of the surroundings of the column, he may also have controlled access to the stairway of the column, admitting visitors and perhaps escorting them on their climb to the top.

How many people had the chance to climb the column? There is no way to determine this, but even if few Romans had the opportunity of actually climbing the stairs, this does not mean that the Romans in general were unaware of this remarkable function of the monument. After all, the symbolic value of the act of climbing the stairs may indeed have been high. *Columnarum ratio*, wrote Pliny, *erat attolli super ceteros mortales*: "The point of columns was that men be raised above other mortals." By climbing one of these monuments, a visitor could put himself, temporarily at least, in just such a position. He would have stood at the very feet of the emperor and enjoyed a view almost as sweeping as his. More importantly, he would have stood far above his fellow citizens below, who could only look up and envy his privilege.[21]

How Great a Column, to Give Evidence of Your Great Deeds

The columns of Trajan and Marcus Aurelius were, in the eyes of contemporary Romans, particularly notable for their extreme height and for the fact that they contained internal staircases. Both were also covered with images recalling military successes and topped by a statue of the emperor; in this they were similar to the *columnae rostratae* of earlier days, but this was not reflected in the Romans' descriptive terms for the new monumental type. Relief sculpture impressed the Romans much less than sheer size. *Quantam statuam faciet populus R(omanus)*, wrote the poet Ennius in a eulogy of Scipio Africanus, victor over Hannibal and conqueror of Carthage at the end of the third century B.C., *quantam columnam, quae res tuas gestas loquatur*?: "How large a statue should the Roman people make, how great a column, to give evidence of your great deeds?"[22] Whether Scipio ever received such a column is not known, but there are no greater columns in all of Rome than those of Trajan and Marcus Aurelius. The Romans were also impressed by architectural novelty. The cochlear columns were the only two monuments of their type in the city and, at the time, in the world. What is more, they offered a remarkable experience to a visitor by means of a previously unknown architectural feature: a spiral internal stairway leading to a lofty belvedere. They were more than honorary monuments: they were functional buildings. The impact of this feature on the Romans was so strong that by the later third century a new term, *columna cochlis*, had developed. This term did not disappear like *columna centenaria* but remained current. It was used into the sixth century A.D. to describe the cochlear columns of Constantinople, and the ancient meaning of the term remained clear into the Renaissance.

chapter four

PLANNING & CONSTRUCTION

The Column of Marcus Aurelius was a complex monument, combining architecture, relief carving, statuary, and an inscription into a single, unified whole. The planning of these different elements would have been a complicated, multistage process, an understanding of which could provide an idea of the relative significance of the column's different parts in the minds of the people who created it. Which elements were given greatest priority in planning? Which details were decided on at the highest level? Were all elements of the column planned at the same time, or were some left to be resolved later? The construction challenges were as great as those of planning: massive blocks of stone had to be quarried in northern Italy, transported to Rome, finished to perfection, lifted to unprecedented heights, and assembled with unfailing accuracy. Some of these challenges, particularly the weight of the blocks and the height to which they were raised, exceeded those faced by the designers of Trajan's Column. How was the Column of Marcus Aurelius assembled, and what would the conditions on the worksite have been? How long did this whole process take? Unfortunately there is no source that tells us how any of this was done. Nonetheless it should be possible, by searching for clues in the finished work, to reconstruct some of the steps by which the designers and builders progressed. If these questions can be even partly answered, it should be possible to form a much clearer idea of what the Romans had in mind when they created the column.

First Steps: Decree and Commission

Significant planning must have gone on in the mind of the man who first had the idea for building the column—what it should look like, perhaps even where it should be. But the first steps in its construction would have had to have been more concrete: to officially decree that it should be built and to commission someone to do the work. Judging from the very few parallels we have, it is likely that the Roman Senate made the official decision to erect the column. This decision would subsequently have been made public in the form of a decree. We are fortunate to have an example of such an order in the decree of an arch in honor of Germanicus, preserved in the *Tabula Siarensis* (A.D. 20/21).[1] The decree orders a marble arch (*ianus marmoreus*) to be built in a specific spot in the Circus Flaminius, adorned with gilded standards of defeated enemies (*cum signis devictarum gentium ina*[*uratis*]), inscribed with a *titulus* whose entire text is given, and topped by a statue of Germanicus in a triumphal chariot flanked by effigies of other members of the imperial family.[2] Summarized, the decree specifies the type of monument, the material, the location, the format and subject matter of the free-standing statuary, and the exact text of the inscription. In contrast to the great attention given to these aspects, and especially to the text of the inscription, some other important details are not mentioned at all, including size and architectural ornament. Presumably it was understood that these were elements to be decided on at a later stage in the planning process. The arch also most likely had relief decoration; La Rocca has identified a number of carved marble fragments found near the Theatre of Marcellus as belonging to the Arch of Germanicus, including a marble block carved with a legionary standard within a *corona muralis*.[3] The text of this decree gives an example of the first level of decision making for a major state monument, and in it we can identify the first division of priorities. Relief sculpture does not even make an appearance.

After the decree, the next step would have been to decide who would supervise the project, who would carry out the actual process of architectural planning, and who would be responsible for construction. To these people would also be left, it seems, decisions about the aspects of the monument that were not spelled out in the decree, especially its exact architectural form and its carved decoration (as opposed to the free-standing, presumably bronze, statuary already specified in the decree). Unfortunately, there is no clear evidence of how this step in the process would have been handled in the case of major imperial monuments in the city of Rome. Augustus put the oversight of public buildings into the hands of consular *curatores operum publicorum*, and Claudius apparently added the administration of *loca publica*, public land, to their duties.[4] These officials usually held office for a short period (in the second century A.D. usually only one year) and there is no evidence to indicate that they were responsible for new projects; rather, their duty was to oversee the upkeep of extant structures.[5] Both Vespasian and Titus appointed equestrians as overseers of major rebuilding projects in the city.[6] But these projects were ordered by the emperor himself and, as Lancaster points out, did not involve new buildings but rather reconstruction.[7]

Under Trajan, all major projects in the capital likely came automatically under the supervision of Apollodorus of Damascus, one of the few Roman architects we know by name; Dio, at least, credits him with all of Trajan's building projects in the city.[8] Dio also reports that Apollodorus was so assertive as to dismiss the future emperor Hadrian with an insulting remark when the latter interrupted an architectural discussion he was having with Trajan. It is doubtful that Trajan would have put an equestrian or even a senator in a supervisory position over such a man. Hadrian, who is accused by Dio of having Apollodorus executed out of jealousy and spite, seems to have fancied himself an architect and to have come up with detailed plans for the site, architecture, and cult images of the temple of Venus and Rome.[9] The *Historia Augusta* records that he relied on the help of the architect Decrianus (otherwise unknown) to relocate the colossal statue of Nero (the Colossus that gave its name to the Colosseum) prior to its rededication to the sun god, and that he also intended to make a similar statue in honor of Luna, the moon, with the aid of Apollodorus.[10] Both ideas seem to have been Hadrian's; the architects were enlisted presumably to provide the needed technical know-how. After Hadrian's reign, evidence for architects in the city of Rome fades.[11] As far as we know, Marcus Aurelius had no Apollodorus, and in fact so much of his column is derivative or plainly copied that it does not give the impression of being the product of a single, brilliantly original mind. Rather it appears more likely that its manufacture lay in the hands of multiple creative actors of varied skill.

But the question for the moment is this: how was the task of planning and executing Marcus's Column assigned? There is tantalizing evidence of the employment of a competitive process in public and private building projects in this period outside of Rome. "Cities," wrote Plutarch around the turn of the first and second centuries A.D., "as we know, when they give public notice of intent to let contracts for the building of temples or colossal statues, listen to the proposals of artists competing for the commission and bringing in their estimates and models, and then choose the man who will do the same work with the least expense and better than the others and more quickly."[12] The representatives of the city knew in general what sort of a building they wanted, but its detailed appearance was only determined at the second stage of the planning process. An essential theme here is competition between designers. The competition was judged on the basis of the appeal of a visual model and on an assessment of speed and economy of execution. The idea of competition is also stressed by Aulus Gellius, writing in the time of Marcus Aurelius: in a description of a private contract to build new baths for Cornelius Fronto (coincidentally the tutor of Marcus Aurelius), Gellius describes Fronto as ill and reclining on a couch. "By his side stood several builders (*fabri*), who had been summoned to construct some new baths, and were exhibiting different plans (*depictas*) for the baths, drawn on little pieces of parchment." Presumably, Fronto was expected to compare these plans and chose a winner in the competition. Visually based competition, if such a process was employed in the design of the Column of Marcus Aurelius, might account for some of the notable differences (for example, the size and configuration of the pedestal) between it and Trajan's Column.[13] A competitive process would doubtless have appealed to officials of a cash-strapped government, which well describes Rome after Marcus's expensive wars and the devastating plague. The extent of the financial crisis is emphasized by the story, recorded in the *Historia Augusta* and by Eutropius, of the emperor even resorting to auctioning off palace possessions to fund his military campaigns.[14] The competitors in this process would have displayed drawings that showed the overall outward appearance of the column, but which most likely did not offer detail of its relief sculpture.

Thus the first two steps in the planning of the Column of Marcus Aurelius were the formation of the idea and the selection (likely by means of a competition) of an expert, an architect, to provide the necessary expertise to design the monument. Lancaster and Martines both argue that the architect himself had a largely advisory role in the construction process.[15] His training, and thus his contribution, was largely technical and artistic. He would likely have advised the patron during the process of contracting out the work, but the actual building would have been organized by a contractor (*redemptor*). For lesser projects such as houses, many contractors must have been able to rely on a fixed body of workers already in their service; for a major imperial project, however, they would doubtless have had to hire extra workers, both unskilled and specialized, as necessary.

Very few examples of a Roman building contract (*locatio conductio*) have survived from the public realm, and the only one preserved in its entirety is a contract of 105 B.C. between the *duoviri* (chief magistrates) of Puteoli (on the Bay of Naples) and a contractor for the building of a wall around a sanctuary of Serapis. It sets out all the requirements of the project in such detail that extremely little is left to the discretion of the builders. For example, the instructions begin with the statement that a gap for a doorway be made in an already existing wall, and continue as follows: "Above the gap let him place a lintel of hard oak, 8 feet long, 1 foot and ¼ wide, ¾ high. Above that and the antae let him project out from the wall on either side for 4 feet, hard oak topping-beams, 2 and ⅔ feet thick and 1 foot high. Above that let him attach the decorated sima with iron."[16] This extreme attention to detail is somewhat at odds with the evidence of imperial building at Rome. For example, significant variation can be detected in often-repeated architectural details in such structures as the Colosseum and the Temple of Vespasian, suggesting that a highly detailed contract was not being followed during their construction.[17] Nonetheless, there is one particularly noteworthy aspect of the Puteoli contract: that the degree of detail given in the instructions is not the same throughout. While materials and measurements (and in other places in this document, weights and even mixture ratios for mortar) are laid out specifically, other aspects of the project are not. The most notable unspecified element is decoration. In the section cited above, it is not made clear exactly how the sima (*simas pictas*) is to be decorated, beyond the fact that this is apparently to be done using paint. Either this sort of decoration was so well-known as not to require detailed instruction, or else it was understood as being left up to a specialist worker to execute according to accepted norms for such a task.

From all this information, it is possible to suggest a reconstruction of the events in the process of decree and commission of the Column of Marcus Aurelius. The basic idea of the column could easily have been conceived by members of the Senate, influenced by the parallels between Marcus's accomplishments and those of Trajan. Their decree to this effect would have included information about the type of monument (a *columna cochlis* or *centenaria*), its material (marble), its location (in the Campus Martius alongside the Via Flaminia), the inscription it was to bear (lost to us today), and the statue (presumably of Marcus himself) which was to be placed on top. Details of the column's appearance and construction, however, would have been determined by the architect and the building contractor, likely in two distinct stages. The first step was to summon architects to present their proposed designs. These designs would have given a general impression of what each architect sought to accomplish.[18] It was at this stage that the form of the pedestal (twice as tall as that of Trajan's Column), the layout of the internal staircase (proceeding directly up from the lower entrance, eschewing the chamber in the pedestal of Trajan's Column), and general format (but not necessarily the particular appearance or content) of the architectural and figural decoration would have been determined.

Then a second competition would have been held for the contract to build this final design, at which time a plan including exact dimensions, proportions, and details of the architecture would have been needed. The question of how much detail this plan included about the sculptural decoration is, however, much more difficult to answer. Neither Germanicus's arch nor the Puteoli sanctuary wall encompassed a decorative element comparable to the frieze of the Column of Marcus Aurelius; however, each did have decoration whose content was not spelled out either in the original decree or in the detailed architectural contract. It would make sense to suppose that the general appearance of the relief carving (a helical frieze) and its overall theme (Marcus's campaigns) would have been specified during planning, but whether its exact design and content was also established at the same time is anything but certain.[19] At the time there were many more pressing pieces of planning to be accomplished, including preparing instructions to be sent to the quarry and calculating the dimensions of the marble elements. Both of these were key parts of the next major phase in the genetic process of the column: the detailed design of its architecture.

Architectural Design

The challenge of designing the Column of Marcus Aurelius was mitigated somewhat by the availability of a model, which would have reduced the amount of innovative thinking (but not practical know-how) needed for the project. The basic model for the architect who designed the Column of Marcus Aurelius was the Column of Trajan. This presents us with a remarkable opportunity to study the thought process of this architect as he adopted or modified various aspects of the earlier monument's structure and decoration along the path to the realization of his new project. By examining both monuments it is possible to determine the extent to which the designer of Marcus's Column emulated Trajan's monument, along with the extent to which he was willing to alter the design provided by his earlier model. It is possible, in effect, to identify and evaluate the degree of original thinking that went into the creation of the column.

To an outside observer, the most immediately striking difference between the two columns would have been the height of their pedestals. The pedestal of Trajan's Column, made of four courses composed of two blocks each, stands 5.27 meters; that of Marcus's monument, made of seven alternating one- and two-block courses, is exactly twice as tall (10.52 meters).[20] Why this great increase in pedestal height? The ground level is lower at this point in the Campus Martius; is it possible that the goal was to create a column of comparable absolute height? The difference in elevation (15.52 meters above sea level compared to 16.90 meters at the base of Trajan's Column) is not great enough to account for the extra five and a quarter meters of pedestal: the Column of Marcus Aurelius stands more than three and a half meters higher at the level of the top of its capital than that of Trajan. Nor can we find any indication that the height of the Marcus column shared the same function as the height of Trajan's Column—*ad declarandum quantae altitudinis mons et locus sit egestus.* The height of Marcus's Column could surely not relate to any such work on the Campus Martius, which as its name (*campus*) indicates is a particularly flat piece of ground. The solution must lie in the doubling of the measurements, from the 17¾ Roman feet of Trajan's Column to exactly 35½ feet on Marcus's monument. This precise doubling can hardly be a coincidence. The goal was apparently to improve on the rather squat appearance of the base of Trajan's Column.

Both columns are built exclusively with white marble from the ancient quarry of Luna, modern Cararra, just north of Pisa along the western coast of Italy. The body of each column, base and capital included, consists of nineteen marble drums approximately 5¼ Roman feet tall, each containing eight steps (both risers and treads); one drum each for the base and capital and the remainder for the column shaft—in theory, at least. The shaft of Trajan's Column tapers significantly as it ascends (from 12½ at the bottom to 11 feet at the top); the diameter of Marcus's Column differs by only half a foot between the bottom and the top (12¾ to 12¼ feet). The seventeen drums making up the shaft of Marcus's Column are slightly taller (the smallest is 152.6, the largest 159.0 centimeters) than the seventeen of Trajan's Column (the smallest is 148.2, the largest 154.7 centimeters). This was required for Marcus's monument because the entire shaft was made up of these seventeen drums, while on Trajan's Column the frieze extends down onto the upper part of the first drum of the column. Wilson Jones has argued that this was the result of an unforeseen problem that came to light in the planning process of Trajan's Column.[21] This problem occurred when the stairs had to change from straight flights in the base to the helix of the column shaft and was unforeseeable because it could not be detected in normal cross-section plans. At this very point, the rising ceiling of the incipient spiral staircase threatened to breach the outer surface of the column where the shaft began, just above the torus. The solution adopted was to increase the height of the column base sufficiently to prevent this threatening puncture. As a result, it was necessary to increase the size of the uppermost course of stonework of the pedestal, and to incorporate the plinth, the rectangular element just below the torus, into it. Thus the uppermost two blocks of Trajan's Column's pedestal incorporate part of the column proper (the plinth), and the first drum of the actual column starts with the torus and includes half of the first winding of the helical frieze. This scheme resulted in a helical stairway that still measured one hundred feet, but in a column that was slightly larger, approximately one hundred and one-half feet. In comparison, the design of the Column of Marcus Aurelius is more successful. All of the column's elements are built from its nineteen drums, one drum for the base, seventeen for the shaft, and one for the capital. Together, these equal exactly one hundred Roman feet (29.62 meters), making the monument a true *columna centenaria*.

The stairway of Marcus's Column is in some ways the most exactly copied part of the monument, but it also departs substantially from its Trajanic predecessor. Each column drum included the same eight risers and treads as did the drums of Trajan's Column, only with a slightly greater rise to correspond to their slightly greater average height. The height of the steps in the drums averages 19.5 centimeters, except when a drum is notably below the average height: for example, in drum seven, with a total height of 152.6 centimeters, the risers are 18.0 centimeters high. This shows that the column's designer put the greatest importance on maintaining the eight-step-per-drum ratio, with the rise of the steps calculated relative to the height of the individual drums. This method allowed for flexibility in the employment of the roughed-out drums newly arrived from the quarry. It is unlikely that the column drums would have arrived all at once, or with exactly the same measurements. The designers could also not rule out the possibility of slight damage during shipment; a chipped edge, for example, may have accounted for the slightly smaller size of drum seven. The slightly smaller size of this drum might then account for the above-average height of some upper drums, as compensation for the shortfall. This careful control resulted in a column shaft that measured 26.39 meters, equivalent to eighty-nine Roman feet. This shows that the ideal drum height was 1.55 meters, or 5½ feet. The base was conceived of as 4½ feet, the capital as 6½, and the whole thus constituted the ideal one hundred feet of elevation.[22]

It is clear that the eight-step ratio for the drum blocks was not taken on lightly, since it required the employment of the complex ratio of fourteen steps per turn. This configuration requires difficult calculations to plot, and simpler alternatives were available: later spiral stairs in Rome employ ratios of sixteen (the Baths of Caracalla) or twenty (the Baths of Diocletian) steps per turn.[23] However, there is an even more puzzling element to the staircase in the Column of Marcus Aurelius: it seems that the fourteen-step ratio was not applied from the beginning, but only from the start of the third turn of the staircase, halfway up the pedestal. Instead of fourteen there are fifteen steps in each of the first two turns of the staircase, their treads executed according to an irregular plan. Moreover, the rise of these steps is also irregular, particularly in the third course where they are 25.5 centimeters tall versus 21.4 in the previous and 20.6 in the following courses.[24] This transition would have been clearly notable for a person climbing the stairs, and one can picture it leading to stumbles in the dark interior of the pedestal, which was not as well lit as the shaft above. One possible explanation is that the column's architect underestimated the difficulty of planning the staircase, attempted to improvise it as he went along, and only resorted to directly copying that of Trajan's Column after construction had already begun. Another possibility is that the designers decided to increase the height of the pedestal after the initial plan was drawn and that, instead of reworking the entire plan, the architect and/or contractor improvised the layout of the stairway in the extra courses. Whatever the case, the extreme irregularity of the lower windings of the Marcus column staircase gives clear evidence of lack of detailed advanced planning of a portion of one of the most important elements of the entire structure.

In summary, the structure of the Column of Marcus Aurelius presents a carefully planned (if less than elegant) exterior combined with an interior that oddly mixes precise copying from Trajan's Column through most of its height with a small portion of uneven and apparently ill-planned staircase in the pedestal. The doubling of the height of the pedestal in comparison to Trajan's Column and the care taken to ensure that all of the elements of the column proper be contained in nineteen drums shows that the designer of the Marcus column had carefully examined his model. What is more, he understood the model well enough to correct an apparent error in it, and he was critical enough to introduce a structural refinement. His treatment of the stairway, however, is more problematic. It may be that the ratio of fourteen steps per turn was copied because this was easier to do than to come up with an entirely new plan for the staircase using a simpler ratio. Careful copying would explain the regularity of the stairway in the standard-sized column drums; the difficult of extending this stairway down into the solid pedestal, where in Trajan's Column a series of straight flights joined by landings was employed, may be another explanation for the remarkable irregularities evident in the bottom two windings of the stair.

From Idea to Monument: Building the Column

Once the plan was (more or less) complete, two main things would have been needed to build the Column of Marcus Aurelius: a prepared site and stone. The preparation of the site (which would have involved not only the digging of appropriate foundations, but also the provision of working areas for the preparation of building elements and facilities for landing and transporting the stone to the site) could have begun immediately after the plans were finished. The quarrying of the stone would have taken longer to get underway, as the plans would have had to have been conveyed to Luna, a suitable source of marble sought out, and the long process of hewing the blocks and drums from the mountainside started.[25]

The Column of Marcus Aurelius is made up of thirty (in ancient times thirty-one) blocks of marble. Ten blocks, arranged in seven levels, form the pedestal; nineteen form the column itself (including its base and capital); and one further block stands atop the capital (there was once one more to cap it off and provide a support for the statue atop, but this was already missing by the time the first drawings of the column were made; presumably it fell in one of the earthquakes that rocked the monument in the Middle Ages). The marble blocks, weighing from about thirty tons each for the drums up to almost eighty tons in the case of the capital, would have been loaded into seagoing ships and sailed down the coast to the mouth of the Tiber. Dionysius of Halicarnassus reports that loads up to about 200 tons could be brought upriver to Rome, but whether these same ships could have entered the city itself is doubtful.[26] Rather, when a large load was brought into Rome (and much larger loads certainly were: for example, the obelisk used by Augustus to form the gnomon of his sundial in the Campus Martius weighed about 440 tons), transfer to river-going craft was probably necessary, ideally a flat-bottomed boat that could simply have been pulled, poled, or rowed up the Tiber.[27] The tasks of loading at Luna and unloading at Rome would have required a massive wooden structure to pick up the blocks, swing them over the boats (they could hardly have been pushed or slid in or out), and lower them safely in place. Such structures likely already existed at both Luna and Rome, given the amount of heavy stone elements, especially monolithic columns, that were shipped to Rome in the first and second centuries.

At Rome there were two main landing areas for goods shipped up the Tiber: at the docks below the Aventine between Monte Testaccio and the Forum Boarium, or at docks on the northwestern bank of the Campus Martius; in both areas partly finished stonework has been found.[28] Lancaster has suggested that the components of Trajan's Column were most likely unloaded below the Aventine and transported to their assembly site around the north side of the Capitol.[29] For the Marcus column blocks, the most likely unloading site would have been the Campus Martius. Certainly we know that the stone for other major monuments in the area was unloaded here: particularly revealing are the plans carved into the ancient pavement in front of the Mausoleum of Augustus that show that elements of the Hadrianic Pantheon's colonnade and pediment were carved here. This suggests that the stone for this project was also unshipped in the same area, along the Tiber just west of the Mausoleum.[30] This would have also been a practical area for the unloading of the Marcus column blocks, as there would have been only a relatively short trip across the Campus Martius to the construction site.

The next task would have been to finish the blocks and drums for assembly. All the elements did not likely arrive at once, but rather by ones and twos as they were progressively quarried, shipped, unloaded, and dragged toward the building site. The final shape of the blocks and drums would have had to have been very carefully controlled, especially with regard to the upper and lower faces of the drums and the sides of any blocks that would come into contact with other blocks. Absolute dimensions, it would seem, could vary somewhat from stone to stone, as long as the final total dimensions of the monument were correct: the column drums, for example, vary from 1.52 to 1.58 meters in height, but the whole shaft still measures 29.62 meters, or exactly one hundred feet. As noted, this sort of flexibility was necessary when working with stone, as natural flaws or accidental damage in shipping could require blocks to be reduced in size on the building site.

To what extent would the column drums have been carved before being set in place? The upper and lower edges of the interior walls of each drum are finished with a narrow, smoothly carved border. The tool marks do not match from drum to drum as would have been the case had the staircase been carved after the drums were in place.[31] This shows that the interior of the drums was carved out before they were lifted—a sensible arrangement that would have spared the unnecessary lifting of literally tons of extra stone. In the case of Trajan's Column, the weight savings won by carving out the staircase in advance have been calculated at about nine tons per drum.[32] The stairwell was not simply roughed out, but carved entirely in its precisely finished form. Such precision must also have been applied to the carving of the upper and lower faces of the drums. These surfaces would have had to have been even and absolutely level to ensure both that excess pressure would not be applied to any part of the carved-out drums and that the column itself would be perfectly vertical.

There is, of course, less information about the finishing of the exterior of the column, since its original surface was removed in the process of carving the relief. As discussed in more detail below, evidence shows that the relief itself was, unlike the stairway, carved after the column drums had been put in place. Unfinished sarcophagi show that Roman relief carvers were accustomed to working from rather rough surfaces, often finished only with a coarse point chisel. It is hard to say whether this would have been the case on the Column of Marcus Aurelius. The task facing the carvers was clearly different than that which faced the carvers of the largely repetitive sarcophagi. In particular, the latter could often work from memory, or by referencing finished sarcophagi already in the workshop. The column surface, on the other hand, likely demanded a finer finish of the prepared work surface so that the course of the frieze and even the details of at least some of its scenes could be sketched out on it before carving began. Architectural considerations were also important in dictating the degree of finish. The Column of Marcus Aurelius, unlike Trajan's Column, has no entasis proper; that is, it does not have a curved profile designed to counter the optical illusion of concavity that can mar the appearance of straight-sided column shafts. However, it does taper along straight lines from bottom to top. This taper would, like the stairway, have been carved before the column was assembled, if only to save weight. To plot the taper, the architects would have likely relied on a template, a drawing of the column's profile with its height dramatically telescoped but with its radius represented at 1:1 scale. From such a template measurements could be mechanically transferred to the drums using a compass. The result may have been a finish similar to what can be seen on the inner wall of the column's staircase—a smooth band at the top and bottom, with a rougher but still fairly even surface in between.[33]

The process of construction would have required an apparatus to put all the elements together. This meant not only lifting but also shifting the blocks horizontally and then lowering them in place, all with great care and precision. The weights involved were not the heaviest that the Romans had ever lifted, but some were substantially greater than those involved in the construction of Trajan's Column, whose capital weighs only 44.7 tons in comparison to 79.1 for that of Marcus's.[34] This work would have been beyond the capabilities of a crane such as depicted on the Haterii relief. Lancaster has proposed a likely arrangement for the assembly of Trajan's Column, based on ancient and Renaissance sources. This would have required two massive wooden towers, square in section and joining each other side by side. The blocks would be positioned under one tower, attached to multiple ropes by means of lewis irons (expanding metal wedges) set into holes cut into the tops of the blocks, and then raised using energy supplied by multiple capstans turned by humans or animals at ground level. Once the blocks had reached the necessary height, they would have had to have been shifted horizontally to the second tower before being lowered carefully into position.[35]

Metal dowels, which must have been set in place in cuttings on the upper face of the column drum below, would secure the two drums together. The next block would be lowered on top and finally the entire assembly would be fixed by pouring molten lead from the outside through a small channel cut in the flat surfaces of the stone. Since the small pouring channels betrayed the presence of the massive and valuable dowels to post-antique metal scavengers, few of these dowels still remain in position. In their place are the numerous pits (at times in the past mistaken for cannon-ball damage) hacked into both Trajan's and Marcus's Columns at the joints between various elements. An excellent example is visible in the figure of Victoria on the Column of Marcus Aurelius (fig. 5.7; other examples in figs. 5.11 and 9.1), where not only can the hole left by looters be seen but also the shifting of the upper and lower column drums that occurred after the dowel had been removed. Despite their value, two such dowels do still survive in place in Trajan's Column, and four in Marcus's.[36]

The final step in assembling the column would have been to raise and place into position the bronze statue of the emperor at its top and to fence in the observation platform. Markings on the upper surface of the capital show that it was provided with a railing supported by four large posts, one at each corner, another large post in the middle of each side, and three smaller posts in each of the intervening spaces. These were presumably made of iron or bronze, possibly gilded, and clearly attest to the function of the column as an observation platform.[37]

Construction Time

Perhaps the single most important factor in the minds of the builders was that of time. Roman monuments were often completed very quickly, a fact that is certainly tied to the desire of the person commissioning them to live to witness their dedication. The cochlear columns of Rome and Constantinople were, it appears, no exception. The Forum of Trajan, including his column, was most likely begun no earlier than late in 106, following the conclusion of Trajan's second Dacian war.[38] This campaign ended with the capture of Decebalus's massive treasury, providing the funds for the project. Epigraphic and numismatic evidence tell us that the Forum and the Basilica Ulpia were dedicated in January of 112. The *Fasti Ostienses*, a historical calendar from Ostia, has an entry for the ides of May A.D. 113 that reads "*id. Mai. Imp. Traianus* [*templum Ven*]*eris in foro Caesaris et . . . m in foro suo dedicavit*," which is to say, "on the fifteenth of May the emperor Trajan dedicated a temple of Venus in the Forum of Caesar and a '. . . m' in his own Forum." The missing word was restored by Calza as *columnam*. Coins commemorate the dedication of the Basilica Ulpia, the Equus Traianus (the great and admired equestrian statue of the emperor), and the Forum itself in the year 112. The column does not appear among these issues, but only later in the year 113, agreeing exactly with Calza's reading of the Ostian Fasti.[39]

This means that the Column of Trajan required, at most, six and a half years to plan, build, and carve. The entire process, from preparing the foundation to finishing the relief, was accomplished at the same time as the much larger project of building Trajan's Forum and Basilica was also being carried out. It is particularly interesting that the column was not completed in time for dedication along with the remaining buildings of the Forum in 112. The main delay was, presumably, the carving of the helical relief. Peter Rockwell has suggested that haste was a main reason for a number of odd inconsistencies visible in the frieze, such as the many instances of empty-handed soldiers who had been meant to receive miniature metal weapons that, as we can tell from the lack of a drilled hole in their hands, were never inserted.[40] One might imagine that as work on other parts of the Forum complex was completed, carvers were transferred to the column in an effort to speed completion.

More evidence comes from the *columnae cochlides* of Constantinople. The Column of Theodosius was begun in A.D. 387 and its crowning statue was placed on top in 393, a period of six years.[41] The whole project almost certainly took somewhat longer than these six years to reach completion, since for the placement of the statue the scaffolding must have still been in place and carving may have been ongoing. The Column of Arcadius, on the other hand, may have taken as long as twenty-one years to complete: it was begun in 401/402 and its surmounting statue was dedicated by Theodosius II in 421.[42] For the Column of Marcus Aurelius, we know only that it was in all likelihood finished before 193, when the procurator of the column, Adrastus, who had already been on the job for some time, was given permission to replace his little hut with a more substantial dwelling. This leaves plenty of time for its completion within the timeframes required by its sibling monuments. Still, even within these dates there would have been little time for delay. Furthermore the latter part of Marcus's reign was marked by bankruptcy and plague, both of which would have put serious strain on the people assigned with making the project a reality.

To achieve the sort of working speed required to accomplish all of this in the time available it would have been essential to perform as many tasks as possible concurrently. This would mean quarrying elements while others were in transport, roughing out blocks and drums while others were being assembled, and beginning the process of frieze carving as soon as possible, perhaps even before the entire monument had been assembled. Although working time for sculptors is very difficult to estimate, Amanda Claridge's calculations give some impression of the magnitude of the challenge. Basing her calculations on the surface area of Trajan's Column expressed as an equivalent number of sarcophagus fronts and supposing four two-man teams at work, Claridge suggested a time of six to eight years for the work of carving the frieze.[43] These six to eight years could begin *only* when much of the work (quarrying, transport, finishing, building) on the structure of the monument itself had already been at least partly completed. The problem is that this estimate is about equal to the actual time it took from the start of the project to the dedication of the finished column. Claridge has suggested that the frieze may actually have been added only later, in the reign of Hadrian.[44] However, coins show the frieze more or less clearly as early as 113 (see for example fig. 3.2), indicating that it was complete at the time the column was dedicated. Perhaps more than eight workers were employed, but even this would not have eliminated the problem. Speed of work during the carving phase would have been of paramount importance, lest an otherwise-completed monument stand for years in scaffolding while the carvers finished their work. To judge from the evidence of coins and of the Fasti this is indeed what happened in the case of Trajan's Column, as its dedication was delayed for a little over a year.

Summary: Evaluating Design Priorities

The primary concerns in the minds of the people who commissioned the Column of Marcus Aurelius were most likely its general appearance, its inscription and freestanding sculpture, and its location. The eventual addition of relief decoration was doubtless assumed at an early stage in the process—the monument was, after all, a copy of the Column of Trajan—but the detail of this sculpture was only decided on later. This at least is the conclusion reached by looking at the role of minor decorative elements in surviving Roman building decrees and contracts. It also corresponds to the priorities reflected in the ancient names for the monument: *columna centenaria, columna cochlis.* Architecture took priority over sculpture, both in the early stages of the design process and in the later appreciation of the monument by Roman viewers. Still, this hardly means that the sculpture was considered unimportant, or that it was devoid of meaning. The remainder of this study focuses on this sculpture: its genesis, its content, and its message.

chapter five

THE FRIEZE CONCEPT & DRAFT

The designers of the frieze of the Column of Marcus Aurelius (its regularity suggests that a single designer was responsible for the general form and layout—the generation of its content is a different matter) did not face the same challenge as did the designer of the frieze of Trajan's Column. They did not have to create an entirely new form of architectural sculpture, but rather were able to rely on a model for guidance. At the same time, the existence of a model (Trajan's Column) did not make the task an easy one. To start with, the designers would have had to rely on their own observation and interpretation of their model. Working seventy years after the Column of Trajan was built, these men would not have been able to rely on the advice or information of anyone who had been involved in the original project. Just how well did the designers of the Column of Marcus Aurelius understand their model? Even today, with the benefit of close-up photography and numerous detailed studies, the frieze of the Column of Trajan is far from fully understood. Differences between the frieze of the Column of Marcus Aurelius and that of the Column of Trajan have been interpreted as attempts to improve on the original, or as conscious and careful alteration made to project a different message. Are such interpretations valid? Examining the planning process of the frieze can reveal some clues.

The first step taken by the designers of the frieze of the Column of Marcus Aurelius was to determine its overall layout. All other factors, including scene placement, were subordinate to this basic step. This simple consideration marks a sharp distinction from the approach followed by the designer of the Column of Trajan and is the first, and in some ways most striking, difference between the decoration of the two monuments. The frieze band of Trajan's Column is irregular: it varies in the angle at which it proceeds up the shaft and exhibits fluctuations in height that are both extreme and unpredictable. Within one single turn about the column shaft, the height of the frieze can vary by as much as 30 percent. Over the course of the entire frieze the fluctuations in height are even more striking, ranging between 145 and 77 centimeters. One might logically expect the frieze height to increase progressively as it winds up the column, in order to make the upper windings more visible from the ground—but this is not the case. Instead, the first thirteen windings of the frieze of Trajan's Column vary between 110 to 125 centimeters in height. After this, the height of the relief band decreases irregularly until a low point of 77 centimeters is reached in the nineteenth winding. Then for the last four windings the height of the frieze jumps, to as much as 145 centimeters in one place, almost double its smallest value just a few windings below.[1]

What are we to make of this? Whatever the course of the relief of Trajan's Column shows, it is not the hallmark of advance planning. This is puzzling, for the Romans were, after all, masters of planning: in their grid-planned colonies, their centuriated agricultural landscapes, the regular and often complex layouts of their monumental buildings. Even such apparently random things as decorative vine carvings were commonly laid over a restricting grid. Whether grand or marginal, the Romans usually took care to think out and plot their work in advance. The frieze of Trajan's Column appears to be anything but carefully planned and plotted. Having no model to follow, the designer of Trajan's Column seems to have improvised the layout of the frieze as he went along.

But there is also clear evidence that at least one part of the frieze of Trajan's Column was carefully planned and its position on the column shaft determined in advance of its carving. This was the Victoria, whose figure is located precisely at the midpoint of the column, exactly along the north axis. Given the unpredictability of the frieze height, it is very unlikely that the figure of Victoria ended up where it did by chance. Rather, her position in the exact midpoint of the column (not, it should be noted, at the exact midpoint of the frieze as measured by its length) was plotted before the course of the frieze. This suggests that these two elements of the frieze—the Victoria and the course of the frieze itself—were plotted independently of each other.

The situation on the Column of Marcus Aurelius could not be more different. There, the helical frieze rises at a steady rate of climb between straight borders (more precisely, one straight helical border), maintaining a constant height from bottom to top. What is more, it does not have an odd number of windings as on Trajan's Column. Though the number of spirals on the Column of Marcus Aurelius is usually given as twenty-one, this miscounts the two truncated windings at the top and bottom of the column shaft. The fundamental division of the column surface appears in fact to have been based on the simpler unit of twenty. The height of the sculpted section of the shaft of Marcus's Column (the portion from the top of the apophyge, the concave transitional area where the drum forming the base meets the first drum of the shaft proper, to the bottom of the band below the fluting) is 88¼ Roman feet, or 1,060 inches (26.11 meters).[2] This number can be divided fully into twenty equal parts each measuring 53 inches, or 4 feet 5 inches. This measurement, repeated twenty times, formed the basis for the layout of the frieze of the Column of Marcus Aurelius. All of this—rigidly straight frieze border, uniform frieze height, and an overall division of the sculpted surface into twenty equal units—is clear indication of careful advance planning.

Why did the designers of the Column of Marcus Aurelius follow this simple approach to planning the frieze, so different from what we see on Trajan's Column? Perhaps the decision was based on aesthetics: the person responsible for the frieze layout preferred a regular pattern to the unevenness he saw in his model. However, it is just as likely that his decision was based on matters of practicality and simplicity, since an even, regularly climbing frieze has two distinct advantages for a designer. First, it can be much more easily drafted than an irregular one, both on a two-dimensional surface and on the curving surface of the column itself. The actual plotting of this regular frieze on the column surface could have been accomplished by marking a series of points 4 feet 5 inches apart up each major axis (north, east, south, and west faces) of the column. These axes would already have to be precisely marked to allow accurate placement of the windows, with which they align. After the points were marked it would then be a simple matter to wind a rope or a cord around the exterior of the column, passing through each of these marks on each of its turns around the column. This line could have been marked on the column surface in paint, or even carved in with a chisel. As long as careful measurements were made, this could even be done drum-for-drum before the entire column was assembled.

Another distinct advantage of an even, regular frieze was that since the height of the frieze was constant, its length could be immediately and definitively known. This would have made very clear the amount of artistic material (that is, the number of figured scenes) needed to fill it, which would in turn have made the advance planning of this material much simpler. Most important, both of these benefits were gained without giving up a rough parity in number of spirals with Trajan's Column, thus ensuring that the overall appearance of the two monuments would be very similar.

This approach gives hints as to the training and background of the person who decided on this type of layout for the frieze. Judging from the evidence we have, Roman sculptors when given a free hand did not tend to organize their work into carefully measured registers: rigid division of frieze units does not appear either on the large historical panels from the Arch of Septimius Severus in the Roman Forum nor on the relief of the Column of Trajan. In both situations the ground lines created by the sculptors were very irregular. The task of laying out the regular frieze we see on the Marcus column called for knowledge of mathematics and geometry, and in particular a clear understanding of the planned overall dimensions of the column itself: this was the domain of the architect, not the sculptor. The rigid, measured technique used to draft the frieze of the Column of Marcus Aurelius is also in keeping with the working methods of Roman architects, who preferred where possible to employ designs based on whole numbers.[3] The same person who designed the structure of the column may also have been responsible for, or at the very least had a hand in, drafting the basic layout of the frieze.

This rigid, architectural approach to planning the frieze of the Column of Marcus Aurelius had major effects on its content. One of these was that the sculpture was constantly constrained by the fixed template of the frieze layout. One of the best examples of how the rigidity of the frieze influenced its content can be seen in comparing the location of the personification of victory on Trajan's and Marcus's columns. On the Column of Trajan, the Victoria is placed exactly halfway up the north axis of the column shaft—the midpoint of the column falls at about the level of her breasts. On the Column of Marcus Aurelius, however, this midpoint falls in between two windings of the frieze. This meant that when it came time to place the Victoria within the established framework of the frieze outline, an exactly central position was impossible since the midpoint of the column fell on the border between two windings of the frieze band. The designers then had to determine where to place the Victoria: above or below the actual midpoint. They chose to place her in the tenth winding rather than the eleventh, thus locating her below the precise middle of the frieze. This choice may have been influenced by a desire to place the Victoria closer to the viewer, and thus make her more prominent, but the very fact that such a choice had to be made is vivid evidence of the subordination of the content to the rigid course of the frieze.

Even though the designers were not able to place the figure of Victory (fig. 5.7) in the exact middle of the column shaft (measured vertically), they clearly took care to position her so that the center of this scene exactly faces the viewer. In comparison, the vast bulk of the remaining scenes on the Col-

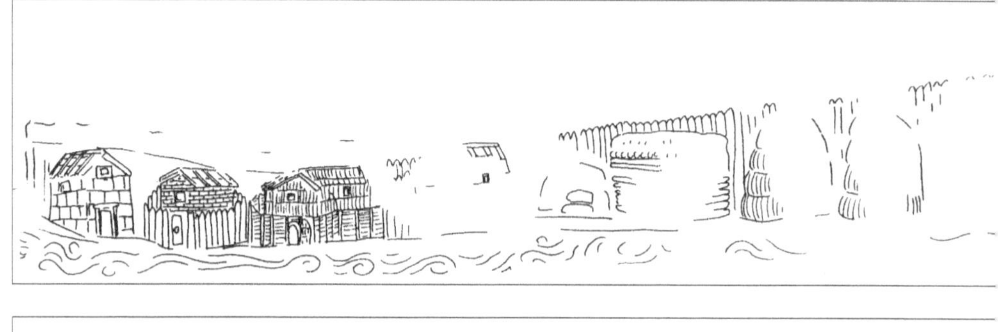

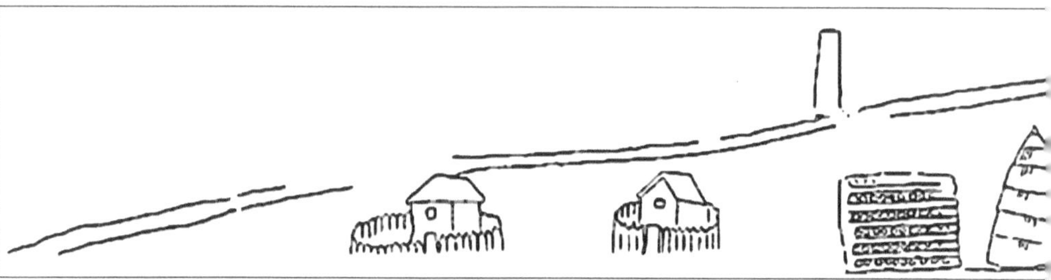

umn of Marcus Aurelius are not centrally aligned: that is, most scenes do not line up directly along any of the main axes defined by the lines of the windows that run up the east, west, south, and north faces of the column. Indeed, the situation is usually exactly the opposite. By far the majority of the column's scenes are portioned into discrete rectangular units, usually taking up one-eighth of a full winding, so that two scenes fit into each quarter-section of frieze between one cardinal axis and the next. This division into eighths becomes more and more regular as the frieze proceeds up the column, until in the upper windings it is almost unbroken. The effect of this organization is that no scene presents itself frontally along the main eastern axis above the Victoria. In other words, along the central axis in the entire upper half of the column there are no important scenes facing the approaching viewer directly.

In the vast majority of cases the positioning of scene units on the Column of Marcus Aurelius was governed by concerns other than a desire to have all scenes face the viewer directly. These concerns were a combination of practicality of arrangement, ease of composition and planning, and facility of execution. By making the entire frieze follow a regular course and then dividing this course into precise rectangular units, the designers of the frieze created a framework perfectly suited to quick and schematic filling. How did the designers go about planning this "filling"—the sculptural content of the frieze?

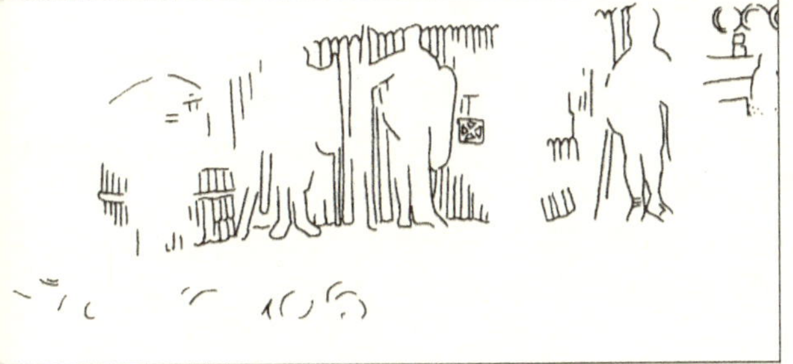

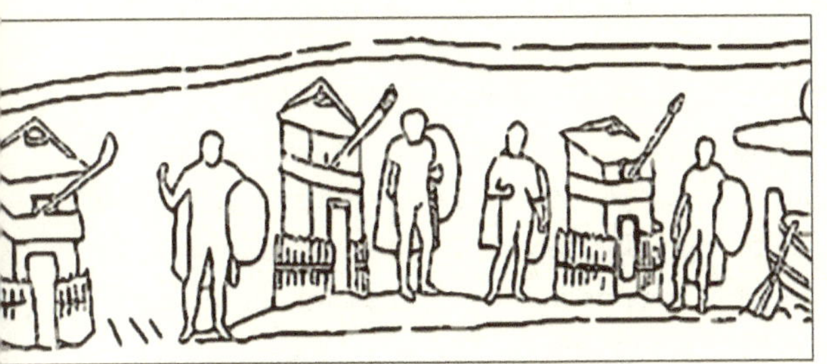

FIGURE 5.1.
The opening scenes on the Column of Marcus Aurelius (above) and on the Column of Trajan (below). Drawings by author.

Planning the Frieze Content

There are two fundamental questions to ask about the planning of the frieze content. First, where did the planners begin? Second, where did they get their visual material from? These questions are related, and so closely that it is possible to fully answer the first and partly address the second by examining just the first one and a half windings of the frieze.

Although the course of the frieze is constant throughout, the division of individual scenes within it is much less regular below than above. This increasing regularity in scene size and placement as one moves up the column suggests a planning process that began with the lowest scenes and moved upward, slowly becoming more schematic as it did so. And the differences between the lower and upper parts of the frieze are striking. The very first scenes we see on the Column of Marcus Aurelius are of a river landscape (scenes I and II, generally accepted as representing the bank of the Danube), followed by a depiction of the river god himself (III), and concluded by a scene of the Roman army crossing the river by means of a bridge of boats (III continued). These scenes show remarkable links to the beginning scenes of Trajan's Column.

Figure 5.1 illustrates the first half-winding of the frieze of both Marcus's and Trajan's columns. The first objects seen on the frieze of the Marcus column are four buildings, the third one built of wattle in the manner common for barbarian huts seen later on the column, the remainder of stone. All have tiled roofs. The first building stands alone, while the remaining three are surrounded by wooden palisades. The second and fourth buildings reproduce with a high degree of accuracy the form, orientation, and placement of the two buildings that stand at the beginning of the frieze of the Column of Trajan; for example, details on the second building (fig. 5.2) mirror those of the first building shown on Trajan's Column (fig. 5.3), down to the lion-head door ornament.

In marked contrast the other two buildings are free inventions (more on the reason for this below). The next object on both friezes is a log pile, which is in turn followed by two haystacks, which are shown as overlapping on Trajan's Column but as standing side by side on Marcus's. Following is a series of wooden, torch-bearing watchtowers, each encircled by a palisade, interspaced with soldiers. Although this section of the Marcus column frieze is heavily damaged, enough remains to see that the same number of towers and soldiers appear on both monuments. The single most apparent difference between these two otherwise nearly identical sections of frieze is that while the background is blank on Trajan's Column, on Marcus's it is filled with a solid wooden palisade.

Next comes a scene of three boats unloading their cargo outside a fortified riverside town (fig. 5.4). At the far left, on shore, lies a row of barrels. Below, two men unload more from a boat. The second ship on the Column of Marcus Aurelius is unmanned, while in the third a soldier unloads what appear to be bundles wrapped in cloth or leather (on the Column of Trajan, both the second and third ships are unmanned). The three structures shown on the Column of Marcus Aurelius reproduce in number and in architectural detail three of the buildings in the corresponding area in the Trajanic cityscape. Most remarkable is a two-story stone structure, the lower story of which looks like a portico with tall, closely spaced rectangular openings, while the upper story contains large, square windows. Behind this porticoed building rise two tall, narrow trees. The correspondence in this scene between the two columns (figs. 5.5 and 5.6) is almost exact; it is clear that the image on the Marcus column was derived directly from that on Trajan's.

The cityscape is followed on both columns by a rendering of a river god bordered by an arch of rocky ground. The image on the Marcus column has not only been damaged but also partly restored in the Renaissance. But enough of the outline remains to show that both gods were similarly clad and were posed in the same way. The next scene immediately after the

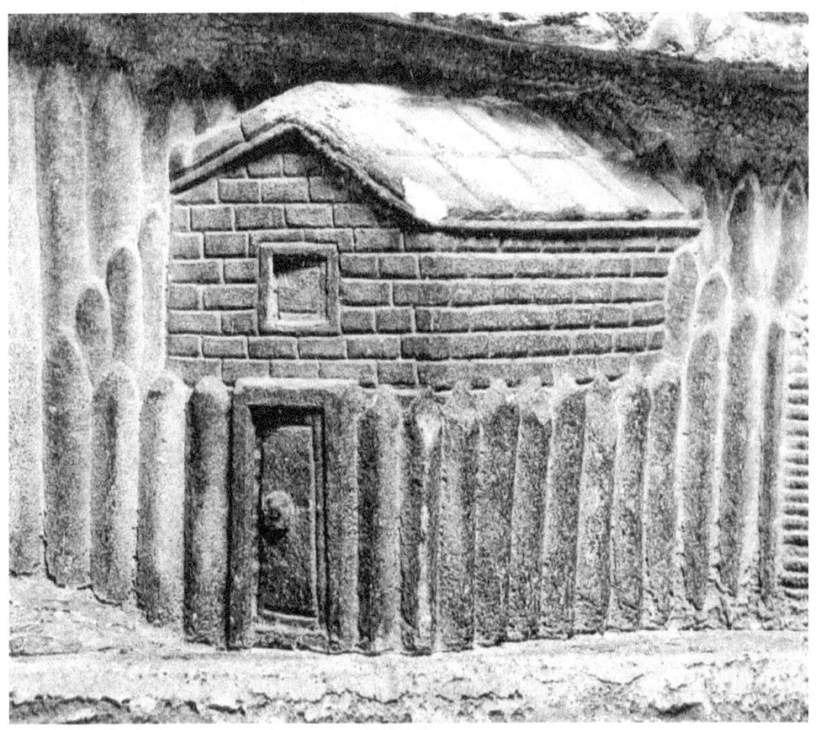

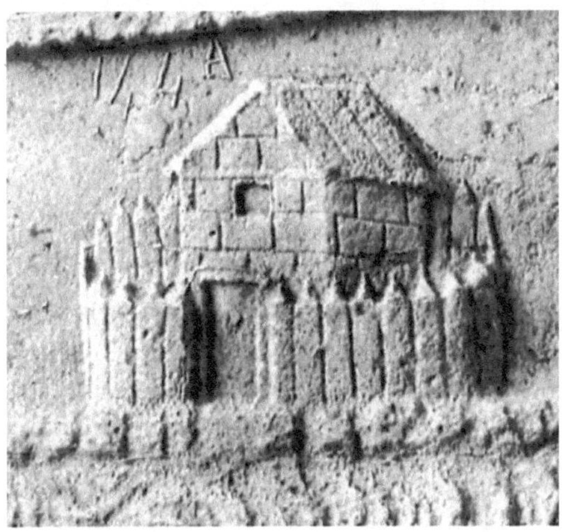

(above) FIGURE 5.2.
Detail of the second house on Marcus's Column. From Petersen et al. 1896, pl. 5A.

(below) FIGURE 5.3.
Detail of the second house on Trajan's Column. From Cichorius 1896/1900, pl. IV.

Danube landscape shows a bridge crossing (III). We can no longer know how the transition from riverside city to march scene took place because this area has been obliterated by a section of Renaissance repair. It is at any rate clear that the method of transition that was used on Trajan's Column was not employed; the troops begin marching in the open and then

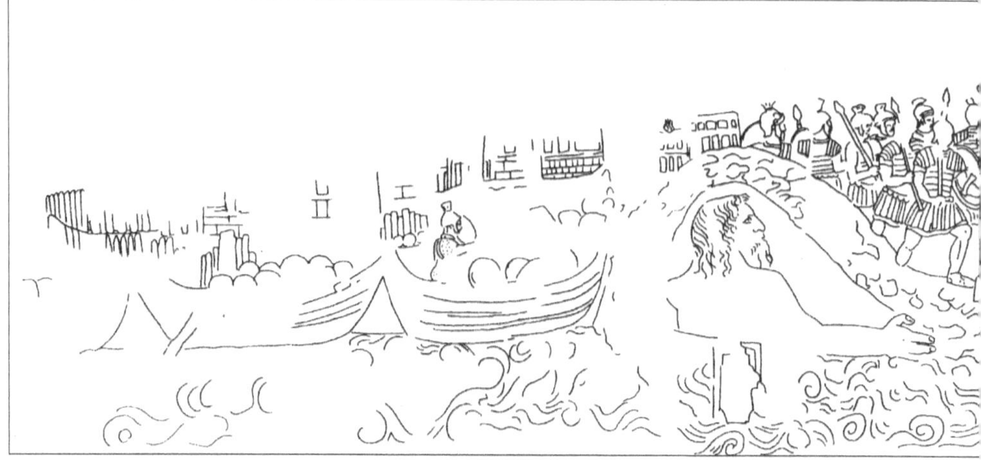

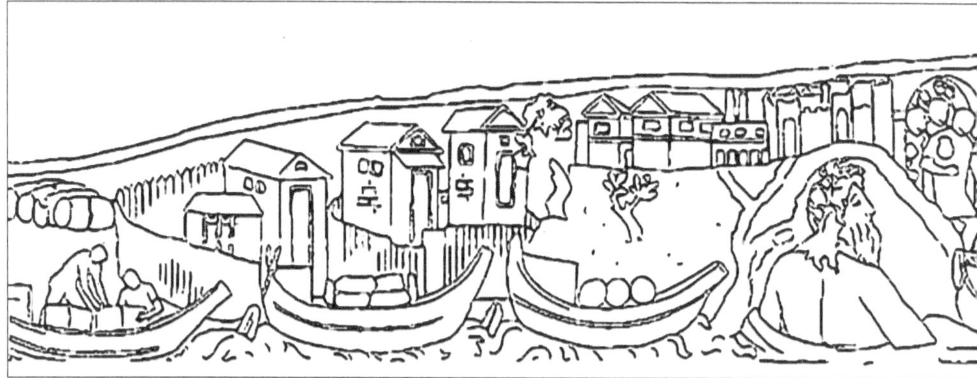

pass through a freestanding gate, rather than exiting from a city gate as on the earlier monument. After passing through the gateway, the Roman soldiers march in a dense mass over a bridge of boats, in the company of the emperor and his attendants, until they reach a second archway through which they proceed onto dry land. The march continues through this gate with the soldiers being accompanied now by horn players and lion-skin-wearing standard- bearers. On Trajan's Column, the corresponding scene is both similar and different. The march is broken into two sections, but not as clearly, and both proceed over a bridge. On Trajan's Column there is no second gateway; instead there appear to be two sections of bridge that do not join. This may be intended to represent a double bridge since the rightmost ends of each structure are supported by pillars, not boats, as if meant to show the end anchored on land. It is easily imaginable that Trajan would

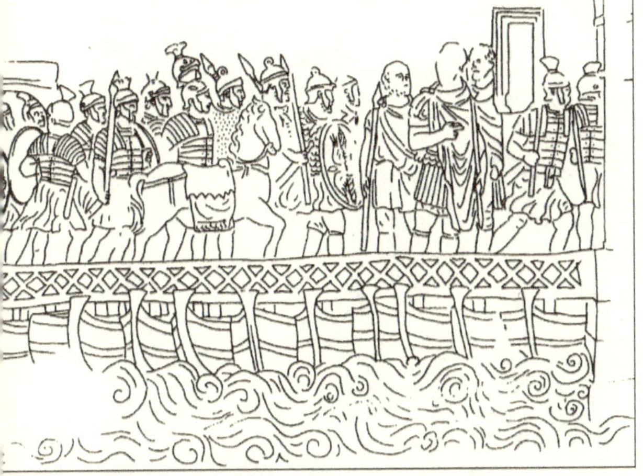

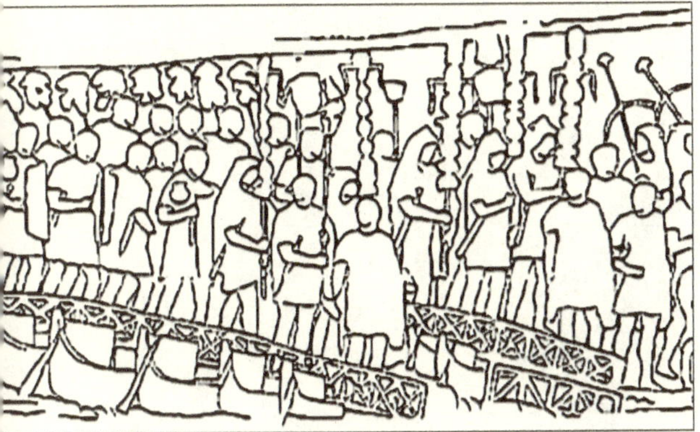

FIGURE 5.4.
The second half of the first winding of the friezes of the columns of Marcus Aurelius (above) and Trajan (below). Drawings by author.

have needed at least two bridges to transport his massive army across the Danube.

What explains the difference in the way this scene is laid out on the Column of Marcus Aurelius? Modern commentators have been uncertain how to interpret the two downward-sloping bridge sections on Trajan's Column. The scene disrupts the sense of left-to-right upward movement and the destination of the first column of marching troops is unclear. It is possible that the designer of Marcus's frieze had similar doubts or, even if he understood the meaning, was simply unhappy with the way in which the image was rendered. The single straight bridge may represent his "solution" to this perceived problem. It is worth noting that the downward-sloping bridge appears elsewhere on Trajan's Column, but on Marcus's there is only the straight, level variety. This suggests that the sloping bridge was a familiar

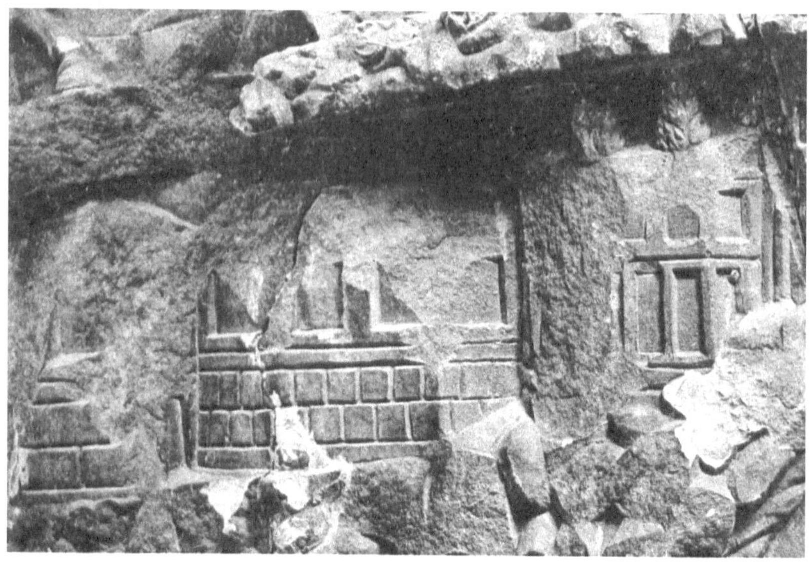

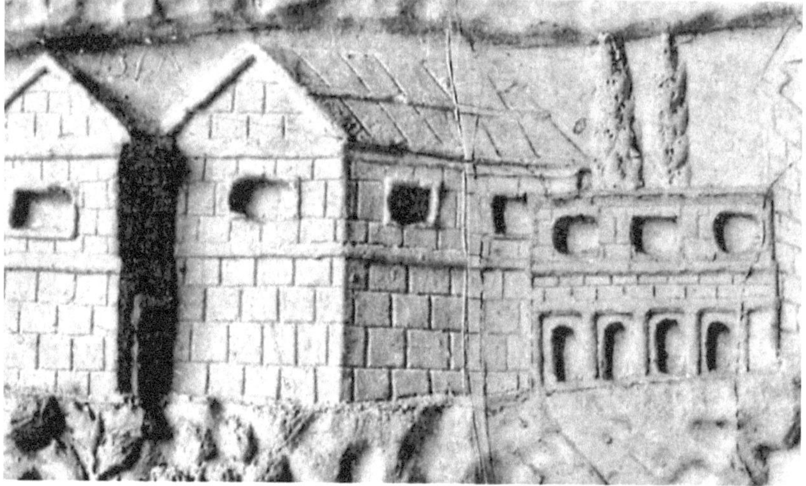

(above) FIGURE 5.5. Detail of two buildings, colonnade, and two trees above and to the left of the River God on Marcus's Column. From Petersen et al. 1896, pl. 9A.

(below) FIGURE 5.6. Detail of the corresponding buildings on Trajan's Column (scene III). From Cichorius 1896/1900, pl. VI.

motif in the repertoire of the designer of Trajan's Column, but not in that of the men in charge of Marcus's monument.

On Trajan's Column, the emperor is not present on either bridge. Rather, each marching column is led by an officer in a muscled cuirass followed by standard-bearers. The next scene, on dry land, does not directly continue (or proceed from) the march shown on the bridge. Here we see a body of mail-clad cavalry, dismounted and leading their horses, whose rear is brought up by two soldiers clad in the lion-skin caps of standard-bearers who carry large, curved horns. The correspondence between the two columns, it would seem, is beginning to break down.

In the following scenes of the Column of Marcus Aurelius this trend continues. The very next scene on the Marcus column (IV) represents an *adlocutio*, an address by the emperor to his troops. This is followed by a damaged marching scene incorporating horsemen and standard-bearers, and then by an even more badly damaged scene in which figures are shown in and around a stone-walled fortification. The overall order and appearance of these scenes corresponds roughly with those in the same position on the Column of Trajan—but only roughly. Scene IV on the Column of Marcus Aurelius is clearly an *adlocutio*: the emperor stands gesturing on a platform, facing his troops who surround him on three sides. On Trajan's Column, on the other hand, the emperor is shown on a platform flanked by two high officials and backed by his lictors, but he is seated, is not attended by soldiers, and appears to be engaged in conversation with the man to his left. Whatever this scene represents (perhaps a council of war), it is not an *adlocutio* as on Marcus's monument. The next scene on Trajan's Column shows standard-bearers walking their horses; on the Marcus column we see a troop of riders. Finally, in scene VIII of Trajan's Column, a beautifully composed depiction of a sacrificial procession making its way around a stone-walled fortress, inside of which the emperor is pouring a libation over an altar. In scene VI on the Column of Marcus Aurelius all that can be made out is a similarly shaped stone structure, in the doorway of which a cloak-wearing figure (Marcus?) stands with one or more attendants. This may be a similar sacrifice scene but if so it lacks the procession seen on Trajan's Column. After this point, copying from the frieze of Trajan's Column essentially ceases.

How is the progression from near-exact copying in the first winding of the frieze to loose imitation in the second to be understood? The direct and more or less exact copying occurs in a place that would not immediately draw the viewer's gaze and did not involve important figures. Only after this introductory, wedge-shaped portion of the frieze does the real action begin, precisely when the emperor makes his first appearance marching with his troops. And it is only then that the exact copying ceases and the imitation—reproduction of the general nature and to a large extent the layout of the scenes but not all of their details—takes over. From the evidence of these correspondences it is clear that the designer of the content of this portion of the frieze of the Column of Marcus Aurelius was in possession of a drawing of the first one and a half windings of the frieze of Trajan's Column. Without any compelling reason to make changes to the contents of the first winding, he chose almost without exception not to. The exceptions are three: two buildings inserted at the very beginning of the frieze, a palisade behind the watchtowers and soldiers on the bank of the Danube, and a number of altered details of objects and figures (especially the execution of chain mail using drill-holes rather than incised lines and the elaborated detailing of the houses at the beginning of the frieze). These details—the precise texture of armor, the decoration of shields and helmets, the materials of buildings—were presumably only roughly indicated or not included at all in the model drawing produced by the designer of the frieze of the Column of Marcus Aurelius. Instead, they were added by the carvers themselves when the design was translated to stone. The differences in detail that resulted are better ascribed to the learned working methods of the carvers of the frieze rather than to the overall designer (see below for early uncertainty in figure detailing on the Column of Marcus Aurelius).

The other two changes made to his Trajanic model by the designer of the Marcus column frieze are of a different nature. They are not alterations to detail, but rather additions to the content of particular portions of the frieze of Trajan's Column, representing entire objects not present in the original. Why were these objects added to the frieze of the Marcus column? The addition of the palisade has been seen by some scholars as a deliberate attempt to reproduce the actual appearance of the Danube frontier in the time of Marcus Aurelius.[4] But there are a number of important objections to this theory. First, if realism was the driving concern, why was only this simple addition made while all other objects (and most of their details) were left precisely the same? The artist cannot have meant to imply that Marcus Aurelius crossed the Danube exactly where Trajan did, since Trajan invaded Dacian territory, while Marcus crossed further to the west into German lands. Why then was the townscape left entirely unaltered? A more important (and ultimately more revealing) objection is that the palisade is not the only addition to the opening scene on the Column of Marcus Aurelius. At the beginning of Marcus's frieze there are four small houses; on Trajan's there are only two, and the remaining portions of the frieze are simply blank. The two extra buildings on Marcus's Column have two different sources: the first (building one in sequence from left to right) is an almost-exact copy of the third building in the townscape of Trajan's

Column (the door with small window above and larger window on the side wall are exactly reproduced, as is the stonework—figs. 5.2 and 5.3); the second (building three) is, on the other hand, an adaptation of building two finished instead in a strange wattle pattern, a type of construction which never is seen on Trajan's Column but is common on Marcus's.

When the additions and modifications to the opening scene on the Column of Marcus Aurelius are considered together—the two new buildings, the palisade filling the background, the increased spacing of the haystacks—a clear motive emerges. The two new buildings do not add any information to the frieze of Marcus's Column, but instead merely serve to fill up the blank space that existed on the corresponding places in the frieze of Trajan's Column. The palisade serves the very same function: to fill the large blank spaces that existed between the various elements of the Danube landscape on Trajan's Column. The two haystacks were moved apart to help fill up the space more evenly. Marcus's artists were apparently afflicted by an acute *horror vacui*. They were extremely uncomfortable with the open spaces they saw on Trajan's Column and sought to fill them up by creating new objects or by adjusting the spacing of objects already present. All of these actions were undertaken not out of a desire to express the genuine historical appearance of the Danube frontier under Marcus Aurelius, but rather to create what the artist considered a visually unified scene.

After the River God, the approach (though not the aversion to empty spaces) of the designer changes, from copying exactly, with some added elements and details, to imitation. The subject matter of scenes III to VI is the same; the figures and composition are, as a rule, not. It seems not to be a coincidence that this change from copying to imitation occurs when Marcus Aurelius makes his first appearance in the frieze. From this point on the designer could not rely entirely on his model, but rather was compelled to introduce new material to replace some of its content. Thus the resulting scenes appear very similar to those on Trajan's Column, and in the same sequence, but they differ substantially in detail. The need to introduce current content, especially images of the emperor and his entourage, resulted in a change from copying to imitation.

Analysis of the opening scenes on both columns reveals much about the working methods of the artists of the Column of Marcus Aurelius but does not tell us why the first one and a half windings consist entirely of copies or imitations of scenes from Trajan's Column, when most of the remaining frieze consists of scenes showing events from Marcus's wars (whether historical or not). The simplest explanation is that the designer of the frieze of the Column of Marcus Aurelius did not know how to begin his task. The regular sections of the bulk of the frieze, mostly divided up into neat rectangles, were working units that would have been familiar to an average Roman relief carver of the time, especially one employed in the sarcophagus industry (see chapter 8). But the beginning of the frieze of Marcus's Column was anything but regular; instead it presented a narrow, tapered section of space that slowly increased in size. The person in charge of this section was faced with the problem of finding some way of filling a very awkward section of relief, one that had the shape of a long narrow wedge. His answer was to go to his model, Trajan's Column, and crib the solution from it.

Scenes around the Victoria

There can be no doubt that the Victoria on the Column of Marcus Aurelius (scene LV, fig. 5.7) was derived from the Victoria (LXXVIII, fig. 5.8) on the Column of Trajan—itself derived, perhaps, from a monument of freestanding statuary from the time of Domitian.[5] There are, however, some important differences. The most readily visible is that the figure of Victoria on Trajan's Column is fully clad, while that on Marcus's is naked to the upper thighs. In this respect Marcus's Victoria is in keeping with traditional representations of the goddess, while Trajan's represented a departure. The shield on which Victory writes is, on the Marcus column, much larger, and it rests not on a pillar but on a window frame. This is a very pleasing and refined solution to the problem of elevating the shield, and it is possible that the position of the window was specially determined to fulfill this purpose. On Trajan's Column the Victoria's left foot rests on a helmet, on Marcus's on a raised lump of ground. These differences in detail make it fairly clear that the Victoria on the Marcus column was not exactly copied from but rather only inspired by the same scene on Trajan's Column. The single major departure of the Victoria on the Column of Marcus Aurelius from more standard images of the goddess is the absence of a helmet beneath her raised left foot. The result is somewhat awkward, her knee raised to no clear purpose and an irregular lump of ground added below as a sort of poor explanation for this situation. The trophies that flank the Victoriae on each column are similar in general form, but they too differ in detail. On Trajan's Column both are topped with open helmets; on Marcus's the left trophy sports a fur cap, the right a closed-face helmet. The left-hand trophies on both columns wear cloaks, but that on Marcus's is fur rather than

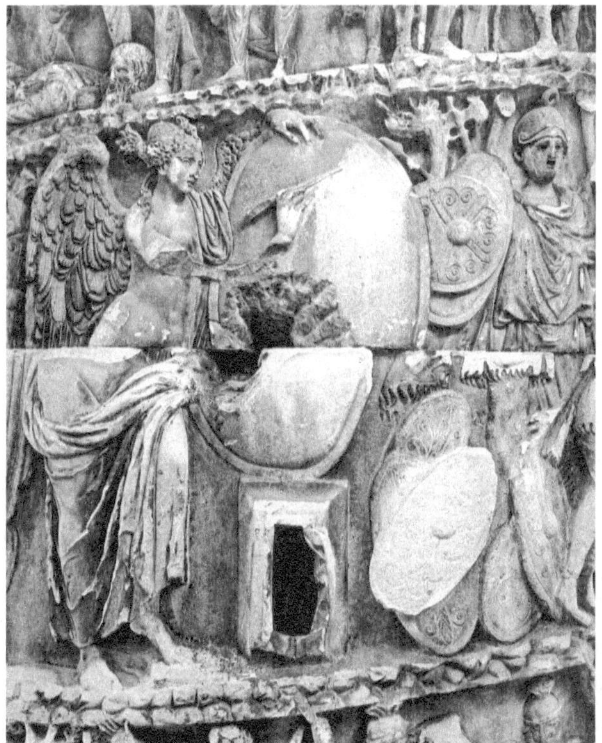

(above) FIGURE 5.7. Victoria (scene LV) on the Column of Marcus Aurelius; note the robber hole at the former location of a dowel between two column drums. From Petersen et al. 1896, pl. 54B.

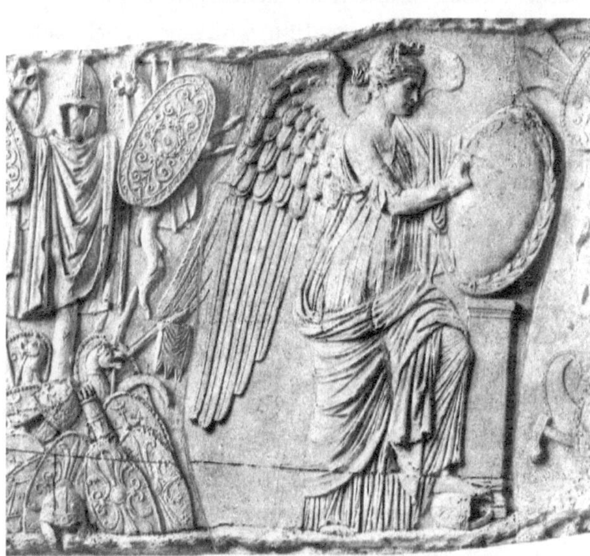

(below) FIGURE 5.8. Victoria (scene LXXVIII) on Column of Trajan.

fabric. Furthermore, the right-hand trophy on the Marcus column wears a tunic rather than a suit of armor as on Trajan's Column. The details of the assembled weapons are also different. In particular there is less variety on the Marcus column, and only shields, no weapons at all, are heaped at the bases of the trophies. The closest parallels for the Marcus column trophies are on contemporary sarcophagi, particularly those showing scenes of battle.[6] In sum it seems that the general appearance of this scene, its composition and placement on the Column of Marcus Aurelius, was taken from Trajan's Column, while its details (including the clothing of the goddess and the equipment of the trophies) were drawn from more contemporary models or the learned repertoire of its designer.

It appears that the artist sent to sketch the opening scenes and perhaps also the Victoria on Trajan's Column also took time to sketch in a few of the other scenes as well. These he then reproduced on the Column of Marcus Aurelius, in similar but not exact position and detail. The clearest example is scene LIV (fig. 5.9) on the Marcus column, showing the only Roman attack on a fortified barbarian position. The barbarian fort is constructed of wickerwork, in the same manner as all of the barbarian houses on the frieze. At the left-hand side of the composition, Roman soldiers throw spears and flaming torches at the barbarian fortification; at the right, two cavalrymen stand watch. The main attack comes from the foreground, where two groups of Romans in *testudo* (tortoise) formation, with shields held above their heads, assault the fortress wall. The barbarian defenders throw spears, swords, torches, rocks, a pot of liquid, and even two cartwheels at them in a desperate attempt to repel the soldiers. This scene is clearly derived from scene LXX/LXXI on Trajan's Column (fig. 5.10); not only is their content very similar, but so is their placement, shortly before the figures of Victory. The configuration of the *testudo* (four shields wide by three deep), the employment of soldiers wearing segmented armor (much less common on Marcus's Column than on Trajan's) to form the *testudo*, and the placement of defenders on top of the wall are all elements common to each. In detail, however, there are many differences. The *testudo* on Trajan's Column has additional shields forming a wall on the side of the formation, protecting the soldiers' flanks. The employment of the *testudo* is also different in each case. On the Marcus column, it seems to be used in a direct attack on the walls. On Trajan's Column, it is set at an angle to the wall itself and may be intended to represent an attack on the gate into which four Dacians are fleeing. The defenders within the fort itself also act in a much more unorthodox manner on Marcus's Column, throwing rocks, swords, fire, and

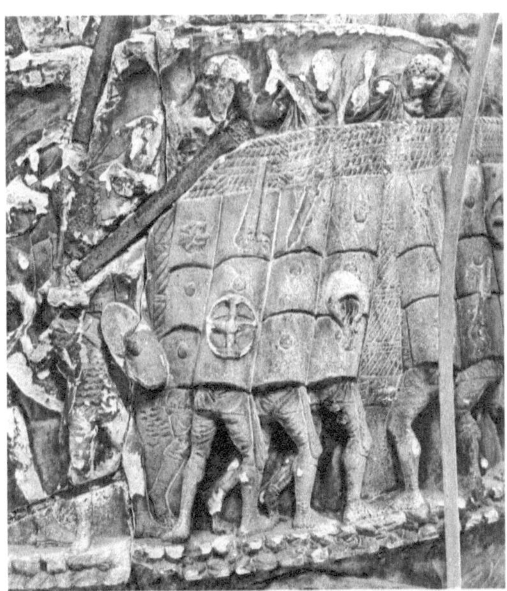

(above) FIGURE 5.9. Testudo (scene LIV) on Column of Marcus Aurelius; note the support bracket of a photographic platform at right. From Petersen et al. 1896, pl. 62A.

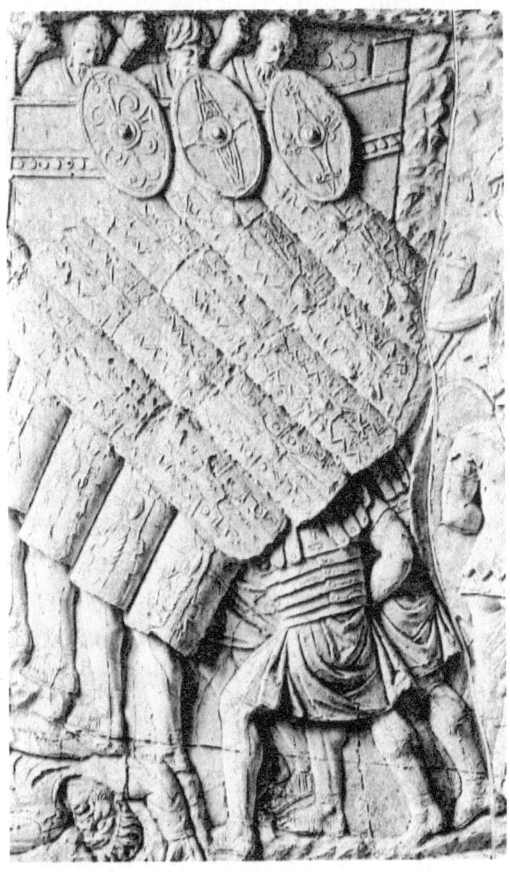

(below) FIGURE 5.10. Testudo (scene LXXI) on the Column of Trajan. From Cichorius 1896/1900, pl. LI.

even wheels upon the attackers. These elements are clearly not derived from the Column of Trajan. The presence of the *testudo* scene on Trajan's Column inspired the placement of a similar scene in a similar position on the Column of Marcus Aurelius, but the actual scene was composed independently. Inspiration from Trajan's Column is also apparent in the following scene, LV, although as in the scene before we are not dealing with a direct copy. Marcus Aurelius is shown standing on a podium flanked by two advisers. He reads from a scroll to his army, which is assembled mainly in front of but also behind the podium. Among the standards are two legionary eagles, and two lictors are visible to the right of the podium. This scene imitates scene LXXVII on Trajan's Column; the details differ, but the general composition is the same.

The Curious Case of Scenes IV, IX, and XXV

A few other scenes on the Column of Marcus Aurelius bear an uncanny resemblance to scenes on Trajan's Column. The first of these is scene XXV (fig. 5.11), showing a Roman soldier bringing a barbarian hostage in front of the emperor while two laden carts pass by above them. Wegner noted many years ago that this scene has a very close parallel in scene XL on the Column of Trajan (fig. 5.12).[7] Although the details differ, the figures and their arrangement in the scenes are almost exactly the same. It almost seems as if the scene on the Column of Marcus Aurelius has been copied from the corresponding scene on the Column of Trajan. What is curious is that this rather unremarkable Trajanic scene does not belong to the beginning of the frieze, nor is it found near the Victoria and *testudo* scenes. The question is, why would this scene have been singled out to be copied?

A clue is provided by other scenes near it. There are remarkable correspondences between some of these scenes on Trajan's Column and various scenes on the Column of Marcus Aurelius. On the opposite side of Trajan's Column from scene XL, but at almost exactly the same height, scene XLII (fig. 5.13) shows an *adlocutio*. The emperor stands on a raised ground line with his body fully exposed to the viewer, surrounded below and on both sides by soldiers. It is the only *adlocutio* scene of this precise format on Trajan's Column—and its composition is a spitting image of the first two *adlocutio* scenes on the Column of Marcus Aurelius (IV and IX—fig. 5.14). Other, smaller details in this area of Trajan's Column also have parallels on Marcus's. A Roman soldier seated on a rock in scene XLII on the Column of Marcus Aurelius resembles the seated Roman in scene XL of Trajan's Col-

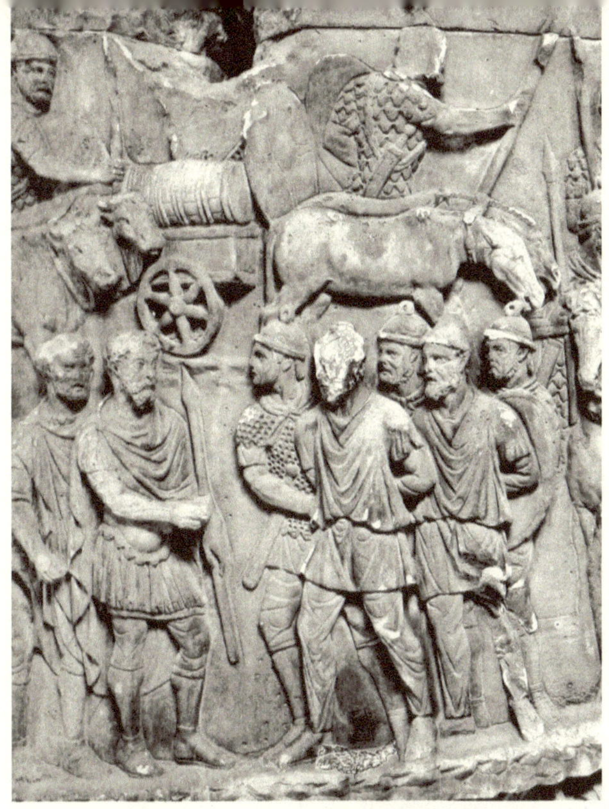

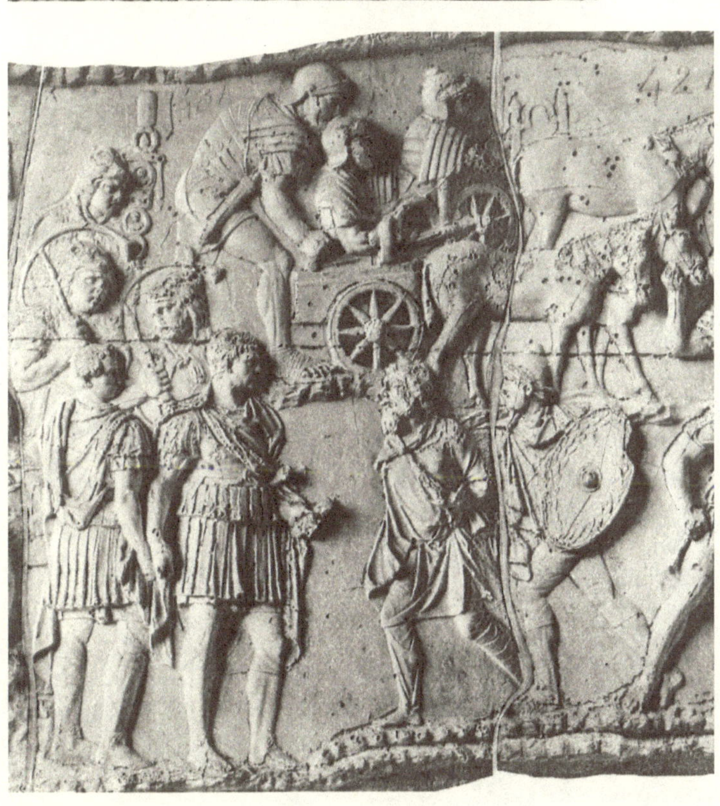

(above) FIGURE 5.11. Scene XXV on the Column of Marcus Aurelius. From Petersen et al. 1896, pl. 33B.

(below) FIGURE 5.12. Scene XL on the Column of Trajan. From Cichorius 1896/1900, pl. XXXI.

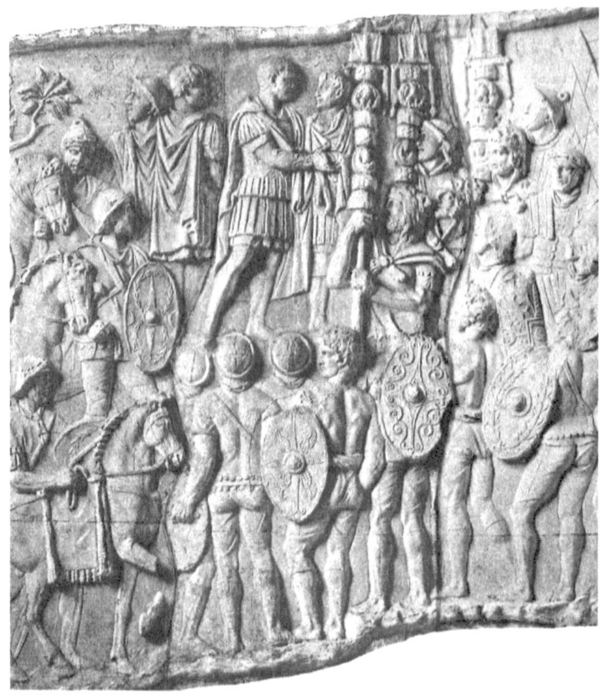

(above) FIGURE 5.13. Scene XLII on Trajan's Column, showing an *adlocutio*; compare fig. 5.14. From Cichorius 1896/1900, pl. XXXIII.

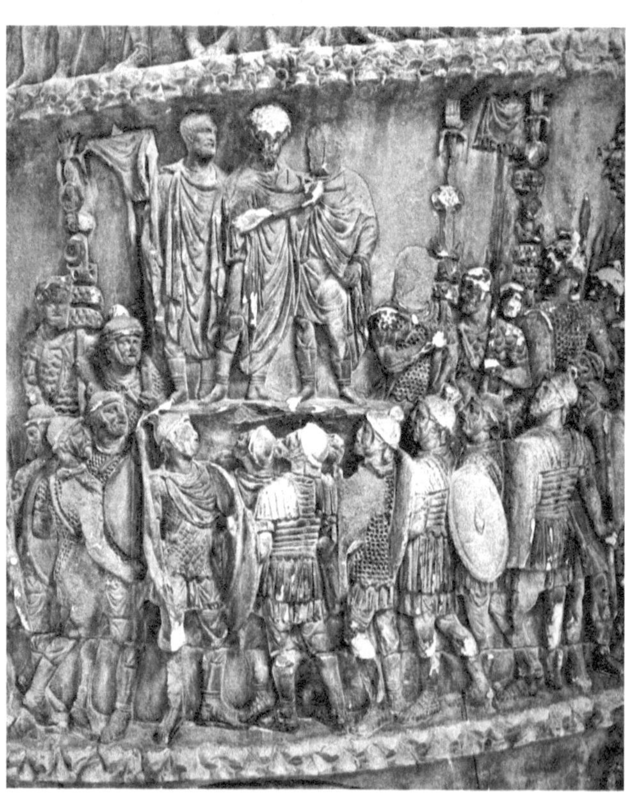

(below) FIGURE 5.14. Scene IX on the Column of Marcus Aurelius. From Petersen et al. 1896, pl. 16A.

umn. The man seated in the last of the three boats at the end of the river scene at the very beginning of the Marcus column frieze (one of the few elements of this section of frieze not paralleled in the corresponding section of frieze on Trajan's Column) has a close parallel in the man unloading a boat in scene XLVII of Trajan's Column. The men in the upper part of this scene, shown carrying tents on their shoulders, have parallels in the similar figures in scene CXI on the Column of Marcus Aurelius. Likewise the soldier advancing through the gate in the scene immediately to the right of this scene is very similar in appearance to the soldier advancing through the second gate of the boat bridge at the start of Marcus's frieze. None of these scenes alone would be enough to rule out simple coincidence as the cause of the similarities, but together they suggest that something more deliberate occurred.

What ties all these parallels together is the area on Trajan's Column from which they are derived: two relatively small surfaces on the west and east faces of the column in the sixth and seventh windings of the frieze. It would seem as if the designer of the later column sketched these particular parts of the frieze of Trajan's Column and then incorporated various elements into different parts of his design. Why were these particular parts of the frieze chosen? The surroundings of Trajan's Column provide an answer: these two areas of Trajan's Column may have been more easily visible than other areas—not from the ground, but from the roofs of the two libraries that flanked the column. The designer of the frieze of the Column of Marcus Aurelius likely ascended to the tops of these libraries (whether their roofs normally served as public viewing platforms, as is sometimes suggested, is not important here) and from these elevated vantage points copied the scenes he could see. He put his sketches at the disposal of the artists and craftsmen in charge of executing the frieze of the Column of Marcus Aurelius. These men employed the sketches where they wished in the frieze, probably unaware of exactly where on Trajan's Column they came from.

This provides a solution to a problem that troubled Per Gustav Hamberg. He noted that there is a more or less clear pattern in the representation of *adlocutio* scenes (addresses to assembled soldiers) on the Column of Marcus Aurelius. The first two (IV and IX) show Marcus elevated on a line of natural ground, surrounded by a curving group of soldiers. The next proper *adlocutio*, scene LV, immediately before the Victoria, is entirely different in composition, showing the emperor elevated on a podium and addressing troops assembled before him. The next (LXXXIII) shows soldiers assembled in a half-arc around Marcus, while the last three *adlo-*

cutio scenes (LXXXVI, XCVI, C) return to the simple podium format as in LV. This presented a problem for Hamberg because although he argued in favor of an evolution in compositional style over the course of the frieze, the podium *adlocutio* scenes are "older" in style than the ones showing the emperor on a ground line in a frontal composition surrounded by soldiers. If such an evolution did in fact exist, and if the frieze was planned and executed from the bottom up (that is to say, from its natural narrative beginning), then the earlier (lower) *adlocutio* scenes should be composed in the older style and the later ones in the new, frontal style. This is clearly not the case, and to explain the discrepancy Hamberg proposed a reverse artistic evolution, with carving of the column's frieze beginning at the top and proceeding to the bottom.[8] But if the lower scenes IV and IX (which to Hamberg appeared to have been carved later in the production of the frieze because of their compositional style) were simply cribbed from Trajan's Column, then the "problem" of an apparently reversed artistic development disappears. Indeed, technical considerations (see chapter 6) make clear that carving of the frieze began at the bottom and not the top, while details of style and content (discussed in this chapter and in chapter 8) show that planning of the frieze content also began at the beginning of the narrative, and not its end.

Was a Plan Available to the Carvers?

Did a full plan of the frieze and its content exist before it was carved? Some sort of model must have been available to the carvers, but theories as to what form this might have taken range widely, with some scholars favoring an exactly detailed full-scale "cartoon," others a group of individual prefabricated scenes, and still others only the most limited preliminary sketches.[9] In the case of Trajan's Column, the existence of a full-scale advance plan seems very doubtful indeed. If a drawing of the entire frieze of Trajan's Column was prepared in advance, why was it executed so irregularly? If a carefully executed plan in fact existed it would be difficult to explain the fluctuations in frieze height, including unpredictable variations of up to 30 percent and the dramatic narrowing of the frieze to 77 centimeters in the nineteenth winding. A commonly held theory attempts to explain the irregularity of the frieze on Trajan's Column by proposing that the idea behind it derives from an illustrated book roll wrapped around a column shaft.[10] The idea is appealing, but two things speak against it. The first is that Roman book rolls were generally neat affairs, with straight edges and

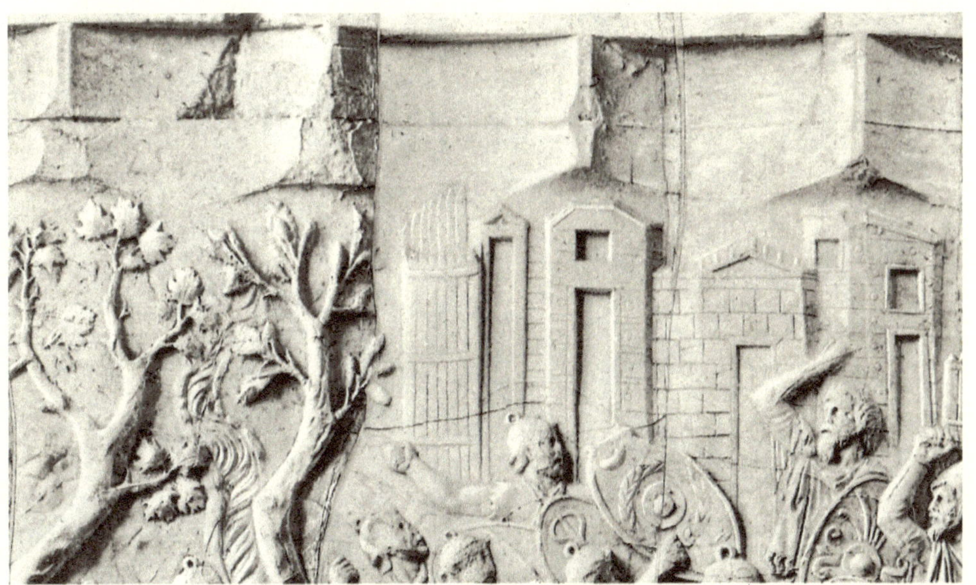

FIGURE 5.15. Detail of the upper edge of the frieze interacting with the fluting at the top of the Column of Trajan. From Cichorius 1896/1900, pl. CX.

even widths. The frieze of Trajan's Column, on the other hand, is not. The second argument against the book-roll theory involves the behavior of the frieze at the top of the column (fig. 5.15). The very top portion of the column shaft is finished with Doric fluting. If the idea behind the frieze was that of a book roll wrapped around the column, then the frieze should appear to cover this fluting. But it does not. Instead, it is cut into it. The frieze even loses its upper border, which is clear evidence that the border was thought of only as a ground line belonging to the bottom edge of the relief band only, not as an upper edge to some manner of scroll.[11]

The extremely uneven frieze of Trajan's Column does not have the hallmark of advanced planning. The most straightforward conclusion that can be drawn from this is that the relief band was not conceived as a whole in advance, but rather was mapped out on the surface of the column as its carving progressed. The fairly steady height in the first thirteen windings, between three and three-quarters and four and one-quarter Roman feet, suggest that a rough guide of four Roman feet had been given to the carvers for the height of the band. The greater fluctuation in the upper ten windings seems to point to a change in the situation—perhaps a relaxation in control as the carving approached the top of the column, although other scenarios, including uncertainty as to the total length of frieze left to fill,

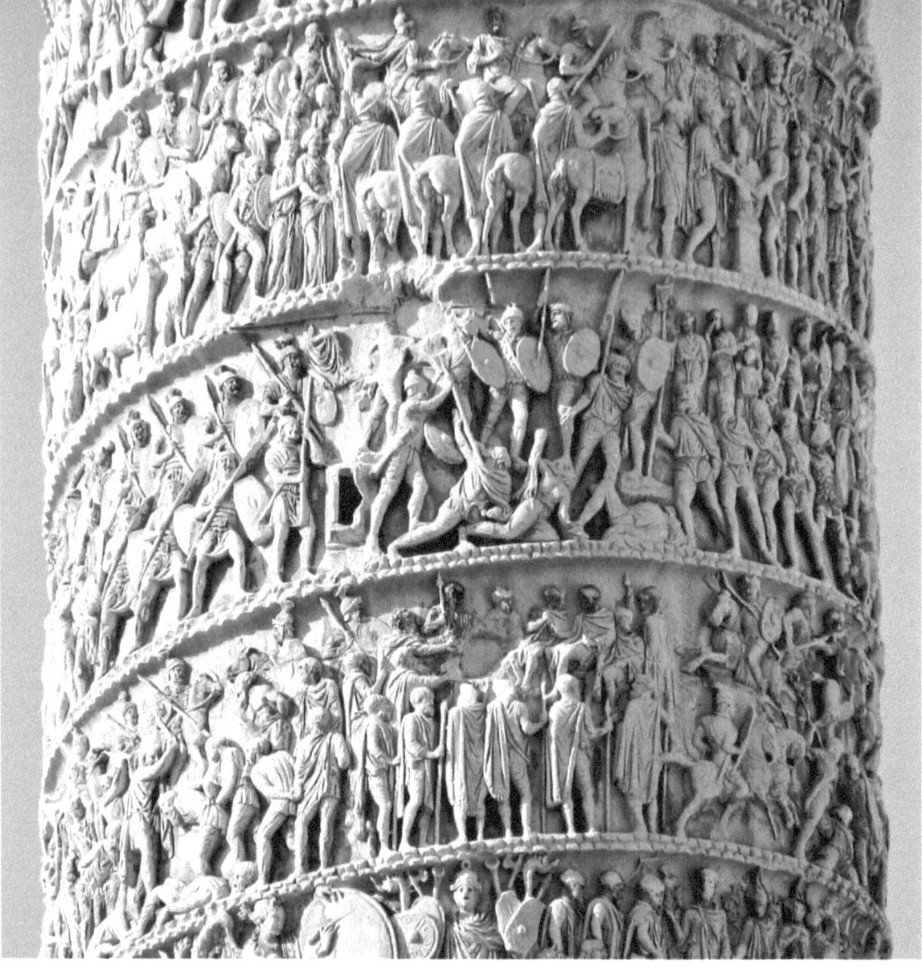

FIGURE 5.16 First three windings of the frieze above the Victoria on the Marcus column; note the line of scene divisions along the window axis. Photo by author.

are possible. Some aids, such as sketches of individual scenes and an overall guide to content, may very well have been available. But a detailed, exact plan almost certainly was not.

The more careful layout of the frieze of the Column of Marcus Aurelius does not necessarily indicate that more preplanning of the frieze content took place. The course of the frieze border is regular over its whole length, but the size, organization, and orientation of the scenes within it is not. In the lower half of frieze, scenes are irregular in size, and a few of the very important ones, particularly the Danube Crossing, the Rain Miracle and the Victoria, are placed more or less astride the east axis so as to face the viewer approaching the "front" of the column. In the upper half of the frieze no scenes are so aligned. After the Victoria the east axis becomes instead a regular line of division between scenes (fig. 5.16), all of which now are subordinated to standard units equal to one-eighth of a winding. A viewer inspecting the frieze above the figure of Victory would see not one scene facing him directly. Perhaps the designers recognized that above a certain point, the scenes would no longer be discernible from the ground. Why bother with alignment to the viewer if the scenes could not be fully appreciated? Even in the bottom half of the frieze, alignment toward the viewer approaching the main axis of the column was the exception rather than the rule.

This suggests that the carvers of the frieze adhered rigidly to their one-eighth rule, except occasionally when, in the lower part of the frieze only, they were required to place certain scenes in such a way that they were centered on what otherwise would have been a dividing line. The course of the frieze was apparently laid out first, the scenes filled in later. There is a striking difference between the bottom and the top halves of the column in how this infilling was done, one that is difficult to square with the idea of a single designer sitting down with the frieze outline and mapping out a unified, coherent narrative including the detailed positioning of all scenes. Instead, it appears that he (if we are in fact dealing with a single designer) plotted a number of key scenes (especially those with important symbolic or historical content) onto a diagram of the column's frieze at an early stage in the project. The vast remainder of the scenes, however, were filled in later: whether a little or much later is difficult to determine. Their standard size (units equal to one-eighth of a complete winding of the frieze) may have been established to allow the drafting of a large number of stock scenes (possibly by multiple artists) that the carvers could later "plug in" to the established framework of the rigid frieze outline where needed—perhaps even while the process of carving was underway. This approach raises important questions concerning the historicity and artistic unity of the resulting frieze. But before addressing these questions (see chapters 7 and 8) it is necessary to consider how this plan was transferred to the surface of the column itself.

chapter six

CARVING THE FRIEZE

For the frieze of the Column of Marcus Aurelius, carving was the final step in the long genetic path from conception to execution. This massive and complicated task is naturally of great interest in and of itself, but the study of its process can also provide many clues about how its iconographic content was created. Carving involved the translation of the ideas of the frieze's designer(s) into stone, and the appearance of the final product depended not only on his wishes but also on the skill, training, and organization of the men charged with the task. How many men were engaged in carving the frieze of the Column of Marcus Aurelius? How were they organized, and how did they go about their task? How did the actual carving of the column's long frieze relate to its planning, and to the construction of the monument? I begin by looking at the people who did this work, and particularly by asking how many sculptors were involved.

The Number of Sculptors

In the absence of building records, the task of determining how many men worked on carving the column's frieze seems at first glance to be an impossible one. But there are ways to answer the question. The most powerful method of determining the number of carvers at work on the column is to look for the signatures of individual carvers—not written signatures, but stylistic ones. This technique, first pioneered by Giovanni Morelli for the identification of Italian Renaissance painters and later used to great effect by Sir John Beazley for the identification of Greek vase painters, usually relies on identifying peculiarities in the treatment of specific body parts—the ear, eye, or hand, for example. The method is much more difficult with sculpture than with two-dimensional painting, especially in the case of the Column of Marcus Aurelius, where most of the work must be done from photographs. But there is one feature of the column's frieze that is eminently suitable to such analysis: its raised border. With a width of about seven to eight centimeters, this border serves to separate the upper and lower edges of the frieze as it winds up the column. The border was created by reserving it from the stone of the column shaft as the carving of the frieze progressed, and its outer face is at more or less the same level as the original surface of the uncarved column. However, the border was not left flat but was carved with a decorative pattern—or rather with a variety of patterns. Easy to overlook when the viewer's attention is focused on the frieze, these patterns are nonetheless often quite distinctive: in some cases there are parallel lines of small lumps, in others erratic, jagged, and random patterns, and in others bricklike schemes (see, for example, fig. 6.1). The apparent intention of this patterning was to reproduce the effect of the rocky border that separates the windings of the frieze of Trajan's Column. There was no column-wide standard for the appearance of the frieze border, nor is there any clear connection to the border design of Trajan's Column, which is more or less uniformly rocklike (that is to say, naturalistic) throughout its length. This suggests that the sculptors, when faced with the task of carving the border, simply adopted a pattern that was comfortable or natural to them, and filled the necessary area with it. The result of this individual, independent approach to an essentially abstract subject gives us a very close view of the sculptors' personal styles. This implies that a count of border patterns should give us a rough minimum count of the individual sculptors who worked on the column. This number, forty-six, is impressive,[1] and is substantially greater than recent estimates of the number of carvers active on Trajan's Column, which has been calculated between seven and twelve.[2] The carvers of Trajan's Column were clearly artists who had higher technical skill than those at work on Marcus's monument, and it would stand to reason that there would have been fewer such artists available. It is important to note, however, that the large count of carvers derived from the border patterns on the Marcus column reflects the sum of carvers engaged over the entire length of the project, and not necessarily the total number engaged at any one time. Much, or perhaps even most, of the frieze carving must have taken place during the reign of Commodus and likely occupied years. It is impossible to conceive of forty or fifty carvers working at one time on the column, but perhaps not so difficult to think that this number of workmen may have come and gone over the length of the project. Perhaps what we are dealing with is a number of working groups or workshops, into and out of which individual carvers came and went. Reasons for such movement are not hard to imagine: the risk of injury from falls or from splinters of stone or metal is certainly one, and the retirement of elderly workers and arrival of new recruits is another.

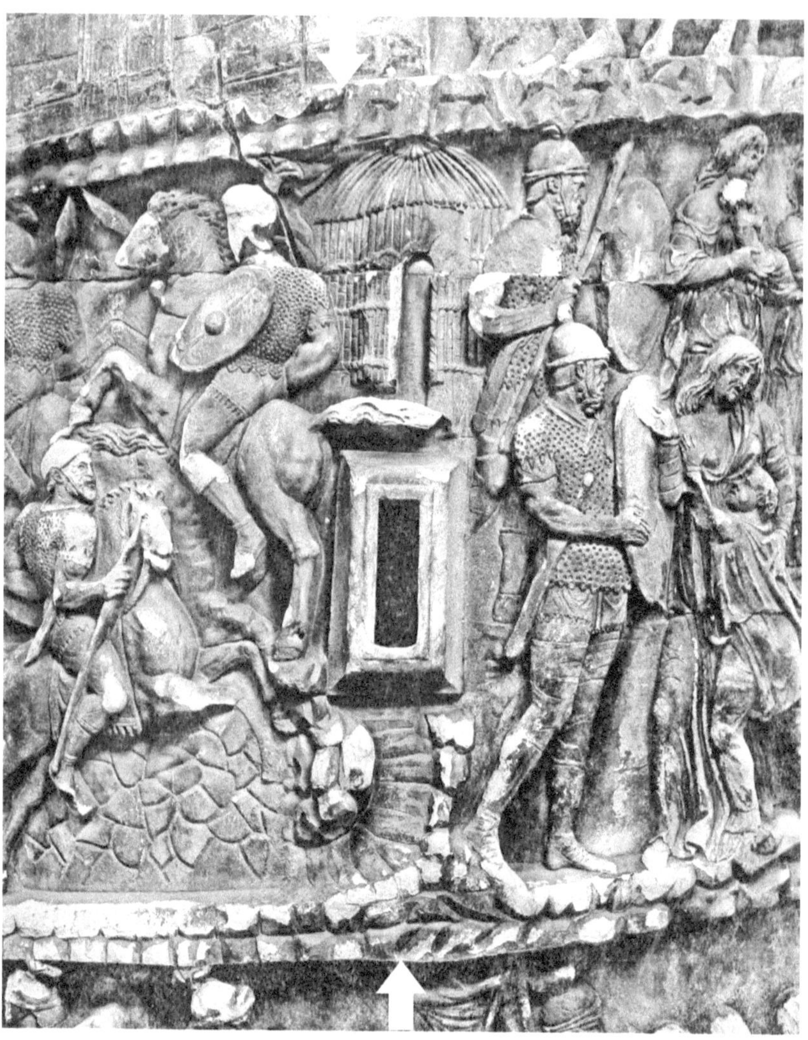

FIGURE 6.1. Division between scenes CIII and CIV, with four different border patterns visible (the points where the border patterns change are indicated with arrows). From Petersen et al. 1896, pl. 112B.

Direction of Carving

The column is composed of a series of drums that had an extensive amount of carving work done on them while they were still on the ground; the first question must be whether the frieze too could have been carved on the drums before they were lifted into place.[3] The benefit to this approach would be the ease of working on the ground; the difficulties would include, but not be limited to, ensuring the carving was not damaged when the drums were lifted and lining up the many figures that crossed from one drum to the next. The greatest difficulty is the latter, positioning the drums so that any figures or objects that crossed drum joints would be exactly aligned. If this process had in fact been used, then at least some errors would be expected to be visible over the lengthy course of the frieze. But there are absolutely no cases of misalignment to be found at drum joins anywhere on the column, and this is the single strongest argument against the idea of precarving.[4] Misalignment might have been avoided, it has been suggested, by leaving a border of uncarved stone at the upper and lower edges of the drums and finishing this once the blocks were in place. This solution, however, negates what is often seen as one of the greatest potential benefits of precarving: to avoid the difficulty of carving the drums after they had been put in place.

So the frieze was carved onto the drums after they had been erected. But in which direction? The clearest evidence comes from the Column of Trajan: numerous examples of objects in the frieze merging with the lower border of the scene (but never with the upper) show that the lower border was carved together with each scene.[5] The upper border was left uncarved, to be finished by the carvers of the scene above. But sometimes objects from the frieze overlap or even penetrate this upper border.[6] This penetration of objects through the border from sections of the frieze below into sections above, generally uncommon but occurring in various places on the column, gives very strong evidence that, in general, lower scenes were carved before ones above. The significance of these instances of border penetration is made clearer when we consider that the reverse is never seen on the column. As Rockwell has pointed out, all the objects that cross the frieze border do so from below, never from above.[7]

Similar interactions can be observed on the Column of Marcus Aurelius, although they manifest themselves in a less pronounced manner. This is at least in part due to the fact that the border which separates the windings of the Marcus column was drafted in a more or less straight and regular inclined line. Unlike on Trajan's Column, it is clear that here the course of the border was fixed before the figures in the frieze were carved, and thus the frieze content has no influence on its path. The Marcus column border is also much wider, so that although some objects from the frieze overlap the upper border, in no cases do they penetrate it entirely.[8] Because the great depth of the Marcus column's frieze (10 centimeters vs. 4 centimeters on Trajan's Column) means that only objects that project very far from the

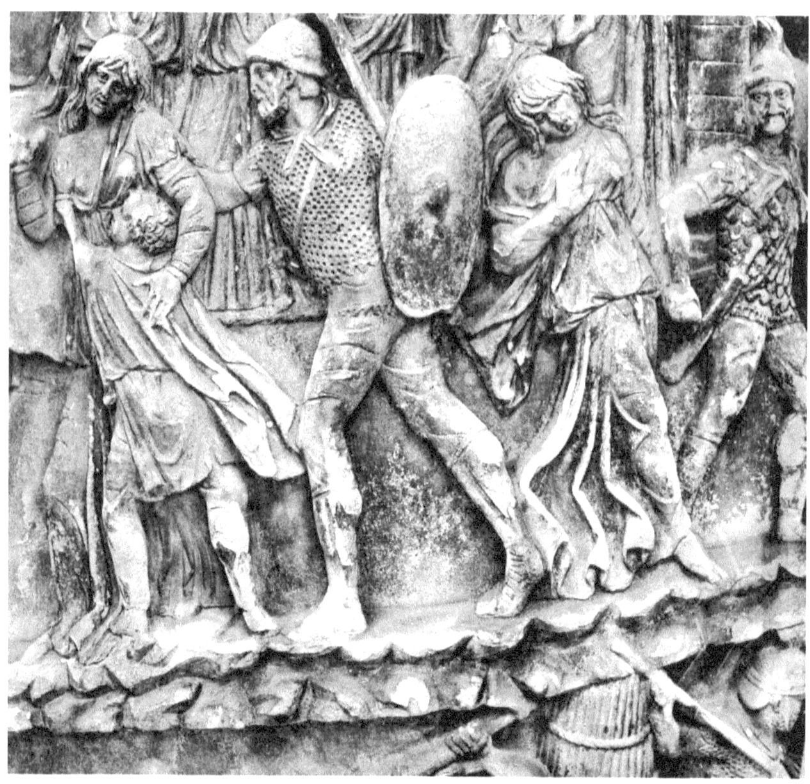

FIGURE 6.2. Scene CIV, showing the lower border integrated with the rocky outcrop on which a child stands, and showing objects from the frieze below penetrating the same border. From Petersen et al. 1896, pl. 113A.

background come near enough to the outer edge to have the possibility of interacting with the border, cases of interaction between objects from the frieze and its lower border are rarer. But they do exist. An example is scene VIII, where below two dead barbarians lying at the lower right the border is integrated with the rocky ground on which the figures lie. A similar situation occurs in scene CIV (fig. 6.2), where a raised lump of ground, fully integrated with the border, has been created to support the figure of a barbarian boy clutching at his mother. Especially interesting here is that two objects, an axe head and a spear butt, overlap this border from the scene below, much in the way seen on Trajan's Column, showing that here too the lower scene was carved before the one above. Bridges also interact occasionally with the border of the column's frieze: in scene XXX, the left end of a low boat bridge enters and partly merges with the border. Finally, there is even some interaction of figures: in scene L the foot of the left of two barbarians fallen at the bottom of the scene is integrated with the border carving. Claridge has suggested that the entire border was carved before the main frieze.[9] But if this had actually been the case, situations such as those visible in figure 6.2 (and 6.3, see below) could never have occurred.

Details of sarcophagi and other monuments of the period show that Roman sculptors were accustomed to carving lower, but not upper, ground lines when they executed both small and large works in relief. Some sarcophagi show this, for example a mid-second-century mythological sarcophagus in the Villa Doria Pamphilj, whose lower border is carved entirely in a rocky pattern.[10] Figures and objects stand atop this border much as they do on scenes from Trajan's Column, and at the right-hand side of the sarcophagus the border merges into a rocky hummock upon which a woman is seated. Similar is the treatment of the lower border on a Protesilaos sarcophagus in the Vatican (the border also incorporates flowing water at the left and right edges), a Dionysiac sarcophagus from the Villa Pamphilj, an early Endymion sarcophagus from the Capitoline Museums, and the Capitoline Amazonomachy.[11] A rocky lower border also appears on other monuments of second-century sculpture in Rome: for example, on relief panels from the Forum of Trajan and on portions of the Great Trajanic Frieze.[12] At no time do we see both lower and upper borders of a single relief panel executed using this technique: either the bottom border is carved with a rocky pattern and the top left blank, or both bottom and top borders are blank. But this blank upper border was not considered "out of bounds" by the sculptors, and sometimes objects protrude into it, as, for example, on the Portonaccio battle sarcophagus.

There are many instances on the Column of Marcus Aurelius of objects from the frieze penetrating the upper border, and doing so in such a way that it is clear that the border pattern must have been carved after, not before, these objects were carved. For example, in the upper border of scene C (fig. 6.3), the tips of two *vexilla* (flaglike military standards) penetrate the carved upper border. The level of both pointed tips is equal to or higher than the border (note weathering on left tip). Had the border pattern been carved first, these *vexilla* could not have been carved in these positions. Another example is found in scene IC (fig. 6.5), where a spear butt penetrates almost the entire height of the border. The spear butt is carved in much higher relief than the center part of the border itself. Had the border been carved first, there would not have been sufficient stone present to carve the spear butt.

Using this evidence we can reconstruct the most likely steps taken by

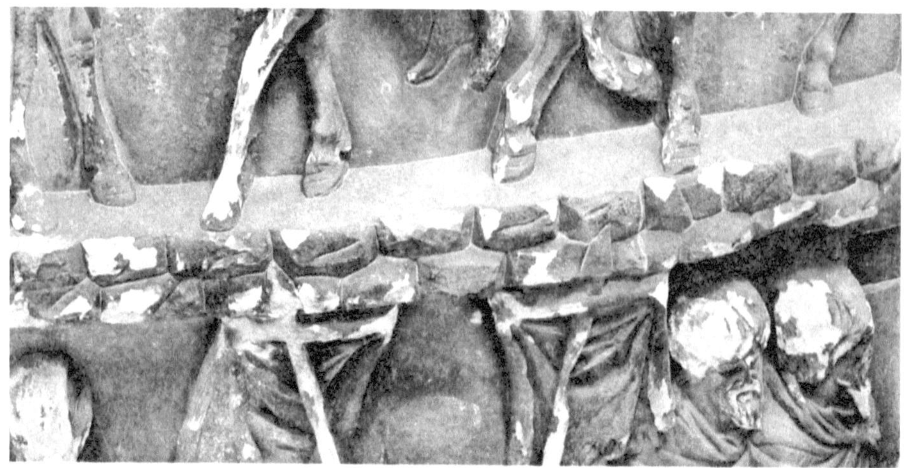

FIGURE 6.3. Scene C, showing tips of two *vexilla* penetrating the carved border. From Petersen et al. 1896, pl. 115A.

the sculptors charged with carving the frieze of the Column of Marcus Aurelius. Before the sculptors started their work, both the general outline of the course of the frieze and the figural content of at least one winding of scenes would have been drafted on the face of the column. The sculptors would have worked between two boundaries. The lower boundary would have been upper edge of the lower winding of the frieze, which had already been carved. The upper boundary would have been firmly established at a constant height. The lower border was unchangeable, since the scene below had been carved. The upper border, however, being no more than a drawn feature, could be breached. That is, it was theoretically possible to extend objects from the frieze into or even beyond it, if needed or desired. This is frequently seen on sarcophagi.[13] Sarcophagi also show that these penetrating objects could be carved into the border using no more than outlines, that is to say, without cutting away any of the surrounding stone.

This technique would have been followed all the way up the column, until the area just below the capital had been reached. Here the ultimate manifestation of the bottom-to-top carving process can be seen. The last few inches of the surface of the shaft of Trajan's Column are carved, not with figures, but with Doric flutes (the situation is similar on the Column of Marcus Aurelius, but a band of uncarved stone divides the frieze from the fluting). At the top of Trajan's Column a number of objects including tree branches, animals, and buildings penetrate the fluted area (fig. 5.15). These objects could not have been carved as they are had the fluting been carved

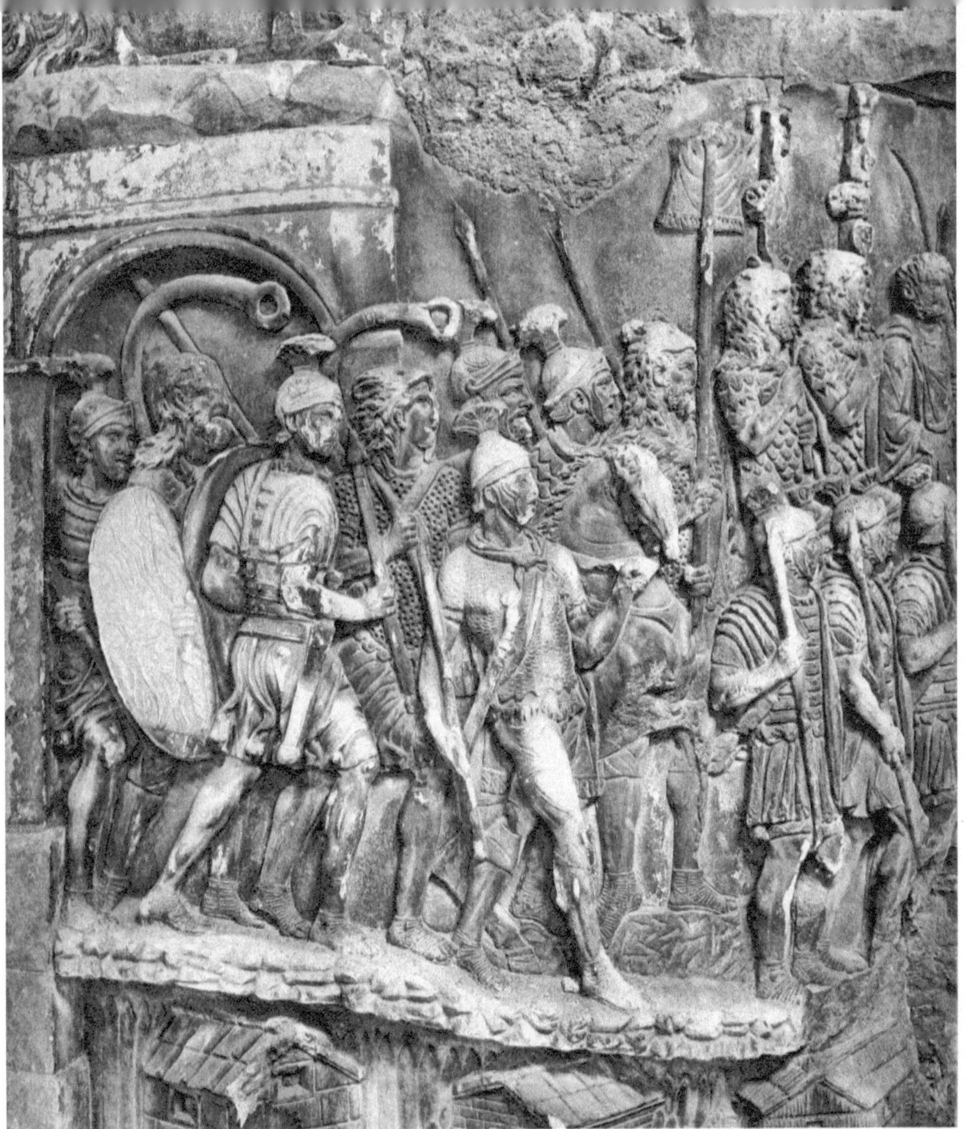

FIGURE 6.4. Scene III, likely the first scene to be carved on the Column of Marcus Aurelius. From Petersen et al. 1896, pl. 11A.

first. Thus the fluting must have been the last detail to be added to the column, after all elements of the frieze had been executed.

The general starting point was at the bottom, but where exactly did carving begin? A remarkable series of figures at the very right-hand end of scene III (fig. 6.4) appears to point to the exact location where carving commenced. The striding figure leading a horse in the foreground at the far right side of scene III is unique. He wears a suit of ring mail, but the mail is here rendered not with numerous small drilled holes, as usual on the column (see for example the figure just behind and to the left of this man). Instead, the ring pattern is rendered using tight rows of curved incisions. This is quite different from scale armor, which on both the columns of Trajan and Marcus Aurelius is made up of large, distinct oval or semicircular plates.[14] It is also not at all the way in which ring mail is rendered on Marcus's Column, where it is indicated by tightly spaced, small, drilled holes. These rows of curved incisions are similar to, but not exactly the same as, the convention of vertical zigzags used to represent ring mail on Trajan's Column; they do, however, have an exact parallel in the armor worn by two standard-bearers on an altar in the Villa Medici in Rome.[15] Also unique on the Column of Marcus Aurelius are the large, curved shields held by the soldiers emerging from the gateway in scene III. Like the ring-mail armor of the unique soldier, the shape and decoration of these shields is much more similar to shields seen on the Column of Trajan than to any other shields on the Column of Marcus Aurelius. This section of scene III is the closest of all scenes to Trajan's Column, and appears to mark the exact spot where the work of carving the Column of Marcus Aurelius began.

Many other details in the first three scenes of Marcus's Column have parallels on Trajan's Column; however, they quickly disappear, never to be used again. This suggests that some specific detail was conveyed in or along with the sketched plan of the first three scenes that were copied in detail from Trajan's Column (see chapter 5). But not every detail was copied: the soldiers in Scene I on Marcus's Column wear ring mail, indicated by tiny drill holes; the roofs of the buildings in the same scene on Marcus's Column have carefully rendered tile coverings, while the corresponding roofs on Trajan's Column are relatively plain. These details were presumably lacking from the sketch of these scenes from Trajan's Column and we should imagine them having been added by the sculptors themselves, to improve on the plain-looking drawing from which they had to work.

Division of Labor

It would have been a crucial concern for the overseer of the project to come up with an efficient and practical way to organize the large number of carvers at work on the column. Even if there was a clear (if not detailed) plan of the frieze to hand, it could not have been left up to the sculptors to execute this as they saw fit—for starters, there were simply too many of them. How was their labor organized? Clues to the division of labor on the Column of Marcus Aurelius can be found, once again, in the frieze border.

This, as already noted, was not left flat but instead was carved with a variety of decorative patterns. What is particularly interesting is that the varied patterns exhibit clear and abrupt breaks between them, and that both the patterns and breaks often have distinct relationships to the frieze itself. In most cases these divisions are sharp and unambiguous, representing the point where one carver left off and another carver carried on in his own personal and distinctive style. Consider, for example, the borders above and below scenes CIII and CIV (fig. 6.1). The lower border on the left consists of two rows of regular blocklike shapes; immediately below the window this pattern disintegrates and is replaced by a random-looking naturalistic pattern resembling, to some extent at least, stone. The upper border is similarly divided at about the same place on the column, between a regular pattern of rows of rounded lumps on the left and a jagged, angular, and random pattern on the right. This one small section of frieze, then, contains examples of four separate border patterns and two divisions.

When these divisions are plotted on the column surface, twenty-five of the total forty-three divisions fall along one of the four axes defined by the vertical lines of windows; fifteen divisions fall along the eastern axis alone, fewer along the north and south axes.[16] The heavy damage to the west face of the column makes the count of divisions along it unrepresentative, but when the divisions in the better-preserved upper windings are counted, it appears that they are as common here as on the eastern axis. Another interesting pattern emerges when the distribution of the various distinctive border patterns are compared with the locations of divisions between them. Most of the identified border patterns appear only once on the column, but four are very common. The most common is a complex but highly repetitive pattern with rows of triangular projections along the top and bottom of the band which give it a serrated appearance, something like a saw blade (an example can be seen in the left half of the upper border of the Victoria scene, fig. 5.7). This pattern is found entirely on the south half of the column and extends over much of the lower two-thirds of the column shaft. A much less common but nonetheless very distinctive pattern is composed of two rows of long, lozenge-like blocks, with fairly regular angled cuts in the centers of the top blocks. It is limited to the northeast quarter of the column and appears in three windings just after the figure of Victory (in fig. 5.16, the first one-eighth to one-quarter sections of the first three borders immediately to the right of the main eastern window axis). Much different is another common pattern where it seems that the carver took pains to create a random effect (in fig. 6.1, the right half of the upper border). There is no clear pattern discernible in this series of angular blocks, executed using sharp, straight cuts of the chisel. This pattern is found almost exclusively in the northeast quarter of the upper third of the column, the one exception being a short length of this border style adjacent to the south axis in the eighteenth winding. The final common pattern is composed of two rows of small rounded lumps in low relief, often with small cuts on their faces (again in fig. 6.1, the left half of the upper border). This pattern is found over much of the entire south face of the column in the upper third of its windings, with the single exception of an appearance of this style in the northwest quarter of the seventeenth winding. The distribution of these patterns over the column surface reveals a clear division down the eastern axis, with each border pattern generally confined to either the left or right side of this divide, which is to say, to either the south or north face of the column. This indicates that, most of the time, carvers worked only on one-half of the column surface—and that they generally never worked on the other half.

How did this division of labor relate to the content of the frieze? Breaks between border patterns most often correspond to breaks between scenes. The border pattern often continues uninterrupted for multiple scenes, while only in rare cases does it break within a scene. A rare example of a break within a scene can be found in scene IC (fig. 6.5), a battle that shows Roman cavalry riding over the bodies of prostrate barbarians. Here, there are clear breaks in the pattern of both the upper and lower borders, at top between an irregular wavy pattern on the left and a series of rectangular blocks on the right, and at bottom between a row of interlocking offset lumps on the left and parallel rows of aligned bumps on the right. The scene itself shows stylistic differences between the figures in its left and right halves. To the left of the two breaks in border pattern we see lively muscular horses with heads held tight against their chests; to the right the animals have heavier bodies and hold their heads forward. The right half of the scene is much less densely composed than the left, and it is not afflicted with awkward figures like the hunched rider in the upper left corner. There are differences in detail, too: in the left half of the scene, the soldiers' mail tunics end at their upper thigh; in the right half, they terminate significantly higher, just below the waist. The soldiers on the left have scabbards slung on low baldrics; those on the right wear theirs tightly about their chests. These differences indicate that different groups of carvers worked on the left and right portions of this section of frieze.

The result of this division of labor was not an entirely happy one. Within the frieze, the dividing line falls just to the rear of the two galloping horse-

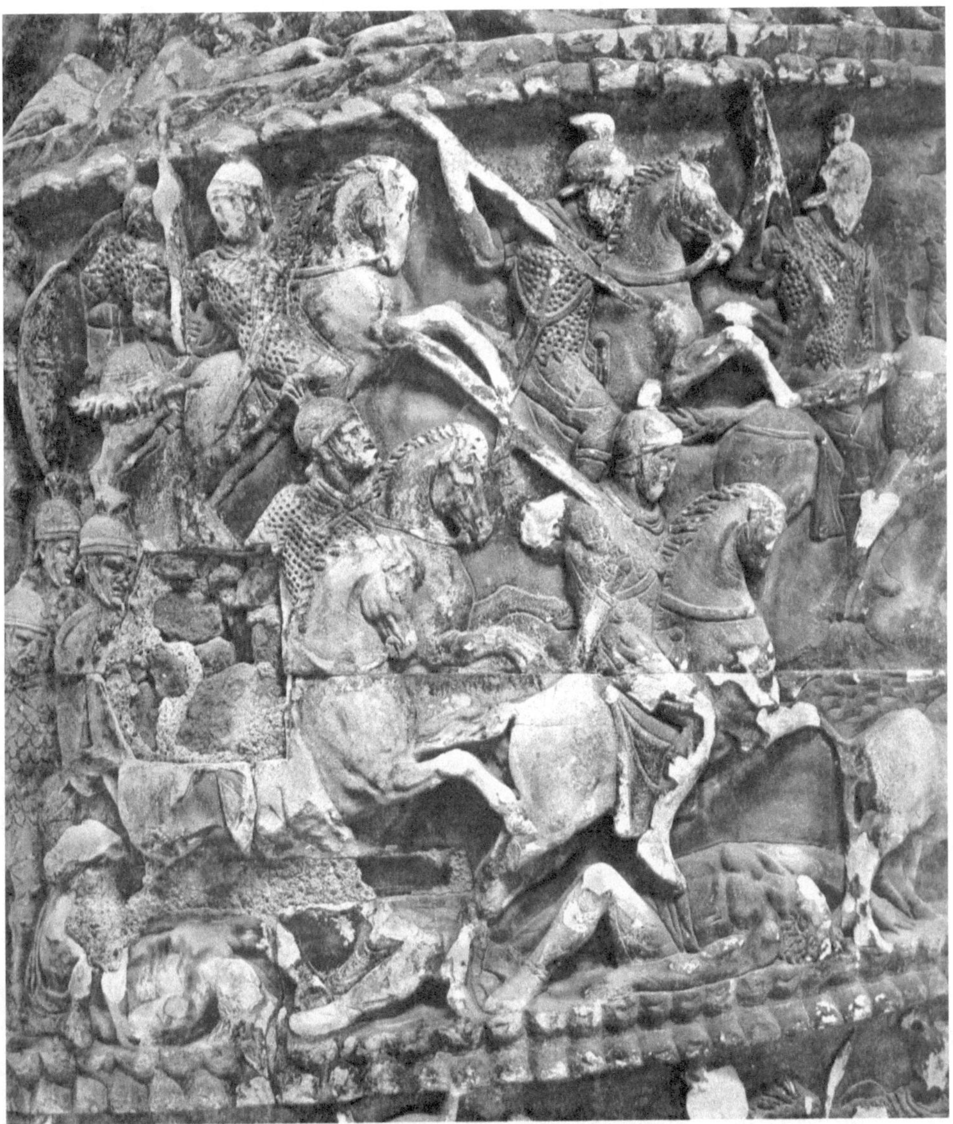

FIGURE 6.5. Scene IC, showing breaks in upper and lower border patterns and carving errors (a pair of human legs with no body at bottom middle, a horse with no rear end in the upper middle). From Petersen et al. 1896, pl. 108A.

men right of center, immediately to the right of the change in the upper border pattern. Two clear mistakes appear along this line of division: the horse of the upper rider lacks a rear end (which all other horses in this scene and generally elsewhere on the column have), while at the very bottom of the scene we have a set of human legs that lacks a body. Errors like this are rare on the column, and it seems that they have occurred here only because one large scene was divided between two teams of sculptors.[17] Presumably each team had some sort of plan of the entire scene, or at least of their portion of the scene; the errors occurred when the work of the two separate teams met. The reason why scene IC was divided between two different groups of carvers seems to be that it, being an exceptionally large scene, straddles one of the main axes defined by the vertical lines of windows. This indicates that the division of labor along vertical lines was considered more important than maintaining single sculptural teams on individual scenes.

Wegner noted that the four main window axes served an important function in dividing up the work of the carvers.[18] The distribution of border patterns allows this conclusion to be refined, as it suggests that two of these axes in particular, the east and west, were especially important. The eastern axis displays a nearly uninterrupted line of border divisions along it, and the undamaged sections of the western axis suggest that a similar distribution existed there, while divisions along the north and south axes do not appear as regularly. Moreover, two border patterns span the whole distance between the west and east axes on the south side of the column. This indicates that the task of carving the column's frieze was divided into two halves, south and north, along lines that ran vertically through the east and west axes (on most of the column at least). The very strong tendency for border patterns to be confined entirely either to the south or to the north sides of the column also argue for this division of labor. Carvers who worked on the north face of the column as a rule did not work on the south face, and vice versa. The division of the column into halves instead of quarters would have been very practical, in that two large teams could have worked with greater freedom than four small ones. This would have allowed for more flexibility of operation and thus potentially for the employment of more carvers at one time. Overall, the distribution of the patterns reveals a rough but apparently firm organization emanating from a central authority.

Relationship of Carving, Construction, and Planning

How did the process of carving relate to the process of construction? Ruling out the possibility that the frieze was carved on the ground (see above), the usual assumption is that the entire column was assembled and then the frieze carved when all drums were in place. This is certainly possible, but there is an alternative: that the carving of the frieze began while the column was still being put together. This would have posed extra problems, especially of safety and organization. But there would also have been a major benefit: time saved. And there is some evidence in the carving itself that indicates that this method, and not the former, was actually the one used. Sometimes, strange things happen to the sculpture of the columns of Trajan and Marcus Aurelius near joins between drums. Usually the progression of the frieze is more or less smooth, with figures crossing over from one drum to the next without any irregularities. But Rockwell has pointed out instances on the Column of Trajan where the upper frieze border follows horizontally along a drum division (instead of crossing it in its normal angled progression). He has suggested that these incidents occurred when certain portions of the frieze were being carved when the upper drum had not yet been placed.[19] A few similar oddities can be identified on the Column of Marcus Aurelius, though they are not as pronounced. Some figures seem to crouch down as if to avoid the upper edge of the drum (scene LXXXI); other times, rows of heads follow along the upper edge of a drum, as if hesitant to cross it (for example, scenes LXI/LXII). This is not enough evidence to prove that this working method was used on the Column of Marcus Aurelius, but the possibility cannot be excluded out of hand.

Claridge objects to this idea on two main grounds: that it would not be possible to plot the course of the frieze until the entire column had been assembled, and that carving during construction would cause such severe delays in the process that the scaffolding and ropes would decay.[20] In the case of the Column of Trajan, the first point would not have been an issue: the course of the frieze is highly irregular, with few hallmarks of careful plotting, having apparently been drafted as the carving proceeded based on rough guidelines. In the case of the Column of Marcus Aurelius, the course of the frieze was based on a very simple and schematic division of the height of the column shaft into twenty equal portions, each four and a half feet high. This frieze could have been drafted from the bottom up (even before the entire column was complete) as easily as from the top down (after completion)—all that would have been needed was a series of measurements based on the already-established rise of the helix to be made along each of the main axes, and a gently sloping line drafted to join them. Claridge's second objection is more serious. However, it assumes that the Romans would have felt the need to halt construction while the carving occurred, either out of concern for safety of the workers or the need for an unobstructed area to work in. Safety of workers seems seldom to have been a concern for Roman builders, or at least little evidence of such concern has come down to us. When it comes to space the crucial question is, would the activities of carvers have taken up space that was needed by the builders during the construction process? This seems highly unlikely, since the carvers would only have needed to work around the part of the column that had already been erected—that is, within the framework of the second tower designed to support the column drums while they were being lowered in place. This is precisely the space where the work of construction was already finished, space that would only have been needed at the time when a new drum was lowered into position and set in place (see chapter 4). It is impossible to prove with certainty that the carvers started work before the column drums were all in place, but it is a powerful explanation for the strange hesitation sometimes seen at drum joints on both columns. The relief carvers could work in the scaffolding during the time when the next drum was being carved out on the ground. They could even, in theory, keep working in the assembly tower while a drum was being raised in the lifting tower. Regardless of the exact sequence of events, the construction site must have been an incredible hive of activity. A series of massive column drums would be being finished for assembly, likely resting on rollers ready to be moved to the assembly site. The rising column would itself have been encased in massive scaffolding, which would likely have risen with the pace of construction. A second scaffold tower would have been joined to the first, for the raising of drums. The entire structure would have swarmed with workers, either engaged in raising the drums, in positioning them, or (perhaps) in carving the relief decoration.

Just as the scene size becomes more regular and the divisions between scenes become more firmly aligned with the main window axes as one goes up the column, so too do the carving divisions. This suggests that the planning of the frieze content (not its overall layout, governed by the division in twenty windings) may have gone hand in hand with its carving. This theory is strengthened when the overall pattern is considered: if a complete plan, say in the form of a scale drawing, was prepared in advance, why would the designer have allowed his creation to become progressively more rigid? The answer is likely tied to the process of carving and its organization: as carving progressed its organization was improved, or at least became more rigid. With speed of the essence, planning and carving became more closely linked. Carvers would have required plans for their upcoming work, and these plans would have had to fit the areas in which they had to work. As carving progressed up the column, both these areas and their contents became progressively more rigidly defined. This process resulted in a composition that detracted from the flow of the narrative and reduced the apparent unity of the frieze. Such an approach was not designed to enhance the narrative content of the frieze, but rather to address practical concerns of efficiency and speed in execution.

Finishing Touches

When the column had been fully assembled and all the carving finished, the project was still not complete: there were still some finishing touches to be applied. We know more about the finish applied to the Column of Trajan than to Marcus's Column. On Trajan's Column, two devices were used to augment the appearance of the carved relief. One was paint. Painting was a common finishing technique for all types of Roman marble sculpture, whether relief or three-dimensional. The Prima Porta Augustus, for example, preserves traces of extensive painting, as do many portrait heads, sarcophagi, and architectural elements. Although no paint is visible on the relief of Trajan's Column, two small potential residues of paint have recently been detected chemically: red on Trajan's cloak in scene XLIV and yellowish-orange from a tree trunk in scene CXXXVIII.[21] We likely should imagine much of the frieze as being brightly painted. The other main extra decorative element used to finish the relief of Trajan's Column was the frequent insertion of miniature metal weapons and tools into the hands of many figures. Unlike painting, this was not a usual technique for augmenting relief sculpture, although it was employed for the provision of objects such as spears in the hands of large free-standing statues. On Trajan's Column all spears, most swords, and many other weapons and implements were made out of metal.[22] Though these inserts have not survived, evidence of them is everywhere on the column in the form of soldiers fighting and working apparently empty handed. The metal weapons and tools were originally inserted into holes drilled into these now-empty fists. The application of the technique was not constant: in some cases tools (and more rarely weapons) were carved rather than left to be inserted. In other cases, where the weapon or tool has not been carved in stone, it is clear that neither was it provided in metal, for there are many instances where hands were never drilled with the holes to provide a setting for the inserts. This suggests that the carvers received instruction to leave most hands empty, and that the addition of metal implements was done as part of the final touches to the frieze, at the same time as (or perhaps even after) painting.

Given the continued popularity of painting on sarcophagi in the later

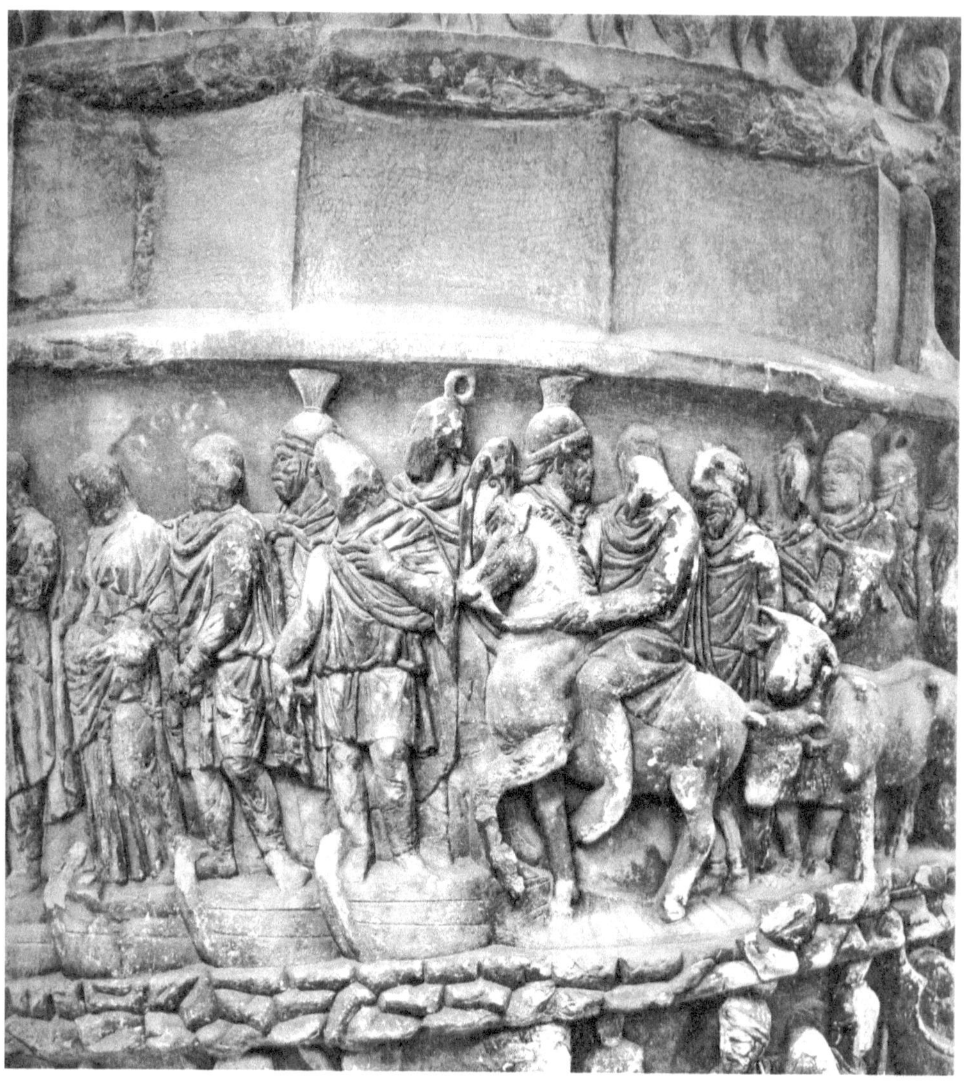

FIGURE 6.6. Scene CXV, showing carving style at very top of the Column of Marcus Aurelius. From Petersen et al. 1896, pl. 125B.

second century we should likely envision the frieze of the Marcus column too as painted. Clearly, however, there was no effort made to add metal weapons or tools. At the time of the construction of the Marcus column, these inserts would still have been plainly apparent on the Column of Trajan, and their absence from Marcus's monument surely would have been notable. This omission must have stood out noticeably to anyone who compared the decoration of both monuments, but perhaps the decision not to include such additions was that on the original model, the frieze of Trajan's Column, they had not been particularly successful. Like the architecture and the helical frieze, they may have been experimental, and not all experiments are successes. Finally, when the work of finishing the column's decoration had been done, the scaffolding could be removed.

After the column had been fully assembled, carved, and painted the final task was to remove the surrounding scaffolding and the various outbuildings that would have served during its construction as workshops for tool fabrication and repair and as storage, offices, and perhaps even accommodation of workers. Slowly the monument would have emerged from this dense web of beams and timbers, until it stood alone in its courtyard. If we can take Adrastus's cannibalization of the various buildings listed in his inscription as evidence of the date at which construction and carving ended, this happened in A.D. 193. To put this period of elapsed time (176 to ca. 193) into perspective, I want to return briefly to a question raised at the beginning of this chapter, that of style. Since carving began on the lowest column drums, possibly as soon as they were put in place, and then carried on up to the top of the monument, a good deal of time, many years at least, separates the lowest and topmost images. And when the style of carving at the very top of the column is examined (fig. 6.6), some differences can be seen. Figures are not as carefully executed: proportions become less realistic, poses awkward, outlines and drapery no longer crisp but instead rough and lumpy. This is similar to the style of carving seen on the great panel reliefs of the Arch of Septimius Severus. Even though sculpture of the Column of Marcus Aurelius had clear Antonine beginnings and was heavily inspired by the art of Trajan's Column, by the time its carving was completed it contained many elements of a Severan style.[23]

chapter seven

THE FRIEZE AS HISTORY

Lactantius, a Christian writer of the early fourth century A.D., tells a revealing story about the sufferings of the Roman emperor Valerian, captured through treachery by the Persian king Sapor in 260. "When King Sapor, who had captured him, wanted to mount a vehicle or a horse, he would order Valerian to kneel on all fours and, placing his foot on his back, he would reproach him, saying with a smile, 'The Romans may paint things on their tablets and walls, but *this* is really the way it is!'"[1] It is doubtful whether Sapor actually said these words, but there must have been enough truth in the idea behind them—that official Roman art often gave a less than accurate account of actual history—to give them convincing bite for Lactantius's readers. The ease with which a painter or sculptor in Rome might misrepresent, deliberately or accidentally, the historical reality of events on a far-flung frontier of the empire is not hard to imagine. Misrepresentation is, however, very difficult to test for. In the poorly documented reign of Marcus Aurelius, this is especially true.

The meager and frequently unreliable sources for the history of the reign of Marcus Aurelius make it almost impossible to reconstruct any more than a superficial account of the main events of his reign. The main literary sources for the period are two: Cassius Dio, a senator and historian who lived in the time of Septimius Severus; and the *Historia Augusta*, a collection of imperial biographies written (it seems) in the fourth century.[2] The *Historia Augusta* is notoriously unreliable, a situation made worse by the fact that its biographic focus means that historical events are normally mentioned out of order. Dio, who should be an outstanding source for this period, has suffered in transmission: his text is only preserved in fragments cobbled together into an abbreviated history in the eleventh century by a Byzantine monk named Xiphilinus. Xiphilinus was varied in his method of abbreviation: descriptions of some major events seem to have been lifted entire from Dio's text, but other parts are the work of Xiphilinus alone. Perhaps the greatest damage has come from the removal of the quoted sections from their original context: because Xiphilinus rearranged the selections to suit his own ends, the dates of these events, even their relative order, are sometimes impossible to reconstruct. A third source is the imperial coinage, but by the time of Marcus Aurelius this had become repetitive and generic in its types. It is useful for dating some few major events—Marcus's victories and imperial acclamations, for example—but gives little or no insight into the detailed course of his reign or his wars.

Given this depressing situation, the Column of Marcus Aurelius has offered generations of scholars the tantalizing prospect of an alternative, visual source for the history (at least part of it) of Marcus's reign. The column seems to present a complete record of the entire course of Marcus's Germanic wars, from beginning to end, in impressive detail. The thinking behind this is that if it is possible to correctly interpret the visual language of the frieze and connect our few historical sources to particular scenes within it, we might then be able to use the rest of the images to reconstruct the entire history of Marcus's wars.

That, at least, is the theory. But can this approach work in practice? The purpose of this chapter is to test the historicity of the column's frieze from a number of different perspectives, from broad patterns of behavior down to the details of arms and equipment. It begins, however, with a focus on testing the historicity of individual scenes. Interest in historical themes is one of the most "Roman" characteristics of Roman art—it could in fact be described as the one that separates Roman art most clearly from the art of the Greeks. To understand the basis of the arguments surrounding the historicity of Marcus's Column, its contents have to been seen in the context of the development of this particular line of Roman art. For this reason, the chapter begins with a survey of the history of Roman historical art. Its medium was (up to the second century A.D.) almost exclusively painting, and our knowledge of it is almost entirely restricted to descriptions in literary sources. Strong arguments have been made that the images of Trajan's Column were drawn directly from painted models that had a high degree of historical content. But can the same thing be said about the frieze of the Column of Marcus Aurelius? In the final portion of this chapter, the analysis moves on to consider the historicity of the frieze at two more general levels: that of the details of arms and equipment shown used by Roman soldiers, and that of general patterns of behavior in combat. The historicity of both can be tested by comparison to textual and archaeological sources, offering the opportunity to evaluate the column's historical accuracy from a broad viewpoint.

A Very Brief History of Roman Historical Art

The record of the Romans' use of art to document and advertise their military victories extends as far back as 264 B.C., when, as the elder Pliny relates (*NH* 35.22), Messala displayed on the side of the senate house a "painting of the battle (*tabula proelii*), in which he had beaten the Carthaginians and Hiero in Sicily." Lucius Scipio is also reported by Pliny (ibid.) to have done much the same thing, setting up a painting of his Asiatic victory (*tabulam victoriae suae Asiaticae*, over Antiochus III, 190 B.C.) on the Capitol. Not long after, we have the first record of the intersection of historical painting with the greatest of Roman military rituals: the triumph. When Lucius Aemilius Paullus returned to Rome after his victory over the Macedonians at Pydna (168 B.C.), he sent to Athens for a philosopher to educate his children and a painter to beatify his triumph (*pictorem ad triumphum excolendum*). The artist's task would presumably have been to paint images of Paullus's victories that would then be carried in the triumphal procession.[3]

An incident of 146 B.C. gives an intensely personal flavor to this distinctive genre of Roman art. Lucius Hostilius Mancinus, a Roman legate recently returned from Africa, set up a large and remarkable painting in the Forum. It showed an image of the city of Carthage, and of the event that had made Mancinus famous: the ill-planned but daring capture and night-long occupation of Megara, a suburb of Carthage, by a small band of Roman soldiers and sailors under the legate's command. Just as extraordinary was what happened next: Mancinus positioned himself beside the painting, curious Romans began to gather round, and the commander of this brave action began to explain its details to them. His goal was political: to ride a wave of popularity to the consulship, as the first Roman (at least, the first Roman of high rank) to enter Carthage by force.[4] Pliny—who tells the story of the display in the Forum—does not tell us exactly what this painting looked like, but if it was improved by explanation then it must have been complex and detailed. Details were undoubtedly tweaked to make Mancinus look as good as possible, but it was certainly historical art.

In the imperial period, triumphal paintings represented the acme of historical art—but we are largely in the dark when it comes to knowing just what sort of images these paintings contained. Most of our records are anecdotal, and there is only one description that offers some enticing (if at the same time somewhat frustrating) detail of the contents of one such set of images. This is Josephus's account of the images, painted on or perhaps even woven into cloth, carried in the triumph of Vespasian and Titus in A.D. 71:

> The war was shown by numerous representations, in separate sections, affording a very vivid picture of its episodes. Here was to be seen a prosperous country devastated, there whole battalions of the enemy slaughtered; here a party in flight, there others led into captivity; walls of surpassing compass demolished by engines, strong fortresses overpowered, cities with well-manned defences completely mastered and an army pouring within the ramparts, an area all deluged with blood, the hands of those incapable of resistance raised in supplication, temples set on fire, houses pulled down over their owners' heads, and, after general desolation and woe, rivers flowing, not over a cultivated land, nor supplying drink to man and beast, but across a country still on every side in flames.[5]

These "numerous representations, in separate sections" sound very much like the individual scenes that make up the contents of the frieze of the columns of Trajan and of Marcus Aurelius. Josephus describes the illustrations in a vivid but imprecise manner, focusing on the overall effect rather than the pictorial or historic details. Nonetheless, there can be little doubt that this art was intensely historical and that it showed events that actually happened in the Jewish War.

Interest in historical themes was not limited to official art: it crossed the entire Roman artistic spectrum, from grand to humble. The famous fresco depicting a riot in an amphitheater that was uncovered in a private house in Pompeii is an excellent example.[6] The amphitheater is Pompeii's own (clearly identifiable by its surroundings and distinctive architecture, especially the arches supporting its external staircases), and the event is without a doubt the deadly brawl between the Pompeians and the visiting Nucerians in 59 B.C., which caused such "frightful bloodshed" that it resulted in the banning of games in Pompeii for a decade and the recording of the event by Tacitus (*Annals* 14.17). And an event need not have been grand or historically significant for a Roman to render it into art: Juvenal tells the tale of a man down on his luck who "must now content himself with a rag to cover his cold and nakedness, and a poor morsel of food, while he begs for pennies as a shipwrecked mariner, and supports himself with a painted storm (*picta se tempestate tuetur*)."[7] The "painted storm" is evidently a small image of a ship foundering in the waves: the historical cause of the unfortunate man's current plight and the exact opposite of Mancinus's proud blustering in the Forum. It suggests that Romans were well accustomed to realistic content in visual art, and to its employment to create specific responses in viewers.

Understandably, no Roman triumphal paintings have survived in the original. It has been suggested, however, that copies (or at least adaptations) of them may survive in such monuments as the Column of Trajan. The idea that the column's relief is derived from triumphal painting is not a new one. It was first suggested in the mid-nineteenth century, and by 1945 Hamberg was able to say that this view was the one most widely held.[8] Koeppel has expressed the argument succinctly: "No relief of this type can be found prior to the reign of Trajan. Why not? If we did not have those few literary descriptions of triumphal paintings, we would be hard put to respond to this question. The answer is, of course, that the column frieze represents an ingenious adaptation to the sculptural medium of compositions which, up to that time, had been rendered only in painting."[9] It is not clear, and obviously cannot be known, how closely the scenes of Trajan's Column might resemble scenes shown on paintings carried in Trajan's triumph. It is possible that the paintings may have originally been executed on strips of fabric, as Josephus's "tapestries", and arranged one above the other as, perhaps, in the Esquiline painting. If this was the case, little adaptation would have been needed before the images could be transferred to the column. But this is only one interpretation of Josephus's evidence; it is also possible that the triumphal paintings were executed on large wooden panels (a format perhaps reflected in the historical reliefs of the Arch of Septimius Severus in the Roman Forum). In this case, the painted battles may have been larger and more complex than the column's depictions and would have required simplification: reduction in number of figures, cropping of certain elements. The fact remains that the compositional schemes seen on the Column of Trajan, and many of the individual figure types, have no parallels in earlier relief sculpture. This strongly suggests that substantial portions of its subject matter were transferred directly from another medium and that painting, perhaps even the genre of triumphal painting, is one of the most likely candidates.

There are two levels at which the historicity of the frieze of the Column of Marcus Aurelius can be evaluated: at a detailed, scene-by-scene level and, more broadly, as a whole. This chapter examines the frieze from both these perspectives, beginning with the individual scenes and moving out to examine the historical accuracy both of realia (details of actual objects such as weapons and armor) and of human actions from a wider viewpoint. The scenes themselves fall into three main categories: certainly historical scenes (of which there are very few); scenes that have been wrongly connected to known historical events; and finally scenes that offer tantalizing evidence of being historical, but for which we have no written source. The best place to begin is with the very few scenes that can be described with confidence as historical: the miracles.

Certainly Historical Images on the Column of Marcus Aurelius

Sandwiched between a description of Marcus's just nature and an account of the revolt of Avidius Cassius, the unknown author of the *Historia Augusta* makes the following remark about his imperial subject: "He summoned lightning from heaven against a siege-engine of the enemy by means of his prayers, and likewise rain was obtained when they [the soldiers] were suffering with thirst."[10] The former of these two miracles is not known from any other source; the latter (the Rain Miracle), however, is also recorded by Dio and other later authors. Both also appear on the Column of Marcus Aurelius, and as such are the only certainly historical scenes in the entire frieze.

The Lightning Miracle consists of two parts: scenes X (fig. 7.1), containing the threatened Roman fort, and XI (fig. 7.2), showing the destruction of the siege tower (Petersen judged them to be separate scenes, but they seem to have been meant to be viewed together). The first component, crucial to setting the scene, is a stone fortress filled with Roman soldiers. Their gaze is directed inward, reflecting their concern for their plight. To the right stands—though for a short time only—a siege tower constructed of three major vertical beams and two sets of horizontal braces. From the upper left corner of the tower a long, narrow object extends to the left at an angle over the wall of the fortress. Only the lowest relief portion of the extreme end of it is visible, and it has the form of a straight, narrow beam or pole with a small square projection on its surface. This may be a ramp or perhaps even a ladder (the projection being then a broken rung, and the entire forward portion of the ladder being lost) used to make a bridge from the siege tower to the fortress. The tower is clearly in trouble: it has been struck by a large thunderbolt, visible above it. The upper story is already engulfed in flames and two of its vertical supports have broken; below are three barbarians, one lying on the ground, a second falling forward, and a third still upright but slumping away from the tower. The small lick of flame on the seat of

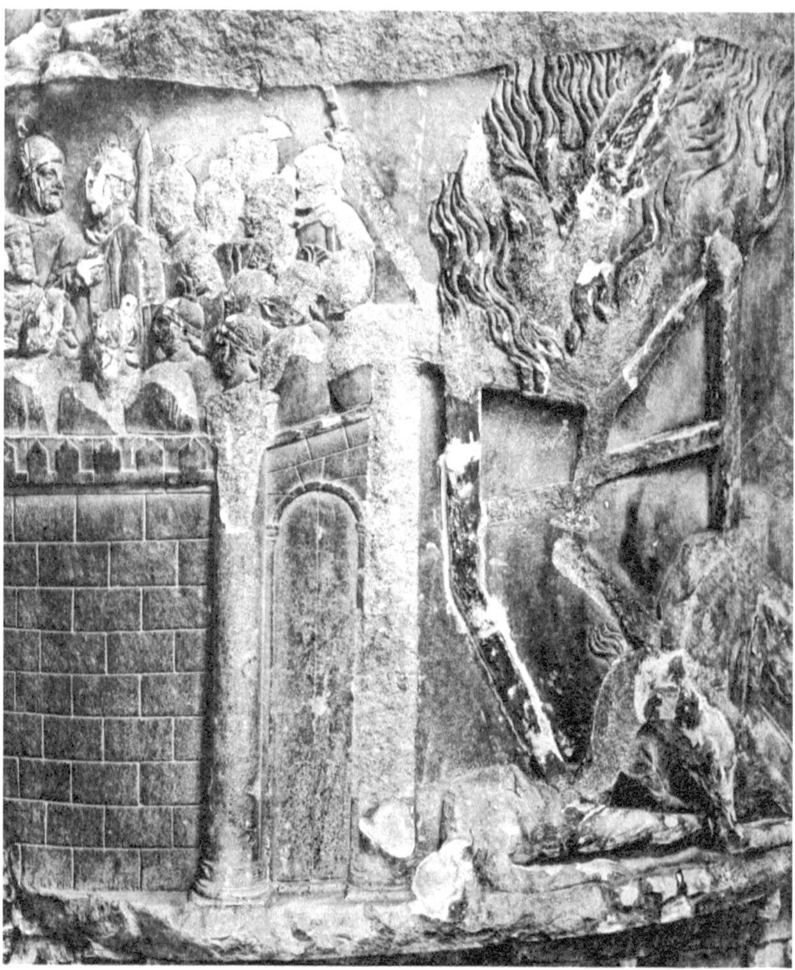

FIGURE 7.1. The Lightning Miracle, left portion. Scenes X (Romans in their fort) and XI (the destruction of a siege tower). From Petersen et al. 1896, pl. 17B.

the second barbarian's trousers suggests that he, and perhaps his comrades, have been struck down from above by the same lightning bolt that has destroyed the tower. This corresponds comfortably with the terse account of the event in the *Historia Augusta*.[11]

The Rain Miracle is located in the very next winding of the frieze, almost immediately above the Lightning Miracle. As much has been written about this one scene as has been about the column as a whole (it has recently been the subject of an entire book), especially concerning the issue of exactly when the event happened; here I focus exclusively on the actual content of the scene and a comparison with the ancient sources that describe the

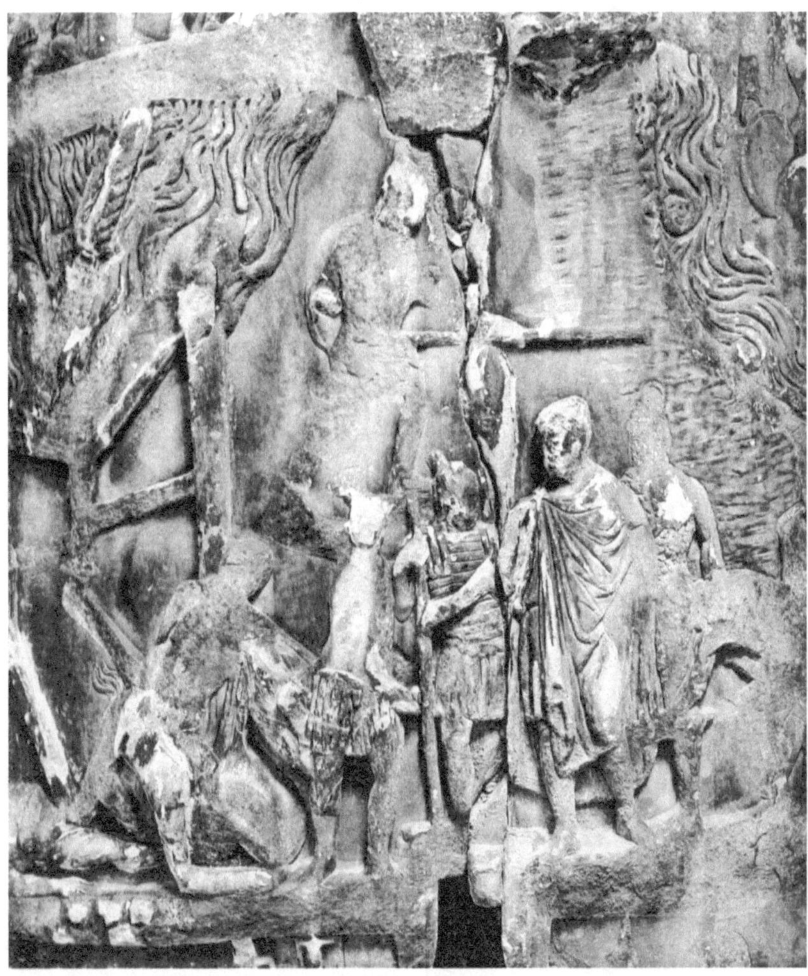

FIGURE 7.2. Scene XI, the right portion of the Lightning Miracle. From Petersen et al. 1896, pl. 18A.

event.[12] The scene (XVI, figs. 7.3 and 7.4; the entire scene is clearly visible in fig. 1.3 as it would appear to a viewer on the ground) does not show any actual fighting; instead, the Roman forces stand in the center and to the left, fallen barbarians and their mounts are scattered at the right. The Rain God himself dominates the scene from his position in the upper right-hand corner. The Romans appear merely to observe the carnage while shielding themselves, literally, against the deluge. The barbarians, represented by only three corpses and two horses, are washed away in a stream of water. This representation differs in a number of ways from Dio's description of the same event:

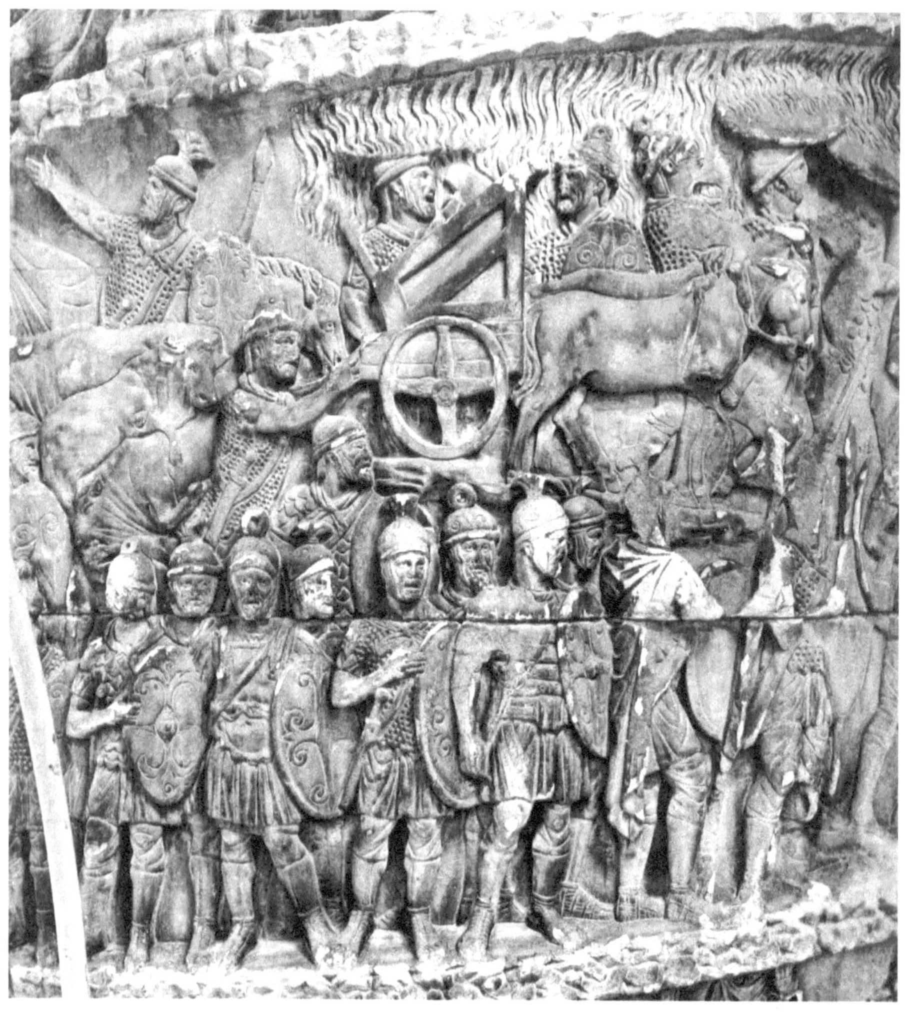

FIGURE 7.3. Scene XVI, the Rain Miracle, beginning of the scene showing rain and a soldier watering his horse (upper left). From Petersen et al. 1896, pl. 22A.

The Quadi had surrounded them at a spot favourable for their purpose and the Romans were fighting valiantly with their shields locked together; then the barbarians ceased fighting, expecting to capture them easily as the result of the heat and their thirst. So they posted guards all about and hemmed them in to prevent their getting water anywhere; for the barbarians were far superior in numbers. The Romans, accordingly, were in a terrible plight from fatigue, wounds, the heat of the sun, and thirst, and so could neither fight nor retreat, but were standing in the line and at their several posts, scorched by

> the heat, when suddenly many clouds gathered and a mighty rain, not without divine interposition, burst upon them. Indeed, there is a story to the effect that Arnuphis, an Egyptian magician, who was a companion of Marcus, had invoked by means of enchantments various deities and in particular Mercury, the god of the air, and by this means attracted the rain. . . . When the rain poured down, at first all turned their faces upwards and received the water in their mouths; then some held out their shields and some their helmets to catch it, and they not only took deep draughts themselves but also gave their horses to drink. And when the barbarians now charged upon them, they drank and fought at the same time; and some, becoming wounded, actually gulped down the blood that flowed into their helmets, along with the water. So intent, indeed, were most of them on drinking that they would have suffered severely from the enemy's onset, had not a violent hail-storm and numerous thunderbolts fallen upon the ranks of the foe. Thus in one and the same place one might have beheld water and fire descending from the sky simultaneously; so that while those on the one side were being drenched and drinking, the others were being consumed by fire and dying; and while the fire, on the one hand, did not touch the Romans, but, if it fell anywhere among them, was immediately extinguished, the rain however, on the other hand, did the barbarians no good, but, like so much oil, actually fed the flames that were consuming them, and they had to search for water even while being drenched with rain. Some wounded themselves in order to quench the fire with their blood, and others rushed over to the side of the Romans, convinced that they alone had the saving water; in any case Marcus took pity on them. He was now saluted *imperator* by the soldiers, for the seventh time; and although he was not wont to accept any such honour before the senate voted it, nevertheless this time he took it as a gift from Heaven, and he sent a despatch to the senate. (Dio 72.8.1–3 and 72.10.1–5, trans. E. Cary)

In Dio's description, the Roman troops are saved from thirst by a rain that falls upon them. The barbarians are at the same time destroyed by thunderbolts and a hailstorm. None of the details of this fantastic description can be found on the column. The Romans do not seem thirsty: in fact, they use their shields to shelter themselves from the rain, not to catch it for drinking. Only one soldier, at the far left of the scene, makes use of the water: he catches it in his shield and offers it to his horse (fig. 7.3, the soldier immedi-

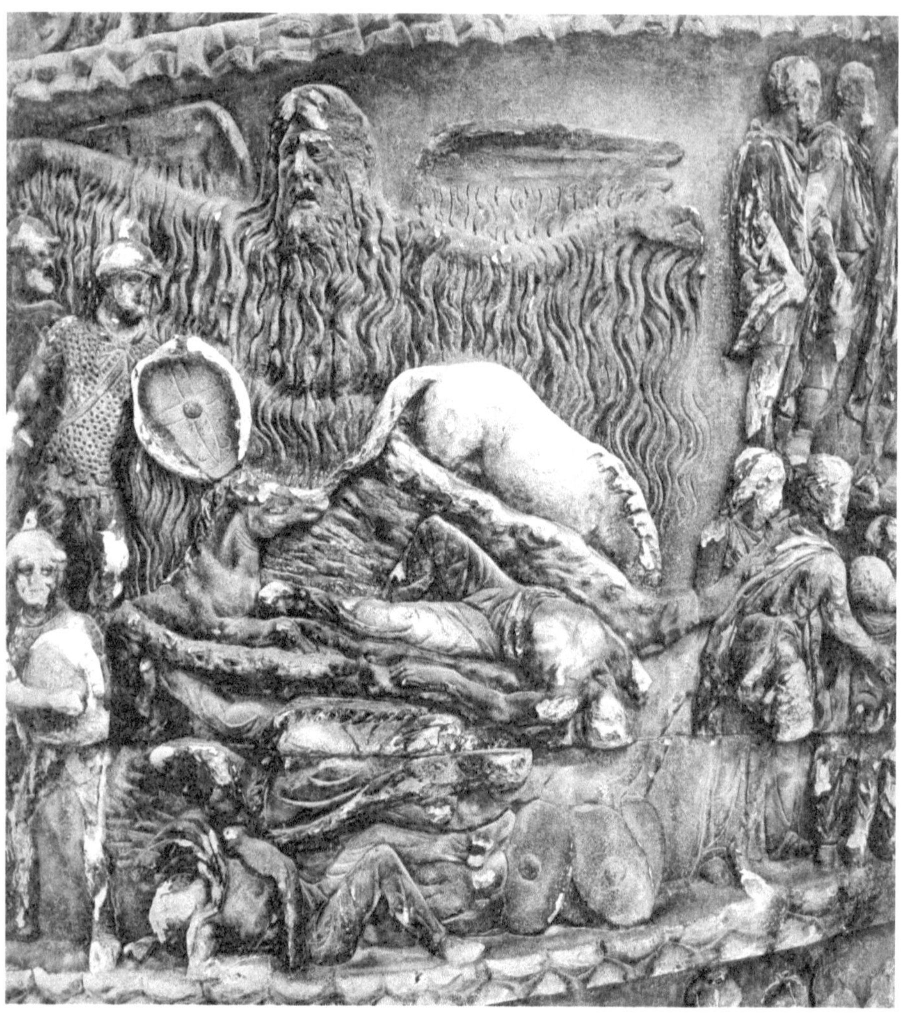

FIGURE 7.4. Scene XVI, the Rain Miracle, final portion of the scene showing the Rain God. From Petersen et al. 1896, pl. 23A.

ately left of the cart). There is no actual fighting taking place, nor is there any sign of hail or of the fire and thunderbolts that in Dio's description play such an important role. No barbarians are shown turning themselves over to the Romans. The barbarians are washed away in the resulting torrent, instead of being consumed by fire. And where is the emperor?

Dio's account of this battle is not the only one we have: there are two other brief descriptions of the same event in later authors. The first is found in the fourth century *Chronicon*, or calendar, of Eusebius. There, he writes that during Marcus's wars, "Pertinax and the army were afflicted with thirst while fighting in the land of the Quadi, when a rain was sent from God, while at the same time lightning-bolts deluged the Germans and Sarmatians and killed many of them." This description is simpler than Dio's and closer to what we see on the column in that it does not include Marcus, but only his general Pertinax. It does however add the detail of lightning bolts killing the enemy, where the column shows only drowning. The second description of this battle, preserved in a speech of the fourth-century rhetorician Themistius, is claimed by its author to be based on a picture that he has seen. This picture showed the emperor standing in the battle line, with hands extended to heaven, and soldiers filling their helmets with the rain. Themistius does not mention the barbarians at all.[13]

How do we determine who—if anyone—is right? Each author agrees on a few details: thirst afflicting the Romans, and their dire position in general. Things are more difficult when it comes to Marcus: Themistius and the *Historia Augusta* mention the emperor's presence specifically; Dio implies it; Eusebius does not refer to him at all. It is possible that by Eusebius's time the event had become associated with a Christian miracle: Christian Roman soldiers were said to have prayed for help, which came in the form of a rainstorm. Xiphilinus also tells this story after he relates Dio's version of events. Themistius and the *Historia Augusta* credit Marcus, Dio a priest working at Marcus's behest, with praying for the miracle. By removing Marcus from his relation of the events and replacing him with the general Pertinax, Eusebius could distance his story from its major pagan connotation and attribute the miracle to the Christian god. But why, when Dio, Themistius, and the *Historia Augusta* place him in the midst of the battle, does Marcus not appear in the Rain Miracle scene on the column? Is this evidence of historical error on the column?

Most likely it is not. To begin with, Themistius's account must be approached very carefully. The speech belongs to a literary genre, very popular in the later Roman period, of *ekphrasis*: descriptions of works of art undertaken as rhetorical exercises. When Themistius says he is discussing a picture he is merely setting up the generic literary *topos*. His information probably came not from an actual painting but from current stories or historical accounts that may have been altered for rhetorical effect. Thus we cannot speak of two sources, but only one, Dio, stacked against the version on the column. What then of Dio? Is his history to be relied on?

Dio's battle descriptions are, unfortunately, regularly embellished with made-up details and elaborated by use of rhetorical *topoi*, derived especially from Thucydides.[14] Some of these tendencies are immediately clear in Dio's description of the Rain Miracle, in particular an excess of generalizations: the Romans first drinking, then fighting, and some then drinking their blood as they fought; the Romans drenched and drinking, the barbarians burning and dying; the fire on one side going out, on the other flaming up. This alone is enough to raise suspicion. What other aspects of the actual events might Dio have altered, elaborated, or invented? Did he invent details, such as the helmets and shields turned up to catch the rain or barbarians giving themselves up to the Romans? Still, all blame should not be laid at Dio's doorstep. He presents the detail of Marcus asking his Egyptian priest to pray for help as "a story told by some," which implies that it was not part of the standard version of events. What of Marcus's presence at the actual battle? Dio merely alludes to it: once in the priest story and later, at the end of the battle, when he says Marcus welcomed the barbarians who fled to the Roman side. Neither is clear evidence of Marcus's presence during the battle: the priest, although a companion of the emperor, may have been alone at the battle, and Marcus's magnanimity to the captured barbarians may have occurred some time after the victory. All in all, we cannot take Dio—or Xiphilinus's version of Dio—as a reliable source with which to compare and test the historicity of the Rain Miracle scene on the column. It is likely best to understand it as a single event that developed a number of variations in the telling over time.

And finally, it may be worth considering the possibility of influence in the other direction—from the column to the author. The *Historia Augusta*'s summary of the miracles is very concise: "He summoned lightning from heaven against a siege-engine of the enemy by means of his prayers, and likewise rain was obtained when they (his soldiers) were suffering with thirst." His short description matches well with what is actually on the column and does not include any of Dio's extra details; he is also the only source to mention the Lightning Miracle. It is conceivable that our author may have taken his information from the column itself. A viewer standing by the northeast corner of the column's pedestal would have seen (and can still see today) both scenes clearly, the Lightning Miracle just below and a little to the right of the Rain God (fig. 1.3). Given the drama of the scenes and the undoubted historicity of one of them, it is easy to believe that these would have been the two scenes most often pointed out to new viewers of the column. Our fourth-century author of the *HA* may very well have first come to associate these events during a youthful visit to Marcus's Column. If this was indeed the case, it deals a blow to the *HA* as evidence for the historicity of the Lightning Miracle.

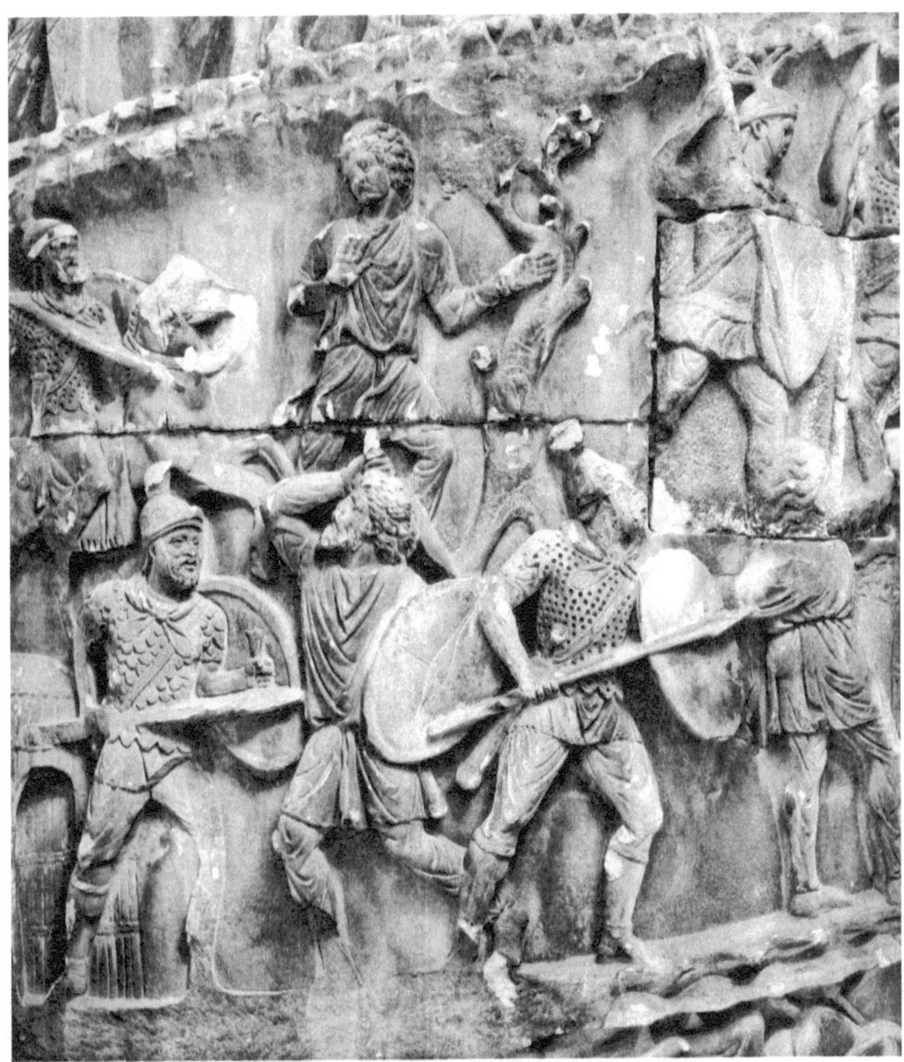

FIGURE 7.5. Scene XLIII, a Roman attack on a barbarian village. From Petersen et al. 1896, pl. 50A.

Wishful Thinking: Falsely Attributed Historical Scenes

In addition to the miracles, two other scenes on the Column of Marcus Aurelius have commonly been interpreted as historical. Rossi argued that two figures in the upper-left corner of scene XLIII (fig. 7.5), a Roman riding down a fleeing, beardless barbarian, are intended to represent the Roman Valerius Maximus and the barbarian prince Valao.[15] The event is recorded in the inscription on Maximus's own tombstone, which tells us

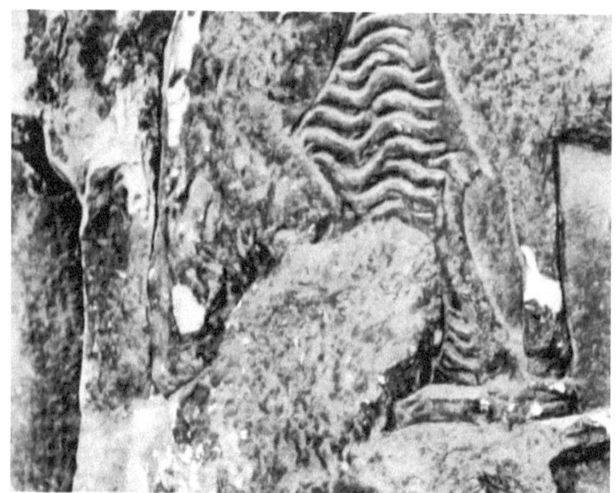

FIGURE 7.6.
Detail of heavily damaged scene XIII, heads of two animals(?) swimming in a river. From Petersen et al. 1896, pl. 20A.

that "he was praised publicly by the emperor Marcus Aurelius, and given a horse, decorations and arms, because he killed Valao, leader of the Narsitae, with this own hand."[16] Can this beardless young man, fleeing from his attacker, be the barbarian leader killed by Maximus, a deed for which the emperor personally praised him? Although Birley finds this plausible, only the lack of a full beard differentiates this barbarian from most others on the column. Instead of looking for a historical connection for these two figures, it is much better to try to understand them in their context: a Roman attack on a barbarian village. The young barbarian merely serves, along with the woman shown later in the scene, to give the impression that the village is populated by barbarian noncombatants. There is no good reason to connect Maximus's endeavors with these figures.

The second supposedly historical scene is the so-called Lion Oracle. Its interpretation rests on a textual source, but the link with the column is even more tenuous. The scene in question is a sacrifice scene, XIII, set on the bank of a wide river. Marcus, immediately to the right of the window that intrudes into the lower portion of the scene, stands in a toga and makes an offering over a tripod, the legs of which are visible in outline. The occasion of the sacrifice is the crossing of the river in boats, visible to the right, and accompanying the boats it seems that there are a number of animals swimming (fig. 7.6). The scene is heavily damaged but Petersen (who was able to inspect the column firsthand) believed that he could see two "lion-like" creatures with horns and cleft hooves in the river, in the upper part of the scene and just below the uppermost boat, in the process of hauling themselves out of the water onto the bank at the right.[17] He identified them as the "maned bison" mentioned by Pliny (*NH* 8.38) in his discussion of unusual animals. Dobias took Petersen's interpretation one step further, by seizing on the supposedly "lion-like" nature of the creatures and proposing a connection to a story in Lucian's fictional work *Alexander Pseudomantis*, "Alexander the False Prophet."[18] Lucian tells a story of how the False Prophet produced an oracle saying that two lions should be thrown into the Danube as part of a sacrifice, and that the Romans would then win a great victory. The lions were thrown into the river, but swam across to the other side where the Germans, mistaking them for a strange type of dog, clubbed them to death. The Romans then suffered a great defeat, losing 20,000 men.[19]

There appears to be nothing to support this interpretation of scene XIII. Besides the fact that the story seems to be a pure invention of Lucian, the very idea that the Romans would place a depiction of an embarrassing defeat on one of their monuments is not backed up by any parallel. The Romans simply did not portray such events in their art. The damage to the frieze in this area is so heavy that it is extremely difficult to interpret, and certainly Petersen's autopsy is to be trusted above Dobias's attempts to interpret the scene from photos. If Petersen detected horns and hooves, these creatures are likely cattle.

Tantalizing Images: Possibly Historical Scenes

The false historical interpretations discussed above were the result of attempts to connect known historical events to scenes on the column. These attempts have not been particularly successful. But some interesting observations can be made by turning the problem on its head, ignoring the fragmentary historical sources and focusing instead on the column. This is because there are some scenes that, for various reasons, possess specific iconographic characteristics that suggest that they may be historical. These are scenes that do not fit into the generic categories such as battle, march, and *adlocutio*, and that seem to show elements that are otherwise unique. Usually these unique elements are less striking than the supernatural wonders depicted in the miracle scenes, but often they are very noteworthy in their own right, so much so that they suggest that either the artist has been uncharacteristically inventive, or that he is depicting a genuine historical event.

The first example is found in scene X (fig. 7.7).[20] Located between a scene (IX) showing Marcus speaking to the troops and the Lightning Miracle, it is centered on the main east axis of the column (Fig. 1.3). In scene X we see an

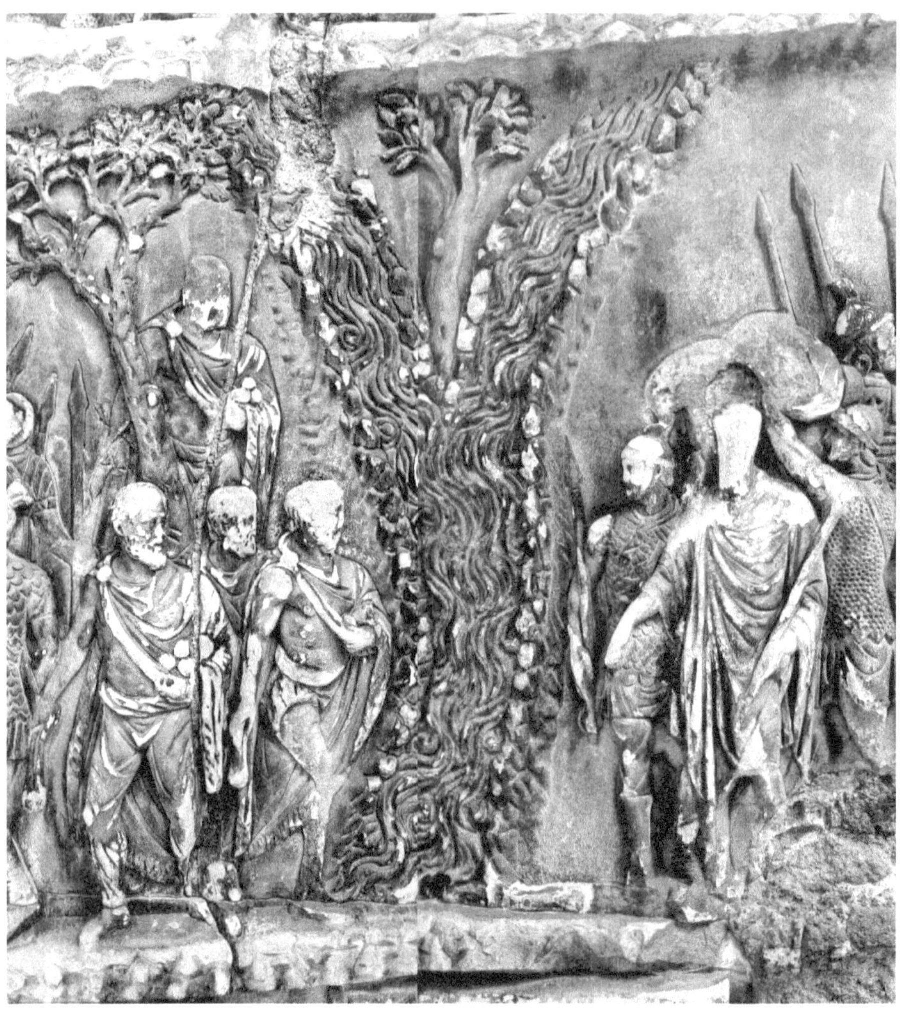

FIGURE 7.7. Scene X, showing Marcus Aurelius being shielded by attendant soldiers while barbarians across the river wield slings. From Petersen et al. 1896, pls. 16B and 17A.

interesting encounter at a fork in a stream. To the left of the stream stand four barbarians holding slings; to the right, the emperor surrounded by soldiers, some of whom hold up shields above his head to protect him from the stones of the enemy slingers. It is not clear whether Marcus is speaking to the barbarians, but the absence of any clear leader figure among the four partly clad slingers makes this unlikely. Scene X does not fit any of the standard genre scenes on the column. This alone does not mean that it is historical (it may simply be a liberal invention), but its location just before another more or less historical scene (the Lightning Miracle) combined with its iconographic uniqueness suggests that it might represent a genuine event. Unfortunately there is no mention of anything similar in our few and fragmentary sources, but perhaps it shows a treacherous surprise attack on the emperor's person, skillfully fended off by his bodyguard, or a daring attempt by the emperor to parlay with a group of aggressive barbarians.

The next potentially historical scene is the right half of XI (fig. 7.2), just after the Lightning Miracle. To the right of the collapsing siege tower (which has just been struck by the lightning bolt), we see a landscape dominated by a curving river. On the far side is a barbarian shield wall (due to damage to the frieze the figures themselves are visible only in outline, but the rounded tops of their heads make it clear that they are not Romans). To the left of the river are two ground lines; on the lower stands the emperor surrounded by soldiers. The leftmost Roman soldier faces away from the Lightning scene, creating a division between it and the river scene. The figures at the right edge of the group are engaged in interesting but enigmatic activities, unconnected to the destruction of the siege tower. Behind and to the right of Marcus stands a soldier; in front and to the right of the soldier is a bent-over figure visible only in outline, near other partial figure outlines. All are Romans—the sheathed sword of the bent figure is visible (barbarians on the column never wear scabbards), and the outlines of helmet crests on the other two figures can be made out.

On the upper ground line is a single Roman soldier who holds an object in a horizontal position. This object—a staff, perhaps—is marked with small holes that Petersen identified as measurement markers, indicating that this soldier is about to measure the depth of the river. The measuring soldier clearly belongs to the river scene and has no connection to the Lightning Miracle—indeed, he does not appear to even notice it. The role of Marcus, however, is less clear. Petersen associated him with the Lightning Miracle; Zwikker and Caprino, on the other hand, included the imperial group with the river scene.[21] Judging from the composition of the two scenes, it seems more likely that the emperor is supervising the operation at the river. Exactly what sort of operation is it? Petersen proposed an interesting reading of the two figures on the far right of the lower ground line: one man holding a staff topped with a helmet and adorned with two shields.[22] He interpreted this as, essentially, a scarecrow whose purpose was to distract the barbarians lined up on the other bank so that the Romans could cross at another, unwatched, location. However, it is just as possible, and perhaps more logical, to interpret all of these figures as living soldiers engaged in activities related to what the soldier with the measuring staff is doing: that is, further preparation for a river crossing. The bent figure may be digging (he appears to hold an object, perhaps a pick or hoe, horizontally), the two to the right carrying material toward the river. Even the figure at the left of the group may be carrying something, for he is shown bent slightly forward with his arms extended below and in front of him. If this is the case, then this scene depicts the initial preparation for the construction of a bridge under the supervision of the emperor, who directs the work with a gesture. This scene has no parallels on the column, nor elsewhere in Roman historical relief, suggesting that it is an attempt to show a particular event from the wars.

Also in the category of possibly historical is scene XXVII (fig. 7.8), a clumsily executed battle scene, but the only one on the column that includes the emperor in person. The emperor, in armor and on horseback, rides to the left up an inclined ground line in the company of Roman cavalry. Marcus Aurelius's head is missing, but his distinctive breastplate, his gesture, and the fact that his companions both turn their heads in his direction make it clear that it is him. In front of his party a Roman soldier stands with sword raised, as if having struck down the barbarian who falls below him; beneath the emperor another Roman attacks a seated barbarian. Petersen sees Marcus and his comrades as clearing the way in advance of the infantry, but this scene may in fact be intended to show the emperor riding to the aid of a group of Roman soldiers.[23] Nowhere else is Marcus shown in the midst of a scene of combat, and it is tempting to think that this scene (positioned exactly on the main east axis of the column and just two windings above the Rain Miracle) depicts a unique event when the emperor faced great danger in combat.

Another novel scene, XLII (fig. 7.9), shows objects not known in any other work of Roman historical relief sculpture. Three structures are shown lined up on the ground (each stands on the ground, as can be seen by the ground line underneath the feet of the second structure). They seem to be wooden frames covered with cloth or leather; ornamental feet are at each bottom corner. They are generally interpreted as litters, although there is no sign of carrying handles. In each sits a person, their heads visible through small windows on the side. Only the face of one, a bearded man in the lowest litter, is preserved; the head of the middle figure has been destroyed, and that of the upper figure is a Renaissance restoration. As far as can be seen from the original portion of the relief, the bottom two figures wear togas; thus Coarelli's reconstruction of the trio as the child Commodus at top, his mother Faustina in the middle, and Commodus's tutor Galen at the

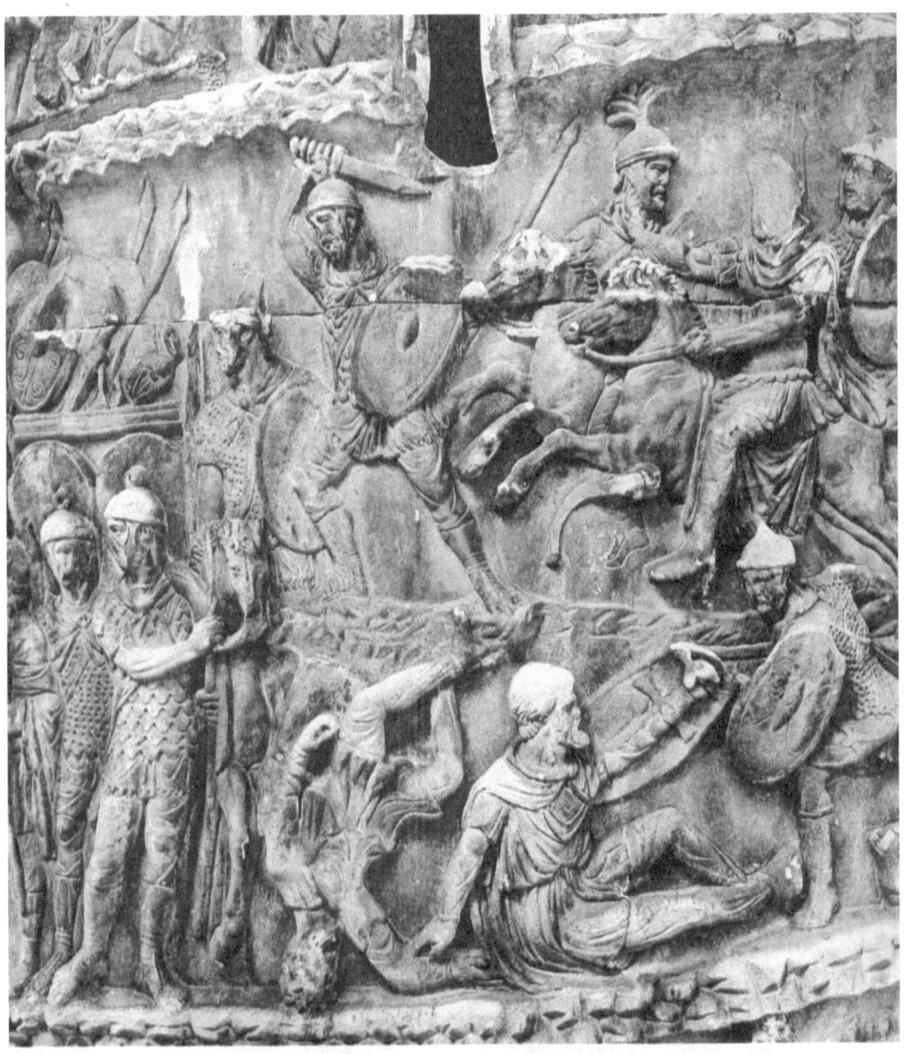

FIGURE 7.8. Scene XXVII, the only battle on the column that involves Marcus Aurelius directly. From Petersen et al. 1896, pl. 34B.

bottom is likely not correct.[24] Traveling in a litter is unmilitary; perhaps, as Petersen suggested, the figures are ambassadors of the senate.[25] The identity of the figure bending down toward the only senator with a preserved face is more of a problem. His dress suggests (but does not guarantee—the stone is worn and damaged) that he is a barbarian. What he is doing is likewise unclear: if he is indeed a barbarian, the scene may represent an attack on senatorial emissaries.

Similarly without parallel are two remarkable scenes of atrocity im-

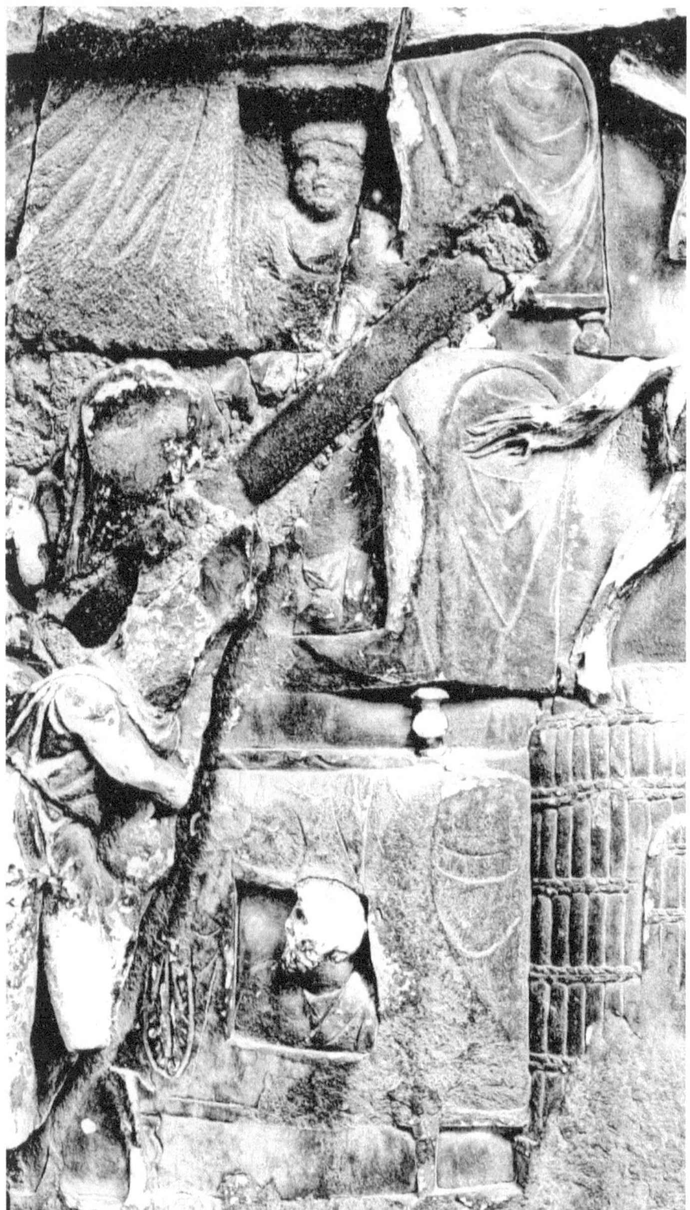

FIGURE 7.9. Scene XLII. Three litters are lined up on the ground. From Petersen et al. 1896, pl. 49B.

mediately above the figure of Victoria: LXI, with barbarians beheading barbarians, and LXVIII, where Roman soldiers massacre what seem to be unarmed prisoners. The story appears to begin with scene LX (fig. 7.10), where Marcus is shown surrounded entirely by barbarians, some of them armed. Certainly he has not been captured. Rather, the emperor is engaged

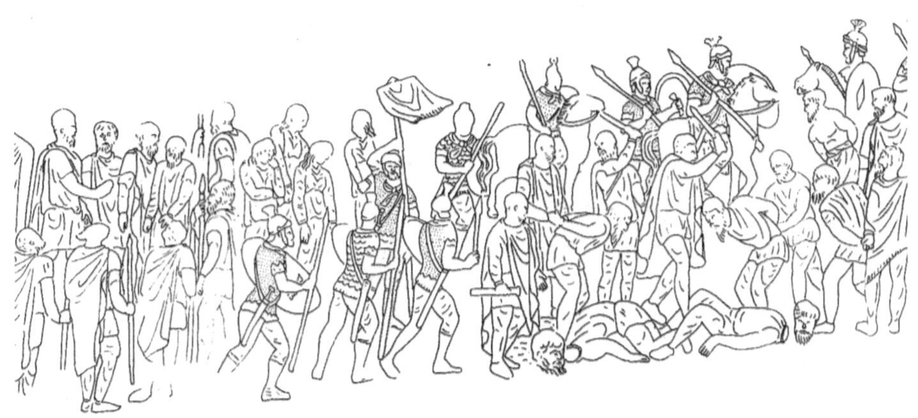

FIGURE 7.10. Scenes LX-LXII, the first execution scene on the column. Drawing by author.

in conversation with one barbarian in particular (third to the right of him) who makes a weak gesture with his arms in return. Perhaps the man is acquiescing submissively to the expulsions and executions that follow. These begin immediately to the right in scene LXI, where a group of barbarian women is escorted away by Roman soldiers. The next scene, LXII, shows a mass execution where, surprisingly, barbarians behead other barbarians under the watchful eye of the Romans. The center of action is focused on two barbarians, swords raised in the air, who are about to strike the heads from two other barbarians held bent over before them. On the ground, two barbarians already lie headless. Roman soldiers can be seen in the background, apparently keeping watch. The placement of this scene between two others showing Marcus speaking to barbarians suggests that it may be intended to represent a dramatic event connected to the surrender of a barbarian nation. Perhaps the execution scene shows the dispatch of former barbarian leaders.

The rare appearance of such unique scenes suggests that the column's frieze contained more direct historical content than the Rain and Lightning Miracles. It is tempting to think that the very few historical scenes we can be sure of were adapted from a medium such as triumphal painting, and that the empty spaces around them were simply filled in with generic material. We do not know for a fact, but might safely assume, that such paintings were carried in Marcus's triumphal procession. We do know that pictures of events from a nearly contemporary war existed: Lucius Verus's war against the Parthians. In a letter to Fronto, philosopher tutor to both Verus and Marcus Aurelius and later apparently historian of Verus's campaigns,

Verus offers Fronto "*picturas*" of events in the Parthian wars, in addition to copies of dispatches and letters, for use as raw source material for his history. These pictures were apparently not displayed in public but were kept in Verus's possession; this suggests that they were made at his command, perhaps during the campaign itself.[26] Marcus, too, may have been in possession of images made during his own campaign, and if so they might have formed the basis of triumphal paintings. They may even possibly have been used for some of the scenes on the column—but not for many. Most of the scenes in the frieze are generic and not historically specific. But it is also possible to analyze their historical accuracy in another way: by examining their details.

History in the Details: Realism in Troop Behavior and Equipment

Two further standards can be used to evaluate, at a more detailed level, the realism of the scenes carved on the Column of Marcus Aurelius. These are the degree of realism in the actions of figures and the accuracy of the real objects shown in daily use. An ideal test case for both these criteria can be found in depictions of the Roman army, and especially in its most commonly depicted employment, battle. Lehmann-Hartleben suggested that the relatively small size (compared to Trajan's Column) of the battles on Marcus's Column may reflect the reality of a war conducted in small skirmishes.[27] However, as argued in chapter 5, the small size of most battles (there are exceptions) was determined by the same factor that resulted in most scenes being small: the division of the frieze into small segments for the purposes of planning. Still, regardless of the size of the encounters, it is possible to evaluate the realism of what soldiers are shown doing in battle by comparing the scenes on the column to what we know of the reality of combat in the second century A.D. It is also possible to objectively judge the accuracy of what the soldiers wear and carry—their arms and equipment—by comparing them to actual archaeological finds from the period.

Although Roman soldiers built roads, bridges, and forts, their fundamental purpose was to fight battles. Roman battles were not free-for-all moblike engagements but rather took place according to established tactics. The core of the Roman armies was the legion, heavily armed infantry regiments with a strength of about 5,000. These were supported by lightly armed infantry and cavalry soldiers drawn from the provinces, called the auxiliaries. We have many ancient descriptions of how these Roman troops were organized and how they fought in battles, and much of it from good sources—Caesar, himself a soldier, wrote detailed descriptions of many of the battles he was involved in personally. Goldsworthy has attempted to reconstruct the usual conduct of Roman battles from these written sources and his conclusions provide a useful "standard of behavior" against which artistic representations of battle can be measured. Goldsworthy shows that in most battles the decisive fighting usually occurred between groups of infantry. It was much rarer for infantry to meet cavalry in battle, especially away from the eastern frontiers of the empire.[28] Encounters between two opposing groups of cavalry, on the other hand, were more common, since these forces often occupied the same positions in opposing armies—usually on the flanks of the main infantry bodies. These patterns—infantry tends to fight infantry, cavalry most often engages cavalry—give us a starting point in evaluating the battle scenes on the column.

These "normal" events of Roman warfare are well reflected in the battle scenes on the Column of Trajan. There, the most common battle scene is one where Roman and Dacian infantry clash face to face in massed groups, well organized in solid bodies and ranks. Cavalry encounters, on the other hand, are much less common and most often show one group of horsemen (always the enemy) fleeing while another mounted force pursues. Only once (scene LXIV) is a body of cavalry shown attacking a body of infantry—a remarkable scene in which Moorish cavalry, identifiable by their ringlet hairstyles and evidently allied to the Romans, drive a group of Dacian infantry to flight. And only in one single scene on Trajan's Column are Roman cavalry shown mixed with Roman infantry. This is scene XXXVIII, and the mixing of troop types seems to have been done with the express purpose of accentuating the confusion of a chaotic nighttime battle in which Night is shown personified, peering down onto a scene of fighting centered around a Dacian supply train, a battle that has degenerated into a melee.[29]

The contrast visible in the battle scenes on the Column of Marcus Aurelius could hardly be more striking. Cavalry and infantry are very often freely mixed within single scenes (e.g., XXVII, XLIII, L, LXIII, etc.), where they are shown performing essentially the same duties in battle. The contrast in troop behavior on the two columns is even stronger when cavalry encounters alone are examined. Ancient sources consistently state that in cavalry battles it was usual for one body of horsemen to lose courage and break off before engaging the opposing horsemen, or to do so after only a brief skirmish. There is a remarkable observation on this point by a British veteran of the early nineteenth-century Peninsular War, in which the cavalry, armed with sword and lance, did not differ greatly from that of the Romans: "Cavalry seldom meet each other in a charge executed at speed; the one party generally turns before joining issue with the enemy, and this often happens when the line is still unbroken and no obstacles of any sort intervene. The fact is, every cavalry soldier approaching another at speed must feel that if they come in contact at that pace they both go down, and probably break every limb in their bodies."[30] The fleeing force would then be exposed to attack from its pursuers and could incur heavy losses thus. This is exactly what we see in scenes XXXVII and CXLIV of Trajan's Column: one body of cavalry fleeing from the other, its rearmost members falling to the swords and spears of the pursuers.

The way that cavalry are employed on the Column of Marcus Aurelius is, in most cases, very different: they engage enemy cavalry and infantry seemingly at random, and in doing so are often indistinguishable in their role from the infantry. The only scene on Marcus's Column that shows a realistic cavalry pursuit is XCII; but the two following scenes (XCVII and CV) depict unbelievable pursuits involving barbarian cavalry being pursued and cut down by Roman infantry. Thus the battle scene compositions on Trajan's Column reflect, in general at least, much of what we know about the reality of Roman battle. The battle scenes on the Column of Marcus Aurelius, on the other hand, do not. This suggests that the oddities in troop behavior in battle seen on Marcus's Column may reflect a difference in knowledge of military reality between the designers of the monuments or a difference in the source material they relied on in creating their compositions.

One of the simplest tests for historicity is to evaluate the realism of details of arms and equipment of the individual soldiers; this is simple (relatively speaking) because these details can be compared to actual archaeological evidence. On the Column of Marcus Aurelius, soldiers are shown wearing either segmented plate armor (made of horizontal strips of metal, articulated like a lobster tail), scale armor (consisting of small iron or bronze scales sewn to a leather backing), or ring mail (individual metal rings joined together to form a complete covering for the body). These differences in armor type have traditionally been interpreted as indicators of the units to which the troops belonged: a soldier in scale armor is identified as a praetorian (a member of the imperial guard), one in segmented armor as a legionary (the citizen-soldier backbone of the army), and one in ring mail as an auxiliary, a member of one of the many noncitizen units of the Roman army.[31] The roots of this approach lie in studies of the frieze of the Column of Trajan. There, the regular Roman troops wear two distinct "uniforms." One type of soldier wears segmented armor, carries a curved rectangular shield, and spends most of his time marching and building things. The other main class of Roman soldier on Trajan's Column wears ring mail, carries a flat oval shield, and does most of the fighting (both on foot and on horseback). The general assumption, based to some extent on textual evidence, is that the former represent legionaries and praetorians, the latter auxiliaries. It is not easy to explain why soldiers wearing segmented armor spend so little time fighting on Trajan's Column. One theory is that this was a deliberately engineered effect designed to reflect positively on Trajan as a general who achieved victory while shedding a minimum of Roman blood (the soldiers in segmented armor, supposedly legionaries and praetorians, being the citizens). This interpretation is supported by reference to Tacitus's description of the battle of Mons Graupius (in northern Britain in A.D. 83), in which the auxiliaries did the bulk of the fighting—and the bleeding, which is remarked upon by Tacitus as the sign of a particularly great victory.[32]

Thus, at first glance it appears sensible to use armor as a key to identifying different troop types on the Column of Trajan. Unfortunately, however, when the details of the representation of the Roman army on Trajan's Column are scrutinized from the perspective of historical accuracy, many of them turn out to be doubtful. The Tropaeum Traiani, on the borders of Dacia itself, provides a stark contrast. The Tropaeum, located in modern Romania about twenty-two kilometers south of the Danube and fifty kilometers west of the Black Sea, was a massive cylindrical monument (thirty meters diameter, eleven meters tall) made up of a rubble and concrete core faced in stone and surmounted by a stone trophy.[33] Dated by its inscription to A.D. 108/109 and dedicated to Mars Victor, the Tropaeum served as a victory monument to one or both of Trajan's Dacian wars.[34] The main figural decoration of the monument was a series of fifty-four figural metopes, each measuring about 1.5 by 1.2 meters, which were found separated from the core of the structure. They are thought to have ringed the middle part of the cylinder, separated by decorative relief slabs. An immediate, striking difference seen on the Tropaeum is that the Dacians are commonly shown wielding a huge, two-handed curved sword. This is the *falx*, a famously feared Dacian weapon, but one which only rarely appears on Trajan's Column and then in a diminutive, one-handed form (Decebalus famously commits suicide with one in scene CXLV). The Romans on the Tropaeum wear ring or scale armor, the latter never seen worn by regular Roman troops on the Column of Trajan. Segmented body armor on the other hand, so common on the column, never appears worn by soldiers on the Tropaeum. But Roman soldiers on the Tropaeum are commonly shown equipped with an arm guard of segmented metal and also wear a helmet reinforced with metal strips running vertically up its front, back, and sides. These refinements to standard Roman equipment were apparently designed especially to protect against blows from the fearsome two-handed Dacian *falx*. Because the Tropaeum metopes show Roman soldiers equipped with special innovations designed to counter specific dangers of the Dacian campaigns, they can be interpreted as realistic in detail.

Why this striking difference in detail on two official, chronologically equivalent monuments that record the very same military campaigns? Robinson suggested that two main divisions ought to be made in the realm of military-themed sculpture: the work, on the one hand, of "military sculptors" who carved soldiers' tombstones near military stations (particularly in the provinces), and on the other hand, the work of the artists in the capital.[35] Jon Coulston took this analysis a step further by noting a disproportionate presence of praetorian standards on Trajan's Column—which suggests that the artists of the column simply copied what was at hand, and when it came to representing the details of the army, they likely relied heavily for inspiration on the most prominent troops at Rome: the praetorians.[36] Coulston also noted the substantial influence of the buildings of Rome (or at least their building technique) on the column's depictions of military architecture.[37] This suggests that the Roman sculptors drew heavily on what they saw in the capital when carving the frieze of Trajan's Column.

How do the Roman soldiers on the Column of Marcus Aurelius compare? They generally resemble the soldiers on Trajan's Column, but add scale armor to the repertoire of protection for both infantry and cavalry (these have generally been interpreted as praetorians). Ring mail is more common than scale armor, but here ease of execution may be a factor, as the former was rendered by simple drill holes, while scales had to be carefully and individually carved, often with elaborated edges. The wearers of ring or scale armor are never formed into distinct units and are generally indistinguishable in their duties; they are often mixed together on the column indiscriminately. There seems to be no basis for singling either of them out as a specific and cohesive group; neither armor type can be interpreted as a "uniform." Soldiers in segmented armor on the other hand *are* commonly shown in homogeneous, distinct formations. Also, soldiers in segmented armor seem to be assigned special duties at times, particularly outside of combat (in which they appear rarely).[38] They are shown as single units marching in the upper half of the column (LXVII, LXXVIII, XCIII, CIII, and CXI), and are the only troop type shown engaged in construction activities (LXXXII [fig. 8.3], XCIV—although this type of scene is much rarer on Marcus's Column than on Trajan's). But were troops in segmented armor genuinely intended to represent a special class of soldier on the Column of Marcus Aurelius? Their concentration in the upper (and overall more generic, less historical) part of the frieze, along with their dominance of the opening march scene (III), suggests that their presence is best explained by artistic influence from other monuments—especially Trajan's Column—used by the Marcus column's designers for inspiration in creating their scenes.

Conclusions

Is the frieze of the Column of Marcus Aurelius historical? The answer to this question is a qualified no. Army equipment and troop behavior as depicted on the Column of Marcus Aurelius does not correspond well to what we know of the historical reality of the period. And while both Marcus's and Trajan's columns suffer from a lack of realism when it comes to equipment, Marcus's Column falls well short of Trajan's when depictions of troop behavior in combat are considered. In this regard, the contrast with the Column of Trajan is often stark: whereas Trajan's soldiers are shown on his column behaving in a more or less realistic manner, Marcus's simply are not. When it comes to the individual scenes, only one of the scenes on the Column of Marcus Aurelius (the Rain Miracle) was clearly inspired by a well-known historical event. In one case, the Lightning Miracle, it is even possible that a historical event of Marcus's wars has made its way into literature via the column itself. But the vast majority of scenes belong to generic categories. Analysis of one of these (battle scenes—see chapter 8) strongly suggests that they were invented as needed by the column's artists with no regard for (or access to) historical source material. But the conclusions are not all negative—there are a number of scenes whose unique nature suggests that they do indeed have some connection to actual history, even if we cannot connect them to any known event.

chapter eight

THE FRIEZE AS ART

"Compared with the noble Column of Trajan, that of Aurelius is in all ways inferior."[1] This was the opinion of Percy Gardner, professor of classical archaeology at Oxford University in the late nineteenth century. His views on the value of the art of the Column of Marcus Aurelius were shared by many of his contemporaries. Eugen Petersen, even after becoming intimately acquainted with the column through many weeks spent on a platform hanging from its capital, still concluded that in comparison to the richness of Trajan's Column "the art of the Marcus Column seems poor and sober, restricted to only the most essential components."[2] In the eyes of these early critics the sole redeeming feature of the Column of Marcus Aurelius was that it was Roman. This seemingly obvious fact is taken for granted today. But Petersen, Gardner, and others of their time viewed Marcus's Column from a special perspective: they saw it less as a monument in its own right than as one of a pair, necessitating constant comparison to the Column of Trajan. And Trajan's Column was for them a monument of Greek art, created by Greek artists; it was even thought to have been made of Greek marble. Marcus's Column, on the other hand, was a truly Roman creation, made by artists from the imperial capital and of Italian stone (which, too, because of the extent of damage to its surface, was judged to be of poor quality). In almost every respect, the Column of Marcus Aurelius was considered to be inferior to Trajan's. But it did offer one thing that Trajan's Column did not: the opportunity to study a work of truly Roman artistic expression.

By the beginning of the twentieth century, the Column of Trajan was recognized to be made of Italian marble after all, and both it and the Column of Marcus Aurelius gradually came to be accepted as Roman monuments. Instead of being seen as polar opposites, the two columns were now looked on as major, important markers along a unified path of artistic development. The discussion of the art of the Column of Marcus Aurelius took a new turn. Rather than marking a contrast between the art of Greece and the art of Rome, Marcus's Column came to be thought of as a crucial piece of evidence for a critical point of change within the history of Roman art itself. Some scholars even saw it as foreshadowing the art of the Middle Ages (and this at the end of the second century A.D.). This viewpoint sounds radical, but it was developed in response to clear and striking characteristics of the column's art. On the Column of Marcus Aurelius, human figures were often carved in ways not seen before—and in ways that contrast sharply with the classical tradition inherited from Greece. Proportions changed, as did methods of working the stone: folds of cloth and locks of hair were deeply carved; extensive use was made of the drill to cut far into the stone, creating a bold play of light and shadow. And the figures themselves were often arranged in new, nontraditional ways: they were crowded into the foreground at the expense of landscape and background, and sometimes they were seen as if from above, in "bird's eye" perspective; they even seemed to some scholars to be grouped and scaled to indicate hierarchy.

These traits were also identified in other artworks of the second and third centuries A.D., leading scholars to conclude that a dramatic change in the style of Roman art as a whole had occurred. This stylistic transition has come to be known in the language of its most eager early discussants—German—as the *Stilwandel.* The term itself simply means "style change" and as such is not period specific, but among English-speaking art historians of the Roman imperial period it has attained iconic status and is often used (sometimes, but not always, with the qualifying adjective "Antonine") to refer to the style change that happened during the late second and early third centuries A.D. The column's undoubted imperial credentials and its prominent public location in the capital naturally gave it great authority as an artistic barometer of Roman art. "To understand the Column of Marcus Aurelius," in the opinion of Massimo Pallottino, "is to understand an entire phase of Roman art."[3] This phase was clearly one of change. Max Wegner, one of the keenest observers of the column's style, believed that the artistic style change that occurred in Rome in the second century A.D. was as important as that which occurred in Greece in the fifth century B.C.[4] The Column of Marcus Aurelius was, in Wegner's opinion, the prime example of this change. There has been much speculation as to why this change occurred (see later in this chapter). Did the appearance of the new style perhaps coincide with a change in the mentality of the Romans who created it? And can special meaning be read from specific elements of it? For example, did the increased employment of the compositional tool of frontality in imperial representations signify a desire on the part of the emperor to be seen in a new light?

The goal of this chapter is deliberately restricted. The focus is on the contributions that a genetic approach to the Column of Marcus Aurelius—a study of design and execution—can make toward understanding this period of artistic change and the column's role in it. Perhaps the most important contribution of this method is the clues that it reveals about how this new style (or more accurately, as will become clear, styles) ended up there in the first place. This in turn has implications for how the new style, and the column's role as a bearer of that style, is interpreted.

I begin by examining the problem of identifying exactly what the style of the column's frieze is. The frieze, in fact, is executed in a number of styles, a situation that makes its analysis extremely difficult. In an attempt to deal with this problem, much of the discussion focuses on the degree of stylistic traditionalism versus innovation in the column's frieze. This approach has two goals: to define exactly what is innovative in the carving, and also to try to understand how and why this innovation came about. Two scene types (construction and *adlocutio*) are used to illustrate the range of tradition and innovation that is visible on the column and to show how both traditional and innovative characteristics could coexist within single scenes. A more detailed examination of the most numerous class of scene on the column, battles, then sheds light on the evolution of compositional style within the frieze. The battle scenes appear to rely on few if any prototypes and thus form a perfect test case to study innovative composition. The question of the source of these innovations is then addressed through an attempt to determine where the artists who created the frieze came from. Finally, I attempt to address the question of interpretation and meaning of the style of the column's frieze and suggest that it may be possible to identify some evidence of nonelite perspectives in the art of this most imperial of monuments. The conclusion considers the afterlife of the column's style and examines the direction taken by the *Stilwandel* after the column was complete.

Defining the Column's Artistic Style

One scholar's concept of style often is not the same as another's. In the case of the Column of Marcus Aurelius, style for some refers specifically to the manner in which figures are carved; others take it as encompassing everything from carving style to the arrangement of scenes. Some even include consideration of iconographic content—for example, the number of times a particular category of subject matter appears. Even when dealing with only one of these individual criteria, not all scholars agree on what exactly defines the *new* style. For example, is the new figural style characterized by short, squat human figures, or tall, thin ones?

In the following, I consider three distinct aspects of style: figural style (the form and proportions of bodies), carving style (how the artist shaped the surface of the stone, especially in his treatment of bodies and clothing), and compositional style (the way in which figures and other objects are arranged into whole scenes). The most detailed and most widely followed definition of the column's figural style was formulated in the 1930s by Max Wegner.[5] He defined the style of the column's carving as "baroque," as painterly rather than sculptural. The column's carvers placed great emphasis on the play of shadows in the deep drill cuts and figural modeling; they carved twisting and turning figures in an attempt to express motion and power. Wegner found the bodies of the figures on the Column of Marcus Aurelius more "sculpted" than those of Trajan's Column. By this he meant not only that they are in much higher relief, but also that the bare flesh, even when seen underneath clothing, was rendered in a more "living" manner. The carvers were particularly fond of modeling folds, hair, and beards, making free use of the drill. The figures themselves stand out boldly from the background, and all levels of depth are used at once—figures in the background may exist as little more than outlines on the marble, while those in the foreground are almost entirely three-dimensional. All this gives the figures in the frieze of the Column of Marcus Aurelius a powerful sense of vigor: while the figures on Trajan's Column seem to dawdle, those on the Marcus column give the impression of a "hurrying river."

Wegner's definition of the Marcus column's style was based on extensive, side-by-side comparison with Trajan's Column. Because his focus was so firmly oriented on this direct comparison, Wegner did not fully take into account developments in art in the period between the two monuments. This lacuna has been filled by Helmut Jung's recent discussion of what he terms the "prehistory" of the *Stilwandel*, in which he traces the development of artistic style in second-century sarcophagus reliefs. Sarcophagi, with their long rectangular front faces carved in deep relief between clear upper and lower borders, offer close physical parallels to the form of the relief carved on Marcus's Column. By comparing sarcophagi from different decades of the second century, Jung was able to trace the development of the new style that eventually appears on the column, and in doing so, he provided a precise definition of what exactly was new—that is, what characteristics exactly define the style change. In the case of figural style, it is slimmer figures, excessively long proportions, and a great interest in displaying contrast between light and shadow.[6]

The other aspect of the column's style, and the one that more often dominates modern discussions of this aspect of the frieze, is compositional style: the way in which the individual figures and other objects in the frieze are assembled to create scenes. The most important characteristics of this aspect of the Antonine style change were defined by Rodenwaldt, especially in his 1940 study of private reliefs: frontality (the arrangement of figures so that they look directly out from the carving), centralized composition (where the most important figures are placed in the middle), and the scaling of figures based on their relative importance (that is, the more important figures appear larger than the less important).[7]

All these characteristics have since been identified in the relief of the Column of Marcus Aurelius (although in some cases, especially that of frontality, there has been debate). And other features have been added to Rodenwaldt's list of characteristics of the new style. One is the tendency to crowd figures together, especially at the expense of background. On the Column of Trajan, there is often a wealth of detail in the landscape through which the figures move; on Marcus's Column, the landscape is sometimes entirely omitted from a scene and the figures become the sole focus. Another more recently emphasized characteristic of compositional style is the repetition, often in the very same scene, of figures of the same type. The classic cases are two of the marching scenes in the upper part of the frieze, LXVII and LXXVIII (fig. 8.1), which consist of overlapping rows of almost-identical figures. Together, these characteristics of carving and composition have come to define the artistic style of the Column of Marcus Aurelius as a whole.

Tradition and Innovation in Style and Composition

None of the characteristics discussed above apply evenly across the whole frieze. The innovative carving and compositional styles identified by Wegner, Jung, and Rodenwaldt all have exceptions. And, more important, they also coexist on the column with more traditional styles. For example, while many of the column's figures show the long, slim proportions pinpointed by Jung as characteristic of the *Stilwandel* (e.g., CIV, fig. 6.2), there are also scenes that employ stout figures of more traditional proportions (in

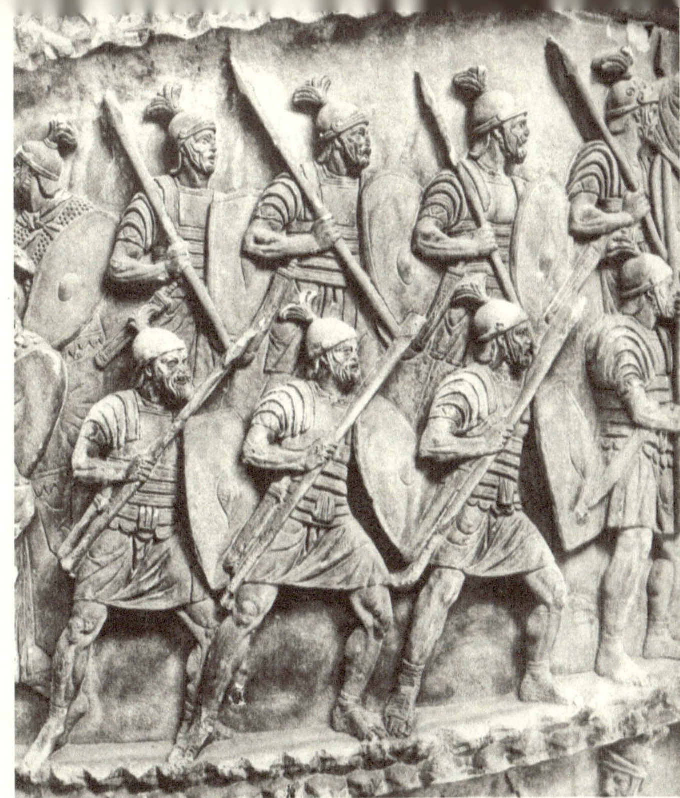

(above) FIGURE 8.1. Scene LXXVIII, showing a marching scene composed of repeated overlapping figures of the same type. From Petersen et al. 1896, pl.76A.

(below) FIGURE 8.2. Scene XXX, a marching scene executed using a variety of figure poses. From Petersen et al. 1896, pl. 38B.

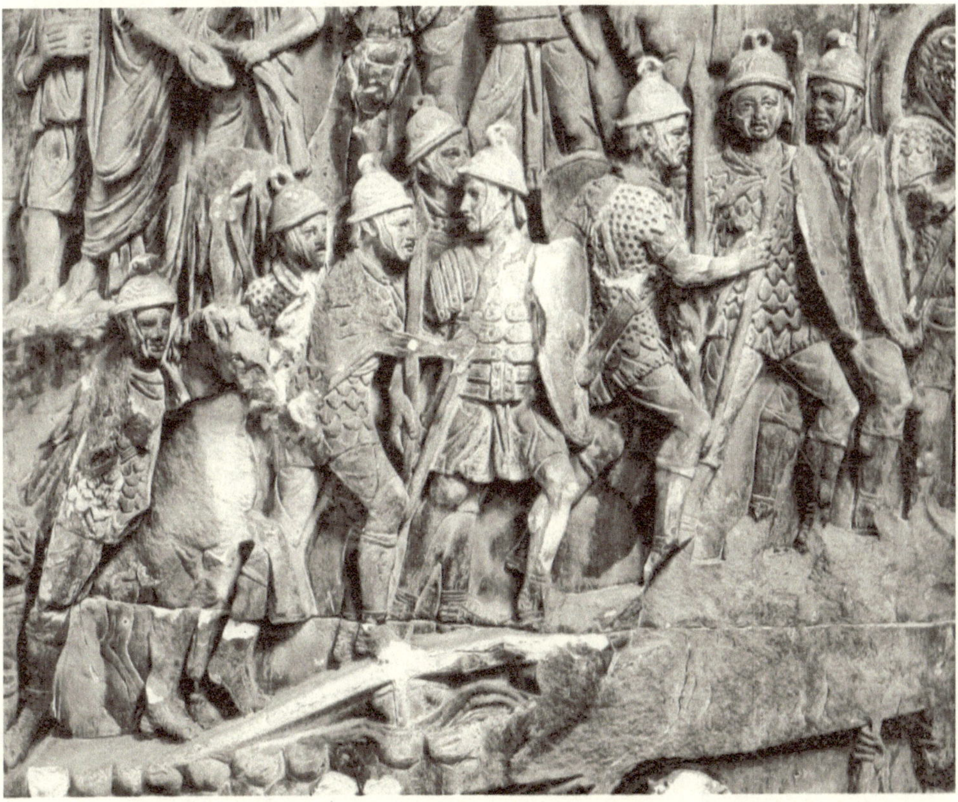

LXXXII, fig. 8.3, for example).[8] When it comes to composition, while some march scenes are composed using the technique of repeating a single figure type (fig. 8.1), others (e.g., XXX, fig. 8.2) show figures in a variety of different poses, with their heads turned at various angles as if they were chatting with each other. This is reminiscent of march scenes on Trajan's Column and even of the turned heads of some figures on the processional frieze of the Ara Pacis. There is often a striking contrast between scenes whose style appears traditional in nature (that is, closer to the classical), and other scenes that embody the characteristics of the *Stilwandel*.

Nor do traditional styles of carving necessarily go hand in hand with traditional styles of composition, and vice versa for the innovative styles. In some cases both the style of the figures and the style of the overall composition have a traditional appearance. Such cases are admittedly rare, but two of the three scenes on the column that show Roman soldiers at work, LXXXII (fig. 8.3) and XCIV, fit this category. They show soldiers in profile or three-quarter view wielding tools, carrying logs, and lifting blocks of stone or turf. The soldiers interact logically with one another, and they are all shown wearing segmented armor—the armor traditionally identified as the prerogative of legionary soldiers (but on this see chapter 7), and the only type of armor worn by soldiers engaged in construction activities on Trajan's Column. What is more, these soldiers wear either short beards or none at all, in vivid contrast to many other depictions of soldiers on Marcus's Column who are often shown with long beards. But short or no beards are the norm on Trajan's Column. In fact, these Marcus column construction scenes would be very much at home on that earlier monument were it not for one detail: there is no clear, logical interaction between the figures and the (very sketchy) background. Not only are landscape elements largely absent, but there is not even any clear indication of what sort of structure Marcus's soldiers might be engaged in building. It seems likely that the figures in these scenes have been lifted bodily from an unknown and presumably earlier model and then placed down in the frieze of Marcus's Column, but without their original background.[9]

In comparison to these traditional-looking construction scenes, the small vignette of three adze-wielding soldiers at the right side of XCVIII (fig. 8.4, the only other work scene on the column) is distinctly novel in both carving and compositional style. Two of the figures are clad in scale armor, one in mail; all wear helmets. They work with vigor not apparent in the two construction scenes and are depicted in energetic, twisted poses; one is shown entirely from behind. This scene has almost no connection

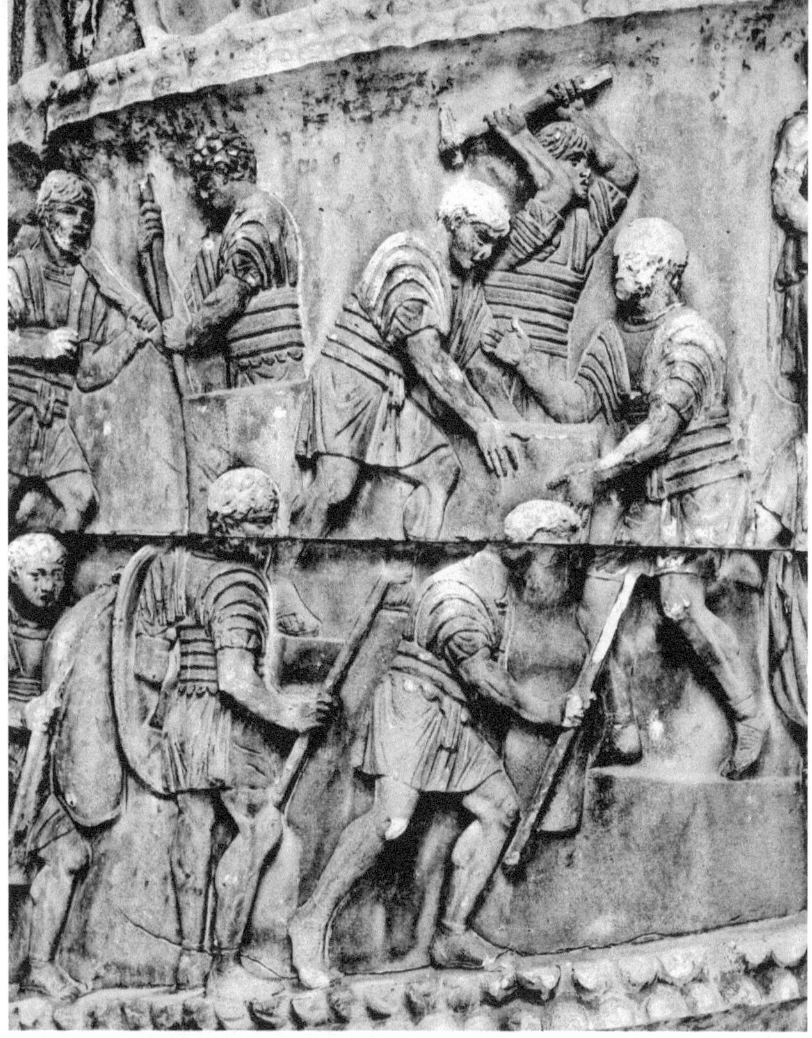

FIGURE 8.3. Scene LXXXII, a construction scene involving soldiers wearing segmented armor. From Petersen et al. 1896, pl. 93B.

to the traditional type of work scene found on Trajan's Column. Instead it brings to mind the convoluted, involved figures seen on second- and third-century sarcophagi, especially those showing scenes of battle.

The combination of traditional compositions with nontraditional figures also occurs, though it is uncommon. The column's *adlocutio* scenes are a good example. The *adlocutio* was a formal address by the emperor to his troops, delivered from atop a platform. On the Column of Trajan, a limited number of solutions were employed to depict these scenes: soldiers were arrayed on one side of the platform, or they were depicted partly or entirely wrapping around the front of the podium in a horseshoe format. On the Column of Marcus Aurelius, most of these scenes echo the same

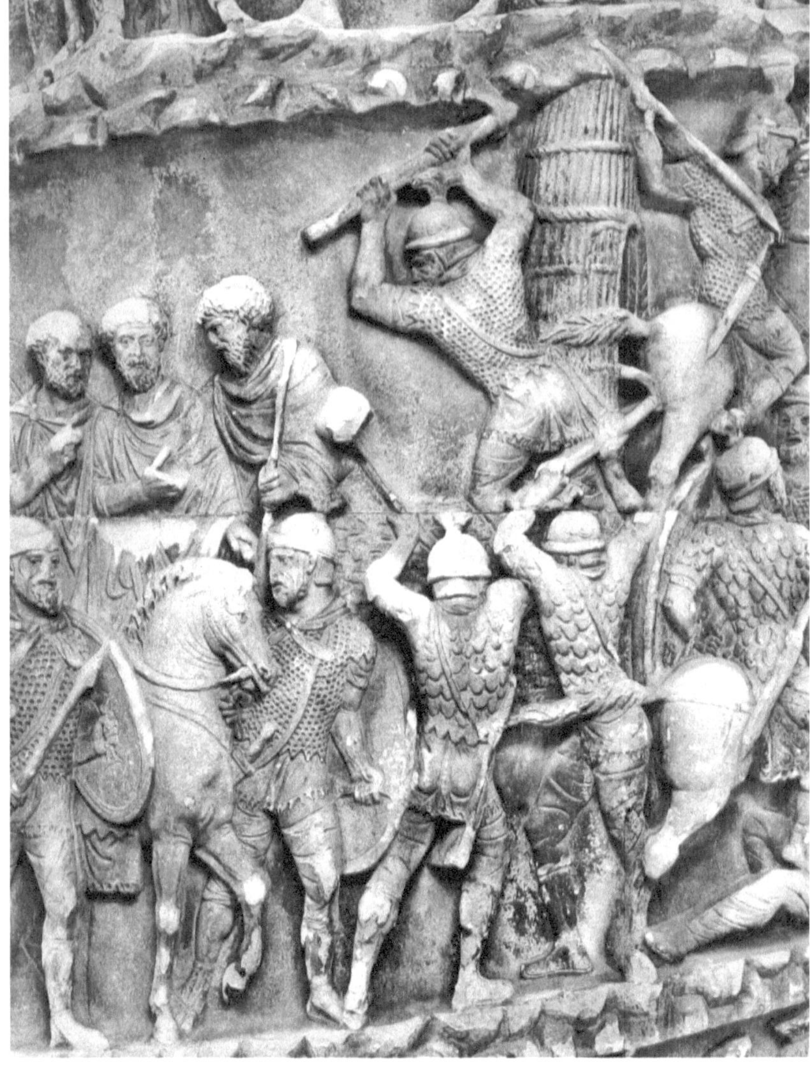

FIGURE 8.4. Scene XCVIII, showing three Roman soldiers working. From Petersen et al. 1896, pl. 107A.

variety of compositions employed on the Column of Trajan. Thus, it can be said that they are composed in a more or less traditional style. Consider scene C (fig. 8.5): the emperor stands on a platform together with two other men, each of whom turn their heads toward him. Marcus himself looks and gestures toward the assembled soldiers gathered in the right half of the scene. Although a smaller group than is typical of *adlocutio* scenes on the Column of Trajan, the soldiers are arranged on multiple overlapping planes, with the heads of those in the background rising above those in the foreground. Their poses are lively and varied; most gaze at their emperor, but

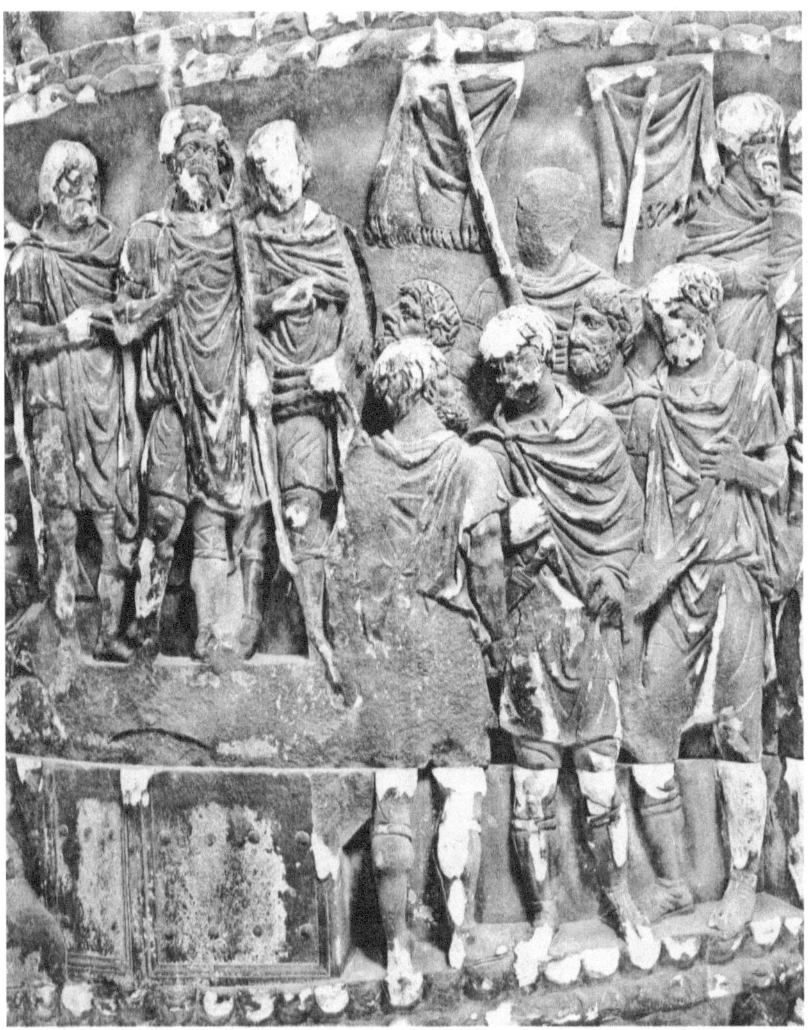

FIGURE 8.5. Scene C, an *adlocutio* in the traditional compositional style. From Petersen et al. 1896, pl. 109A.

two in the left foreground turn toward each other. None of this would be out of place on the Column of Trajan. The style of figure carving, however, is another matter. The bodies of the soldiers in the audience are remarkably elongated; they are taller, in fact, than the emperor atop the platform. The details of figure carving show great emphasis on creating volume and a dramatic contrast between light and shadow. Facial features and the folds of clothing are deeply and roundly carved, as is the fluttering cloth of the two

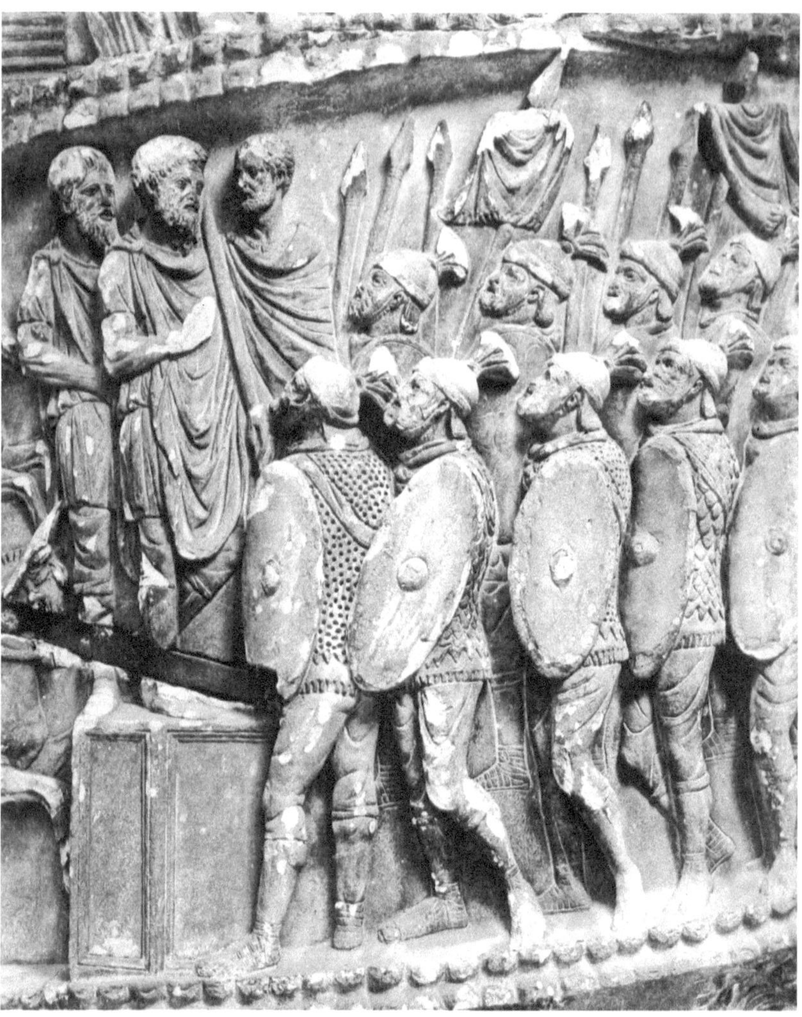

FIGURE 8.6. Scene XCVI, an *adlocutio* showing a combination of traditional and innovative styles. From Petersen et al. 1896, pl. 104B.

vexilla, or standards, that the soldiers hold. This is a very traditional scene from the point of view of compositional style, but one populated by figures carved with the innovative style characteristic of the *Stilwandel*.

The *adlocutio* in scene XCVI (fig. 8.6) shows a more complex combination of traditional and innovative styles. The emperor and his two companions are depicted in much the same way as in scene C (fig. 8.5), but their audience is a very different matter. Instead of natural poses and varied planes, there are two rows of soldiers, the one in the foreground overlapping the one in the background, every single man with their eyes fixed on the emperor. The two static rows of soldiers remind the viewer of the repetitious type of march scenes, LXVII or LXXVIII, except that here the soldiers are standing still in front of a podium. The style of carving is also nontraditional, though in not exactly the same way as in C. The bodies are elongated, but in a less naturalistic manner, with shorter legs relative to torsos and, in the front rank at least, with broad shoulders and very squat necks. Overall these figures are less three-dimensional, and this impression extends to the details: clothing, armor, and equipment tend to be indicated with incised lines rather than drill work or deep, plastic carving. This scene does have some traditional aspects: the overall layout, with the emperor atop a podium and the soldiers arrayed to one side, is common on Trajan's Column; however, the composition of the audience and the overall style of figural carving are both new.

There are likely two reasons why no *adlocutio* scene on the Column of Marcus Aurelius is entirely novel in its composition. The first is that the general ceremony of *adlocutio* did not vary greatly in reality—the emperor stood atop a platform in front of or surrounded by his soldiers—and had not changed over time; thus its depiction in art was similarly restricted to a few basic forms of composition. The second is that there were many clear and easily available models for this type of scene that the column's designers could draw on.

Innovation in Action: The Battle Scenes

While the later *adlocutio* scenes retain many traditional traits in their compositional style, other types of scene are much more innovative. The best example is the battle scenes. Numbering thirty in all, battles are the most numerous scene type on the Column of Marcus Aurelius, and their composition is the most varied of all scene types.[10] From the point of view of overall compositional style, these scenes clearly did not rely on traditional models of battle art. Instead, they show strong evidence of having been created specifically for the column.

Battle scenes were a common theme in classical and Hellenistic art and were frequently depicted in relief sculpture and vase painting. The unifying factor in almost all Greek battle depictions was that they were assembled by grouping together a number of individual, one-on-one encounters.[11] These scenes did not show armies clashing, but rather a collection of single combats; needless to say, this contrasts sharply with how battles actually happened.[12] Exceptions of course existed. Some vase paintings show ranked Greek hoplite soldiers, and the Alexander Mosaic from the House of the Faun in Pompeii, generally accepted as a copy of a Hellenistic painting, depicts a highly realistic battle seen from the eye-level viewpoint of an imaginary viewer.[13] The combatants are massed in groups with the figures overlapping and receding into the distance, and relatively few of the soldiers are actually shown fighting. The focus of the action is on Alexander, mounted at left, and Darius, fleeing in his chariot at right. Adding to the sense of realism is the fact that all soldiers are wearing clothing and armor (battle scenes of the period more normally employ heroic nudity). The composition of the Alexander Mosaic is absolutely unlike that of any earlier surviving battle scene of the period, a factor that is one of the most important arguments for it being a copy of a lost painted masterpiece.

The battle scenes on the Column of Trajan share some important characteristics with the Alexander Mosaic. Almost all of them are composed on the basis of two opposing groups of soldiers depicted in massed and orderly ranks, a rare technique employed to produce a realistic effect. This method of composition is so uncommon that it is impossible to trace the development of the battle scenes of Trajan's Column from any of the works of ancient battle art that survive today.[14] It is highly unlikely that a brand-new, highly complex and varied compositional style was invented just for the frieze of the Column of Trajan. The most reasonable conclusion is that the battle scenes of the column were an adaptation in stone of similar art in another medium that has not survived: painting, and in particular the paintings that were carried in Trajan's triumphal processions (see chapter 7 for a discussion of the tradition of Roman historical painting).[15] Although Trajan almost certainly exhibited paintings in his triumphs, nothing proves that they were the models for the frieze of his column. However, there is a very strong circumstantial argument: the content of much of the frieze, the battle scenes included, is entirely novel. This raises the fundamental question of why no parallels can be found in relief sculpture for so many of the scenes on Trajan's Column. The answer, well expressed by Gerhard Koeppel (see chapter 7), lies in the ultimate derivation of the scenes.[16] Literary references to large-scale battle paintings make clear that an entire genre of Roman battle art existed, of which we have no surviving examples. The Column of Trajan provides a glimpse of this genre, just as the Alexander Mosaic illuminates the lost masterpieces of Hellenistic painting. Not every battle scene fits this criterion of novelty (scenes CXII and CLI, for example, have clear parallels in classical and Hellenistic sculp-

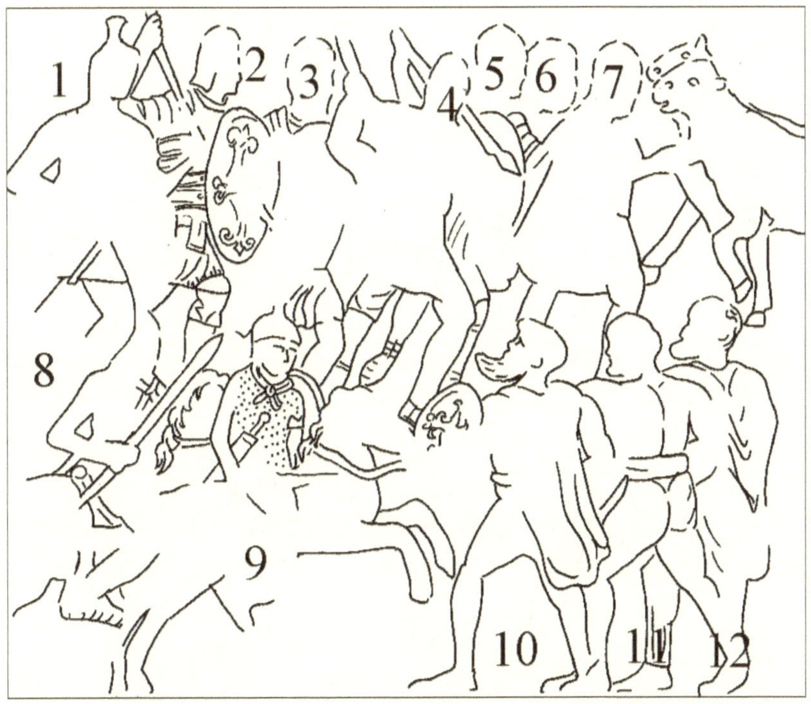

FIGURE 8.7. Scene XIX, a battle between ranked forces. Drawing by author.

ture), but most do, and this strongly suggests that these scenes are derived from painted originals.

The battle scenes on the Column of Marcus Aurelius are very different. The first and perhaps most important difference is that while some Marcus column battle scenes show engagements between solid formations of troops, many others show battles made up of clusters of one-on-one encounters. These represent two distinctly different approaches to scene composition. Battle scene XIX (fig. 8.7) is a good example from early on in the frieze of a clash between solid formations. Figures 1 through 5[17] are Roman soldiers wearing segmented armor, three of whom (2, 4, and 5) brandish their spears against the row of barbarians (figures 10 through 12) at the lower right. Figures 6 and 7 are apparently not part of the battle line, but are attending to the oxen at right, which are pulling a cart holding a captured barbarian couple. Figures 8 and 9, both Roman cavalrymen wearing ring mail, are advancing to attack the solid line of barbarians who face their Roman adversaries shoulder to shoulder. The composition is simple, and one has the impression that battle is about to be joined.

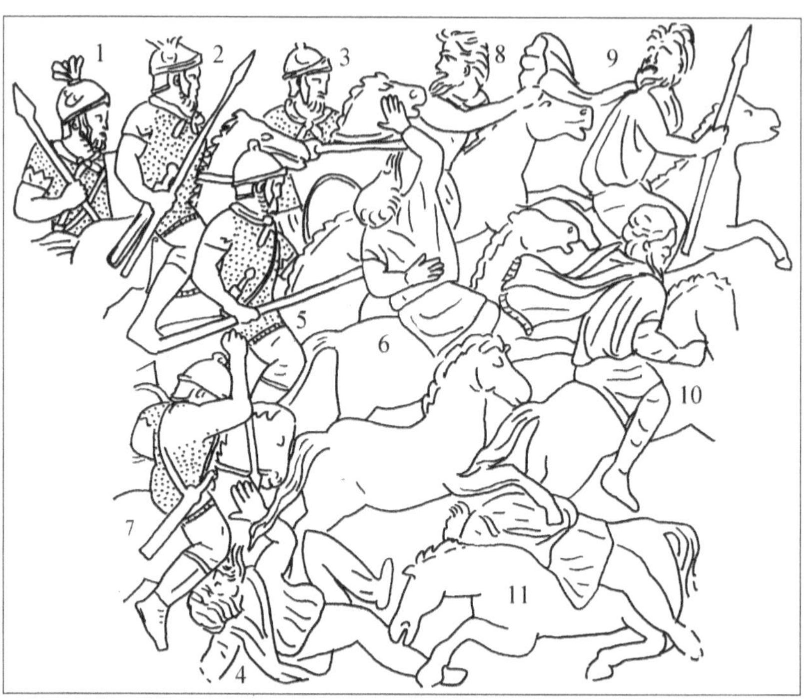

FIGURE 8.8. Scene XCII, a battle showing massed formations. Drawing by author.

Scene XCII (fig. 8.8) is reminiscent of battle XIX, in that clear and solid formations dominate, but here the formations are shown as dense masses rather than linear ranks. The front line of the Roman force is formed by figures 3, 5, and 7, each of whom employs his spear against a barbarian adversary. Roman 7 raises his spear over barbarian 4, who has fallen from his horse (shown galloping off to the right); 5 has already lodged his spear in the back of 6, who rears back and gestures upward; and 3 appears just about to make contact with 8, who looks behind at his attacker. Barbarians 9 and 10 are already in flight, while in the lower right another barbarian (11) falls along with his mount beneath the hooves of his fleeing comrades. The face-up position of barbarian 11 is awkward and can only be explained if he was sitting backward on his horse. Barbarian 9 is the only one shown with a weapon in his hand. The combatants resolve into three registers, and the figures in the first two are all connected to each other by the use of careful interweaving. The four figures in the lowest register form, together with the riderless horse, a nearly circular pattern.

In stark contrast, battle scene XXIV (fig. 8.9) can only be described as chaotic. Here a group of Roman infantry is engaged in combat with a group

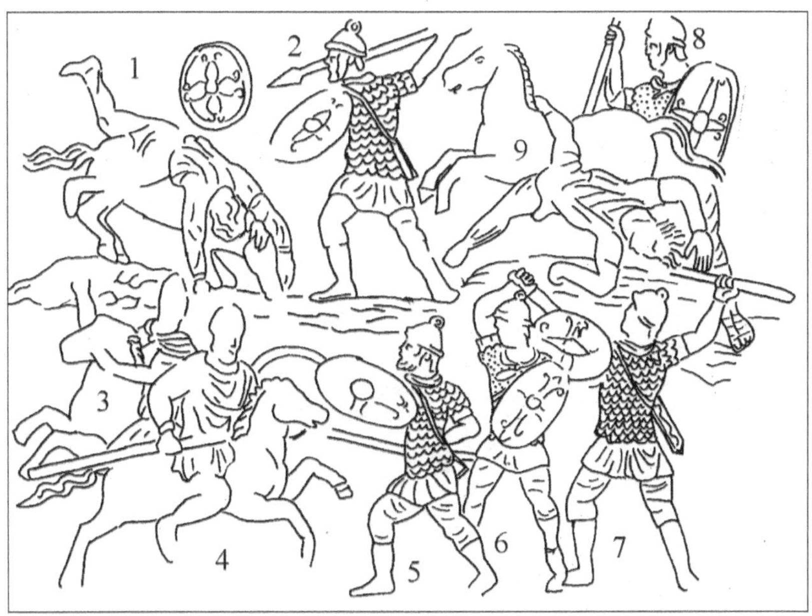

FIGURE 8.9. Scene XXIV, a chaotic and illogical battle between pairs of combatants. Drawing by author.

of barbarian cavalry. The widely spaced figures are arrayed on two registers, the upper one defined by an artificial ground line reminiscent of the relief on the base of the Column of Antoninus Pius. At the upper left, a barbarian (1) careens headlong over the neck of his falling horse, while his shield flies up into the air. Roman 2 is apparently attacking him, advancing with his spear raised. Below, a cloaked barbarian (figure 3) gallops off to the left while gesturing with his right hand. In front of him, another similarly clad comrade (4) advances on a Roman (5) with spear and shield at the ready. Behind Roman 5 stands another Roman with his sword raised above his head; the purpose of this gesture is not apparent. Behind him another Roman (7) makes a menacing gesture with his spear; this is perhaps, but by no means certainly, aimed at falling barbarian 9, above. Barbarian 9 has tumbled right off his mount's back, with only one leg left draped over the neck of the horse, behind which a Roman soldier (8) spears downward. Questions abound: Why is figure 8's spear behind the horse? Why is Roman 2 gesturing with his spear when barbarian 1 has already fallen from his mount? And what enemies are Romans 6 and 7 supposed to be attacking?

Scene LXIII (fig. 8.10) is composed using yet another method. It is formed almost exclusively of fighting pairs and is divided into two registers

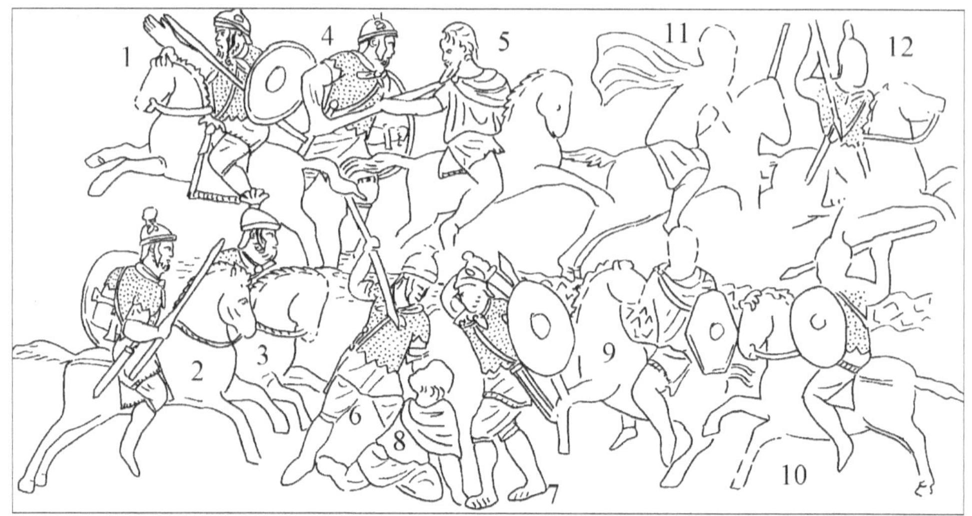

FIGURE 8.10. Scene LXIII, a chaotic but highly symmetrical battle scene. Drawing by author.

much as scene XXIV; however, instead of the chaos of XXIV, there is a very careful and balanced composition. Two Romans, figures 2 and 3, appear to be just riding in from the left, while above them another Roman (figure 1) rides off gesturing. To the right of these figures are two fighting groups: in the foreground, two Roman infantrymen (6 and 7) attack a fallen barbarian with spear and sword; above them, a Roman infantryman (4) spears a fleeing barbarian (5). Further to the right in the foreground is another fighting pair composed of a Roman cavalryman (10) who chases a shield-bearing barbarian (9). Above and behind this pair are two mounted figures, a barbarian (11) riding to the right and a Roman (12) riding in front of him in the same direction, with spear raised as if to stab an opponent. What is most remarkable about this scene is that it is very difficult, if not impossible, to discern any coherent, unified action on the part of the combatants. Romans and barbarians ride to and fro, sometimes fighting, sometimes not. It is essentially impossible to grasp any solid narrative of events in this battle. But the overwhelming sense is not one of chaos; instead, the division into two registers helps spread the figures clearly over the field and serves to unite what otherwise would be a confusingly uncoordinated composition. The lower register has a clear focus toward the triangular central group (figures 6 through 8), which is emphasized by the pairs of riders converging on it from each side. The upper register has an opposite, outward sense of flow, as figures 1, 11, and 12 gallop away from the central scene of Roman 4 stabbing barbarian 5. Logically, it makes little sense, but compositionally the scene has a clear, even pleasing order.

This wide range of compositional styles is not at all similar to what is seen on the Column of Trajan. There, battles are as a rule quite large, with opposing groups often containing between ten and twenty soldiers. Almost all of the battle scenes show clashes between more or less homogeneous formations of Roman and enemy troops, in which both sides are shown fighting more or less fiercely. These groups are not simply massed together face to face but instead are often arrayed in realistic ranks as if viewed from an angle above. The Trajanic battle scenes also frequently incorporate architectural and landscape elements and make sophisticated use of perspective techniques. There is often an attempt to show more than one phase of a single battle in a more or less unified scene: for example, the main clash and the subsequent rout of the enemy. The lack of clear parallels between the battle scenes on the Column of Marcus Aurelius and those on the Column of Trajan suggests not only that direct influence from that monument can be ruled out, but also that the influence of large-scale triumphal painting can (with reservations stemming from our entire lack of preserved originals) be excluded.

Another potential artistic influence for the battle scenes on the Column of Marcus Aurelius was the repertoire of the sarcophagus industry. The second century A.D. saw a massive growth in production of relief-decorated sarcophagi in the city of Rome, connected with a change in burial practice, from cremation to inhumation.[18] These sarcophagi were large marble containers whose main front panel was carved with ornamental decoration or figural scenes from myth or daily life. The scale of production of these sarcophagi is shown by the large number of examples that survive today: about 6,000 dating between the second and fourth centuries.[19] The majority of these sarcophagi are dominated by a small number of artistic themes: there are 700 sarcophagi decorated with Erotes, for example, another 700 with depictions of the Seasons, and about 400 with Dionysiac themes. Scenes of battle are relatively few and usually mythical in origin; the most common are those showing an Amazonomachy, a fight between Greeks and the mythical warrior women, sometimes given a Trojan setting by the inclusion of the figures of Achilles and Penthesilea. These number about sixty. Another twenty show scenes of battle between Greeks and Gauls, and a very few show encounters between figures identifiable by their dress as Romans and Germanic barbarians.[20] Most of these sarcophagi were created by copying a single model (a very common working method in the sarcophagus industry), which may have existed as a painting or a drawing of an unknown archetype.[21] All of the Amazonomachy and Greek-versus-Gaul sarcophagi are composed of specific pairs of fighting figures, repeated from one sarcophagus to the next. In this one respect, they resemble some of the battle scenes on Marcus's Column that also use paired combatants; however, exact parallels are few, and entire compositions are never repeated. While there is some evidence to link the sarcophagus industry as a whole to the column (including a number of specific figure parallels from battle sarcophagi—see below), there is no compelling evidence that the content or composition of the column's battle scenes was significantly influenced by the repertoire of battle scenes depicted on sarcophagi.

If the column's carvers did not take cues for their battle scenes from contemporary monuments, whether public or private, then we must consider the main remaining possibility, which is that they created the battle scenes from scratch. This is a difficult theory to prove, but there are some significant clues within the frieze itself that suggest that this was indeed the case. Especially important are the relationships between the scenes: first, there is a clear tendency for scenes that share a common compositional principle to appear close to each other in the frieze; second, there are indications of a development in compositional style within the battle scenes as the frieze progresses.

Ten of the battle scenes on the Column of Marcus Aurelius, all scenes based on clashes between solid formations of troops, show evidence of this sort of evolution in design. These scenes group together in clusters of two or three, each group sharing a particular approach to composition. The first such cluster consists of scenes XV and XIX. Both show linear formations of barbarian infantry actively resisting attack from linear formations of Roman troops. In scene XV two barbarians stand back to back in order to resist an attack by archers from both sides. The barbarians are shown in fighting poses, one particularly aggressive. In scene XIX the barbarian formation maintains a close shoulder-to-shoulder line in the lower right corner of the scene. The Romans attack in two lines, two cavalrymen from the left and five infantrymen from above. Though outnumbered, the barbarians stand their ground and await the attack with raised shields. Both scenes use linear formations that are arranged horizontally along a ground line at the bottom of the frieze or in its middle. A hint of perspective is given by the overlapping of figures, but the overall effect is static.

The next cluster consists of scenes XXIII and XXXIX. They each share the common component of a group of three barbarian riders in a stacked, overlapping formation fleeing from a massed force of Romans arrayed in line. Scene XXIII consists effectively of two separate encounters: to the left, three Romans on two superimposed registers attack a group of barbarians, some of whom have fallen to the ground and some of whom flee on horseback. The right half of the scene is organized in a similar manner, but with more orderly formations of troops. Two lines of Roman and allied soldiers attack a line of three barbarian horsemen who flee. Scene XXXIX employs a nearly identical method of composition, though with attackers and fugitives on different sides of the scene. At the left, two lines of Roman troops and barbarian allies in superimposed registers attack a vertical line of barbarian cavalrymen who flee to the right. In both scenes, one of the fleeing barbarians extends his arm back in a pleading gesture.

Scenes L, LII, and LXXII employ a different and more complex compositional technique. The main battle in scene L occurs at the far right, where four Romans attack a group of barbarians, all but one of whom have already fallen. The Romans are arrayed in a staggered line and engage the barbarians on their front; the Roman line hooks around their enemies at the top of the scene. Scene LII is composed in a similar manner. There, a group of Romans on horseback attacks a pair of barbarians, only one of whom still resists. The barbarians are physically enclosed by the Roman formation, which hooks around the top of the scene; one Roman even attacks his enemy from the rear, seemingly having completed the envelopment. In scene LXXII four Romans attack a group of barbarians from the left and from above; both the composition and even many of the fighting figures in this scene are nearly identical to those in scene LII and L.

Finally, a group of three scenes (XCII, XCVII, CV) shares the compositional theme of a group of barbarian cavalry fleeing to the right, pursued by a group of Romans who inflict casualties upon them. Scene XCII is the most complex of these and shows a dense group of Roman cavalrymen (and perhaps one infantryman) occupying the left part of the field. They attack a massed group of barbarians, also on horseback, who flee to the right. The other two scenes show Roman infantry attacking fleeing barbarian cavalry; they are simpler but are based on the same general compositional principle. In each of these three scenes, two barbarians are shown fallen on the ground. The nature of the pursuing Roman troops varies (infantry in two cases, cavalry in one), but this does not appear to have any particular effect on the way in which the two groups interact: the Romans advance and attack with their spears, while the barbarians flee, are speared, and fall to the ground (see chapter 7 for a discussion of the realism of these scenes).

A pattern emerges if these scenes are ordered in the sequence in which they appear on the column. First, battles using the same compositional technique tend to be located close to each other on the column. Moreover, the use of such techniques follows a sequence. One technique appears, is used for two or three scenes, and then drops out of use, to be replaced sooner or later by another. The sequence proceeds from simple, linear formations lower on the column to more complex arrangements higher up. This may be evidence of a learning process at work, perhaps combined with a conscious decision to avoid excessive repetition when composing the battle scenes. The artists responsible for these scenes did not draw on earlier prototypes or learned tradition (more on this below); instead, they produced original compositions created specifically for the Column of Marcus Aurelius. The next question is who were these artists?

The Source of the Column's Style

The style of a carving comes into existence through the actions of its carver—or, in the case of the Column of Marcus Aurelius, carvers. At least forty or fifty individuals were engaged in carving the column's frieze (see chapter 6), although not all need have been involved in carving the figures. Who were these men? Were they already living and working in Rome, or were they brought to the capital from somewhere else? In the absence of written records the only way to determine the origin of the craftsmen who carved the column is to look for parallels between the frieze and other examples of relief carving of the period. If similar stylistic traits can be identified on both the column and another genre of relief carving—especially if this other carving is earlier in date—this might suggest where the column's carvers came from.

There are no clear connections between the column's frieze and the only major work of historical relief from the reign of Marcus Aurelius: the so-called Panel Reliefs. These large, rectangular reliefs presumably adorned a triumphal arch set up in honor of Marcus after his triumph in the year 176; eight were reused to decorate the Arch of Constantine; three more found their way into the Capitoline Museums.[22] Naturally enough there are some general connections in theme, but almost every stylistic aspect of the Panel Reliefs is different from what is seen on the column. Although Marcus Aurelius is always the center of attention, he never appears exactly in the middle of the compositions. Instead, his central importance is indicated in the same manner as used for Trajan on his column—other figures in the scene turn their faces toward the emperor. Nor does Marcus ever look directly out from the relief; there is no frontality. Also strikingly different is the constant use of background, whether trees or buildings, to give the human figures a firm setting. And most important, the figure style of the Panel Reliefs is classical, and the thin, elongated proportions characteristic of the *Stilwandel* are never seen. This is strong evidence that the column's carvers were not drawn from the ranks of the men who created the Panel Reliefs.

But there are numerous parallels to be found in another major body of contemporary relief carving: private sarcophagi. The most striking link between the sarcophagi and the column is one of figural style. Some sarcophagi exhibit such close parallels with the carving of certain figures on the Column of Marcus Aurelius that Gerhard Rodenwaldt and Giovanni Becatti both suggested that it might be possible to find the "hand" of one of these sarcophagus carvers on the column itself.[23] The similarities in style are sometimes striking indeed, but no one has as yet succeeded in identifying a common hand and thus making a definite connection between column and sarcophagi. Even the sarcophagi that seem most similar to the column turn out, when inspected in detail, not to be the work of the same hands.[24] The fact that such a direct connection has not been found should not surprise, for even in the field of sarcophagus study itself it is almost never possible to identify common hands on different sarcophagi. As a result sarcophagi are not grouped by artist, but rather in broader stylistic assemblages called "workshops," with this term left loosely defined at best.[25] But more than just stylistic similarity connects the column's carvers and the sarcophagus industry. First, some of the Marcus column's more peculiar iconographic details have notable parallels in sarcophagus decoration: for example, the trophies flanking the Victoria figure. On Trajan's Column, both trophies wear helmets of a distinctly non-Roman form. On the Column of Marcus Aurelius, on the other hand, the left-hand trophy wears a fur cap and the right-hand trophy a Roman-style helmet with full facial mask. Both of these features appear commonly on sarcophagi in the second and early third century A.D., suggesting that the Marcus column's carvers ignored the detail of their model (Trajan's Column) and instead took inspiration from sarcophagi.[26] The Marcus column scenes with boats are also exceptional. While the warships and transports on Trajan's Column are executed in realistic detail (though with little attention to scale), those on the Marcus column are often ludicrously rendered. The worst offender is scene XXXIV (fig. 8.11), where ships transporting Roman soldiers across

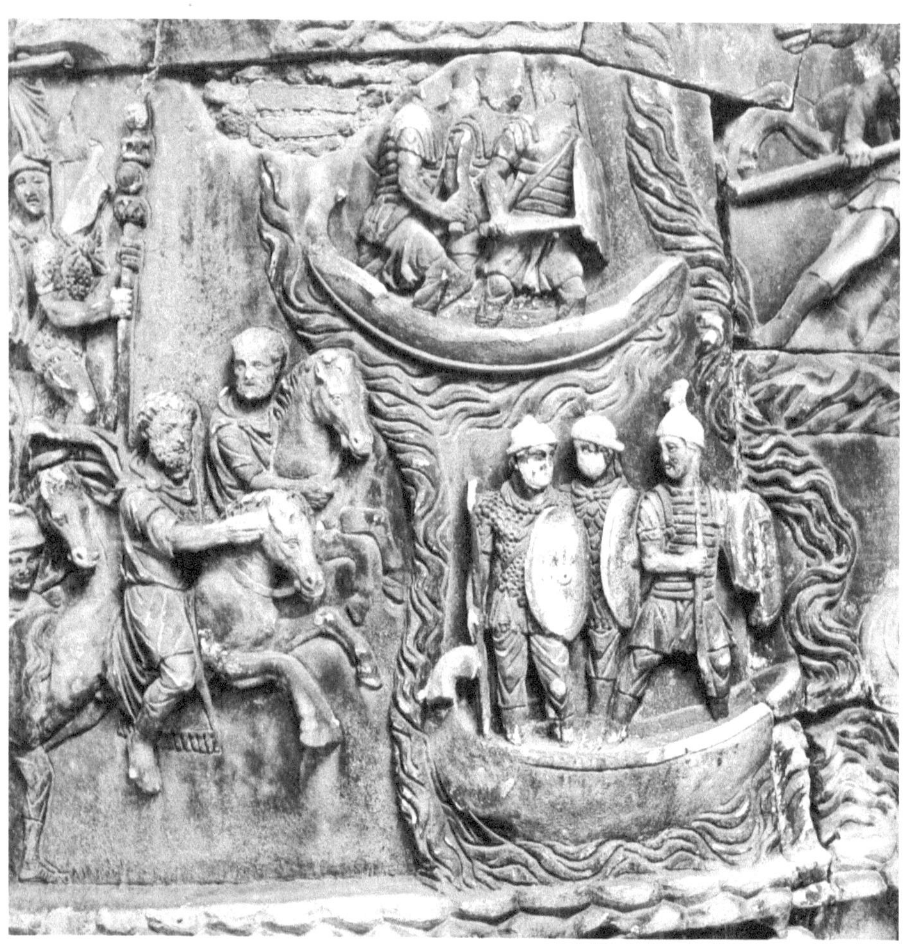

FIGURE 8.11. Scene XXXIV, showing Roman soldiers crossing a river on boats. From Petersen et al. 1896, pl. 41A.

a river look more like gravy boats; scene LXXXI renders the boat more successfully, but the passengers adopt comically un-nautical attitudes. Proper oared warships are never shown, though they would have played a role in campaigns along the Danube. Parallels for such unrealistic vessels can be found in sarcophagi depicting Erotes, where dumpy ships are crewed by cavorting passengers.[27] A more restricted but still compelling parallel involves the head of the Rain God in scene XVI, which is closely paralleled in sarcophagus depictions of Oceanus. These show the god's face in the center of the sarcophagus's front panel, with flowing hair and beard forming a stream of water that feeds a sea beneath.[28]

There are also a number specific parallels between the figural repertoire of the column's carvers and that of the men employed in the sarcophagus industry. The first is in the pose of the two very similar barbarian swordsmen from scenes LII and LVII, who hold round shields as they fight with an approaching Roman horseman. This figure is common on Amazon and Achilles sarcophagi and is very closely paralleled on two Amazon sarcophagi, where not only is a very similar pose used for the swordsman, but he is also paired with a very similar mounted attacker.[29] Even more informative is the common figure of a Roman or barbarian swordsman with sword raised behind the head (e.g., fig. 7.5). On the column this figure is (with only one exception) shown facing left.[30] This same figure type, also facing left, is frequently found on Amazonomachy, Meleager, and Herakles-themed sarcophagi.[31] Another Marcus column figure type with parallels in the sarcophagi is a barbarian lying on his back with his right arm extended back over his head (scenes LXXIX, IC, e.g., fig. 6.5). This type is common on Herakles sarcophagi (where it is used for a defeated Amazon) and on Amazonomachy sarcophagi.[32] A final connection between the column and sarcophagi can be identified in the lone trumpeter in scene IC, a figure seen in Amazonomachy sarcophagi.[33]

Finally, evidence of a connection between sarcophagus carvers and the column can be found in the traces left by the tools used in their creation. Roman stone carvers employed a fairly standard set of tools in their work: a point chisel for the earliest and roughest stage of carving, then toothed chisels, flat chisels, scrapers, and rasps, and in some cases polish as the final stage. On the Column of Trajan traces of a number of these tools can be found: for example, the marks of flat chisels that were commonly used on the background and on features such as hair and beards, and rasps that were used to give a smooth finish to human flesh. The Panel Reliefs of Marcus Aurelius also preserve evidence of varied tool marks, including extensive use of polish to give a very smooth surface to both human flesh and certain flat inanimate objects.[34] Antonine sarcophagi tend to have either a mixed rough and polished or an entirely rough (that is, rasped) finish.[35] On the Column of Marcus Aurelius, all surfaces appear slightly rough, finished with the scraper or rasp.[36] This tool use is consistent with that found on sarcophagi, but not with the technique employed on the Panel Reliefs.

The parallels between sarcophagi and column, though not many, are quite close and speak strongly for a connection between the artists involved in creating each. A connection between the column's carvers and the Roman sarcophagus industry is valuable because it give us a good idea of what kind of artists the men who worked on the column were. They were trained from youth in workshops dedicated to carving sarcophagi, which meant that they worked for years on end at the task of repeating a relatively small number of more or less standard compositions dominated by mythological themes. It is difficult to say exactly how much of the repetitiveness of sarcophagus production was due to the carvers themselves or to their patrons, but the frequent finds of sarcophagi with portrait heads left uncarved suggests that the carvers generally carved first and sold their product later. These craftsmen naturally brought their working methods and learned habits with them when they were employed to execute the frieze of the Column of Marcus Aurelius.

It is not likely that these carvers were deliberately chosen because of the style in which they worked, not at least in the way that the artists of the Ara Pacis were probably selected because of their skill in executing relief carving in a classical style.[37] This can be most easily seen by the fact that not all carvers who worked on the Column of Marcus Aurelius produced carving in the same style. Standards of composition and figure carving fluctuate over the frieze as a whole, suggesting that a standardized style was not the goal of the column's designers or of its carvers. This indicates that other factors lay behind the choice of which sculptors to employ. One of the designers' foremost concerns would have been completing the project in a timely manner, and for this to happen, a large number of workers experienced in executing relief carving in marble would have been required. The designers of the column turned to the Roman sarcophagus industry because the carvers employed there were the most easily accessible large pool of skilled figure-carving labor available in the city. When these carvers came to the project, they brought their working methods and their style—or more accurately, styles—with them. And this affected more than merely the style of the carving: it seems to have had influence on the overall layout of the scenes. On the Marcus column, scenes are divided into small, regular units, typically equal to one-eighth of a full winding of the frieze. This tendency to break the frieze into small units may indicate the influence of a designer accustomed to working in discrete units of standard size, which is exactly the sort of canvas that sarcophagus fronts offer.

The employment of a large number of sarcophagus carvers to execute the frieze of the Column of Marcus Aurelius both makes practical sense and explains why so many of the characteristic markers of the Antonine *Stilwandel* appear on the column. It also helps to explain why there is so much variety in the style of the frieze. But above all, the employment of craftsmen whose work had previously been largely confined to the private sphere has two important implications for our understanding of the column's art. The first is that it clarifies the reasons behind the often-striking mixture of traditional and novel aspects of its style. The second is that it provides a sound footing for tentative conclusions to be drawn about the meaning of the new style.

The Column, Art, and Society

Much has been read from—and into—the column's style. Gerhard Rodenwaldt, focusing on frontality and centralized compositions, called the new style visible on the Column of Marcus Aurelius "Italic" and argued that this was "no transition, but rather a prelude to the last phase of ancient art."[38] For Rodenwaldt, the new style was a manifestation of a change in mentality, in how the Romans viewed the world, precipitated by a crisis of confidence and identity in the late second century. Thirty years later, Ranucchio Bianchi Bandinelli interpreted the change in style in a different light. For him the artistic novelty of the Column of Marcus Aurelius was not so much the result of a general change in mentality, but rather was representative of the triumph of one style—what he called "plebeian"—over another, traditional style that he labeled "patrician." Bianchi Bandinelli argued that plebeian art contained many aspects of the Late Antique before they emerged into official art at the time of the death of Marcus Aurelius.[39]

These dichotomies—Italic/classicizing, plebeian/patrician—are the two best-known models that have been advanced to explain the column's remarkable style, but they are not the only ones. Picard argued that it is wrong to identify an "Italic" style in the column's art, and that the style of the frieze of the Column of Marcus Aurelius should instead be traced to a renewed interest in the 160s A.D. in the art of Pergamum, an interest that was also reflected in the popularity of sarcophagus decoration featuring battles of Greeks against Gauls. It was this influence, Picard argued, that combined with artistic influences from the Rhine and Danube provinces to bring about the *Stilwandel* around A.D. 180.[40] Lehmann-Hartleben also argued against the Italic interpretation but saw the true influence as coming not from abroad but from Rome itself, especially from the tradition of triumphal painting. He concluded that the "wonderful baroque/expressive elements of the Column of Marcus Aurelius . . . are a new spiritual achievement of their own time and artists," with its roots partly in the Hellenistic and Flavian artistic traditions.[41] And Becatti simply rejected theories of provincial or oriental influence and economic or social explanations in favor of the view that the style of the frieze of the Column of Marcus Aurelius was the result of a natural progression—in fact, a decline—in Roman art.[42]

More recent attempts to address the column's style generally reject simple dualistic explanations or theories of external (provincial or foreign) artistic influence. Instead, the concept of a deliberate choice made by the designer or commissioner has come to the foreground. Felix Pirson has argued that "the formation of the 'new' style of the Column was due at least partly to the need for more explicit messages."[43] The style of the column's carving was a new creation made up using a number of stylistic elements that already existed in Roman art. In a similar vein, Hölscher argues that the column's style "fundamentally signifies the dissolution of the traditional body-form, with the goal of producing a stronger expressive effect."[44] For both Hölscher and Pirson, style served to make the message of the frieze clearer and easier to understand.

But the conclusions drawn from analysis of the column's genesis—especially the large number of carvers, their origin in the sarcophagus industry, and the great variety in style and composition actually seen on the column—suggest an alternative interpretation. The great variety in style, both of carving and of composition, likely stems not from a deliberate choice by the monument's commissioners (not directly, at least) but rather from the varied background of the many individual carvers employed. These craftsmen were more or less ordinary—and as a few cases of very poor carving show, sometimes substantially less than that. They were not master artists of the caliber of the sculptors responsible for the Panel Reliefs. This applies, however, only to the main helical frieze—the pedestal relief is composed in a different manner, more similar to the Panel Reliefs than to the column frieze, and may have been executed by different craftsmen. The situation may have been similar to that of the carving of the Arch of Septimius Severus, where the style of the main panels and the small "triumphal" frieze is very different from that of the scenes on the column pedestals. This suggests that the style and composition of the Marcus column's frieze were not deliberately chosen by a high authority. Instead, the new style that appeared in some scenes did so of its own accord, because of the craftsmen who were selected to do the work. This in turn suggests that we should understand the frieze of the Column of Marcus Aurelius as being, in effect, a mirror that reflects part (a large part, but not the whole) of one major Roman sculptural industry during the 180s, in all (or at least much of) its variety.

This does not change the basic, fundamental importance of the column as key evidence of the Antonine *Stilwandel*, but it refines our understanding of its role within this process. The Column of Marcus Aurelius did not introduce a new style to imperial art; it might even be possible to say that the art of the column's frieze is not, really, "imperial art" at all. Rather, it is an attempt by artists trained in the private sphere to create a suitable decoration for a public monument. John Clarke has argued with respect to artworks commissioned by nonelite Romans that there was in fact no such thing as a special class of Roman art "that *consciously* went against the grain of Hellenistically inspired imperial art. Instead, when patrons called on artists of ordinary (or less-than-ordinary) skills to create an original representation, the product often failed to look like imperial art."[45] Lack of a model—or the ignorance or unwillingness on the part of the artists to use one—could result in the creation of art that has been variously described as folk, plebeian, or freedman art.

The idea that a work of art could end up having a "nonstandard" appearance if, at the time it was commissioned, it had no established classical model is directly relevant to the interpretation of the carved frieze of the Column of Marcus Aurelius. The analysis here suggests that when the column was created, the task of designing and carving the frieze was assigned to a group of craftsmen who were not experienced in such work. They were given few models (likely restricted to images of a few historical events such as the Rain Miracle), and they drew on Trajan's Column for others (particularly the opening scenes), but for the bulk of the scenes they struck out on their own. Most common of all are scenes where both composition and figure style are new to the genre of imperial "historical" relief. Some (sometimes striking) parallels for the figure style can be found on sarcophagi; parallels for the compositions, however, are nowhere to be found. They do not match compositional techniques used on sarcophagi, on other works of historical relief from Marcus's reign, or in the scenes (derived from painted models) on the Column of Trajan. The implication is that the figural style of most of the Marcus column's scenes came directly from the many carvers engaged on the project, who learned their craft in the workshops of the Roman sarcophagus industry. A small part of their compositional style came from traditional models; most, however, was the result of their own novel creative effort. The result was a frieze filled with scenes of almost-incredible variety: some marches are lively and interesting, others repetitious and monotonous; some battles are arranged from pairs of figures (reminiscent of Greek-versus-Gaul sarcophagi), others are massed encounters evocative of later Roman-versus-barbarian sarcophagus scenes; some *adlocutio* scenes would seem more or less at home on Trajan's Column, others seem to foreshadow the *adlocutiones* on the Arch of Septimius Severus. In working like this, the artists of the Column of Marcus Aurelius did not deliberately seek to break with the tradition of imperial reliefs; in fact, by copying the beginning scenes of Trajan's Column (even down to details of equipment), they showed clear intentions of trying to follow in this tradition. But either they were not capable of continuing this for the entire length of the frieze or they were compelled to adopt a more simplified approach, perhaps in order to speed up the process of carving. The result was a frieze that, when compared to the Column of Trajan, had a distinctly "nonstandard" appearance.

The implications of this alternate viewpoint are well illustrated by one of the most problematic aspects of the style of the Column of Marcus Aurelius: frontality. The occasional appearance of frontality in the column's frieze has been interpreted as stemming from a desire to transmit a message originating from a high authority, perhaps even from the emperor himself.[46] This message could be that the emperor did not have to be directly engaged in events to be victorious—that he could turn his attention away from the events around him, focus on the viewer, and thus display godlike powers.[47] But what if this frontality was not deliberately planned at a relatively early stage in the design process of the frieze but actually came instead from the innate impulses of a small number of the column's artists who, because of the nature of the planning process, were left to execute many scenes without specific models? Most scenes showing the emperor do not depict him in truly frontal poses; if frontality was indeed intended as a message, why does it not occur more often? In this alternate interpretation, the use of frontality can be understood not as a conscious attempt to go against the classical/Hellenistic tradition of imperial art, but instead as the result of a trend among a small number of the column's carvers to produce images that deviated from the traditional format. If this was indeed the case, then frontality may be read as evidence of the personal attitude of some individual artists toward their emperor. These men, left on their own to design a proper scene, decided to depict the emperor in a pose looking out from the relief, detached from events. Only small changes to a traditional *adlocutio* scene would be required to achieve this effect: a slight shift of the body of the emperor, a turn of his head. Seen in this light, frontality may well reflect the intense, personal concept on the part of some artists of the time of the sanctity of the emperor, and as such would constitute rare evidence of the personal attitudes of nonelite craftsmen toward their ruler.

Conclusion: The Afterlife of the Column's Style

The Column of Marcus Aurelius was a large canvas on which many artists worked. Some were influenced by a new style moving through the sarcophagus workshops of Rome, while others adhered to a more traditional approach to carving. The result was a relief that exhibits many different styles, both in figure carving and in composition. We must be cautious when interpreting these novelties of style, especially when asking the question of whether they represent a major new impetus in the overall direction of Roman art. Elongated body forms, one of the most important characteristics of the new figural carving style identified by Jung in his study of the "prehistory" of the *Stilwandel*, continue to appear on Roman sarcophagi into the early third century. But they are absent from the next major work of imperial state art: the Arch of Septimius Severus. The arch was built in the first decade of the third century to honor Severus for his successful military exploits in Parthia.[48] The most important battles of the campaigns are depicted there in four large relief panels, and a victorious procession (not a triumph, which Severus did not accept) is shown in a smaller frieze that circles the arch just below the attic. In both the great panels and the smaller frieze, short squat figures predominate. The reliefs on the pedestals at the base of the arch's columns, on the other hand, are in lower relief and a much more traditional style, with classically posed bodies and barbarians whose faces show emotion in a Hellenistic manner. There is no sign—in carving style at least—of many of the key characteristics of the *Stilwandel*.

The compositional style of the main panels of Severus's Arch is decidedly nontraditional, but there is good reason not to look for its origin in the realm of relief sculpture. Susann Lusnia makes a strong argument that the arch's panels are actually "sculptural reproductions" of paintings and suggests that they may even copy specific paintings mentioned by the contemporary historian Herodian: "After this good fortune [the capture of Ctesiphon, capital of the Parthians], which succeeded beyond his wildest dream, he [Severus] dispatched a report to his senate and people, making much of his achievements and ordering that his battles and victories should be painted and publicly exhibited."[49] If these paintings indeed formed the models for the arch panels, then the compositional style of the relief carving depends on artistic trends in painting, not sculpture. The carving style, on the other hand, likely came from the sculptors themselves—who were fewer in number than those who worked on the Column of Marcus Aurelius, accounting for the greater homogeneity in style. The marked difference between the scenes on Severus's Arch and most of those on Marcus's Column make clear that the *Stilwandel*, such as it was, by no means followed a clear path of evolution. The most enduring aspects of the new style (which must have followed its own, unknown course in the medium of painting) were compositional: frontality, hierarchical scaling of figures, and bird's eye perspective. That some of these traits can be seen in the Column of Marcus Aurelius, but not all and not everywhere, is due to the fact that its carving reflected the work of a large and diverse body of artists who were trained in one particular medium.

chapter nine

VIEWING THE COLUMN

Up to this point, I have concentrated on questions related to how the Column of Marcus Aurelius was created. This last chapter has a different focus and asks a more problematic question: what did the column mean? For the modern viewer, the main message of the column at first seems to be contained in the frieze: a vast expanse of detailed images, inviting equally detailed interpretation. But the frieze is a frustrating artwork, full of contradictions. It appears to tell a story, yet very few of its scenes are historical. It is detailed, but many of the details are wrong. It was on prominent display yet shows many signs that great care was not lavished on it by its carvers. It is apparently intended to give the impression that it chronicles Marcus's campaigns yet contains substantial elements copied directly from Trajan's Column. And the frieze is never mentioned in any of our ancient sources.

All of this suggests that we should not assume that the frieze of the Column of Marcus Aurelius had the same degree of prominence in the minds—or eyes—of the ancient Romans who created or viewed the monument as it does in ours today. But, at the same time, the frieze represents the investment of an undoubtedly large amount of time and effort. What was its purpose? Surely it must have been intended to contribute something important to the external appearance of the monument. This chapter begins by asking the question of what, exactly, an ancient visitor to the column would have seen. Viewing the frieze would have been very difficult, and I argue that many features that other scholars have interpreted as innovations to aid visibility were not that at all. I then turn to the content of the frieze. Regardless of how difficult they may have been to see, the fact remains that many scenes differ sharply in the tone of their content from those on Trajan's Column. This new tone—harsher and more violent—has been seen as reflecting a change in mentality, or as intended to project a reassuring message of Roman power in times of increased uncertainty.

But our sources tell us that this violent tone is not new at all, that it had been used before and is exactly what we would expect to find on the column given the nature and goal of Marcus's wars. Finally, I suggest that the challenge of interpreting the helical frieze has drawn attention away from a much more prominent and visible component of the column's decoration: the pedestal relief. When interpreting the column's overall decoration, the pedestal relief's simple yet powerful message must be considered along with—or even before—that of the helical frieze.

What the Viewer Saw

To begin with, an ancient Roman would not have had to approach the column closely to be able to see it. Unlike its position today, so hemmed in by tall buildings that it is hardly visible from anywhere outside the Piazza Colonna, in the year 193 it would have dominated the Campus Martius from the Hadrianeum to the Mausoleum of Augustus. Standing so close to the Via Flaminia, it would have been the most impressive single monument that a visitor—or an inhabitant—entering the city from the north would have seen. Trajan's Column, in comparison, was largely hidden, tucked into its little courtyard behind the Basilica Ulpia.

To see the Column of Marcus Aurelius up close a visitor would have had to ascend a series of steps from the Via Flaminia. The initial view of the column would have been dominated by the pedestal, its door (perhaps invitingly open), and its busy decoration. A visitor's eyes would have travelled quickly up the column to the statue of the emperor, a larger-than-life-size image in gilded bronze. Of the statue, nothing remains today except (perhaps) the first two joints of the middle finger of one of its hands: this broken bronze finger was found in 1873 under the Palazzo Ferrajoli on the south side of the Piazza della Colonna. It is about twice life-size, and Petersen believed that it may have broken violently from Marcus's statue when it tumbled to earth in one of the quakes that shook the column.[1] After admiring the statue of Marcus, our visitor may then have noted the fenced-in capital, his eye perhaps drawn to it by the animated gestures of visitors on the viewing platform.

Only then would he have turned his attention to the frieze. What would he have seen? Despite Karl Lehmann-Hartleben's suggestion that ancient Romans' eyes may have been sharper than ours, we can be fairly certain that they saw much of what we can see today.[2] Paint, if it had been applied, might have helped make certain elements in the carving more visible—the emperor, for example, if he were marked out by a purple cloak.[3] But even with such visual aids the frieze of the Column of Marcus Aurelius must have remained very difficult to view. It is fairly easy when standing in front of the column to point out some of the major scenes in the lowest portion of the frieze—the Rain Miracle, for example—to a person unfamiliar with the monument. The Victoria is more difficult, but not impossible, to bring to a viewer's attention. Other scenes, especially those above the third winding of the frieze, are hard to point out, let alone to explain. This difficulty would have been amplified in ancient times when the ground level was significantly lower. The pedestal is currently buried to about half its total height, and the lowest scenes on the column were twice as far away from the ancient viewer as they are today.

If he wanted to follow the narrative progression of the helical frieze, a visitor would have to walk around the column, while looking up, a total of twenty times. Few are likely to have done this, since the rewards would have decreased with each turn. While most ancient visitors likely did walk around the column, much the same as visitors today, their main point of inspection would have been from the direction from which they approached, from the east. The column's designers gave some thought to making some of the scenes more or less easily visible from this perspective: the Danube Crossing, the Rain Miracle, and the Victoria all share the eastern axis on the column. These main scenes can be viewed from one position, standing in front of the main face of the monument. Clearly, the placement of these scenes was carefully considered and intentional. This is especially true for the figure of Victory, which is lined up directly over the doorway—a deliberate modification of the layout on the Column of Trajan, where Victory is on the opposite side from the column's entrance. The location of these few scenes was carefully planned, and the reasoning behind it not difficult to see. The big question is, why was there not *more* of this sort of planning?

Some scholars have argued that indeed there was more of this sort of planning—at least on Trajan's Column, which has garnered the lion's share of attention. One approach, advocated especially by Gauer and Brilliant, has been to search for and identify vertical correspondences between scenes and figures on various faces of the column that were created to allow a viewer standing in one spot to read a series of events in the campaign simply by looking up.[4] More recently, Settis identified what he believed to be a complex network of scene sequences, directional impulses, converging compositions, and vertical alignments of scenes on Trajan's Column.[5] The most obvious vertical alignment, on the northwest axis of Trajan's Column, is clear and easy to identify from the ground. This involves a strange scene, interpreted as an omen, in the second winding where a barbarian falls from a mule in front of the emperor, the Victoria halfway up the column, and the death of Decebalus near the top. But Settis's other, more complex alignments, especially those involving diagonal connections, are difficult or impossible to discern from the ground.

Approaches such as this create a paradox: the relief is supposedly organized according to a complex system, but this can hardly be appreciated by an observer on the ground. There have been two main responses to this paradox. One has been to deny one of the very conclusions on which the paradox is based and to assert, as Veyne does, that this sort of overanalysis makes the frieze seem much more complex than it really is.[6] The frieze of Trajan's Column, in Veyne's view, contributes little more than a decorative component to the monument, the overall purpose of which is to proclaim in a more general way the glory of Trajan.[7] Hölscher on the other hand characterizes Veyne's theory as "a frontal attack on sophisticated archaeological research methods."[8] He proposes instead that the dichotomy between a complex narrative structure and a visually confounding method of display—the helical frieze—does not indicate a shortcoming in design. Even if no more than a third of the frieze was legible, he argues, this was enough for the observer to know the general content, and he or she could be sure that what followed contained similar subject manner.[9]

Working with the evidence of Trajan's Column alone, it is difficult to decide which interpretation is closer to the truth. But the Column of Marcus Aurelius may provide some clues. In a way, the Marcus column provided Roman architects and artists an opportunity to "remake" Trajan's Column and to improve on any characteristics they found deficient. Did they in fact do this? Some scholars believe so and have pointed to differences between the two columns as evidence of just such improvements. One of the most cited instances of improvement is the decrease in the number of spirals, from twenty-three to twenty. Fewer spirals meant taller ones, and taller spirals meant larger figures, which were presumably easier to see. Related to this is the idea that the dramatically different manner of carving of the Column of Marcus Aurelius may also have been intended to aid visibility. The deep relief (about ten centimeters deep, compared to about four on Trajan's Column) may have been designed to make individual figures easier to see from the ground by creating stronger shadows and contrasts. And at least since the time of Rodenwaldt (the 1930s), scholars have suggested that some scenes were composed to render them more easy to see: the figures are large, less numerous, and often arranged in simple patterns.[10] For example, marching groups of soldiers are often rendered in simplified double columns of repetitious figures (LXVII, LXXVIII, XXXIX, XLIV, and CIII). All these novelties—increased spiral height, deeper carving, larger figures arranged in simpler patterns—might be interpreted as components of a concerted attempt to make the frieze of the Column of Marcus Aurelius easier to understand than that of the Column of Trajan. As Paul Zanker put it: "The imperial columns provide indisputable evidence for a conscious awareness of the viewer's experience. The relief on the column of Marcus Aurelius is clearly more pronounced than that on the column of Trajan; the figures are fewer but larger; the composition obviously attempts to achieve more of a billboard effect."[11]

But were these features really the product of a conscious effort on the part of the designers of the Column of Marcus Aurelius to improve the visibility and intelligibility of the frieze? Analysis of the genetic process of the column and its frieze suggests a rather disappointing conclusion: they were not. The reduction in number of spirals was most likely the result of the employment of a simple mathematical scheme to plan the layout of the frieze on the exterior of the column shaft. Twenty was close enough to twenty-three to create the same effect as on the Column of Trajan, and it had the advantage of being much easier to plot on the available surface. This lower total spiral count did result in a slightly greater average frieze height: the frieze on Trajan's Column varies extremely in height but averages about four feet tall; that on Marcus's Column is closer to four and a half. But it is uncertain that this significantly increased the legibility of the frieze—especially keeping in mind that the height of the pedestal of Marcus's Column had been increased to double the height of that of Trajan's, handicapping the new monument immediately from the point of view of legibility. To genuinely make the frieze easier to decipher from the ground a much more dramatic increase in frieze height would have been needed. This was actually done for the Column of Arcadius in Constantinople (see epilogue), where the frieze had only thirteen windings. This uneven number of turns was certainly not based on a simple mathematical formula and would have been much harder to lay out on the column—and thus was much more likely the result of a deliberate attempt to improve legibility.

Similarly for repetitive scenes: when seen from the ground, the nature of these scenes is relatively easy to make out, as long as they are not too high up. The repetition of the figures also adds a sense of motion and progress to the frieze.[12] The question is, were these effects calculated or were they more or less unintentional results of a method of composition that had other goals? It is much simpler, for example, to create a marching scene using rows of standard, repetitive figures than it is to create one with a high degree of variety. If the use of repetitive figures and simplified composition in march scenes was indeed a strategy designed to increase visibility and narrative flow, then it would be expected that they would be the dominant (or only) type of march scene in the frieze. They are not. Scenes III, XXX, XXXIII, LXXXIV, and CXI are all good examples of marches that incorporate variety in their figures and composition—and they are not, as the scene numbers show, concentrated exclusively in the lower, more easily visible, part of the frieze. The main advantage offered by repetitive scenes to the creators of Marcus's Column were similar to those offered by the choice of twenty rather than twenty-three windings: ease of execution. The fact that repetitive scenes do not entirely dominate the frieze suggests that different planning or carving teams approached their assigned tasks differently: some used more traditional compositions; others preferred repetitive scenes that were easier and faster to compose (and also to carve) than complex ones.

There is a strong connection here to the working environment of the sarcophagus carvers, in whose workshops a small number of set designs was repeated almost endlessly with minimal variety. In a sarcophagus workshop, repetition was not intended to aid the viewer's understanding of the whole; rather, it was intended to make production easier. But the products of this industry were never meant to be viewed together, lined up side by side. What was an advantage in the sarcophagus industry—and what may well also have been an advantage during the actual process of carving the column's frieze, at least as far as speed of design and execution went—was not so very advantageous when it came to producing a continuous frieze.

These supposed refinements can thus be seen in proper perspective: they are the result of various practical decisions make by the column's designers, mainly with the goal of simplifying and speeding their task. That is not to say that the designers had no interest in visibility. Quite the opposite: they appear to have been very much aware of it, as can be seen from the fair degree of variety and originality combined with the limited use of vertical alignment in the bottom half of the column, features that contrast strongly with the steadily increasing regularity of the scenes, their size, and their content as the frieze proceeded up the column. This may all be read as a tacit admission on the part of the designers of the Column of Marcus Aurelius that viewers were not expected to be able to appreciate the content of the frieze in its upper parts. The ancient viewer certainly could not have fully appreciated the detailed content of the column's entire frieze. But this was not the main objective of the designers. They did what they could, working with a small number of simple goals in mind: first, that of reproducing the appearance of Trajan's Column; second, that of placing a small number of genuinely historical scenes in clear view of the public. In both these tasks they succeeded.

There was one major area where the designers of Marcus's Column did not succeed, one that has important implications for our understanding of the knowledge and capabilities of Marcus's artists and architects. On the Column of Trajan, the order of scenes is clear and is repeated in a careful structure—campaigns begin with marching, followed by construction, then sacrifice and an address to the troops, and finally battle and the subsequent submission of prisoners.[13] But on its Aurelian successor this order becomes, as Hölscher expressed it, decomposed.[14] The same repeated sequence of scenes found on Trajan's Column cannot be identified on the Column of Marcus Aurelius, at least not with the degree of regularity in which they are employed on the earlier monument. Hölscher has argued that Marcus's Column dispenses with much of the ideologically based framework of Trajan's Column frieze because it did not have the same ideological message to deliver.[15] There is, however, another possible explanation for this "decomposition" of structure: that the designers of the Marcus column were unable to appreciate (and perhaps were simply unaware) that such a system existed at all on Trajan's Column. Could the designers of the Column of Marcus Aurelius have been aware of the complex narrative structure of the frieze of Trajan's Column when the frieze was so difficult to view? A detailed plan of the entire frieze was most likely not available, even in Trajan's day (see chapter 5). The frieze has every sign of having been created loosely, without firm prototypes or models; modern suggestions that such models existed are entirely unfounded. The numerous irregularities in the frieze itself, some quite shocking, demonstrate that the opposite was in fact the case. This means that an understanding of the internal structure of the frieze of Trajan's Column may very well have died with its designer, and that in the absence of modern aids such as photography there was no easy way for the designers of the Column of Marcus Aurelius to grasp this structure, let alone replicate it.

Debellare Superbos: The Message of the Column's Frieze

The basic function of the frieze of the Column of Marcus Aurelius was to show, by means of a mass of military imagery, that Marcus's achievements were equal to Trajan's. But a casual visitor, even if he would only notice the details of the lowest spirals and some of the scenes clustered around the figure of Victory, would still notice some differences between the frieze content of the two columns. What strikes many viewers first is the high degree of violence shown on Marcus's Column. Most shocking are incidents of violence toward unarmed opponents and noncombatants: the killing of a woman in scene XCVII (fig. 9.1), the repeated depictions of devastation and killing in barbarian villages (scenes XVIII, XX, XLIII; see fig. 1.3, immediately above Rain Miracle), and the truly unique scenes of execution and slaughter of unarmed barbarians (LXI and LXVIII, fig. 5.16).[16] These last two execution scenes are unlike anything seen in surviving Roman art of any genre. Neither is connected directly to a battle; instead, each follows a similar sequence: first a presentation of barbarian prisoners before the emperor (LX and LXVI), then a short march by Roman troops, and then the slaughter. That these scenes of brutal slaughter appear only twice and in different forms suggests that they, like the miracle scenes, are intended to reflect historical events. This idea is strengthened by their position on the column: directly beside the main east axis above the figure of Victory, one of the main foci for the eye of the viewer.

Why this violence? Are these scenes perhaps symptoms of a change in the Roman psyche, brought on by the mental shock of the barbarian invasions and plagues of the late second century A.D.? Felix Pirson has stressed the message of Roman superiority projected by the scenes of violence on the column, connecting them to a "need for self-affirmation in insecure times."[17] Another possibility is that these scenes reflect the actual reality of Marcus's Germanic wars, which according to the images on the column were much more brutal than Trajan's Dacian campaigns.[18] Or should we turn the entire question on its head, as Sheila Dillon does for images of violence shown toward women on the Column of Marcus Aurelius, scenes that present a striking contrast to the peaceful scenes on Trajan's Column. Dillon argues that these scenes are not so much a reflection of greater violence toward women in Marcus's wars as the result of a cover-up of the actual treatment that women would have received in Trajan's Dacian campaigns.[19] Did the frieze of Trajan's Column gloss over or play down the un-

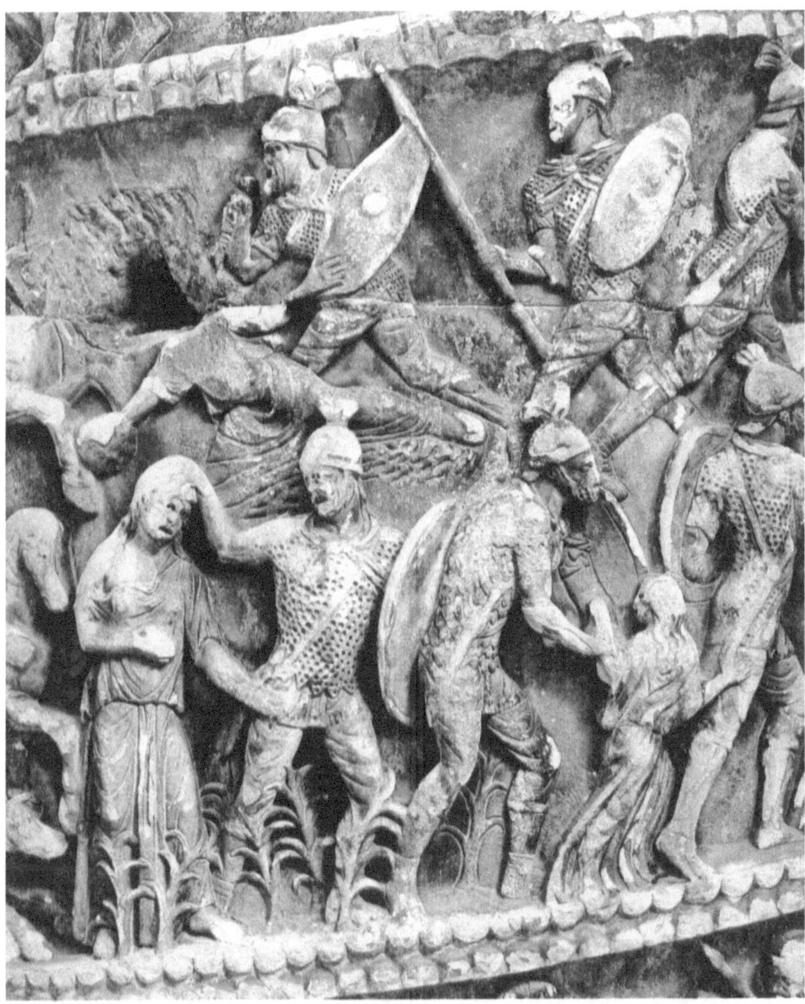

FIGURE 9.1. Scene XCVII, showing a Roman soldier stabbing a falling barbarian woman (her head has been obliterated by a robber hole cut to remove a metal dowel). From Petersen et al. 1896, pl. 106A.

pleasant aspects of the Dacian wars, while the Column of Marcus Aurelius pulled no punches and told the story exactly as it happened?

The best way to evaluate these ideas is to consider what expectations the Romans themselves would have had when they viewed the column. One requirement of this approach is to consider the scenes of violence on the Column of Marcus Aurelius in the context of the late second century A.D. and against the historical background of Marcus's wars. A second requirement is to consider how the Romans were culturally and historically accustomed to react to such events. The wars of Marcus Aurelius—hard, often brutal, and at times (especially at their beginning) desperate—were very different from the wars of Trajan. But for our purpose—understanding the message of the scenes—even more important is understanding the motivation behind the increased violence. The cause of Trajan's first war against king Decebalus and the Dacians is not entirely known but was likely rooted in an interest in Roman frontier security, a need for gold, or Trajan's own desire for personal glory.[20] The war was initiated by the Romans, and its first action was the Roman invasion of Dacia. The second Dacian war had clearer causes: Decebalus was declared an enemy by the Senate after it was reported that he broke a number of terms of the peace treaty that concluded the first Dacian war.[21] As a result, the Romans again invaded, and the final result was the incorporation of Dacia into the Roman empire. Both wars were effectively preemptive. The goal in each case was to subjugate a potential threat and to make physical gains, whether of money or territory, for Rome. The second war also involved punishment for minor transgressions, but this was more of a pretext for invasion than the ultimate goal of the campaign.

In the case of Marcus's wars, the situation was dramatically different. Marcus's campaigns against the Germans started with a barbarian invasion. This triggered a Roman campaign of punishment and revenge. The conduct of a Roman army in a war of punishment was very different from that of one in a war such as those fought by Trajan against the Dacians. Brutality and punishment were expected, and indeed required. This was because the barbarians had themselves started the war, and by the most horrific means imaginable to a Roman at the time, by invading Italy itself. In the course of this invasion they had laid siege to Aquileia, destroyed the smaller town of Opitergium, and defeated a Roman force and killed its leader, the praetorian prefect Furius Victorinus.[22] The barbarians had thus committed a double crime against the Romans: they had broken the peace, and they had invaded Roman lands and slain Roman citizens.

There was clear precedent for appropriate Roman action in response to such events. As Germanicus said to his troops before their battle against the rebellious Germans under Arminius, the treacherous chieftain who had led the slaughter of Varus's three legions in the Teutoberg Forest: "There is no use in taking prisoners; only the destruction of the race will end the war."[23] In that case, the battle resulted in a slaughter of the barbarians that did not cease till nightfall. Similar were the instructions of the Roman commander Paulinus to his troops before their battle with the forces of Boudicca: to "furnish to the rest of mankind an example, not only of benevolent clemency toward the obedient, but also of inevitable severity toward the rebellious."[24] The followers of Boudicca had earned this severity not only by their rebellion, but also by their sacking of a number of Roman cities and the atrocities committed against captured Roman noncombatants. What to us may seem unwarranted savagery was to the Romans a normal and necessary response to rebellion. When the general Corbulo finally captured the key city of the rebellious Armenians in A.D. 62, he slaughtered all the adults and sold the rest of the population into slavery.[25] Domitian himself is reported to have taken pleasure at the report that his governor of Numidia had succeeded in annihilating the rebellious Nasamones, "even destroying all the non-combatants."[26] The Nasamones had earned this treatment by revolting and killing Roman tax collectors.

The purpose of such treatment of the enemy was twofold. For one thing, slaughter and, if possible, extermination was the prescribed (if unwritten) penalty for such offenses. In addition, such treatment was meted out to send a message to others. Agricola clearly had this purpose in mind when he nearly exterminated the Ordovices, a tribe that had massacred a troop of Roman cavalry, "knowing that he depended on the issue of his first campaign to terrorise the enemy for the future."[27]

The connection between rebellion and horrible punishment was even clear to the vanquished. Josephus describes images very similar to the scenes of violence on the column in his account of the paintings carried in the triumph of Vespasian and Titus in A.D. 71. These included depictions of slaughter, the destruction of buildings (some with their inhabitants still within), and a generally devastated landscape (see chapter 7).[28] This vivid description recalls scenes shown in the frieze of the Column of Marcus Aurelius (and it is entirely unlike most of the scenes on the Column of Trajan). But Josephus does more than simply describe these images: he also does a very rare thing for an ancient author and gives us his own personal opinion of the message of Vespasian's paintings, one that reflects the intensity of his feelings on seeing these horrors but also is based on an understanding of why they came about: "For to such sufferings were the Jews destined when they plunged into the war."

Events such as these must certainly have sprung to the minds of the Roman citizenry of Marcus's day. Their trust and their lands had been violated, their citizens killed, and for this the offenders had to pay a harsh penalty. According to Dio, this sentiment was very much in the front of the mind of Marcus Aurelius himself. When the fighting began to go the Romans' way, "envoys were sent to Marcus by the Iazyges to request peace, but they did not obtain anything. For Marcus, both because he knew their race to be untrustworthy and also because he had been deceived by the Quadi, wished to annihilate them utterly."[29] When the Iazyges finally obtained a surrender, the emperor still "wished to exterminate them utterly," because "they were still strong and had done the Romans great harm."[30] Even individual barbarians were singled out for Marcus's wrath. "Against Ariogaesus [leader of the Quadi] Marcus was so bitter that he issued a proclamation to the effect that anyone who brought him in alive should receive a thousand gold pieces, and anyone who slew him and exhibited his head, five hundred."[31] The direct involvement of Marcus in acts of punishment and brutality is clearly shown on the column. In scene XX, for example, the emperor presides over an execution of a barbarian, crouched on the ground (fig. 1.3, immediately above the image of the Rain God); in scene LXVI (fig. 9.2), two Roman soldiers present Marcus Aurelius with severed barbarian heads.

This message, one of harsh and brutal punishment, is just the sort of message we should expect to see on the frieze of Marcus's Column. It is also not an innovation unique to Marcus's reign, but rather reflects an established tradition of violent Roman reprisal against rebels. Art had served as a vehicle for these violent messages before: Vespasian's triumphal paintings "portrayed the incidents [of the war] to those who had not witnessed them, as though they were happening before their eyes."[32] The slaughter, the rivers running red, the burned and destroyed landscape were all displayed to the Roman public as signs of a job well done. That we see very little of this on Trajan's Column has to do directly with the nature of Trajan's wars, which were wars of conquest rather than wars of reprisal. The Column of Marcus Aurelius is another case altogether. It commemorates an entirely different type of war, even if it was fought in a similar geographical area. The Roman audience in the time of Marcus would have expected a much different message from its leaders than would a similar audience in the time of Trajan. This was the standard message of empire, expressed so vividly by Vergil through the mouth of Anchises: the Romans' glory was not to be art or architecture, but *pacis imponere morem, parcere subiectis et debellare superbos*: "to impose the custom of peace, to spare the conquered and to 'war down' the haughty."[33]

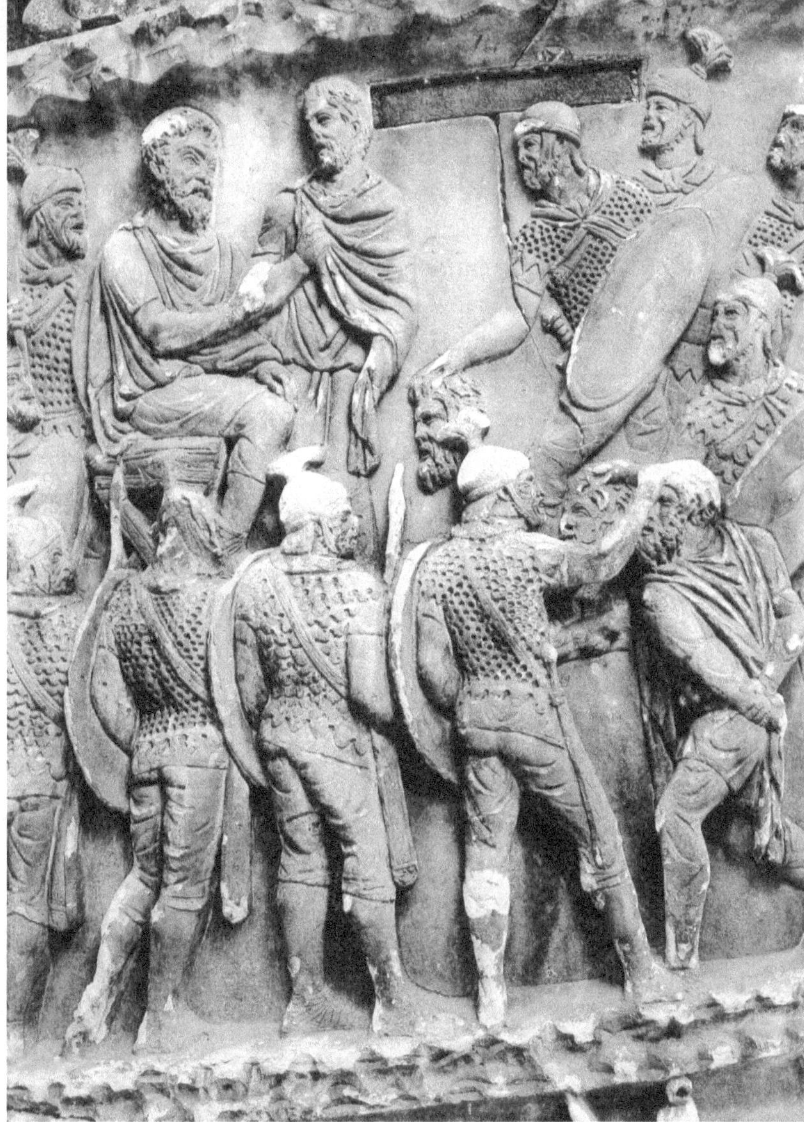

FIGURE 9.2. Scene LXVI, showing Roman soldiers presenting severed barbarian heads to Marcus Aurelius. From Petersen et al. 1896, pl. 75B.

The Effect on the Viewer

The location of the Column of Marcus Aurelius, in the Campus Martius alongside the Via Flaminia, would have opened up its frieze to a wide range of spectators. The significance of the imagery of the frieze for Roman citizens has been outlined above; but what might it mean for a foreigner, a slave employed in the capital or a visitor from abroad? Did the violent scenes of punishment and enslavement on the column perhaps reflect Roman fear of outsiders, and were they intended to help keep a potentially rebellious foreign-born slave population in its place by cowing them with visual threats? It is helpful in this context to look back at the first step in the genesis of the column: it was decreed, most likely by the Senate, to honor Marcus Aurelius for his victorious German campaigns; this was the primary message of the monument. While the column's frieze was not rigidly historical, it did incorporate a limited number of genuine events and, in a more general way, reflected the tone and mood of the campaigns. Scenes of violence toward barbarians covered the monument not because the Romans felt frightened and in need of sending a message of superiority to their enemies; rather, the violence of the frieze reflected the actual violence of the war it depicted, a violence whose necessity was dictated—in Roman eyes—by the tradition of hard dealing with rebels. The main message was for the Romans who had won the war, not for the barbarians who had lost it.

Still, the impact that this monument and others like it may have had on visiting foreigners, especially official embassies, may have been significant. One particularly interesting consideration that arises from the location of the column along the Via Flaminia is that it would have made the monument much more prominent in the eyes of certain groups of foreigners—those approaching Rome along the principal land route from the north. An embassy from Germany, for example that of the Buri in the time of Commodus, would have traveled down the Via Flaminia and entered the city through the Campus Martius.[34] Along their way to meet with the Senate they would have passed by the Column of Marcus Aurelius, adorned with graphic scenes of their own people's defeat (the Buri had taken part in the original invasion of Roman territory, along with the Marcomanni). It is hard to say to what degree this sort of effect on visiting barbarians might have been considered when the column was designed in 176, but it is not hard to imagine that it had the potential to deliver a strong message, whether calculated in initial planning or not.

Regardless of this potential effect on foreigners, the main intended audience was a Roman one—but which Romans? A recent trend in scholarship has been to consider more carefully the effect of the scenes on the column on nonelite viewers. Clarke has suggested that the repetitive scenes, for example the many marching scenes, may have been designed to send Romans a message of unity and military efficiency, a guarantee of certain victory in an increasingly disordered time.[35] But consideration from a perspective of design suggests that, at least in the case of the Column of Marcus Aurelius, the lack of variety and frequent repetition of scene and figure type is more likely a result of different factors. These were the working methods adopted by the creators of the frieze and the training of the carvers who executed it. Simplified working methods do not necessarily mean a deliberate simplification of message. The frieze of the Column of Marcus Aurelius was, after all, not the main bearer of message; that was the column itself, the statue of the emperor on top, and the clear parallel with Trajan's Column. For the ancient Romans, the frieze contributed to but did not define the main message of the monument.

Some impression of the relationship between medium, message, and audience can be gained from an examination of the ways in which the events of Marcus's wars were reported in other media, especially literature. One glaring discrepancy is immediately visible: the wars of Marcus Aurelius were harsh and long, and filled with Roman danger and sometimes horrendous defeat. Written histories record these negative events; the Column of Marcus Aurelius does not. Instead, the column focuses exclusively on Roman victories. This difference in viewpoint between literature and visual arts is common throughout Roman history: Roman setbacks or defeats are openly addressed by authors but are scrupulously avoided by artists. This is a trend that can be traced back in classical literature and art as far back as the Persian Wars in the early fifth century B.C. and seems to reflect an unwritten but universally understood rule of thumb throughout classical history. When genuinely historical (rather than mythical) events were depicted, a barbarian could never be shown in art as victorious over a civilized person. This suggests that the author had a different audience in mind than did the artist, one capable of understanding and processing the news of a Roman defeat, one who appreciated truth in reporting, and one who could put information about Roman setbacks into historical perspective. The artist, on the other hand, could apparently not assume that his audience would be able to process negative images in the same way that an informed reader would be able to process a description of a Roman defeat.

The frieze does more than omit negative aspects of the wars. Lucian, a contemporary of Marcus Aurelius, in his treatise on the proper way to write history, criticized reports of battle casualties that contradict official reports and that, he says, would not be believed by anyone of sound mind.[36] His example, drawn perhaps from a history of Lucius Verus's Parthian war, is a report of a battle that resulted in 70,236 enemy casualties versus 2 Roman dead and 9 wounded. What then must a viewer have thought when looking on the battle scenes of the Marcus column, where not a single Roman is even wounded? Another of Lucian's admonishments is that a good historian ought to have practical knowledge of things military, either from personal experience or from observation.[37] As detailed in chapter 7, military accuracy is an area where the Marcus column relief falls short. Some observers of the Column of Marcus Aurelius must have noted these shortcomings, and the designers of the column themselves were almost certainly aware of them, too. Was this situation the result of a conscious, deliberate choice on the part of the designers? Part of it, in fact, could hardly have been a choice at all. There was not and had never been an alternative to showing Romans as totally victorious in historical battle on a Roman monument. What a historian might interpret as a shortcoming may well have been a positive feature in the eyes of an artist.

When it came to the audience, the same man might very well have expected different things from a work of history than he did from a work of art, even if the theme of both was the same. William Harris has examined the depiction of Roman soldiers in literature and concluded that one characteristic, ferocity, is regularly downplayed.[38] Harris makes the interesting observation that the same ferocity that is avoided in literature is sometimes very clearly shown in art. The Column of Marcus Aurelius offers this in plenty. The basic message of art and literature may fundamentally have been the same, but the language they each used to transmit that message differed, very possibly as a result of a conscious consideration of the likely audience.

Conclusion: The Role of the Pedestal Relief

Up to now I have focused on the content of the helical frieze. But this was not the only, and perhaps not even the most important, part of the column's iconographic content. This consisted of three distinctly different components: the statue of Marcus Aurelius on top, the historical frieze covering the shaft of the column, and the allegorical scene that occupied a very prominent position on the east face of the pedestal above the entrance to the internal stairway. It is natural that the column's helical frieze has attracted the lion's share (indeed, often all) of the attention of modern scholars. But it is almost certain that before the ancient viewer ever turned his attention to the helical frieze, he would have examined the decoration on the pedestal. Today the pedestal is plain and unadorned, but in ancient times it would have made a striking impression, faced with decorative marble panels, perhaps in bold colors. And in a broad band between these panels, about halfway up the pedestal and directly above the entrance to the column, was a striking allegorical frieze.

The destruction of this frieze by Domenico Fontana has effectively banished this major relief from most modern discussions of the column's iconography. Still the fact remains that it almost certainly was the first element of relief sculpture that a visitor to the column would have noticed—and perhaps the only one that he would have been able to understand in detail. Today, the pedestal relief has generally been relegated to discussion only by those with antiquarian interests or by chronological revisionists seeking an image of Commodus somewhere in the column's decoration. But this relief was in a very prominent position, and, when compared to the Column of Trajan, it is one of the most innovative (and hence presumably important) components of the Marcus column's decoration. This raises the possibility that it may even have been considered by the column's designers more important than the helical frieze itself.

Although the majority of the pedestal's substance is antique, its exterior was entirely refaced under orders of Pope Sixtus V between the years 1588 and 1589.[39] Even before this, the base was already in a serious state of decay, with only a portion of its original surface surviving; this much we know from a small selection of drawings made before 1588. The most useful of these is that made by Antonio Lafreri (fig. 1.7), who published an etching whose original artist is disputed. It shows a view of the column from the east, dates to about 1550, and preserves the only surviving image of this face of the pedestal. The drawing shows that five of the pedestal's seven courses were visible above ground in the sixteenth century (the lowest two, containing the original entrance, had already been buried by the rising ground level of the Campus Martius). The main visible feature in all of these drawings is the middle (fourth) course of stone. This course (actually a single block—see fig. 3 in the introduction) projected beyond the others, was fairly well preserved, and was covered with sculpted figures. Above and below this projecting block, the surface of the pedestal was very rough. It seems most likely that this area was originally covered with a cladding of another type of stone, perhaps colored marble or even porphyry, which had at some point been removed. The metal clamps necessary to hold such a cladding in place would have been reason enough for it to have been plundered, and the holes in which they were previously fastened can be seen on Lafreri's etching.[40]

This ragged surface, with one course of marble (the fourth, the one bearing the relief) projecting so far beyond the others, presented Fontana with a serious problem—how could the entire pedestal be restored so as to present a uniform face? His solution was to fill up the space above and

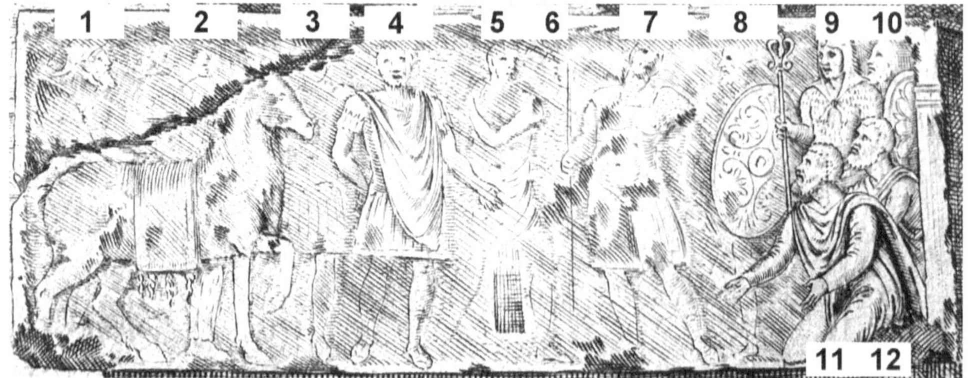

FIGURE 9.3. The relief on the pedestal of the Column of Marcus Aurelius (detail of fig. 1.7). From A. Lafreri, *Speculum Romanae Magnificentiae*, ca. 1550 (no date), p. 34 (no pagination).

below the fourth course of the pedestal with marble taken from another Roman monument, the Septizodium, which was destroyed in the process. Presumably, Fontana was not comfortable with the contrast between the smooth face of this new marble cladding and the worn, damaged condition of the relief sculpture on the original fourth course. So he decided to simply chisel it off, leaving a flat surface that now forms the middle part of Fontana's restored pedestal.

From the drawings we know that the fourth course of the pedestal was carved on all sides. Three of them (the south, west, and north faces) had the same repeated motif of Victories supporting garlands. This imagery, paralleled on coins and reliefs of the 160s and 170s, has clear connotations of military victory.[41] The sculpture on the east face, however, was different. It consisted of a single long rectangular scene (fig. 9.3), marred by a crack extending from the middle right edge diagonally to a point one-third of the way across the top. The bottom left and right corners were damaged, and a window pierces the relief in the lower centre. The left border of the relief was a narrow band, the right wider and carved in the form of a pilaster representing one side of an archway. The upper and lower borders were simple uncarved bands. In the main field were twelve human figures and one horse.

How reliable is this etching as evidence of the actual appearance of the relief? Judging from his rendering of the sculpture on the lowest part of the column shaft, the etching of the pedestal relief is likely fairly trustworthy with regard to detail. The first winding of the helical frieze is well rendered (compare figs. 1.3 and 1.7), with particularly exact detail in the archway at the end of the boat bridge; the second winding shows the forked river above this arch, but from there on up there is much more improvisation. This suggests that the artist of the drawing on which the etching was based took care to reproduce the lower scenes of the column accurately. The pedestal relief, which was almost at eye level in the sixteenth century, would have been the most accurate part of this drawing.

In Lafreri's etching, the first two figures on the left (1 and 2 in fig. 9.3) are visible in profile behind the horse, facing right. Figure 1 wears a helmet and carries, perhaps, a shield; one leg is visible between the horse's two hind legs. Of figure 2, no more than a profile and a leg are visible. Figure 3 stands frontally behind and just right of the horse; the lower part of his face, most of his torso, and one leg are visible. He wears a muscled cuirass. Figure 4 is much clearer and must have stood in high relief. He wears a muscled cuirass and a military cloak; his left arm is extended toward the right, his right hand propped on his right hip. His face, possibly bearded, is turned toward the viewer. Figure 5 is less clearly visible. His (or her) head is turned to the right, and he steps in that direction. His left arm, however, is bent over his chest, as if gesturing toward figure 4. Drapery is visible around the figure's hips, and perhaps over the right shoulder. In the space between the head of figure 5 and the top of the spear carried by 7 is the faint outline of a head in profile, probably wearing a helmet, facing right—this is figure 6. Figure 7 stands, like 4, frontally, but his head is turned back toward the right. He wears a muscled cuirass, belt, and helmet, and he carries a spear or a staff in his right hand. His left arm seems to hang down more or less at his side. Of figure 8 only a profile, facing left, along with a shield and a leg can be seen. Figure 9 also faces left, wears an armored shirt (ring mail?) and a lion-skin headdress. In his right hand he carries a staff topped with volutes. Behind him stands figure 10, of whom only a profile head and a shield are visible. The last two figures, 11 and 12, kneel on the ground below; figure 11 extends both his arms to the left, hands open.

The theme of the scene is a submission: two barbarians (figures 11 and 12, identifiable by their long-sleeved tunics and trousers) offer themselves to the emperor (figure 4). Behind the horse are Roman soldiers; between horse and emperor we see an officer. Figures 8 through 10 are also soldiers; 9 is identifiable as a standard-bearer from his headdress. Figures 5 and 7 are more difficult to identify. Figure 7 is the better detailed of the two: he balances the figure of the emperor in the composition, and his full frontal pose marks him out as being similar to him in importance. As discussed in chapter 1, this could not be Commodus since his image would not have survived the *damnatio memoriae* put into action after his death in 192. Who then is he? The roughly contemporary Panel Reliefs of Marcus Aurelius (from a lost arch dedicated in the honor of the emperor and Commodus, likely in A.D. 176) offer a number of informative parallels.[42] In the Clementia Relief, a figure to the left of the mounted emperor, similar to figure 7 on the column base, appears from his dress and prominence to be an officer. In the Adventus Relief a similarly equipped male figure is present, but this time he is clearly Mars, dressed like the officer from the Clementia scene but wearing a Corinthian helmet and the lion-skin boots that mark him out as divine. A third parallel is found in the Profectio Panel, which shows the emperor preparing to depart Rome. Behind the personification of the Via Flaminia, reclining on a wheel, are four figures: three are ordinary soldiers, but the fourth is different. He is depicted in a frontal pose holding a *vexillum* (a military standard topped with a rectangular piece of fabric or leather). An officer's belt is tied over his armor; his helmet is Corinthian; his face clean shaven; and his hair long and curly. Soldiers are rarely shown smooth shaven on the Panel Reliefs or the column and never wearing long hair or a plumed Corinthian helmet. These features, along with the figure's prominent position, suggest that he is a personification.

Any of these solutions—an officer, the god Mars, or a personification—would suit the unidentified figure 7 on the column pedestal. A similar solution can be proposed for figure 5, who is perhaps a draped female such as Victory. If so, her right hand (held toward Marcus) may have held a wreath. The imagery, both here and on the wreath-and-Victory reliefs on the other three sides of the pedestal, was explicitly linked to military victory. Thus, the pedestal frieze showed the emperor and his army, accompanied by a personification, receiving the submission of defeated barbarians who are being presented by another god or personification, perhaps Mars. This is not a historical scene, but rather an allegorical representation of the triumph of the emperor and the army over rebellious barbarians. But there is more. The barbarians are not, as so often on the supposedly historical frieze of the column above, being brutally punished or slaughtered, nor is there any indication that they are about to be. Thus, the second message of this relief is the clemency of Marcus Aurelius, a theme that is strengthened by its contrast with the imagery of the frieze above. The message of clemency can also be found in the helical frieze; its prominence on the pedestal suggests that it was thought of as even more important than the message of just punishment.

epilogue

THE COLUMNS OF TRAJAN, MARCUS AURELIUS, & ARCADIUS

The Romans saw things differently than we do today. When looking at the Column of Marcus Aurelius, the modern observer usually thinks first about the remarkable helical frieze, wonders what events it might record, and then wishes that he could see them better. The Roman first thought of a snail. He looked at the column and was captivated not by the spiraling frieze on the exterior but by the dark, winding passage inside, a hidden passage leading up within the monument to a lofty balcony atop its capital. Our priorities were not necessarily theirs.

Evidence of these priorities is unfortunately often hard to come by—but it is there, if one looks closely enough, in the details of the monument itself. The approach followed in the chapters above has been to attempt to reconstruct these priorities by examining the process by which the column was created. The tasks involved in the design and construction of the Column of Marcus Aurelius were numerous and of various degrees of difficulty. Much of the architectural detail could be copied from Trajan's Column, and was: the height of the column shaft, for example, and the layout of the staircase. Some elements were simplified: the chamber in the base was eliminated; entasis was traded for a much simpler tapering of the column shaft. The helical frieze was a much more serious challenge. Its execution was made easier where possible, particularly by drafting the course of the frieze according to a simple mathematical ratio and by copying some of its content directly from the model, Trajan's Column. The remainder of the frieze, all 700-odd feet of it, was filled with scenes drawn sometimes from history, but more often from the minds of the designers. We will never know just how much history went into the frieze of the column as a whole, but analysis points to a high generic component and to a lack of accuracy in details, suggesting that the degree of historical accuracy overall was relatively low.

When the column was complete, it became the most conspicuous monument along the Via Flaminia. Elevated above the road, it beckoned passersby to approach. Some lingered around the base of the pedestal, where they sat by the doorway and played games on a *tabula lusoria* scratched into the marble. Others, more fortunate, made the climb through the dark, winding stairway to the top of the column. Perhaps they first knocked at the door of Adrastus's house and waited for the *procurator columnae* to appear, then walked with him back to the column and waited for him to open the door. At some point, they certainly looked up at the column's impressive frieze. Much of it would have remained obscure to them, as it does today, but the Danube Crossing would be clear (perhaps they recalled a similar beginning on Trajan's Column), so too the Rain Miracle, of which they surely had heard stories. A more careful inspection would be enough to reassure our Roman visitors: good, the barbarians have been properly punished, as they deserve.

In the introduction I asked whether, perhaps, the Column of Marcus Aurelius can be seen as a work of Roman artistic and architectural criticism, with the object of criticism being Trajan's Column (its one and only model) and the goal of criticism to create a better successor. This is not likely. Clearly the designers of Marcus's Column relied heavily on their model, and clearly, too, they altered and changed certain aspects of their model while adapting it to their own needs. But, overwhelmingly, these changes were not ones of careful critique and refinement but instead were fundamentally rooted in a powerful desire for simplification. The frieze height is greater on average because a simple ratio of twenty windings was settled on for its layout. The carving is deeper because this had become the norm in relief carving by the late second century A.D. Entasis was dispensed with because it was easier to carve a linear taper. The careful structure of scenes visible in the frieze of Trajan's Column is not reproduced because this structure was not understood. And so on. There were certainly changes, but these were generally not for the better.

Nonetheless, although it is possible to criticize details of refinement and finish on the column it is also fairly clear that Marcus Aurelius's artists and architects were doing their best with the skills, resources, and knowledge they had at their disposal. As best as can be judged from the end product, their skills were varied. The architect was generally competent if not sophisticated (thus the employment of a taper rather than genuine entasis), and his planning was not always thorough (witness the problems with the first windings of the staircase). The sculptors, drawn in large numbers from the mass-production sarcophagus industry, were not the highest quality carvers available in Rome. Our historical sources suggest that the resources available to these men would have been stretched, given the wars, plague, and financial crisis of the Roman Empire in Marcus's reign. Somewhat surprisingly there is little evidence that this had a great effect on the column; apparently, its construction was given the highest priority. Perhaps the most difficult problem facing the column's creators was their knowledge: not general architectural knowledge or technical skills, but rather specific knowledge of their model, Trajan's Column. This lack of knowledge is most evident in the frieze. The careful, repeated sequence of standard scene types in the frieze of Trajan's Column did not appear again on Marcus's. Vertical alignment vanished after the figure of Victoria, indicating a lack of concern about the order and the appearance from the ground of the upper scenes. The designers of the Column of Marcus Aurelius even seem to have been unsure of how to begin filling their frieze, so much so that they resorted to copying the beginning sequence of the frieze of Trajan's Column in exact detail until they had left the awkward, triangular-shaped first spiral behind.

The monument had more than one layer of meaning, and the frieze was in more than a literal way superficial. The main function of the monument—and thus its primary message—was honorific, and this is how most Roman viewers would have understood the column. Most important, the parallel with the Column of Trajan would have been immediately apparent to any viewer with the least knowledge of the imperial capital. In the eyes of the ancient Romans, Trajan was one of the two most revered emperors who had ever lived. Eutropius records how Trajan's name was so esteemed that up to his day, in the later fourth century, when emperors were acclaimed in the Senate they were greeted with the cry "*Felicior Augusto, melior Traiano*!"—"may you be happier than Augustus, and better than Trajan!"[1] The Column of Marcus Aurelius was, in effect, a parallel salute in stone. What is more, it outdid Trajan's Column in one very obvious way: it was significantly taller. This added height came from a doubling in the height of the base, a feature that would not have been missed by any observer familiar with Trajan's monument.

The fact that the helical frieze was in many ways secondary in importance for the creators of the column does not mean that modern interest in it is misplaced—only that its contents should be seen in perspective, and particularly from the perspective of the people who designed and built the column. Still, it could be argued that the designers of the Column of Marcus Aurelius partly wasted a great opportunity to provide their audience—and posterity—with an accurate, detailed representation of the events and achievements of Marcus's wars. Instead of striking out boldly on an original narrative, they resorted to rote copying and the creation of many repetitive, generic scenes. Was the Column of Marcus Aurelius, in some ways at least, a failure? This was, it seems, the opinion of the team of architects and artists that came to Rome from Constantinople in the late fourth century A.D. to survey both columns. Their purpose was to plan and build, in Constantinople, a *columna cochlis* for the emperor Arcadius, son of Theodosius the Great, a project that they began in 401.[2] (Theodosius had his own cochlid column, which is now entirely lost, torn down in the sixteenth century by the Sultan Bayazit II to provide space—and some materials—for his new baths.) The Column of Arcadius, heavily damaged by earthquakes, was partly pulled down in 1715, but its fire-scarred pedestal still stands in Istanbul today. Even better, an anonymous draftsman recorded detailed views of it from three angles at some point before its destruction (fig. e.1). To judge by comparison with the surviving remains, these drawings are accurate. Two things are immediately clear: first, the architecture of the Column of Arcadius was modeled not on Marcus's Column but rather on Trajan's. Second, Arcadius's artists, the men in charge of planning and composing the frieze, showed far more originality and independent thinking that did Marcus's. The pedestal of Arcadius's Column has the same architectural form as Trajan's (though it is a little taller). There is a chamber inside, off to the left as one enters the pedestal. The purpose of this chamber is unknown (the ceiling is carved with a massive Christogram, but this is of little help), but its inspiration is clear.

The frieze of the Column of Arcadius is unlike either Trajan's or Marcus's. It seems to have had only thirteen windings, regular in height and each much taller than those on either of the Roman columns, and its content was entirely original. The opening scenes (fig. e.2) show views of Constantinople, and in the second winding the emperor and his army march out of a city gate, escorted by a flying Victory. The remainder of the frieze chronicles the events of a single and relatively short war (against the Goths near Constantinople in A.D. 400) that seems to have included only one major sea battle and one on land; no Victoria divides the frieze in the middle, and the final scenes show the victorious emperor surrounded by his court.

The most striking difference between the Column of Arcadius and the

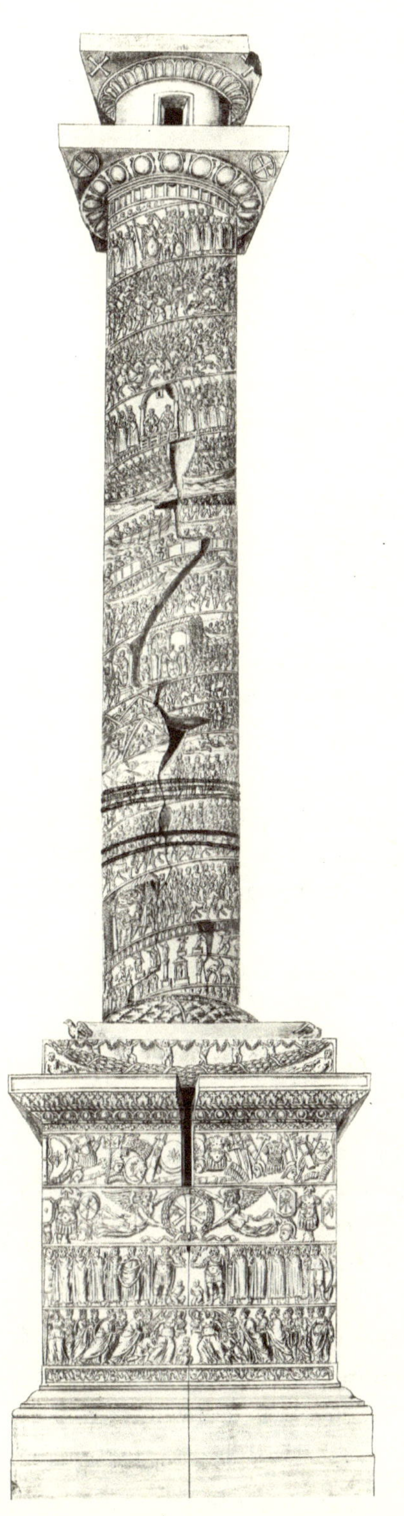

FIGURE E.1.
The Column of Arcadius, Constantinople, early fifth century, south face. Composite from Freshfield 1922, pls. XV, XVI, and XVIII.

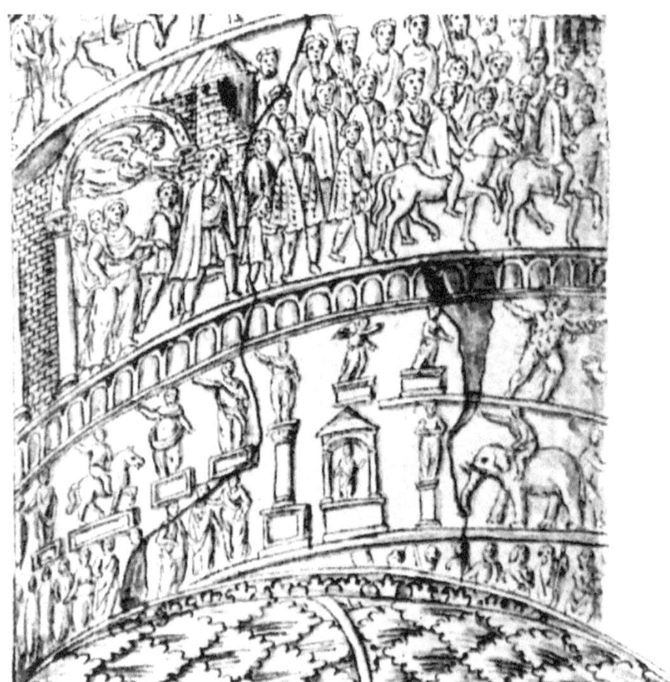

FIGURE E.2. The Column of Arcadius, detail of beginning of frieze on the south face. From Freshfield 1922, pl. XVI.

Column of Marcus Aurelius is in the approach to designing the frieze. The designers of the Column of Arcadius struck out on their own and created an entirely novel narrative that accurately reflected the events for which Arcadius was given this remarkable honor, his campaign to defeat the Goths. The men responsible for the frieze of Marcus's Column, on the other hand, showed markedly less originality. They did not create a new and original frieze, as did Arcadius's artists, but rather produced an altered copy of the frieze they saw on Trajan's Column. Certainly, original and truly historical scenes were added. But many opportunities were missed by Marcus's artists, opportunities that were boldly seized by Arcadius's craftsmen. The designers of the frieze of the Column of Marcus Aurelius could have shown the emperor's departure from Rome, they could have shown a truly historical version of his crossing the frontier into barbarian territory, and they could have shown scenes of his ultimate triumph. That they did not is perhaps partly due to the confused nature of Marcus's campaigns, which began not with a bold Roman sortie but rather with a disastrous barbarian invasion of Italy, and ended not in a clear triumph but rather in a hastily negotiated deal designed to buy time for the emperor to deal with a usurper. A desire to gloss over these details might excuse the designers of the column for being less than historically accurate, but it does not excuse them for relying so heavily on copied and generic material. One intriguing possibility is that, perhaps, the designers of the Column of Arcadius had a greater expectation that their relief would be actively viewed and interpreted by the public. This would explain the dramatic increase in frieze height seen on that column, and the entirely original and much more easy-to-follow narrative.

The Column of Marcus Aurelius, on the other hand, was different. Its designers had different ideas, both architecturally and artistically, and the comparison of these three monuments—Trajan's Column, the Column of Marcus Aurelius, and the Column of Arcadius—shows clearly that they cannot be regarded merely as steps in the linear evolution of a new monumental form. Rather, the appearance of each monument was determined by their distinctly different geneses, by their designers' and artists' goals and skills, by the mood and the situation of the times.

Notes

Abbreviations

ASR XII.1	D. Grassinger, *Die mythologischen Sarkophage* 1. *Achill bis Amazon.* Berlin 1999.
ASR XII.2	H. Sichtermann, *Die mythologischen Sarkophage* 2. *Apollon bis Grazien,* Berlin 1992.
BMC	H. Mattingly, *Coins of the Roman Empire in the British Museum* (multiple volumes). London.
BMCR	H. A. Grueber, *Coins of the Roman Republic in the British Museum.* London 1910.
CAR	*Carta Archeologica di Roma.* Tavola II. Florence 1964.
CIL	*Corpus Inscriptionum Latinarum.*
ILS	*Inscriptiones Latinae Selectae.*
SHA	*Scriptores Historiae Augustae,* also known as the *Historia Augusta.*

Introduction

1. Gibbon [1782] 1862: 216–17.

2. *SHA Marcus* 1.5.

3. On the military preparedness of the new coemperors, see Birley 2000: 159.

4. For recent (and disagreeing) studies of the chronology of Marcus's wars, see Wolff 1990 and Kerr 1995. For a comprehensive narrative treatment see Birley 1993: 163–83 and 2000: 165–76.

5. *SHA Marcus* 13.

6. *SHA Marcus* 21.6–7.

7. The story is related by Lucian, *Alexander the False Prophet* 48.

8. Ammianus Marcellinus 29.6.1. On the dating of the invasion of Italy, see Birley 1993: 250–51 and Scheidel 1990.

9. *SHA Marcus* 21.10.

10. Ibid., 25.5-6.

11. Dio 72.17.1; *SHA Marcus* 25.1.

12. Dio 72.30.1.

13. The pyre and altar are both shown on contemporary coins: *BMC* Marcus 1552 for the pyre, 1580 for the altar.

14. *SHA Marcus* 27.9–10, *SHA Commodus* 12.6. See Morris (1952: 34–37) and Birley (1993: 198–210) for discussions of the main events of the later wars and their sources.

15. *SHA Marcus* 2.1.

16. On how Marcus's thoughts and goals may be read from the *Meditations,* see Brunt 1974.

17. The list exists in two forms, called the *Curiosum urbis Romae* and the *Notitia urbis Romae*: see Jordan 1907: 2.2, 539–74, and the more detailed discussion here in chapter 1.

18. On Bartoli's and Piranesi's prints, see Petersen 1896: 12–17.

19. Mommsen 1896: 21.

20. Petersen 1896: 46 ("Ja für uns das Wichtigste ist, die Gegner der Römer zu betrachten und nach ihrer Charakteristik zu unterscheiden."). On this aspect of Petersen's work, see Beard 2000: 265–66.

21. Wegner 1931.

22. Petersen 1896: 18: the "kuenstlerisch freilich so ausserordentlich viel hoeher stehenden Reliefs der Trajanssaeule."

23. See especially his comparison of the two Victory figures, Wegner 1931: 63–71.

24. Rodenwaldt 1935 (for a résumé in English see Rodenwaldt 1936).

25. For example, Pallottino 1938: 34; Hamberg 1945: 158.

26. Rodenwaldt 1936: 796.

27. Caprino et al. 1955.

28. Vermeule 1956: 317.

29. Pirson 1996; Hölscher 2000; Scheid and Huet 2000; Coarelli 2008. The reader who is interested in the details of the frieze should be aware that the quality of Petersen's original plates is vastly superior to the reproductions in Scheid and Huet (2000) and Coarelli (2008).

Chapter 1

1. On the excavations, conducted by C. Féa, see Daguet-Gagey (1998: 902). Unfortunately nothing was recorded of the structure of the house. For more on the inscription and what it reveals about the topography of the area, see chapter 2. The inscription is *CIL* 6.1585.

2. *CIL* 6.1585a, lines 5 and 7.

3. "*Tegulas omnes et inpensa<m> de casulis item cannabis et aedificiis idoneis adsigna Adrasto procuratori Columnae Divi Marci, ut ad voluptatem suam hospitium sibi ex struat,*" *CIL* 6.1585, lines 15–21.

4. Petersen (1896) felt that a date of either 176 or 180 was possible; a date of 180 is advocated for by, for example, Caprino et al. 1955: 18; Becatti 1957: 1; Richardson 1992: 95; Maffei 1993: 302; Davies 2000: 45–48; Elsner 2000: 253–55. Birley (1993: 252–53) feels Rossi's arguments (1977) may favor a dating of 172–75 for the contents of the frieze, but he remains undecided on the date of the column.

5. For Victor's life, see Bird 1984: 6–13.

6. For Victor as urban prefect: Ammianus 21.10.6, *ILS* 2945.

7. Marcus's gift of citizenship: Victor *De Caesaribus* 16.12. On Victor's errors in general, see Bird 1984: 16–23.

8. Victor *De Caesaribus* 16.8.

9. Dio 72.10.4. Many coins dated TRP XXVIII bear the title IMP VI instead of IMP VII, indicating that this was awarded later in 174 rather than earlier.

10. Petersen (1896), who followed von Domaszewski's (1896) dating of the Danube Crossing to 171, favored a date for the Rain Miracle in the same year. Zwikker (1941: 240) and Wolff (1990) argued for redating the Danube Crossing to 174 in order to accommodate the Rain Miracle.

11. Wolff 1990: 12–13. Wolff presents a numismatic parallel (his plate 2.5) to back up

a connection between the Victoria on the column and Marcus's triumph of 176, but on Wolff's parallel the Victoria is seated, not standing. Victoria, at any rate, is a very common coin type throughout Marcus's reign.

12. My thanks to Tonio Hölscher for suggesting this interpretation.

13. *SHA Marcus* 22 records the summoning of Commodus to the frontier by Marcus Aurelius, at which time he was vested with the *toga virilis*, the toga of manhood. *SHA Commodus* 2.2 records that Commodus's assumption of the *toga virilis* occurred at the time when Cassius revolted. Birley (1993: 254) takes *AE* 1982.778, a dedication in the sanctuary of Jupiter in Carnuntum dating to 172 for the wellbeing of Marcus Aurelius and Commodus as showing that both men were present there at that time. However, it would seem equally plausible that the name of Commodus (who was Caesar at the time) was simply added to the inscription because it was thought appropriate, whether he was there in person or not.

14. *SHA Commodus* 6.5.

15. For the Panel Reliefs, see Ryberg (1967) and Koeppel (1986). Koeppel's (1986: 47–75) description of the reliefs is to be prefered to that of Ryberg, from the point of view of accuracy.

16. Birley (1993: 267) tentatively identifies Commodus in scenes XLIX, standing on platform left of Marcus; LXXV, standing left of Marcus, who is sacrificing; XCVIII, standing right of Marcus, holding lance; and CX–CXI, standing right of Marcus. Morris, too, (1952: 42 and n. 7) suggests that Commodus may be represented in some scenes, but the examples he gives (LXX, LXXXVI, LXXXVII, C, CVII) are scenes in which the heads of both Marcus and his companions are so heavily damaged that no features at all can be identified, and in one case (LXX) the detail in question is a Renaissance restoration.

17. The development of Commodus's numismatic portraiture is clearly illustrated by Wegner (1939) on his pl. 62, with a discussion on pages 68–69. Plates 62a–d show portraits of Commodus between 176 and 179.

18. *BMC* Marcus 625, pl. 66.2.

19. *BMC* Marcus 1606 and 1648, pls. 87.8 and 88.6.

20. Wegner 1939, pl. 62e and f (A.D. 180), k and 1 (185).

21. Birley 1993: 267.

22. The primary example is a bust of Commodus as Sol in the Museo Nazionale Romano (inv. 56128; see Cioffarelli 1988: 300–303; and Wegner 1939: 67, 69–70, 265, and pl. 50). Varner (2004: 147–48) lists the related busts.

23. Wegner 1939: 69; Varner 2004: 147.

24. Marcus's own portraits on the column belong to Wegner's fourth type, with hair brushed up off the forehead and a full, long beard (Wegner 1939: 43–47), which dates to the last decade of the emperor's reign.

25. On Fontana's work on the column, see Colini 1955: 34–38; Martines 2000: 64–68; and Martines in Coarelli 2008: 73–78 (with a very useful summary in English of Martines's research into the modern history of the column, including Fontana's restoration).

26. In favor of Commodus's representation on the pedestal: Petersen 1896: 8; Becatti 1960: 48–49; Bianchi Bandinelli 1969: 324.

27. The historical, epigraphic, and artistic sources on Commodus's *damnatio memoriae* are collected by Varner 2004: 136–48. The quotation from Dio: 74.2.1.

28. For the Panel Reliefs, see Koeppel (1986) and Ryberg (1967).

29. Morris 1952: 43.

30. Compare, for example, the treatment of drapery, hair, and facial features in CXII (one of Morris's "Roman" inserts) with the Renaissance figures in the almost entirely restored scene CXIII immediately following.

31. The portion of the Vatican manuscript relevant to the carving work on the Marcus column is reproduced in Caprino et al. 1955: 121–24, especially the entries connected to pls. LXVII (p. 124) and LXVIII (p. 123). On the restoration, Colini 1955: 34–36; Martines 2000: 64–68.

32. Victor *De Caesaribus* 1.9.

33. Suetonius *Augustus* 52.1; see also Dio 51.20.7.

34. Victor *De Caesaribus* 16.12.

35. Dio 72.34, E. Cary trans.

Chapter 2

1. Strabo 5.3.8, translation by H. L. Jones, slightly adapted. Strabo wrote at the time of Augustus, the latest building he mentions being the portico of Livia, built 7 B.C.

2. Dio 55.8; Aulus Gellius 14.5.1.

3. *CIL* 6.702 (base inscription); Buchner 1982: 358 and figs. 12–14.

4. Suetonius *Augustus* 100.4.

5. See Dio 60.22.1 for the arch; Almeida 1993, and Richardson 1992: 24 for the identification of its location.

6. Wiseman 1993.

7. On the fire of A.D. 80, see Dio 66.24.2.

8. Maischberger 1997: 139 and fig. 68.

9. Buchner 1982: 372; Rakob 1987: 691–98 and list of elevations on 707–12. Rakob suggests that the Domitianic reconstruction of the Horologium may not have been as wide as the Augustan.

10. *SHA Hadrian* 19.9–10.

11. Coarelli 1974: 264–65; Richardson 1992: 247.

12. *SHA Hadrian* 19.11.

13. Haselberger 1994.

14. Rakob 1987: 698 and 708–9.

15. Brick stamps in the retaining wall around the Ara Pacis date to A.D. 123 (Moretti 1948: 198).

16. Rakob 1987: 698–705; Gatti 1989.

17. Blake and Bishop 1973: 53.

18. The insula beneath San Lorenzo in Lucina is dated to the Hadrianic period by its construction and frescoes; see Bertoldi 1992: 128 and fig. 12, and Rakob 1987, fig. 7 for elevations.

19. *SHA Pius* 8.2. Remains of the courtyard have been found: Richardson 1992: 184.

20. For these remains see Hülsen (1889), who published the records of the eighteenth-century excavations of the column of Antoninus Pius and the associated altar by Francesco Bianchini.

21. For a summary of the 1907–10 excavations see Mancini 1913. The in situ remains have been most recently surveyed by Kampmann (1985) and have been given a precise

topographic location by Danti (1984). The architectural remains are published by Danti (1985) and are also illustrated in Nash (1968: 488–89).

22. See Buzzetti 1984 for these twin altars.

23. The architectural remains of this altar are published by Danti (1985: 423–33) and are also illustrated by Nash (1968: 488–89).

24. The term *ustrinum* was first applied to the Antoninus Pius altar in the eighteenth century by Bianchini, whose work is reproduced and analyzed by Hülsen (1889). Frischer (1983: 74) notes that the stone altar complexes in no way resemble ancient descriptions of imperial *ustrina*; Boatwright (1985: 496) observed that a new descriptive term was needed, and suggested "consecration memorials." Kampmann (1985: 78) has recently suggested that the travertine and marble structure might have been present at the time of cremation, protected by an insulating layer of stone or similar material, but this seems unlikely and at any rate unnecessary.

25. On the form of imperial funerary pyres: Herodian 4.2.6–8.

26. Dio 75.5.3–5, E. Cary trans.

27. Buzzetti (1984: 27) notes that the altars were found at a depth of 5–6 meters below the modern level, which is approximately equivalent to the Hadrianic ground level.

28. *CIL* 6.1004.

29. See Hülsen 1889: 41–48, and in general for the monument, Vogel 1973. Although the column itself was subsequently damaged and broken up, its base can still be seen in the Vatican.

30. For Faustina I, see Richardson 1992: 149; for Pius see Danti 1993.

31. As, for example, recently by Danti (1984).

32. Maffei (1993: 303) notes the problem in orientation, while Frischer (1983: 74) points out the problem of distance, a factor also remarked on by Ward-Perkins (1976: 345).

33. Buzzetti 1984: 28.

34. *BMC* Hadrian 960–63, pl. 66.8–10.

35. Faustina I: pyre (*BMC* Pius 1429–31, pl. 34.10), altar (*BMC* Pius 1464–67, pl. 35.6 and 8), temple (*BMC* Pius 319–23, 1454–57, pl. 7.17, 8.2, 35.3 and 4, and many others).

36. Verus: pyre *BMC* Marcus 505, 1363–70, pl. 62.20, 81.7 and 8.

37. *SHA Verus* 4.6–7.

38. Faustina II: pyre (*BMC* Marcus 698–99, 701–3, 1550, 1552, 1553, pl. 67.12 and 14, 86.1), altar (*BMC* Marcus 725–27, 1579–83, pl. 68.5, 87.2).

39. Marcus: pyre (*BMC* Commodus 25–28, 399–402, pl. 91.14, 15, 101.10 and 11). The remainder of his divus coinage is interesting and varied, including an elephant cart and the symbolic eagle in various guises—with thunderbolt, bearing Marcus, and standing alone on a globe or a small garlanded platform (in no way to be confused with the large funerary altars with their acroteria, doorways, and staircases).

40. A series of coins struck under Trajan Decius depicts portraits of various deified emperors, going back to Augustus, with a common reverse showing a flaming altar with the legend CONSECRATIO. There is no reason to believe that these represent actual individual altars belonging to each emperor so honored.

41. Zanker 2004: 56 and 66–68.

42. For the temple of Faustina, *SHA Marcus* 26. For its possible location on the Palatine, see Cecamore 1999.

43. No solid evidence for such a colonnade is known, but its existence is proposed by

Sediari (1997: 216) and by Richardson (1992: 96); Maffei (1993: 303) neither supports nor attempts to refute the idea of a surrounding colonnade.

44. Gatti 1955: 22–24 and figs. 4 and 5. See also Calderini in Petersen et al. 1896: 36–38; and Martines 2000: 20.

45. Gatti (1955: 27), the marble surface at the base of the column has an elevation of 15.35 meters, compared to an elevation of 12.30 meters for the surface of the street that ran below the two second-century *insulae* immediately across the road, beneath the Palazzo della Galleria. For other Hadrianic and Antonine elevations in the area see the table in Rakob 1987: 709.

46. Martines 2000: 20.

47. Cipollone 1996: 8 and figs. 4 and 5.

48. See Davies 2000: 167–69.

49. *Curiosum* and *Notitia* Regio IX, line 19; see Jordan 1907 (vol. 1.3): 539–74.

50. For the location of the temple to the west of the column, see most recently Sediari 1997: 216; and Maffei 1993: 303. A number of fragments of coffered ceiling found immediately to the west of the column have been tentatively identified as coming from this structure. Most of these fragments are collected in *Carta Archeologica di Roma* II, 189 and 191–2. La Rocca (2004: 228–29) finds the rosettes in the ceiling panel fragments to be stylistically closer to carving from Trajan's Forum than to the (supposed) altar of Marcus Aurelius and feels they likely date to around the mid-second century, making their association with a temple built after 180 quite unlikely.

51. C. Fea, cited in Daguet-Gagey (1998: 902). The approximate location is given on the *CAR*.

52. François Chausson (2001: 374) recently suggested that because the column is called *columna divi Marci, columna centenaria*, or *columna centenaria divi Marci* in the preserved parts of the letters from the *rationales*, Mommsen's reconstruction of the house of Adrastus as being *post colu[mnam centenariam divorum] Marci et Faustinae* is incorrect, and should read instead *post columnam centenariam et templum divorum Marci et Faustinae*. La Rocca (2004: 231) finds this a sensible and intelligent solution but still feels that there was not enough space for a temple structure. It seems to me that the nomenclature of the column is so variable in the preserved parts of the inscription that we cannot argue from that evidence that Mommsen's restoration (presenting yet another variation) is wrong. Why would Adrastus have mentioned *both* the column *and* the temple, instead of only the temple, if his house was actually directly behind the latter monument?

53. Dio on Augustus and the Via Flaminia: 53.22.1.

54. Dio ibid., *CIL* 11.365.

55. *Inscriptiones Italiae* 13.2: 176 for the altar; for the boundary of *imperium*, see Patterson 1999: 136.

56. On the Ara Fortunae Reducis, see Augustus's own *Res Gestae* 11.

57. On the Arch of Claudius: Dio 60.22.1.

58. Martial 8.65, trans. D. R. Schackelton Baily.

59. The elephant arch of Domitian is identified by some, e.g. Koeppel (1986: 56) and Richardson (1992: 25), as the Porta Triumphalis. Against this identification, see Ryberg 1967: 32–33.

Chapter 3

1. On Roman honorary columns in general, see Becatti (1960): 33–45; and Jordan-Ruwe (1995):53–73. Pliny (*Natural History* 34.10.21) records a *columna honoraria* for L. Minucius Augurinus, *praefectus annonae* in 439 B.C., and a column of unusual construction but topped by a statue is shown on coins issued by two moneyers from the same family in the second century B.C. (*BMCR* 952, 1005). However it is by no means certain that this monument was actually erected in the fifth century; it may be a Hellenistic creation. See Torelli 1993.

2. For Greek columnar monuments, see Jordan-Ruwe (1995): 11–14, also Becatti (1960): 37–39.

3. Maenius's column: Pliny *Natural History* 34.10.20. Maenius's colleague Camillus may also have received a similar statue in his honor; see Hölscher 1978: 338.

4. For Diulius's column: Quintillian *Institutes* 1.7.12, Pliny *Natural History* 34.10.20.

5. Aemelius Paulus: Livy 42.20.1. Octavian: Appian, *Civil War* 5.130.

6. Vespasian's coins with rostral column: *BMC* Vespasian 253 and 254, pl. 7.17 and 18. Vespasian also reproduced other Augustan types, including the globe and Capricorn (ibid. 251, pl. 7.16).

7. The inscription on the pedestal of the column (*CIL* 6.960) gives Trajan's titulature as it was between January 112 and September(?) 114, and the *Fasti Ostienses* almost certainly record its dedication in May 113 (see below, chapter 4). Claridge's (1993) suggestion that the frieze was carved under Hadrian has been argued against by La Rocca (1998: 167, who is followed by Hölscher 2002: 132) on the basis that Hadrian would not have excluded Trajan's Parthian war from such a carving. At any rate, coins of A.D. 113 (e.g., fig. 3.2 here) clearly show the figural frieze and constitute conclusive evidence that it was complete when the monument was dedicated.

8. On Trajan's burial in the base, see Eutropius 8.5.3 and Dio 69.2.3. Gesemann (2003) has recently argued that Eutropius cannot be taken as evidence that Trajan was buried inside the actual *pomerium*, and that the actual *pomerium* border ran in such a way as to exclude both the column and the Basilica Ulpia from it. Eutropius is not speaking technically, and may well not have been aware of the exact course of the *pomerium*.

9. Dio 68.16.3.

10. The inscription on the pedestal of Trajan's Column is *CIL* 6.960. The precise meaning of this inscription has been often discussed; see especially Settis 1988: 49, and Packer 1997: 117. Stucchi (1989: 239–51) surveys previous attempts to reconstruct the missing portion, a number of letters in its last line (*tant . . . ribus*), and suggests a new solution (*tantis viribus*), which would translate, "with such great labors" rather than "for these great works (i.e., the forum complex)."

11. On the measurements of Trajan's column and the significance of the hundred-foot unit in it, see Wilson Jones 1993. The Adrastus inscription (*CIL* 6.1585a and b = *ILS* 5920) is discussed by Daguet-Gagey (1998) with a focus on the administrative aspects thereof. The very earliest reference of any sort is, of course, the depictions of the column of Trajan on that emperor's coinage (e.g., *BMC* III: 449, pl. 14.19; 972, pl. 38.3). For the significance of the height of the columns, see Martines 2000: 39–46.

12. *Curiosum urbis Romae* and the *Notitia urbis Romae*: see Jordan 1907: 2.2.539–74.

Richardson (1992: xx) follows Nordh 1949 in dating the *Curiosum* to the time of Diocletian, the *Notitia* to the reign of Constantine.

13. Isidore *Origines* 15.2.38.

14. Vulgate *Kings* 6.8.

15. Placidus *Corpus Glossarum Latinarum* 5.351.43.

16. P. Gilles, *De Topographia Constantinopoleos,* 3.3. Gilles's fascinating text is available in English translation, reissued by Musto (1988). In Greek, Procopius (*Persian Wars* 1.24.43) provides a similar interpretation of the word from the sixth century A.D. Celsus's description of how to wrap a bandage (*Med.* 8.10.1.E) is sometimes cited as an argument for *cochlis* referring to the frieze, but here the term was employed by Celsus as a simile, not in a technical manner as in our other sources. For detailed discussion of these and other sources see Beckmann 2002.

17. Ammianus Marcellinus 16.10.14, text from Teubner edition of W. Seyfarth. For the *Notitia urbis Constantinopolitanae,* see Seeck 1876. Marcellinus Comes (sixth century) *Chronicon* (II 480.92.8) for the year 480: *statua Theodosii Magni in foro Tauri super cochlidem columnam posita corruit.* For the column of Arcadius, see *Chronicon Paschale,* year 421 (*Corpus Scriptorum Historiae Byzantinae,* ed. L. Dindorf, 16: 579).

18. Formigé's (1949) reconstruction of the Trophy of Augustus at Turbie includes five spiral staircases, but the basis for this reconstruction is not made clear. There is a single fragment of travertine carved with three steps of a spiral staircase lying near the Arch of Titus in the Roman Forum, but date and provenance are unknown. For Selinus (Temple A) see Mertens 1984: fig. 37; and Ginouvès 1998: p1.86.3. For the temple of Bel at Palmyra (commonly dated to the first century A.D., although a date in the second to third century has been suggested for parts of it; see Murray 1917: 24), Ginouvès 1998: pl. 20.1, and Lyttelton 1974: fig. 22.

19. For the S. Silvestro inscription, see Petersen 1896: 4 n.1 and, for a translation, Gregorovius 1903: 686–87n1. Lanciani (1897: 507) suggested that the revenue may have come from pilgrims and tourists wanting to ascend the monument.

20. *CIL* 6.1585; see chapter 1.

21. Pliny: *Natural History* 34.12.27.

22. *SHA Claudius* 7.7. My thanks to Tonio Hölscher for bringing this source to my attention.

Chapter 4

1. For the Tabula Siarensis, see González and Arce 1988: 307–8. It is preserved in the form of a bronze plaque found in Spain and records honors voted to Germanicus after his death.

2. The relevant section reads: *supraque eum Ianum statua Ger[manici Caesaris po] / neretur in curru triumphali et circa latera eius statuae D[rusi Germanici patris ei] / us naturalis fratris Ti(beri) Caesaris Aug(usti) et Antoniae matris ei[us et Agrippinae uxoris et Li] / viae sororis et Ti(beri) Germanici fratris eius et filiorum et fi[liarum eius].*

3. La Rocca (1993: 84–87) identifies the arch described in the Tabula Siarensis as the monumental entrance to the Circus Flaminius shown on the Severan Marble Plan, located in front and slightly east of the entrance to the *Porticus Octaviae* near the Theatre of Marcellus.

4. On the development of building administration in Rome, see Kolb 1993: 28–32.

5. On the length of curatorial appointments see Kolb 1993: 96–97. Bruun (1996: 737) argues that, in addition to the lack of positive evidence, the short time in office of the *curatores* speaks against their involvement in new construction projects.

6. Tacitus *History* 4.23 on Vespasian's reconstruction of the Temple of Jupiter Optimus Maximus after the civil wars, and Suetonius *Titus* 8 on that ruler's reconstruction work in the city after the fire of A.D. 80. On supervision of building work in general, see Lancaster 2002.

7. Lancaster 2002: 372.

8. Dio 69.4. Procopius (*Buildings* 4.6.12–13) identifies Apollodorus as coming from Damascus; through him we also know that Apollodorus's Danube bridge was still famous in the sixth century A.D. For a description of the bridge, see Dio 68.13.

9. Dio 69.4.

10. *SHA Hadrian* 19.12–13.

11. Anderson 1997: 65.

12. Plutarch *Moralia* 498e, trans. W. C. Helmbold.

13. For Fronto's baths, see Aulus Gellius, *Noctes Atticae* 19.10.2–3, (translation here by J. C. Rolfe). Wilson Jones (2000: 52–56) discusses the evidence for the use of drawings and models in Roman architectural planning.

14. *SHA Marcus* 21; Eutropius 8.13.

15. Lancaster 2004: 20–21; Martines 2000: 49–52

16. The Puteoli building inscription: *CIL* 1.608 = *ILS* 5317. Translation in Humphrey et al. 1998: 269–70. Commentary in Anderson 1997: 71–74.

17. For the Colosseum see Lancaster 2002; for the Temple of Vespasian, Rockwell 1988.

18. For Roman building plans, their materials and scales, see Lancaster 2000: 760–62.

19. In the case of the Ara Pacis, Conlin (1997: 84) suggests that the designers of the frieze were left alone to create different compositions for the north and south friezes.

20. For comparative measurements of both columns, see Martines 2000, tables 9 and 10.

21. The profiles of the columns are compared by Wilson Jones (1993, figs. 3 and 4), who also (ibid. and 2000: 169–73) discusses potential problems in the planning of the staircase in Trajan's Column. Relative dimensions can be found in Martines 2000, tables 9 and 10.

22. Step heights: Calderini 1896: 30–33.

23. Martines 1983: 61.

24. Martines (2000: 24) notes that these first two turns of the staircase do not correspond to one another if superimposed.

25. On the process of quarrying, see Rockwell 1993: 156–64.

26. The capacity of Tiber-borne transports is based on a passage in Dionysius of Halicarnasus (3.44.3–4), the interpretation of which is debated; see Maischberger 1997: 30.

27. See Maischberger (1997: 25–31) for discussion of issues involved in shipping stone to Rome.

28. On docks used for unloading stone, see Clayton Fant 2001 for the Emporium docks by the Aventine, and Maischberger 1997: 61–151 for the Campus Martius locations.

29. On the route used to transport elements of Trajan's Column, see Lancaster 1999: 437–39.

30. On the construction of the Pantheon, see Haselberger 1994.

31. Petersen (1896: 39) describes the surfaces of the staircase walls.

32. Wilson Jones 1999: 241.

33. On the method of and weight-saving potential for precarving of entasis, see Wilson Jones 1999: 239–48.

34. The weights of individual elements given here are those calculated by Martines (2000: 75 and 77); Lancaster (1999: 426) calculates a higher weight for the capital of Trajan's Column, 53.3 tons.

35. On methods of construction, Lancaster 1999: 426–37 and figs. 8 and 9.

36. Martines (2000: 83) lists the positions of surviving dowels. Two of the surviving pouring channels, in scene LXXVI between drums 12 and 13, are illustrated in his fig. VI.

37. Martines 2000: 58.

38. On the events surrounding the end of Trajan's second Dacian war, see Dio 63.14.4.

39. Calza 1932: 201, 11.33–34 and 53–56; the modern edition of the *Fasti Ostienses* is Bargagli and Grosso 1997. For the relevant coinage see Beckmann 2000 and 2007.

40. Rockwell 1993: 240–42.

41. The Column of Theodosius: Theophanes *Chronographia* I.70.20 for the beginning of construction; the *Chronicon Paschale* (I.565.6–8) for the placement of the statue.

42. The Column of Arcadius: Theophanes *Chronographia* I.77.24, and *Chronicon Paschale* I.579.15. The sources are conveniently collected by Jordan-Ruwe (1995: 218–22).

43. Claridge 1993: 19. Claridge calculates a surface area of 264 square meters, equivalent to the fronts of 150–200 figured sarcophagi, and estimates that each two-man team worked at a pace of a minimum of two months per sarcophagus equivalent.

44. Claridge 1993.

Chapter 5

1. On the variation in frieze height on the Column of Trajan, see Rockwell 1993: 239.

2. Martines (2000: 88, table 10) gives 2623.4 centimeters for the height of the historiated shaft, but he includes in this the 12.2 centimeter tall apophyge.

3. See Wilson Jones 2000: 74.

4. Zwikker (1941: 256), though he saw "inspiration" from the Column of Trajan, argued against taking the Danube crossing as a copy. Instead he proposed that the palisade reflected the actual state of the late second-century *limes*, and reflected an attempt by the Marcus column designers to introduce an aspect of contemporary reality into the scene.

5. On the possible Domitianic model for the composition, see Lehmann-Hartleben 1923. Wegner (1931: 64–69) compares the depictions of Victoria on each column from a stylistic point of view, with reference to numismatic representations of the goddess.

6. Parallels for the Marcus column trophies are found on the Ammendola sarcophagus (Koch and Sichtermann 1982: 91n5, fig. 74) and the sarcophagus from the Villa Doria Pamphilj (91n7, fig. 75). On Hellenistic derivation of these trophies, see Picard 1957: 443. From the group of Roman vs. German battle sarcophagi, particularly similar is the Portonaccio sarcophagus (Museo Nazionale inv. # 112327; Musso 1985); for others of this type, see Andreae 1956: 15–16, catalogue nos. 9–17.

7. Wegner 1931: 160.

8. Hamberg 1945: 141–45, especially 143.

9. For arguments in favor of large-scale cartoons, see, e.g., Lepper and Frere 1988:

29–31. Hamberg (1945: 138) advanced the theory of individual prefabricated scenes, while Rockwell (1985b) and Coulston (1990b:301) argue for limited sketches only.

10. Becatti (1960: 13–24) traces the history of this idea, which originated in the nineteenth century.

11. Note though that the frieze was completed before the carving of the flutes: see chapter 6.

Chapter 6

1. For an analysis of the border patterns, see Beckmann 2005.

2. Claridge (1993: 19) proposed four teams of two men each; Peter Rockwell (pers. com.) has identified seven hands, and Conti (2001: 204) has also arrived at a total of seven carvers.

3. The precarving of drums is suggested for Trajan's Column by Lepper and Frere (1988: 29–31) and for Marcus's Column by Hamberg (1945: 143 and 158).

4. Rockwell 1993: 238–40.

5. Examples from Trajan's Column of objects from scenes merging with the lower border include rocky formations (scenes LXXVI, XXXIX, LXXII, CI, and CXXXVI), trees (XCII and CXLIII), and water (XXI and XXXIII). On the direction of carving for both columns, see Beckmann 2006.

6. The main examples are legionary standards, scenes LIII/LXII, LXVI/LXI, LXIII/LXVII.

7. Rockwell 1985b: 104.

8. Examples from the Column of Marcus Aurelius of objects overlapping the upper border of the frieze are found in scenes L, LXIII, XCVIII, IC, and C.

9. Claridge 2005: 313–16.

10. Calza and Bonanno 1977: 170–71, #198, pl. 121.

11. Vatican Protesilaos: Koch and Sichtermann 1982: 184, fig. 218 (A.D. 160–70); Villa Pamphilj Dionysus: Calza and Bonanno 1977: 175–76, #203, pl. 124; Capitoline Endymion: ASR XII.2 #27, pl. 26, 1; Capitoline Amazonomachy: ASR XII.1 #94, pl. 91 (A.D. 140–50).

12. Forum of Trajan: Packer 1997, fig. 79 and 80 (note however that the lower portion of fig. 79 is a later restoration). The panels perhaps belong to the colonnade of the temenos of the Temple of Divine Trajan. Great Trajanic Frieze: Leander Touati 1987, pls. 4 and 16.

13. Examples are quite common and include such famous works as the Portonaccio sarcophagus (Koch and Sichtermann 1982: 92, fig. 76), the greater Ludovisi battle sarcophagus (ibid., fig. 78), and the so-called sarcophagus of Balbinus (ibid. 101–2, fig. 100).

14. On Trajan's Column scale armor is worn only by barbarians (e.g., scene XXXVII) and by the trophy in the Victoria scene (LXXVIII); on Marcus's Column it is one of the three common types of armor, together with ring and segmented, worn everywhere by Roman soldiers. On armor types on Trajan's Column, see Coulston 1989: 31–44.

15. De Azevedo 1951: 86–87, #119, pl. XXXVI.65. My thanks to a reviewer of this press for drawing my attention to this parallel.

16. For details of the border patterns and their arrangement on the column, see Beckmann 2005.

17. Another possible error is in scene XVI (the Rain Miracle), where the soldier directly below the window has an uncarved suit of armor, left flat with neither scales nor holes.

18. Wegner 1931: 161–66.

19. Rockwell 1993: 239.

20. Claridge 2005.

21. Del Monte et al. (1998).

22. For examples of holes drilled in hands to hold weapons or tools, see Coarelli 2000, pls. 19, 31, or 40.

23. See Wegner 1931: 160 and 167 for discussion of stylistic development on the Marcus column.

Chapter 7

1. Lactantius, *de Mortibus Persecutorum* 5.3. Lactantius's words for the last portion are: *illud esse verum dicebat exprobans ei cum risu, non quod in tabulis aut parietibus Romani pingerent.*

2. On the problems of the sources, especially Dio and the *SHA*, see Birley 1993: 228–30.

3. Pliny, *Natural History* 35.22 for Messala and Scipio, 35.135 for Paullus. On early references to paintings and other objects carried in Roman triumphs, see Holliday 1997 and 2002.

4. For the action in Carthage, more a foolish venture with a fortunate ending, see Appian, *Roman History* 17.113–14; for the painting, Pliny, *Natural History* 35.23.

5. Jewish Wars 7.139–48; trans. H. Thackeray, Loeb edition.

6. For the Pompeii amphitheatre riot painting, see, for example, Ramage and Ramage 2009, fig. 5.51.

7. Juvenal XIV.298–302; trans. G. Ramsay.

8. The connection between the frieze of Trajan's Column and triumphal painting was first suggested by Semper in 1860 (295). For Hamberg, see Hamberg 1945: 125. See also Rodenwaldt 1921/22: 82.

9. Koeppel 1985: 92. See Coarelli 2000: 13–16; and Settis 1988: 86–100 for recent surveys of these and other theories regarding the source of the images on Trajan's Column.

10. *SHA* Marcus 24.4: *fulmen de caelo precibus suis contra hostium macinamentum extorsit, suis pluvia impetrata cum siti laborarent.*

11. Birley (1993: 172) associates the Lightning Miracle with coins of Marcus as Jupiter crowned by Victory, but this numismatic motif is, as I argue elsewhere, almost certainly intended to recall a specific honor given to Trajan and also represented on that emperor's coinage.

12. For the most recent contributions to the debate over the exact date of the Rain Miracle and the significance of its position within the narrative frieze see Wolff 1990; Löhr 2009: 131; and above all Kovács 2009. Despite relatively abundant (though admittedly often problematic) evidence, historical approaches have still yielded no clear solution to the problem. This suggests that one of the main assumptions of the historical approach—that the position of the miracle on the column has a chronological significance—is itself in error.

13. Eusebius: *In quis (bellis) semel Pertinaci et exercitui, qui cum eo in Quadorum regione pugnabat, siti opressis pluvia divinitus missa est, cum e contrario Germanos et Sar-*

matas fulmina persequerentur et plurimos eorum interficerent. (*Chronicon* A.D. 173, Helm 1984: 206–7, also Schoene 1866: 173). Themistius: *Orationes* 15.191.b–c.

14. On Dio's use of *topoi*, see E. Cary in his introduction to the Loeb edition of Dio, xiv. On Thucydidean elements, see Paul 1987: 309–10.

15. Rossi 1977.

16. *Année épigraphique* 1956.124, 11.9–11: *Ab Imp. Antonino Aug. coram laudato et equo et phaleris et armis donato quod manu sua ducem Naristarum Valaonem intermisset.*

17. Petersen et al. 1896: 58.

18. Dobias 1932: 150.

19. *Alexander the False Prophet* 48.

20. Most commentators include the fortress to the right of the emperor's party as being part of scene X, but the soldiers in the fort are turned away from the action at the river, suggesting that it is right to understand an entirely new scene beginning with the fortress wall.

21. Zwikker 1941: 262, Caprino et al. 1955: 85.

22. Petersen et al. 1896: 56.

23. Petersen 1896: 63.

24. Coarelli 2008: 195.

25. Petersen 1896: 68.

26. Fronto *ad Verum* 2.3 (in the Loeb edition: vol. II, 195).

27. Lehmann-Hartleben 1926: 88.

28. See Goldsworthy 1996: 191–227 for discussion of Roman infantry battle, 228–35 for fights between cavalry and infantry.

29. In scene XL on Trajan's Column, the two Roman cavalrymen who ride in from the edge of the battle at the upper right are not an example of mixing troop types, but rather a depiction of the Roman cavalry riding to the aid of the infantry in the concluding phase of the battle, the pursuit (Dacians are shown fleeing immediately to the right).

30. Nolan 1860: 234. See also Goldsworthy (1996: 236–37) for comment on Nolan and examples of cavalry encounters from Caesar, Plutarch, and Arrian.

31. For example, by Petersen (1896) and Caprino (1955). Not all agree: Romanelli (Caprino et al. 1955: 68) registers his doubt as to the validity of specific troop-type assignments for ring- and scale-wearing soldiers. Praetorians in Italy in the early second century do not seem to have been distinguishable from the regular soldiery except by their use of specific emblems, especially the scorpion; for this in sculpture, see Fowler 2001: 635–36. Dio (79.37.4) describes praetorians in the time of Macrinus (ca. A.D. 218) wearing scale breastplates, but at the same time describes them as bearing large curved shields, which the scale-wearing troops on the Marcus column do not. On legionary versus auxiliary equipment in general, see Bishop and Coulston 2006: 254–59.

32. Tacitus's account of the battle of Mons Graupius: Agr. 35. For the ratio of bloodshed interpretation, see most recently Coulston 1989: 32. Another suggestion is that the auxiliaries were in the forefront at Mons Graupius because the terrain was unsuited for legionaries in formation, and that the tactical nature of the war in Dacia may have dictated a similar use of auxiliary soldiers (Cheesman 1914: 103–4, esp. 104nn2 and 3).

33. The fundamental work and source of published illustrations is Florescu 1965. For

a recent discussion, including coverage of the 1977 reconstruction made after Florescu's theories, along with arguments for and against it, see Bianchi 1997.

34. For the inscription of the Tropaeum, see Florescu 1965: 61–67. The Trajanic dating is accepted by the vast majority of scholars (see list in Florescu, 9). On the function of the monument, see Florescu 18–20.

35. Robinson 1975: 7.

36. Coulston 1989.

37. Coulston 1990a.

38. Troops in segmented armor appear in only one scene (XIX) fighting as a unit, and then only once (XCVII) outside of the *testudo* attack (LIV) as an individual soldier in a larger battle.

Chapter 8

1. Gardner 1897: 221.

2. Petersen 1896: 18 and 101; "die künstlerisch freilich so ausserordentlich viel höher stehenden Reliefs der Trajanssäule" . . . "All diesem Reichtum gegenüber erscheint die Darstellung der Marcussäule arm und nüchtern auf das Notwendigste beschränkt."

3. Pallottino 1938: 35 "Comprendere la colonna aureliana," wrote Massimo Pallottino, "significa comprendere tutta una fase dell'arte romana."

4. Wegner 1931.

5. Ibid., 146–53.

6. Jung 1984: 59.

7. The most important early discussion of the new style is by Rodenwaldt (1940 in German, with shorter discussions in English in volumes XI and XII [first edition] of the *Cambridge Ancient History*).

8. It is crucial to note that extra care must be taken not to confuse Renaissance restorations executed in a neoclassical style with the original frieze.

9. Unfortunately, but perhaps not surprisingly, there are no direct parallels between scenes LXXXII and XCIV and the construction scenes on Trajan's Column.

10. The battle scenes are: VIII, XII, XV, XVIII, XIX, XX, XXIII, XXIV, XXVII, XXVIII, XXIX/XXX, XXXV, XXXIX, XLIII, XLVIII, L, LII, LIV, LVII, LXIII, LXX, LXXII/LXXIII, LXXVII, LXXIX, LXXXIX, XCII, XCVII, IC, CV, CIX. Pirson (1996: 140) counts thirty-six battle or small combat scenes, but he includes four (XXXIV, XL, LXXVI and XLVII) Renaissance restorations that may or may not reflect the original scene content, and he counts LXXII/LXXIII as two scenes.

11. On Greek battle art, Bie (1891) is still unsurpassed for the identification of its overall characteristics; for a more recent analysis of its evolution, see Hölscher 1973.

12. See especially Hanson 1989 on Greek hoplite warfare.

13. A third- to second-century date for the original on which the Alexander Mosaic was presumably based has been proposed by Pfrommer (1998: 216), mainly on the basis of antiquarian details. Cohen, on the other hand, argues that the mosaic is a copy of a painting of the time of Alexander (1997: 2).

14. The closest any earlier monument comes to the type of battles seen on Trajan's Column is the so-called Mantua Relief, which may have been part of an Augustan-period

temple in the Roman Forum. It shows a group of Romans fighting with a group of largely naked barbarians. The figure types are classical and Hellenistic in derivation, but the grouping of combatants is innovative. See Strong 1961: 91; Koeppel 1983b: 132–33 (especially for bibliography); and Marszal 2000: 219.

15. The connection between the frieze of Trajan's Column and triumphal painting was first suggested by Semper in the nineteenth century (1860: 295). See also Rodenwaldt 1921/22: 82.

16. Koeppel 1985: 92. See Coarelli 2000: 13–16; and Settis 1988: 86–100 for recent surveys of other theories regarding the source of the images on Trajan's Column.

17. The numbering employed here is specific to the figures involved in the battles and is independent of Petersen's full-scene numbering scheme.

18. See Koch and Sichtermann 1982: 27–30 for the evidence for this change in funerary tradition.

19. For the numbers of different genres of sarcophagi, see Koch 1993: 94.

20. Andreae (1956: 14–16) catalogs seventeen examples, including the Large Ludovisi sarcophagus (not treated here because of its much later date). Koch and Sichtermann (1982: 91) use the figure of "about twenty"; Koch (1993: 66) uses the figure of "etwa 30," but with no indication of where the extra ten sarcophagi come from. See below for a detailed discussion of numbers.

21. On the models employed by sarcophagus carvers, see Koch 1993: 53–54. Jung 1984 provides striking examples, conveniently collated, of rote repetition of figure types and scene composition on sarcophagi over periods as long as half a century: figs. 2–4 for Medea sarcophagi, 5–7 Leukippides sarcophagi, 8–10 and 11–13 for Endymion sarcophagi. Andreae (1956) proposed that Greek-vs.-Gaul sarcophagi copied a famous but now lost Hellenistic painting.

22. For the Panel Reliefs, see Ryberg 1967.

23. Rodenwaldt 1935: 23; Becatti (1960: 77–79) follows Rodenwaldt, and speculates that some carvers from the same workshop responsible for the column also executed sarcophagi like the Frascati Wedding sarcophagus (Koch and Sichtermann 1982: #94). Traversari (1968) attempted to connect sarcophagi showing the death of Meleager to the "Maestro" responsible for the Marcus column's frieze.

24. Becatti's (1960) plates 42 and 43 provide an excellent opportunity for comparing the style of barbarian heads on the Marcus column, the Frascati Wedding sarcophagus, and the Portonaccio battle sarcophagus. This comparison, selective though it is, suggests fairly close stylistic similarity between the column and the Frascati sarcophagus, but not the work of the same artists. The distorted, triangular, elongated faces of the Portonaccio sarcophagus are further removed from the style of the column.

25. On workshops, see Koch and Sichtermann 1982: 259–67.

26. The fur cap on the left-hand trophies of the Ammendola (ibid., 91n5, fig. 74) and Doria Pamphilj sarcophagi (Calza and Bonanno 1977: 202–4 (P. Pensabene) cat. #233, pls. 137, 138; Andreae 1956: 14, #12), the full-face mask on the right-hand trophy is paralleled on the Palermo (Tusa 1995, #77, pp. 76–77) and Portonaccio (Musso 1985) sarcophagi.

27. Koch and Sichtermann 1982: fig. 249. Pure seafaring scenes on sarcophagi are rare, are mainly dated to the third century, and tend to be more realistic (ibid., 124–25; figs. 132–35).

28. Rumpf 1939: 11–19, #s 32–54, especially 32 = pl. 11 (Ostia, Fondo Aldobrandini, third quarter of second century A.D.), which is similar to the Rain God in both form and style.

29. Vatican Museo Chiaramonti 1735 and Vatican Belvedere 896 (dating to A.D. 170 and 180) = *ASR* XII.1 cat. 100 and 101, pp. 239–40, pls. 96.6 and 97.2. Also on an Amazon sarcophagus in the Berlin Antikensammlung (*ASR* XII.1 cat. 102, pp. 241–42, third quarter of the second century, pl. 101.5) and an Achilles sarcophagus in Rome, Villa Albani, circa A.D. 190 (inv. 223, *ASR* XII.1 cat. 41, pp. 209–10, pls. 32.4, 33.2).

30. The exception is Roman figure 20.11, who is not in exactly the same pose as the rest of this group, with his shield held out before his body.

31. Hübner 1990: 21–27, figs. 1.2a–j.

32. Herakles: Robert 1919, cat. 102, 105, 107, 112, 120; Amazon: *ASR* XII.1: 140, type "Gefallene Q," with an especially good parallel in cat. 114, pl. 107.1.

33. Trumpeter on Amazon sarcophagi: *ASR* XII.1: 141, "Tubicen Y."

34. See Rockwell 1993: 31–54 for a description of ancient stone-carving tools and 233–42 for tool marks on Trajan's Column. For the finish on the Panel Reliefs, see Ryberg (1967) pls. 10, 12, 18, 19, and 21 and Chilosi and Martellotti 1987: 46–47, pls. 1–3.

35. For example, the Vatican Chiaramonti Alcestis sarcophagus, dated by inscription to 160–70, is finished all over with a scraper and rasp (*ASR* XII.1 cat. 76, pl. 78.2 for a good close-up).

36. The rasp appears to have been applied to almost all flat surfaces: flesh, drapery, armor, and the background (see, for example, Becatti 1957, figs. 39, 41, 50). Channeling (the outlining of figures with a narrow round-headed chisel) is ubiquitous. Clear marks of a flat chisel can only be seen on the fluting at the very top of the column (ibid., fig. 70, and here fig. 6.6).

37. On the carving of the Ara Pacis, see Conlin 1997.

38. Rodenwaldt 1935 (for a résumé in English, see Rodenwaldt 1936, whence the quotations, p. 796) and Rodenwaldt 1940: 43.

39. Bianchi Bandinelli 1969.

40. Picard 1962: 292.

41. Lehmann 1956: 518.

42. Becatti 1957: [3–4] (pages unnumbered).

43. Pirson 1996: 170.

44. Hölscher 2000: 101. "Der Stil der Marcus-Säule bedeutet grundsätzlich eine Auflösung der traditionellen klassischen Körperformen, mit dem Ziel eines stärkeren expressiven Ausdrucks."

45. Clarke 2003: 273.

46. Genuine frontality is rarer than often supposed; as Elsner (2000: 255–59) notes, perceived cases of frontality are often the effect of misleading angles in the photographs used by modern scholars.

47. Clarke 2003: 52–53.

48. On the Arch of Semptimus Severus, see Brilliant 1967.

49. Lusnia 2006: 283–91. Herodian 3.9.12 (trans. C. R. Whittaker, Loeb ed.). Lusnia (291–93) makes a compelling connection between the location of the arch—near the Senate House—and the tradition of exhibiting such paintings in the Forum.

Chapter 9

1. On the finding of the finger, see Petersen 1896: 3.

2. Lehmann-Hartleben 1926: 1..

3. No evidence for paint has been found on the Marcus column, but Del Monte et al. (1998) have cautiously identified what they believe may be two small potential residues of paint on Trajan's Column: red on Trajan's cloak in scene XLIV and yellowish-orange from a tree trunk in scene CXXXVIII.

4. Gauer 1977: 45–48; Brilliant 1984: 90–116.

5. See Settis 1988: 130–88 for discussion of compositional schemes; 202–19 for vertical correspondences.

6. Veyne 1991.

7. Ibid., 321–22.

8. Hölscher 1991: 262; and Hölscher 2002: 140n7: "einem Frontalangriff auf die anspruchsvollen Untersuchungskriterien der Archäologen."

9. Hölscher 2000: 90.

10. Rodenwaldt 1936: 796; Becatti 1960: 282; Zanker 1997: 189.

11. Zanker 1997: 189.

12. Balty 2000: 201—though note the skeptical view of Beard (2000: 269) in the same volume.

13. The stock scenes of Trajan's Column were first identified by Lehmann-Hartleben (1926), whose scheme was built upon by Gauer (1977), who demonstrated that these stock scenes tended to be arranged in standard, repetitive sequences. Hölscher (1980 and 1991) and Settis (1988) have led the way in interpreting these sequences from an ideological perspective.

14. Hölscher (2000: 94) uses the adjective "*zersetzt.*"

15. Ibid., 95, 105, and throughout.

16. See Zanker 2000 for discussion of violence toward noncombatants on the column. For violence against women in particular, see Dillon 2006.

17. Pirson 1996: 174.

18. Hölscher 2000: 97–98.

19. Dillon 2006.

20. See Lepper and Frere 1988: 277–89 for discussion of these and other possible motivations for the first Dacian war.

21. Dio (68.10.3–4) records that Decebalus was rebuilding forts, strengthening his army, and conniving with his neighbors.

22. Ammianus (29.6.1) mentions the invasion briefly, and the *SHA* (*Marcus* 14) records Victorinus's death.

23. Tacitus *Annals* 2.21: *nil opus captivis, solam internicionem gentis finem bello fore.*

24. Dio 62.11.2, trans. E. Cary, Loeb ed.

25. Tacitus *Annals* 13.39. See Gilliver 1996: 225–26 for slaughter as a usual outcome of a successful Roman siege of a holdout enemy fortification.

26. Dio 67.4.6, trans. E. Cary. See also Shaw 2000: 379.

27. Tacitus, *Agricola* 18; trans. M. Hutton, Loeb ed.

28. *Jewish Wars* 7.139–46. See chapter 7 for the full quotation.

29. Dio 72.13.1–2, trans. E. Cary, Loeb ed.

30. Ibid.

31. Dio 72.14.1, trans. E. Cary, Loeb ed.

32. Josephus, *Jewish Wars* 7.146, trans. H. Thackeray, Loeb ed.

33. Vergil, *Aeneid* VI.847–43.

34. On the embassy of the Buri, see Talbert 1988, whom I thank for raising the idea of the column's impact on visiting dignitaries.

35. Clarke 2003: 50–53.

36. Lucian, *How to Write History*, 20.

37. Ibid., 37.

38. Harris 2006.

39. On this work, carried out by Domenico Fontana, see Colini 1955: 34–38, and Martines 2000: 64–68.

40. The main attempts at reconstructing the original appearance of the pedestal are those by Calderini (1896, pl. 2), Gatti (1955, fig. 5B), and Jordan-Ruwe (1995, fig. 24; see also Jordan-Ruwe 1990).

41. Victories bearing garlands are particularly common on coins marking the Parthian victory in 166 (*BMC* Marcus 399, pl. 60.11 etc.); the motif also appears on the Adventus panel of Marcus's arch reliefs (Ryberg 1967, pl. XXIII).

42. For the Panel Reliefs, see Ryberg 1967.

Epilogue

1. Eutropius *Breviarum* 8.5.

2. It is possible that the designers of the Column of Arcadius took their inspiration solely from the Column of Theodosius, which was completed in Constantinople in or about A.D. 393—and in fact, these are so close in time that some architects and artists are likely to have worked on both projects. Then it would have been the designers of Theodosius's Column who would have gone to Rome to gather data for their project. I use Arcadius's Column here because our evidence for its original appearance is overwhelmingly better. The most detailed discussion of the Column of Arcadius is Becatti 1960 for the frieze, Konrad 2001 for the architecture.

Bibliography

Almeida, E. R. 1993. "Arcus Claudii." *Lexicon Topographicum Urbis Romae* 1:85–86.

Amy, R. 1962. *L'arc d'Orange*. Paris.

Anderson, J. C. 1997. *Roman Architecture and Society*. Baltimore.

Andreae, B. 1968–69. "Imitazione ed originalità nei sarcofagi Romani." *Atti della Pontificia Accademia Romana di Archeologia: Rendiconti* 41:145–66.

———. 1956. *Motivgeschichtliche Untersuchungen zu den römischen Schlachtsarkophagen*. Berlin.

Balty, J. 2000. "L'armée de la colonne Aurélienne: Images de la cohésion d'un corps." In Scheid and Huet 2000: 197–204.

Bargagli, B., and C. Grosso. 1997. *I Fasti Ostienses*. Rome.

Beard, M. 2000. "The Spectator and the Column." In Scheid and Huet 2000: 265–79.

Becatti, G. 1960. *La Colonna Coclide Istoriata*. Rome.

———. 1957. *Colonna di Marco Aurelio*. Milan.

Beckmann, M. 2007. "Trajan's Gold Coinage, A.D. 112–117." *American Journal of Numismatics* 19:77–130.

———. 2006. "The Direction of Carving on the Columns of Trajan and Marcus Aurelius." *Römische Mitteilungen* 112:225–36.

———. 2005. "The Border of the Frieze of the Column of Marcus Aurelius and Its Implications." *Journal of Roman Archaeology* 18:302–12.

———. 2002. "The *Columnae Coc(h)lides* of Trajan and Marcus Aurelius." *Phoenix* 56:1–10.

———. 2000. "The Early Gold Coinage of Trajan's 6th Consulship." *American Journal of Numismatics* 12:119–56.

Bertoldi, M. E. 1992. "L'area archeologica di San Lorenzo in Lucina." *Bollettino di Archeologia* 13:127–37.

Bianchi, L. 1997. "Tropaeum Traiani." *Enciclopedia dell'Arte Antica*, suppl. 5:862–64.

Bianchi Bandinelli, R. 1969. *Roma: L'arte romana nel centro del potere*. Milan.

Bie, O. 1891. *Kampfgruppe und Kämpfertypen in der Antike*. Berlin.

Bird, H. W. 1984. *Sextus Aurelius Victor: A Historiographical Study*. Liverpool.

Birley, A. R. 2002. Review of Scheid and Huet 2000. *L'Antiquité Classique* 71:504–6.

———. 2000. "Hadrian to the Antonines." In A. Bowman, P. Garnsey, and D. Rathbone (eds.), vol. 11 of *Cambridge Ancient History*, 2nd ed. New York. 132–94.

———. 1993. *Marcus Aurelius: A Biography*. London.Bishop, M. C., and J. N. C. Coulston. 2006. *Roman Military Equipment*. 2nd ed. Oxford.

Blake, M. E., and D. T. Bishop. 1973. *Roman Construction in Italy from Nerva through the Antonines*. Philadelphia.

Boatwright, M. 1985. "The 'Ara Ditis-Ustrinum of Hadrian' in the Western Campus Martius and Other Problematic Roman Ustrina." *American Journal of Archaeology* 89:485–97.

Briggs, C. C. 1930. "The Pantheon of Ostia." *Memoirs of the American Academy in Rome* 8:161–69.

Brilliant, R. 1984. *Visual Narratives: Storytelling in Etruscan and Roman Art*. Ithaca.

———. 1967. *The Arch of Septimius Severus in the Roman Forum*. Rome.

Brunt, P. A. 1974. "Marcus Aurelius in His Meditations." *Journal of Roman Studies* 64:1–20.

Bruun, C. 1996. Review of Kolb 1993. *Bonner Jahrbücher* 196:735–40.

Buchner, E. 1982. *Die Sonnenuhr des Augustus*. Mainz.

Buzzetti, C. 1984. "Ustrini imperiali a Montecitorio." *Bullettino della Commissione Archeologica Comunale di Roma* 89:27–28.

Calderini, G. 1896. "L'architettura della colonna." In Petersen et al. 1896: 21–28.

Calza, G. 1932. "Un nuovo frammento di Faste Annali (anni 108–113)." *Notizie degli Scavi* 6, no. 8:188–205.

Calza, R., and M. Bonanno. 1977. *Antichità di Villa Doria Pamphilj*. Rome.

Caprino, C., A. M. Colini, G. Gatti, M. Pallottino, and P. Romanelli. 1955. *La Colonna di Marco Aurelio*. Rome.

Cecamore, C. 1999. "Faustinae Aedemque Decernerent (*SHA*, Marcus, 26). Les Fragments 69–70 de la Forma Urbis et la Première Dédicace du Temple de la Vigna Barberini." *Mélanges de l'École Française de Rome* 111:311–49.

Chausson, F. 2001. "Deuil dynastique et topographie urbaine dans la Rome antonine." In N. Belayche (ed.), *Rome, les césars et la ville aux deux premiers siècles de notre ère*. Rennes. 293–395.

Cheesman, G. L. 1914. *The Auxilia of the Roman Imperial Army*. Oxford.

Chilosi, M. G., and G. Martellotti. 1987. "I Relievei della Chiesa di S. Martina. Dati sulle techniche esecutive." In E. La Rocca (ed.), *Relievi Storici Capitolini*. Rome. 46–60.

Cichorius, C. 1896 and 1900. *Die Reliefs der Traianssäule*. Berlin.

Cioffarelli, A. 1988. "Ritratto di Commodo-Sol." *Museo Nazionale Romano: Le Sculture* I/9.2:300–303. Rome.

Cipollone, M. 1996. "Hadrianus, Divus, Templum; Hadrianeum." *Lexicon Topographicum Urbis Romae*, 3:7–8.

Claridge, A. 2005. "Further Considerations on the Carving of the Frieze on the Column of Marcus Aurelius." *Journal of Roman Archaeology* 18:313–16.

———. 1993. "Hadrian's Column of Trajan." *Journal of Roman Archaeology* 6:5–22.

Clarke, J. R. 2003. *Art in the Lives of Ordinary Romans: Visual Representation and Non-elite Viewers in Italy, 100 B.C.–A.D. 315*. Berkeley.

Clayton Fant, J. 2001. "Rome's Marble Yards." *Journal of Roman Archaeology* 14:167–98.

Coarelli, F. 2008. *La Colonna di Marco Aurelio. The Column of Marcus Aurelius*. Rome.

———. 2000. *The Column of Trajan*. Rome.

———. 1997. *Il Campo Marzio dale origini alla fine della Republica*. Rome.

———. 1974. *Guida archaeologica di Roma*. Verona.

Cohen, A. 1997. *The Alexander Mosaic: Stories of Victory and Defeat*. Cambridge.

Cohon, R. 2002. "Form and Meaning: Scrollwork on the Ara Pacis, Grotesques in Furniture Design." *Journal of Roman Archaeology* 15:416–28.

Colini, A. M. 1955. "Vicende della Colonna, dall'antichità ai nostri giorni." In C. Caprino et al. 1955: 29–42.

Conlin, D. A. 1997. *The Artists of the Ara Pacis: The Process of Hellenization in Roman Relief Sculpture*. Chapel Hill.

Conti, C. 2001. "Gli Scultori della Colonna Traiana." In F. Festa Farina et al. (eds.), *Tra Damasco e Roma: L'architettura di Apollodoro nella Cultura Classica*. Rome. 199–215.

Coulston, J. C. 1990a. "Three New Books on Trajan's Column." *Journal of Roman Archaeology* 3:290–309.

———. 1990b. "The Architecture and Construction Scenes on Trajan's Column." In M. Henig (ed.), *Architecture and Architectural Sculpture in the Roman Empire*. Oxford. 39–50.

———. 1989. "The Value of Trajan's Column as a Source for Military Equipment." In *Roman Military Equipment: The Sources of Evidence*. BAR International Series 476. 31–44.

Curle, J. A. 1911. *A Roman Frontier Post and Its People, the Fort of Newstead in the Parish of Melrose*. Glasgow.

Daguet-Gagey, A. 1998. "Adrastus et la Colonne Antonine: L'administration des travaux publics à Rome en 193 ap. J.-C." *Mélanges de l'École française de Rome* 110:893–915.

Danti, A. 1993. "Arae Consecrationis." *Lexicon Topographicum Urbis Romae* 1:75–76.

———. 1985. *Museo Nazionale Romano: Le Sculture* I/8.2. Rome.

———. 1984. "Nuove acquisizioni per la topografia antica del Campo Marzio settentrionale (Ustrino di Marco Aurelio)." *L'Urbe* 47:143–46.

Davies, P. J. E. 2000. *Death and the Emperor: Roman Imperial Funerary Monuments from Augustus to Marcus Aurelius*. Cambridge.

De Azevedo, M. C. 1951. *Le Antichità di Villa Medici*. Rome.

De Fine Licht, K. 1966. *The Rotunda in Rome: A Study of Hadrian's Pantheon*. Arhus.

DeLaine, J. 1997. *The Baths of Caracalla: A Study in the Design, Construction, and Economics of Large-Scale Building Projects in Imperial Rome*. Ann Arbor.

Del Monte, M., P. Ausset, and R. A. Lefèvre. 1998. "Traces of Ancient Colours on Trajan's Column." *Archaeometry* 40:403–12.

Demougin, S. 1987. "Élections et électeurs à la fin de la république." In *L'Urbs: Espace urbain et histoire*. Rome. 305–17.

Dillon, S. 2006. "Women on the Columns of Trajan and Marcus and the Visual Language of Roman Victory." In Dillon and Welch 2006: 244–71.

Dillon, S. and Welch, K. E. 2006. *Representations of War in Ancient Rome*. New York.

Dobias, J. 1932. "Le monnayage de l'empereur Marc-Aurel et les bas-reliefs historiques contemporaines." *Revue Numismatique* 1932:127–72.

Domaszewski, A. 1896. "Erläuterung der Bildwerke." In Petersen et al. 1896: 105–25.

Dufraigne, P. 1975. *Aurelius Victor, Livre des Césars*. Paris.

Elsner, J. 2000. "Frontality in the Column of Marcus Aurelius." In Scheid and Huet 2000: 251–64.

Ferris, I. M. 2000. *Enemies of Rome: Barbarians through Roman Eyes*. Sutton.

Florescu, F. B. 1965. *Das Siegesdenkmal von Adamklissi, Tropaeum Traiani*. Bonn.

Formigé, J. 1949. *Le Trophée des Alpes: La Turbie*. Paris.

Fowden, G. 1991. "Constantine's Porphyry Column: The Earliest Literary Allusion." *Journal of Roman Studies* 81:119–31.

Fowler, H. I. 2001. "A Tale of Two Monuments: Domitian, Trajan, and Some Praetorians at Puteoli." *American Journal of Archaeology* 105:625–48.

Freshfield, E. H. 1922. "Notes on a Vellum Album Containing some Original Sketches of Public Buildings and Monuments Drawn by a German Artist Who Visited Constantinople in 1574." *Archaeologia* 62:81–104.

Frischer, B. 1983. "Monumenta Honoris Virtutisque Causa. Evidence of Memorials for Roman Civic Heroes." *Bullettino della Commissione Archeologica Comunale di Roma* 88:51–86.

Froning, H. 1980. "Die ikonographische Tradition der kaiserzeitlichen mythologischen Sarkophagreliefs." *Jahrbuch des Deutschen Archäologischen Instituts* 95:322–41.

Gardner, P. 1897. "The Column of Marcus Aurelius." *Classical Review* 11, no. 4:221–23. Gatti, G. 1989. "Caratteristiche edilizie di un quartiere di Roma nel II secolo d.C." In G. Gatti, *Topografia ed elilizia di Roma antica*. Rome.

———. 1955. "La Columna Divi Marci, nelle sue caratteristiche architettoniche e nel suo ambiente." In Caprino et al. 1955: 13–28.

Gauer, W. 1981. "Die Triumphsäulen als Wahrzeichen Roms und der Roma secunda und als Denkmäler der Herrschaft im Donauraum." *Antike und Abendland* 27:179–92.

———. 1977. *Untersuchungen zur Traianssäule*. Berlin.

———. 1973. "Ein Dakerdenkmal Domitians: Die Trajanssäule und das sogenannte grosse trajanische Relief." *Jahrbuch des Deutschen Archäologischen Instituts* 88:318–50.

Gesemann, B. 2003. "Zum Standort der Traianssaeule in Rom." *Jahrbuch des römisch-germanischen Zentralmuseums Mainz* 50, no. 1:307–28.

Gibbon, E. [1782] 1862. *History of the Decline and Fall of the Roman Empire*. Ed. W. H. Smith. London.

Gilles, P. [P. Gyllius]. 1561. *De topographia Constantinopoleos*. Lyon. Reprint, 1967, Athens.

Gilliver, C. M. 1996. "The Roman Army and Morality in War." In A. B. Lloyd (ed.), *Battle in Antiquity*. London. 219–38.

Ginouvès, R. 1998. *Dictionnaire méthodique de l'architecture grecque et romaine*. Vol. 3. Rome.

Goldsworthy, A. K. 1996. *The Roman Army at War*. Oxford.

González, J., and J. Arce (eds.). 1988. *Estudios sobre la Tabula Siarensis*. Madrid.

Grassinger, D. 1999. *Die mythologischen Sarkophage* 1. *Achill bis Amazon*. Berlin.

Gregorovius, F. 1903. *History of the City of Rome in the Middle Ages*. Trans. G. W. Hamilton. London.

Grueber, H. A. 1910. *Coins of the Roman Republic in the British Museum*. London.

Guglielmo, G. 1961. "Caratteristiche edilizie di un quartiere di Roma del II secolo d. Cr." *Quaderni dell'Istituto di Storia dell'Architettura*. Serie 6–8, fasic. 31–48, pp. 49–66. Republished in *Topografia ed edilizia di Roma antica*, Rome 1989: 283–300.

Hamberg, P. G. 1945. *Studies in Roman Imperial Art*. Copenhagen.

Hanson, V. D. 1989. *The Western Way of War: Infantry Battle in Classical Greece*. Berkeley.

Harris, W. V. 2006. "Readings in the Narrative Literature of Roman Courage." In Dillon and Welch 2006: 300–320.

Haselberger, L. 1994. "Ein Giebelriss der Vorhalle des Pantheon. Die Werkrisse vor dem Augustusmausoleum." *Römische Mitteilungen* 101:279–308.

——— (ed.). 1999. *Appearance and Essence: Refinements of Classical Architecture: Curvature*. Philadelphia.

Hassel, F. J. 1966. *Der Trajansbogen in Benevent*. Mainz.

Helm, R. 1984. *Die Chronik des Hieronymus*. Berlin.

Holliday, P. J. 2002. *The Origins of Roman Historical Commemoration in the Visual Arts*. Cambridge.

———. 1997. "Roman Triumphal Painting: Its Function, Development, and Reception." *Art Bulletin* 79:130–47.

Hölscher, T. 2002 "Bilder der Macht und Herrschaft." In A. Nünnerich-Asmus (ed.), *Traian*. Mainz. 127–44.

———. 2000. "Die Säule des Marcus Aurelius: Narrative Struktur und ideologische Botschaft." In Scheid and Huet 2000: 89–105.

———. 1991. "Vormarsch und Schlacht." In L. E. Baumer, T. Hölscher, and L. Winkler, "Narrative Systematik und politisches Konzept in den Reliefs der Traianssäule: Drei Fallstudien." *Jahrbuch des Deutschen Archäologischen Instituts* 106:287–95.

———. 1987. *Römische Bildsprache als semantisches System*. Heidelberg.

———. 1980. "Die Geschichtsauffassung in der römischen Repräsentationskunst." *Jahrbuch des Deutschen Archäologischen Instituts* 95:265–321.

———. 1978. "Die Anfänge römischer Repräsentationskunst." *Römische Mitteilungen* 85:315–57.

———. 1973. *Griechische Historienbilder des 5 und 4 Jahrhunderts v.Chr.* Würzburg.

Hübner, B. 1990. *Ikonographische Untersuchung zum Motifschatz der stadtrömischen mythologischen Sarkophage des 2. Jhs. n. Chr.* (*Boreas* Beiheft 5). Münster.

Hülsen, C. 1889. "Antichità di Monte Citorio." *Römische Mitteilungen* 4:41–64.

Humphrey, J. W., J. P. Oleson, and A. N. Sherwood. 1998. *Greek and Roman Technology: A Sourcebook*. London and New York.

Johnson, S. 1983. *Late Roman Fortifications*. London.

Jordan, H. 1871–1907. *Topographie der Stadt Rom im Alterthum*. 2 vols. in four parts. Berlin.

Jordan-Ruwe, M. 1995. *Das Säulenmonument: Zur Geschichte der erhöhten Aufstellung antiker Porträtstatuen*. Asia Minor Studien 19. Bonn.

———. 1990. "Zur Rekonstruktion und Datierung der Marcussäule." *Boreas* 13:53–69.

Jung, H. 1984. "Zur Vorgeschichte des spätantoninischen Stilwandels." *Marburger Winkelmannprogramm*. 59–104.

Kampmann, H. 1985. "The Ustrinum in the Palazzo del Parlamento in Rome." *Opuscula Romana*. 15:67–78.

Kerr, W. G. 1995. *A Chronological Study of the Marcomannic Wars of Marcus Aurelius*. Diss., Princeton.

Koch, G. 1993. *Sarkophage der römischen Kaiserzeit*. Darmstadt.

Koch, G., and H. Sichtermann. 1982. *Römische Sarkophage*. Munich.

Koeppel, G. 1991, 1992. "Die historischen Reliefs der römischen Kaiserzeit VIII: Der Fries der Trajanssäule in Rom." Part 1: *Bonner Jahrbücher* 191:1–78; part 2: *Bonner Jahrbücher* 192:61–122.

———. 1989. "Die historischen Reliefs der römischen Kaiserzeit VI." *Bonner Jahrbücher* 189:17–71.

———. 1986. "Die historischen Reliefs der römischen Kaiserzeit IV." *Bonner Jahrbücher* 186:1–90.

———. 1985. "The Role of Pictorial Models in the Creation of the Historical Relief during the Age of Augustus." In R. Winkes (ed.), *The Age of Augustus*. Providence. 89–106.

———. 1983a. "Two Reliefs from the Arch of Claudius in Rome." *Römische Mitteilungen* 90:103–9.

———. 1983b. "Die historischen Reliefs der römischen Kaiserzeit I." *Bonner Jahrbücher* 183:61–144.

Kolb, A. 1993. *Die kaiserliche Bauverwaltung in der Stadt Rom*. Stuttgart.

Konrad, C. B. 2001. "Beobachtungen zur Architektur und Stellung des Aäulenmonumentes in Istanbul-Cerrahpasa—'Arkadiossäule.'" *Istanbuler Mitteilungen* 51:319–401.

Kovács, P. 2009. *Marcus Aurelius' Rain Miracle and the Marcommanic Wars*. Leiden.

Lancaster, L. 2004. *Concrete Vaulted Construction in Imperial Rome: Innovations in Context*. Cambridge.

———. 2002. "The Organization of Construction for the Superstructure of the Colosseum." *Römische Mitteilungen* 109:361–74.

———. 2000. "Building Trajan's Markets 2: The Construction Process." *American Journal of Archaeology* 104:755–85.

———. 1999. "Building Trajan's Column." *American Journal of Archaeology* 103:419–39.

Lanciani, R. 1897. *The Ruins and Excavations of Ancient Rome*. Boston.

La Rocca, E. 2004. "Templum Traiani et columna coclhis." *Römische Mitteilungen* 111:193–238.

———. 1998. "Il foro di Traiano ed i fori tripartiti." *Römische Mitteilungen* 105:149–73.

———. 1993. "L'arco di Germanico 'in Circo Flaminio.'" *Bullettino della Commissione Archeologica Comunale di Roma* 95:83–96.

Leander Touati, A. M. 1987. *The Great Trajanic Frieze*. Skrifter utgivna av Svenska Institutet i Rom 45. Stockholm.

Lehmann, K. 1956. Review of Caprino et al. 1955. *Gnomon* 28:515–19.

Lehmann-Hartleben, K. 1926. *Die Trajanssäule: Ein Römisches Kunstwerk zu Beginn der Spätantike*. Berlin and Leipzig.

———. 1923. "Ein Siegesdenkmal Domitians." *Römische Mitteilungen* 28/29:185–92.

Lepper, F., and S. Frere. 1988. *Trajan's Column: A New Edition of the Cichorius Plates*. Gloucester.

Löhr, H. 2009. "Zur Botschaft und Datierung der Markussäule." In R. Einicke, S. Lehmann, H. Löhr, A. Mehnert, G. Mehnert, and A. Slawisch (eds.), *Zurück zum Gegenstand: Festschrift für Andreas Furtwängler*. Langenweissbach. 123–35.

Lusnia, S. 2006. "Battle Imagery and Politics on the Severan Arch in the Roman Forum." In Dillon and Welch 2006: 272–99.

Lyttelton, M. 1974. *Baroque Architecture in Classical Antiquity*. New York.

Maffei, S. 1993 "Columna Marci Aurelii Antonini." *Lexicon Topographicum Urbis Romae* 1:302–3.

Maischberger, M. 1997. *Marmor in Rom: Anlieferung Lager- und Werkplätze in der Kaiserzeit*. Rome.

Mancini, G. 1913. "Le recenti scoperte di antichità a monte Citorio." *Studi Romani* 1:3–15.

Marszal, J. R. 2000. "Ubiquitous Barbarians: Representations of the Gauls at Pergamon and Elsewhere." In N. T. de Grummond and B. S. Ridgway (eds.), *From Pergamon to Sperlonga*. Berkeley. 191–224.

Martines, G. 2000. "L'architettura." In Scheid and Huet 2000: 19–88.

———. 1983. "La struttura della Colonna Traiana: Un'esercitazione di meccanica alessandrina." *Prospettiva* 32:60–70.

Mattingly, H. 1923–62. *Coins of the Roman Empire in the British Museum*. 6 vols. London.

Mertens, D. 1984. *Der Tempel von Segesta und die dorische Tempelbaukunst des griechischen Westens in klassischer Zeit*. Mainz.

Mommsen, T. 1896. "Der Marcommanen-Krieg unter Kaiser Marcus." In Petersen et al. 1896: 39–104.

Moretti, G. 1948. *Ara Pacis Augustae*. Rome.

Morris, J. 1952. "The Dating of the Column of Marcus Aurelius." *Journal of the Warburg Institute* 15:33–47.

Murray, S. B. 1917. *Hellenistic Architecture in Syria*. Princeton.

Musso, L. 1985. "Sarcofago da Portonaccio." In *Museo Nazionale Romano: Le Sculture* I/8.1: 177–89. Rome.

Musto, R. 1988. *Pierre Gilles: The Antiquities of Constantinople*. 2nd ed. Trans. John Ball. New York.

Nash, E. 1968. Vol. 2 of *Pictorial Dictionary of Ancient Rome*. London.

Nolan, L. E. 1860. *Cavalry: Its History and Tactics*. London.

Nordh, A. 1949. *Libellus de regionibus urbis Romae: Notitia urbis Romae regionum XIV*. Skrifter utgivna av Svenska Institutet i Rom 8. Lund.

Packer, J. E. 2001. *The Forum of Trajan in Rome: A Study of the Monuments in Brief*. Berkeley.

———. 1997. *The Forum of Trajan in Rome*. Berkeley.

———. 1994. "Trajan's Forum Again." *Journal of Roman Archaeology* 7:163–82.

Pallottino, M. 1955. "L'arte della Colonna." In Caprino et al. 1955: 43–60.

———. 1938. "L'orientamento stilistico della cultura Aureliana." *Le Arti* 1:32–36.

Paul, G. M. 1987. "Two Battles in Thucydides." *Classical Views* 31:307–12.

Patterson, J. R. 1999. "Via Flaminia." *Lexicon Topographicum Urbis Romae*. 5:135–37.

Petersen, E. 1896. "Beschreibung der Bildwerke." In Petersen et al. 1896: 39–104.

Petersen, E., A. von Domaszewski, and G. Calderini. 1896. *Die Marcus-Säule auf Piazza Colonna in Rom*. Munich.

Pfrommer, M. 1998. *Untersuchungen zur Chronologie und Komposition des Alexandermosaiks*. Mainz.

Picard, G. C. 1962. Review of Becatti 1960. *Gnomon* 34:290–95.

———. 1957. *Les Trophées romains*. Paris.

Pirson, F. 2002. "Vom Kämpfen und Sterben der Kelten in der Antiken Kunst." In H.-U. Cain and S. Rieckhoff (eds.), *Fromm-fremd-barbarisch: Die Religion der Kelten*. Mainz. 71–78.

———. 1996. "Style and Message on the Column of Marcus Aurelius." *Papers of the British School at Rome* 64:139–79.

Poulter, A. G. 1988. "Certain Doubts and Doubtful Conclusions: The Lorica Segmentata from Newstead and the Antonine Garrison." In J. C. Coulston (ed.), *Military Equipment and the Identity of Roman Soldiers*. Oxford. 39–48.

Rakob, F. 1987. "Die Urbanisierung des nördlichen Marsfeldes: Neue Forschungen im Areal des Horologium Augusti." In *L'Urbs: Espace urbain et histoire*. Rome. 687–712.

Ramage, N. H., and A. Ramage. 2009. *Roman Art: Romulus to Constantine*. 5th ed. Englewood Cliffs, N.J.

Richardson, L. 2000. *A Catalog of Identifiable Figure Painters of Ancient Pompeii, Herculaneum, and Stabiae*. Baltimore.

———. 1992. *A New Topographical Dictionary of Ancient Rome*. Baltimore.

Robert, C. 1919. *Die antiken Sarkophag-Reliefs*. III.1. Berlin.

Robinson, H. R. 1975. *The Armour of Imperial Rome*. London.

Rockwell, P. 1993. *The Art of Stoneworking: A Reference Guide*. Cambridge.

———. 1988. "Carving Instructions on the Temple of Vespasian." *Atti della Pontificia Accademia Romana di Archeologia: Rendiconti* 60:53–69.

———. 1985a. "Report on Carving and Construction Techniques of Several Monuments in Rome." Unpublished report.

———. 1985b. "Preliminary Study of the Carving Techniques on the Column of Trajan." *Studi Miscellanei* 26:101–11.

Rodenwaldt, G. 1940. "Römische Reliefs: Vorstufen zur Spätantike." *Jahrbuch des Deutschen Archäologischen Instituts* 55:12–43.

———. 1936. "Art from Nero to the Antonines." In A. Bowman, P. Garnsey, and D. Rathbone (eds.), vol. 11 of *Cambridge Ancient History*, 2nd ed. New York. 775–805.

———. 1935. "Über den Stilwandel in der antoninischen Kunst." *Abhandlungen der Deutschen Akademie der Wissenschaften zu Berlin* 3:1–27.

———. 1921/22. "Eine spätantike Kunstströmung in Rom." *Römische Mitteilungen* 36/7:58–110.

Rossi, L. 1977. "Sull' iconografia e storiografia celebrativa di Marco Aurelio dall' epigrafe di M. Valerio Massimiano." *Quaderni ticinesi di numismatica e antichità classiche* 6:223–32.

———. 1971. *Trajan's Column and the Dacian Wars*. London.

Rotili, M. 1972. *L'Arco di Traiano a Benevento*. Rome.

Rumpf, A. 1939. *Die Meerwesen auf den antiken Sarkophagreliefs*. Antiken Sarkophagreliefs 5.1. Berlin.

Ryberg, I. 1967. *Panel Reliefs of Marcus Aurelius*. New York.

Schäfer, T. 1986. "Römische Schlachtenbilder." *Madrider Mitteilungen* 27:345–64.

———. 1979. "Zum Schlachtsarkophag Borghese." *Mélanges de l'École Française de Rome* 91:355–70.

Scheid, J., and V. Huet (eds.). 2000. *Autour de la Colonne Aurélienne*. Turnhout.

Scheidel, W. 1990. "Der Germaneneinfall in Oberitalien und die Emissionsfrage der kaiserlichen Reichsprägung." *Chiron* 20:1–18.

Schoene, A. 1866. *Eusebi Chronicorum Canonum*. Zurich.

Schulten, P. N. 1979. *Die Typologie der römischen Konsekrationsprägungen*. Frankfurt.

Sediari, M. 1997. "La topografia della Regio IX di Roma in età severiana." *Bullettino della Commissione Archeologica Comunale di Roma* 98:215–48.

Seeck, O. 1876. *Notitia Dignitatum*. Frankfurt. Reprint, 1962.

Semper, G. 1860. Vol. 1 of *Der Stil in den technischen und tektonischen Künsten.* Frankfurt.
Settis, S. 1994. "Colonna Coclide Istoriata." *Enciclopedia dell'Arte Antica*, 2, no 2:230–33.
———. 1988. *La Colonna Traiana*. Rome.
Seyfarth, W. 1968. *Ammianus Marcellinus: Römische Geschichte.* Berlin.
Shaw, B. D. 2000. "Rebels and Outsiders." In A. Bowman, P. Garnsey, and D. Rathbone (eds.), vol. 11 of *Cambridge Ancient History*, 2nd ed. New York. 361–404.
Sichtermann, H. 1992. *Die mythologischen Sarkophage 2. Apollon bis Grazien.* Berlin.
Stewart, P. 2003. *Statues in Roman Society: Representation and Response.* Oxford.
Strong, D. E. 1961. *Roman Imperial Sculpture*. London.
Stucchi, S. 1989. "TANTIS VIRIBUS: L'area della colonna nella concezione generale del Foro di Traiano." *Archeologia Classica* 41:237–92.
Talbert, R. 1988. "Commodus as Diplomat in an Extract from the Acta Senatus." *Zeitschrift für Papyrologie und Epigraphik* 71:137–47.
Torelli, M. 1993. "Columna Minucia." *Lexicon Topographicum Urbis Romae*, 1:305–7.
———. 1992. "Topografia e iconologia: Arco de Portogallo, Ara Pacis, Ara Providentiae, Templum Solis." *Ostraka* 1:105–31.
Traversari, G. 1968. "Sarcophagi con la Morte di Meleagro nell'Influsso Artistico della Colonna Aureliana." *Römische Mitteilungen* 75:154–62.
Tusa, V. 1995. *I Sarcofagi Romani in Sicilia*. 2nd ed. Rome.
Valentini, R., and G. Zucchetti. 1940. *Codice topografico della città di Roma*. Rome.
Varner, E. 2004. *Mutilation and Transformtion: Damnatio Memoriae and Roman Imperial Portraiture.* Leiden.
Vermeule, C. 1956. Review of C. Caprino et al. 1955. *American Journal of Archaeology.* 60:315–18.
Veyne, P. 1991. "Propagande expression roi, image idole oracle." In *La Société romaine.* Paris. 311–42.
Vogel, L. 1973. *The Column of Antoninus Pius.* Cambridge.
Ward-Perkins, J. B. 1976. "Columna divi Antonini." In P. Ducrey (ed.), *Mélanges d'histoire ancienne et d'archéologie offerts à Paul Collart.* Lausanne.
Wegner, M. 1939. *Die Herrscherbildnisse in antoninischer Zeit.* Das römische Herrscherbild II.4. Berlin.
———. 1931. "Die Kunstgeschichtliche Stellung der Marcussäule." *Jahrbuch des Deutschen Archäologischen Instituts* 46:61–174.
Wilson Jones, M. 2000. *Principles of Roman Architecture.* New Haven.
———. 1999. "The Practicalities of Roman Entasis." In Haselberger 1999. 225–49.
———. 1993. "One Hundred Feet and a Spiral Stair: The Problem of Designing Trajan's Column." *Journal of Roman Archaeology* 6:23–38.
Wiseman, T. P. 1993. "Campus Martius." *Lexicon Topographicum Urbis Romae* 1:219–24.
Wolff, H. 1994. "Die Markus-Säule als Quelle für die Markomannenkriege." In H. Friesinger, J. Teral, and A. Stuppner (eds.), *Markomannenkriege: Ursachen und Wirkungen.* Brno. 73–83.
———. 1990. "Welchen Zeitraum stellt der Bilderfries der Marcus-Säule dar?" *Ostbairische Grenzmarken: Passauer Jahrbuch für Geschichte, Kunst und Volkskunde* 32:9–29.

Zanker, P. 2004. *Die Apotheose der römischen Kaiser: Ritual und städtische Bühne.* Munich.

———. 2000. "Die Frauen und Kinder der Barbaren auf der Marcussäule." In Scheid and Huet 2000:163–74.

———. 1997. "In Search of the Roman Viewer." In D. Buitron-Oliver (ed.), *The Interpretation of Architectural Sculpture in Greece and Rome.* Hanover, N.H. 179–92.

Zwikker, W. 1941. *Studien zur Markussäule.* Amsterdam.

Index

Italicized numbers refer to pages on which illustrations appear.

Adlocutio. *See* Scenes on Column of Marcus Aurelius: *adlocutio*

Adrastus (Roman official), 19, 22, 37, 82, 127, 208, 216 (n. 3); inscription, 19, *20*, 37, 51, 60; residence, 51, 208, 220 (n. 52); duties as *procurator columnae*, 65–66

Aemilius Paulus, Lucius, 130

Agricola, Gn. Julius, 197

Alexander Mosaic, 168

Alexander the False Prophet (Lucian), 3, 143

Altar of Fortuna Redux, 52

Altars, 49; of Faustina the Younger, 46; of Lucius Verus, 46; of Marcus Aurelius, 46; on coins of Trajan Decius, 219 (n. 40). See also *arae consecrationis*; Ara Pacis

Ambassadors: on Column of Marcus Aurelius, 147; of Buri to Rome, 200

Anchises, 198

Apollodorus of Damascus, 64, 70, 223 (n. 8)

Apotheosis imagery, 34, 42, 45. *See also* Campus Martius: as "apotheosis landscape"

Aqua Virgo, 53

Aquileia, 3, 196

Arae consecrationis, 42

Ara Pacis, 39, 41, 49, 52, 162, 180

Arcadius (Roman emperor), 210

Arch of Claudius, 53

Arch of Constantine, 176

Arch of Domitian, 53

Arch of Germanicus, 69, 73

Arch of Septimius Severus, 87, 127, 132, 184, 185–86; style, 182

Ariogaesus (leader of the Quadi), 198

Armenians, 197

Armies, behavior of, 150–51

Arminius (German chieftain), 196–97

Armor: segmented, 100, 152–55, 162, *163*, 169; ring mail, 117–18, 152–54, 162, 169, 205; on column reliefs, 117–18, 205; scale, 152–54, 162, 225 (n. 14); on Alexander Mosaic, 168

Atrocity, 147, 197

Aurelius Antoninus, Marcus. *See* Marcus Aurelius

Auxiliary soldiers, 152–53. *See also* Military equipment, variation in

Avidius Cassius, rebellion of, 4, 29, 133

Bartoli, Pietro Santi: drawings of Column of Marcus Aurelius, 8–9

Baths: of Agrippa, 40, 51–52; of Nero, 40, 51–52; of Caracalla, 63, 75; of Diocletian, 63, 75; of Trajan, 64

Bayazitt II (Ottoman sultan), 210

Bellum Germanicum, 2–3

Bellum Marcomannicum, 2–3

Boats, on Column of Marcus Aurelius, 177, *178*. *See also* Bridge of boats

Book roll, 106–7

Boudicca, revolt of, 197

Bridge of boats, on Column of Marcus Aurelius, *92–93*, 114, 205

Building contracts, 71

Buildings, on Column of Marcus Aurelius, 89–90, *91*, 96–97. *See also* Scenes on Column of Marcus Aurelius: construction

Buri (tribe), 200

Campus Agrippae, 39, 53

Campus Martius: rising ground level,

38, 40–41, 189, 203; stonemasons' work areas and, 40, 41, 127; Hadrianic ground level, 41; plan, under Septimius Severus, *43*; as "apotheosis landscape," 47; transporting stone to, 78
Carnuntum (city), 4
"Cartoon," 106
Cassius Dio. *See* Dio
Chisel, 86, 120, 179; point, 79, 179; flat, 179; toothed, 179
Coch(l)is. See *Columna coch(l)is*
Cocleae, 61–62
Coinage, as dating evidence, 129
Colonne de la Grande Armée, *21*
Columna centenaria, 19, 60, 61, 62–63, 67, 72, 75, 83
Columna coch(l)is, 5, 7–8, 17, 51, 55, 60, 61, 63, 67, 72, 81, 83, 210; meaning, 62–63
Columna rostrata, 55, *56*, 57, 60, 66
Column of Antoninus Pius, 36, *45*, 47, 49; comparison to Column of Marcus Aurelius, 34, 50, 171, 187
Column of Arcadius, 18, 62, 191, 210, *211*, *212*, 213; construction time, 81
Column of Constantine, 62
Column of Gaius Diulius, 55
Column of Gaius Maenius, 55
Column of L. Minucius Augurinus, 221 (n. 1)
Column of Marcus Aemilius Paulus, 55
Column of Marcus Aurelius: mentioned in literature, 5; description, 5, 7, *8*; designers, 17, 63, 70, 76, 84, 86, 87, 88, 96, 105, 109, 110, 124, 152, 155, 167, 180, 189, 193, 202, 203, 208, 210, 212; *columna divi Marci*, 22; inscriptions, 22; sixteenth century restoration, 31, 34, 90–91, 146, 203, 217 (n. 25), 228 (n. 8); view from top, 49; climbing, 50; funerary associations, 50, 52, 59; height, 60, 63, 74; *procurator*, 65 (*see also* Adrastus); process of decree and commission, 72, 200; elevation, 74; marble, 74; entasis, lack of, 74, 79, 207–8; capital, weight of, 79; railings, 80; metal inserts, lack of, 126; figure types, 179; statue, 188, 202
—battles: size of, 150; skirmishes, 150
—blocks: number of, 77; weight, 77; unloading site, 78
—carvers, 79, 81–82, 96, 106–7, 109, 113, 120, 122, 124, 159, 176–77, 179, 180, 182–84, 201, 209; from sarcophagus industry, 179–80, 182, 183, 192
—carving: before assembly, 78, 79, 82; steps in, 116, 122–23; teams, 120, 122, 192
—construction, 21, 37; preparation of site, 77; finishing blocks and drums, 78, 112–13; lifting apparatus, 79; time, 80, 82, 123
—damage: fire, 16; earthquake, 16, 77, 188
—date: of completion, 22, 81–82; of decree, 22–24, 36
—design: architectural, 73–76, 87; priorities, 82, 109
—doorway: lower, *8*, 16, 48, 189, 202, 208; upper, *9*, 49, 50–51
—dowels, 16, 80, 203; scavenging of, 16, 80, *99*, *195*
—drums, 74, 112–13, 124; height, 7, 74–75, 76, 78; joins, effects at, 123–24
—frieze. *See* Frieze of Column of Marcus Aurelius
—images: casts, 10; photography, 10, *11*, 12, 13, 84, 110
—location, 52, 61, 83; axis of approach, 48, 189; elevation, 48, 220 (n. 45); surrounding area, 48–49; relationship to Via Flaminia, 48–50, 52, 54, 72, 188, 199, 200; relationship to funerary altars, 49–50, 52, 54
—message, 198; to foreigners, 200
—pedestal, 7, *8*, 31–32, *33*, 48, 72, 77, 188–89, 202–3, *204*, 208; height, 73–74, 76, 191; relief, 182, 188, 202–6
—planning: decree, 69; lack of, 76, 193
—relationship to Column of Trajan: differences/contrasts, 12–13, 50, 72, 74–75, 85–86, 126, 151–52, 154, 156, 159, 163–65, 173, 177–78, 184, 189,

193, 194, 203, 207; improvements on, 190–91, 208. *See also* Frieze of Column of Marcus Aurelius—relationship to frieze of Column of Trajan
—staircase, 7, 49, 50, 61, 62, 72, 202; ratio of steps per turn, 63, 75–76; importance, 63–66; access to, 64, 208; rise of steps, 75; planning, 76, 191; first two turns irregular, 76, 223 (n. 24); carving, 78; tool marks, 78, 230 (n. 36)
—style: of carving, *126*; Severan and, 127; definition, 158–60; innovative versus traditional, 158–86 passim, *161*, *165*, *166*. See also *Stilwandel*; Style
—Victoria, 194; position on column, 189
—windows, 50, 64, 86, 88, 119, 204; relationship to frieze, 98, *108*, 119, 122, 124
Column of Octavian, 55
Column of Scipio Africanus, 66
Column of Theodosius, 62, 210, 232 (n. 2); construction time, 81; fall of statue, 222 (n. 17)
Column of Trajan, 22, 87; casts, 9–10; as model for Column of Marcus Aurelius, 12–13, 15, 17, 26, 28, 58, 63, 73, 76, 84, 201, 207; climbing, 50; funerary associations, 50; windows, 50, 57; concept of, 56; date of dedication, 56, 81; on coins, *57*; chamber in pedestal, 57; Trajan's burial beneath, 57; height, 57, 60, 209; view from top, 58, 64, *65*; doorway, upper, *59*; pedestal, 73–75; elevation, 74; entasis, 74; marble, 74; capital, weight of, 79; construction, time, 81; metal weapons, 81, 125; designer, 84–85; fluting, *107*, 116; painted, 125; message, 196, 198; relation to *pomerium*, 221 (n. 8); inscription, 221 (n. 10)
—drums, 74, 78; joins, effects at, 123–24
—frieze: length, 7, 107; on coins, *57*, 82; inconsistencies, 81; time to carve, 82; irregular layout, 84–85, 106, 123, 191; height, 85; lack of planning, 85, 106–7; plan, 106–9; border, 107, 111, 113, 114–15, 123; direction of carving, 113; depth, 113–14; order of scenes, 193; date of completion, 221 (n. 7)
—scenes: Victoria (LXXVIII), 27, 85, 87, 98, *99*, 100, 189–90; XXIV, 28; III, *94*; VIII, 95; XL, 102, *103*, 227 (n. 29); XLII, 102, *104*; XLVII, 105; CXXXVIII, 125; XLIV, 125, 151; XXXVIII, 151; battle, 151–52, 155, 168; XXXVII, 152; CXLIV, 152; CXLV, 153
—staircase, 57, 58, 64; ratio of steps, 63; importance, 63–66; access to, 64; problem planning, 74, 209
Commodus, 1, 2, 4, 111, 200; and Column of Marcus Aurelius, 22; absent from Column of Marcus Aurelius, 24, 29–34, *30*, 203, 205–6; on coins, 29, *31*; busts, 30; *damnatio memoriae*, 31, 32–34, 206; assumes *toga virilis*, 217 (n. 13); present in field, 217 (n. 13)
Corbulo (general), 197
Curator operum publicorum, 69
Curiosum urbis Romae, 60–61, 221 (n. 12)

Dacian wars, 26, 81, 153, 194–96
Danube frontier, on Column of Marcus Aurelius, 96–97
Defeat, in Roman art and literature, 143, 201
Design, architectural, as competitive process, 70–71
Dio (Roman historian), 36, 128, 135–38
Domitian, 1, 40, 53, 98, 197
Dowels, metal, 80, *99*, *195*. *See also* Column of Marcus Aurelius—dowels
Drawings: used for planning, 96, 108, 109; of column, 203–4

Ekphrasis, 139
Expeditio Germanica secunda, 27

Falx (Dacian weapon), 153–54
Faustina the Elder, 146; funerary altar, *44*, 46–47
Faustina the Younger, 19; death, 4, 50; funerary altar, 46–47, 49, 51; pyre, 47
Fontana, Domenico, 203–4

Frieze of Column of Marcus Aurelius: design, 84, 86, 109; layout, 84–88, 180, 191; length, 85–86; plotting on column, 86, *108*, 109, 123, 207; placement of Victoria in, 87, 88; orientation of scenes to viewer, 87, *108*, 109, 189; number of sculptors, 110–11, 118; depth, 113–14; order of scenes, 193. *See also* Visibility, of Column of Marcus Aurelius
—border, 85–86, 108, 110–11, *112*, 113, 115, 119, 120; patterns, 110–11, *112*, 115, 118–20, 122
—carving: prior to assembly, 112–13; direction, 113; starting point, 117; errors, *121*, 225 (n. 17); during construction, 123–24
—plan, architectural, 86–88, 106–9, 123, 124, 150, 184, 193, 200; use of drawing in, 96, 105, 109, 118, 124
—relationship to frieze of Column of Trajan: copying and imitation, 28, *88–89*, *91*, *92–93*, *94*, 97, 98, *99*, *101*, 102, *104*, 106, 118, 184, 193, 207, 208; while planning, 89–97 passim, *88–89*, *91*, *92–93*, *94*, 183, 208
—scenes. *See* Scenes on Column of Marcus Aurelius
Frontality, 157, 160, 177, 181, 184, 186, 230 (n. 46)
Fronto, Marcus Cornelius, commissions bath, 71
Furius Victorinus (praetorian prefect), 196

Germanicus, attitude to prisoners, 196
Germanic Wars, 36, 54, 200; chronology, 3–4
German races, 12

Hadrian, 40–41, 42, 82; as architect, 70
Haterii relief, 79
Historia Augusta, 128, 133–34
Historical art, Roman, 130–33
Historicity, of column friezes, 155, 200
Horologium of Augustus, 39, 41, 49; transport of obelisk, 77
Hostilius Mancinus, Lucius (Roman legate), 130

Iazyges (people), 198
Insulae, in Campus Martius, 41

Labor, division of, 118–22
Lafreri, Antonio: etchings of, on Column of Marcus Aurelius, 32, *33*, 203, *204*, 205
Legionary soldiers, 152–53, 162. *See also* Military equipment, variation in
Lewis irons, 80
Libraries, in Forum of Trajan, 105
Litters, 146–47, *148*
Locatio conductio (contract), 71
Luna (quarry), 74, 77

Mantua Relief, 228 (n. 14)
Marble of Column of Marcus Aurelius, 156; transport to Rome, 77
Marcomannia (province), 4
Marcus Aurelius: "Germanicus", 4, 26; "Sarmaticus", 4, 26; crossing the Danube, 24; funeral pyre, *44*, 47; financial crisis, 71; depicted in battle, 146, *147*; involvement in acts of punishment and brutality, 198; wrath of, 198; *divus* coinage, 219 (n. 39)
— history of reign, 1–4; sources, 128
Meditations (Marcus Aurelius), 4–5, 215 (n. 16)
Messala (Roman consul), 130
Military equipment, variation in, *117*, 120. *See also* Armor
Miracles, 133. *See also* Scenes on Column of Marcus Aurelius
Mons Graupius (battle), 153, 227 (n. 32)
Morelli, Giovanni, 110

Notitia urbis Constantinopolitanae, 62
Notitia urbis Romae, 36, 51, 60–61, 221 (n. 12)

Opitergium (city), 3, 196
Ordovices (tribe), 197

Painting: historical, 130–32, 139, 185
—triumphal, 130–32, 149, 150, 168, 173, 180; message of, 197; of Vespasian, 131, 197–98
Paint on columns, 125–26, 188
Palisades, 90, 96
Panel reliefs of Marcus Aurelius, 16, 29, 32, 34, 176–77, 179, 182, 206; Adventus, 53, 206; Profectio, 53, 206; Clementia, 206
Pantheon, plans on Mausoleum pavement, 78
Pertinax (Roman emperor), 138–39; cremation of, 43–44
Piazza Colona, 19, 188
Piazza Montecitorio, 19, 42, 51
Picturas (sing. *pictura*), 150
Piranesi, drawings of Column of Marcus Aurelius, 9, 12
Place Vendôme, 21
Plague, 3, 71, 82, 194, 209
Planning, architectural: use of drawings in, 223 (n. 13)
Polish, 179
Porta Triumphalis, 220 (n. 59)
Praetorian soldiers, 152–54, 227 (n. 31). *See also* Military equipment, variation in
Procurator columnae. See Adrastus
Puteoli magistrates, contract for sanctuary of Serapis and, 71–72, 73
Pyres, 42–43, *44*, 46–47

Quirinal Hill, 58

Rasp, 179
Realism, in battle depictions, 150–51, 168–73, *169*, *170*, *171*, *172*

Sapor (Persian king), 128
Sarcophagi, 178, 180, 185; carving, 79, 82, 98, 115, 116, 125, 180; style, 159, 163; industry, 173–74, 180, 183; carvers, 177, 179; "workshops," 177, 180, 185, 192; Oceanus, 178; figure types, 179; Frascati Wedding, 229 (nn. 23, 24); Portonaccio, 229 (n. 24)
Sarmatia (province), 4
Sarmatians (people), 4, 26, 27, 54, 139
Scenes on Column of Marcus Aurelius: marching, 13, 89, 91–92, 95, *117*, 155, 160, *161*, 162, 167, 191, 192, 194, 200; historical, 24, *25*, 26–28, 129, 133–50 passim, 193, 194; battles, 27, 100, *101*, 115, 120, *121*, *141*, 146, *147*, 150, 151–52, 158, 167–76, *169*, *170*, *171*, *172*, 179; *adlocutio*, 95, 102, 105–6, 158, 163, *165*, *166*, 167; executions, *108*, 148, *149*, 194, 198, *199*; size and alignment of, 108–9; construction, 146, 155, 158, 162, *163*, *164*, 193; creation of, 174
—Danube Crossing (III), 24, *25*, 26, 28, 48, 89, 91, 97, 108, *117*, 118, 155, 189, 192, 208
—Lightning Miracle (X–XI), 133, *134*, *135*, 140, 143, 144, 145, 149, 155, 226 (n. 11); historicity, 140
—Rain Miracle (XVI), 10, 13, 24, *25*, 26, 48, 108, 133, *134*, 134–40, *136*, 137, *138*, 146, 149, 155, 178, 183, 189, 208; position in frieze, 28; date, 226 (n. 12)
—Victoria (LV), 24, *25*, 26, 27, 28, 48, 80, 87, 98, *99*, 102, 105, 108, 119, 189, 209; setting in narrative, 27, 100
—other scenes: I, 89, *91*, *94*, 118; II, 89, *91*, *94*; III (*see* Scenes on Column of Marcus Aurelius—Danube Crossing); IV, 95, 97, 102, 105–6; VI, 95, 97; VIII, 114; IX, 102, 105–6, 143; X (river scene), 143–44, *144*, 227 (n. 20); XI (river scene), 145; XIII (Lion Oracle), *142*; XV, 174; XVI (*see* Scenes on Column of Marcus Aurelius—Rain Miracle); XVIII, 194; XIX, *169*, 170, 174; XX, *25*, 194, 198; XXIII, 174–75; XXIV, 170, *171*, 172; XXV, 102, *103*; XXVII, 146, *147*; XXX, 114, *161*, 162, 192; XXXIII, 192; XXXIV, 177, *178*; XXXIX, 174, 191; XLII, 102, 146–47, *148*; XLIII, *141*, 179, 194; XLIV, 191; XLIX, 29, *30*; L, 114, 175; LII, 175, 179; LIV, 27, 100, *101*; LV (*adlocutio*), 102, 105–6; LVI, 27; LVII, 27, 179; LX, 148,

149, 194; LXI, 123, 148, *149*, 194; LXII, 123, *149*; LXIII, 171, *172*; LXVI, 194, 198, *199*; LXVII, 160, 167; LXVIII, 148, 191, 194; LXX/LXXI, 100, *101*, *103*; LXXII, 175; LXXVII, 102; LXXVIII, 160, *161*, 167, 191; LXXIX, 179; LXXXI, 123, 178; LXXXII, 155, 162, *163*; LXXXIII, 105; LXXXIV, 192; LXXXVI, 106; XCII, 152, *170*, 175; XCIV, 155, 162; XCVI, 106, *166*; XCVII, 152, 175, 194, *195*; XCVIII, 162, *164*; IC, 115, 120, *121*, 179; C, 106, 115, *116*, 164, *165*, 166, 167; CIII, *112*, 119, 191; CIV, *112*, *114*, 119, 160; CV, 152, 175; CXI, 105, 192; CXII, 34, 168; CXIV, 34; CXV, *126*; CLI, 168
Scipio Asiaticus, Lucius (Roman general), 130
Sculptors, Roman: working methods, 87, 110–27 passim
Septimius Severus, 19, 31–32
Severed heads, 198, *199*
Slings, *144*
Staircases, spiral, 63, 64, 222 (n. 18); ratio of steps per turn, 75. *See also*, Column of Marcus Aurelius—staircase; Column of Trajan—staircase
Stilwandel, 12–13, 157–58, 160, 162, 166, 177, 180, 181, 185–86; prehistory of, 159, 185; Column of Marcus Aurelius as evidence of, 183–84, 186
Style: compositional, 159, 160, 162, 168–76, 180, 182, 183, 186; carving, 159–60, 162, 167, 180, 182; figural, 159–60, 165–67, 177, 180, 183, 185; centralized composition, 160; scaling of figures, 160; meaning of, 181–84

Tabula lusoria, 48, 208
Tabula Siarensis, 69, 222 (n. 1); text, 222 (n. 2)
Temple of Marcus Aurelius, 51–52, 220 (n. 52)
Temple of Fortuna Redux, 53
Temples of Hadrian and Matidia, 40–41, 42, 47, 49
Testudo, 100, *101*, 102
Tools, carving, 179. *See also* Chisel
Topoi (sing. *topos*), 139
Trajan's Column. *See* Column of Trajan
Trajan's markets, 58
Triumph, 130; of Vespasian and Titus, 131, 197. *See also* Painting—triumphal
Tropaeum Traiani, 153–54
Trophies, 98; on Column of Marcus Aurelius, 100, 177, 224 (n. 6); on sarcophagi, 100, 177, 224 (n. 6); on Column of Trajan, 177

Uniform, 152, 153
Ustrina (sing. *ustrinum*). *See* Pyres

Valao (Narsitan prince), 141–42
Valerian (Roman emperor), 128
Valerius Maximus, Marcus (Roman soldier), 141
Vertical alignment of scenes, *25*, 189–90, 192–93, 209
Vexilla (sing. *vexillum*), 115, *116*, 166, 206
Via Flaminia. *See* Column of Marcus Aurelius—location: relationship to Via Flamina
Victor, Sextus Aurelius (Roman historian), 22, 35–36; background, 23
Victoria, 204, 206, 210; on coins, 217 (n. 11). *See also* Column of Trajan—scenes: Victoria; Frieze of Column of Marcus Aurelius: placement of Victoria in; Scenes on Column of Marcus Aurelius—Victoria
Viewers, 199–202, 203
Violence, 194–200
Visibility, of Column of Marcus Aurelius, 48, 50, 108–9, 188–93, 200, 203

Wilhelm II (emperor of Germany), 10, 12

Xiphilinus (Byzantine monk), 128–29, 139–40

www.ingramcontent.com/pod-product-compliance
Lightning Source LLC
LaVergne TN
LVHW050952080826
845145LV00005B/1482

* 9 7 8 1 4 6 9 6 6 8 6 3 5 *